The Health of Nations

THE HEALTH OF NATIONS.

A REVIEW OF THE WORKS

OF

EDWIN CHADWICK,

WITH A BIOGRAPHICAL DISSERTATION.

BY

BENJAMIN WARD RICHARDSON.

IN TWO VOLUMES.

VOL. II.

LONDON:
LONGMANS, GREEN, AND CO.,
39, PATERNOSTER ROW.
1887.

Printed by Hazell, Watson, & Viney, Ld., London and Aylesbury.

TABLE OF CONTENTS OF SECOND VOLUME.

INTRODUCTORY NOTE.

PART I.

SANITARY AND PREVENTIVE OF DISEASE.

CHAPTER I.

CHAPTER II.

CHAPTER III.

CHAPTER IV.

CHAPTER V.

CHAPTER VI.

CHAPTER VII.

CHAPTER VIII.

CHAPTER IX.

CHAPTER XXVII.

CHAPTER XXVIII.

CHAPTER XXIX.

CHAPTER XXX.

CHAPTER XXXI.

CHAPTER XXXII.

PART II.

PREVENTION OF PAUPERISM AND POVERTY.

CHAPTER I.

PART III.

PREVENTION OF CRIME.

CHAPTER I.

INTRODUCTORY NOTE.

PREVENTIVE SCIENCE.

BY common consent Mr. Chadwick is esteemed as the pioneer of that modern sanitary science which has worked in the course of half a century such true marvels for the prevention of disease. In the field of his work in this direction we trace out designs not always finished, indeed not often finished in detail, but so projected, that others may labour on them and bring them to perfection. His universality is unique. He is found dealing with building and construction as if he were an architect; with engineering as if he were an engineer. In treating of diseases he might be often taken for a physician, in matters of administration for a politician, while he is always in his right place as a statistician. By a strange fortune he is least prolific on the legal side of sanitary work, though by education and profession a lawyer called to the bar.

This universality of industry renders it difficult to place his sanitary work in anything like systematic order, because in point of fact it has been produced just as the occasion called it forth, without plan or premeditation. It has come from the fulness of knowledge,—knowledge good from the first, but gaining in power and extension as facts were observed, accumulated, and mastered.

In presenting the sanitary labours of the author to a public now largely advanced in a knowledge of sanitation, I shall, in the first twenty chapters of the present volume, pith, if I may so express myself, the report on the sanitary condition of the labouring classes. In this way, without troubling the reader with the necessary official style of the original document, I shall place under distinctive heads the practical ideas of the writer as they were and are still applicable to sanitary science as a whole. This plan will serve, at the same time, to show the remarkable originality of thought and action which too often lay concealed in the official record.

In the succeeding chapters I shall select from Mr. Chadwick's other works those which appear to be most instructive to students of public health at the present time.

By pursuing this course the reader of the present day will be able to form an idea, not only of the changes which have taken place for good, but of those which still remain to be effected before the realisation of the aspirations of our author have been fulfilled. Following the plan adopted in the previous volume, inverted commas are placed at the head of each paragragh that contains the *ipsissima verba* of Mr. Chadwick.

VOLUME II.

PART I.

SANITARY AND PREVENTIVE OF DISEASE.

CHAPTER I.

IN the month of May, 1838, the Poor Law Commissioners presented to Lord John Russell a report relative to certain charges which had been disallowed by the auditors of Unions in England and Wales, together with two supplementary reports; one a "Report on the prevalence of certain physical causes of fever in the Metropolis, by Dr. Neil Arnott and Dr. James Phillips Kay, afterwards Sir James Kay-Shuttleworth;" the other a "Report on some of the physical causes of sickness and mortality to which the poor are exposed, and which are capable of removal by sanitary regulations," by the late Dr. Southwood Smith.

In April of the following year the commissioners received from Dr. Southwood Smith a further "Report on the prevalence of fever in twenty Metropolitan Unions or Parishes during the year which ended on the 20th of March, 1838."

As a result of these, Lord John, in August, 1839, issued another letter, directing, from Her Majesty "A commission of enquiry as to the extent to which the causes of disease, stated to prevail amongst the labouring classes of the Metropolis, prevail also amongst the labouring classes in other parts of the United Kingdom."

The commissioners, George Nicholls, George Cornewall Lewis, and Edmund Walker Head, thereupon issued directions for an elaborate enquiry and report, and requested Mr. Chadwick, at that time their secretary, "to peruse the information which they had received, and by comparing the different statements with such authentic facts bearing upon the question as he might collect from other sources, to frame a report which should exhibit the principal results of the enquiry."

In obedience to this instruction, our author constructed the now historical volume known as his "Report on the Sanitary Condition of the Labouring Classes of Great Britain." This work, consisting of four hundred and fifty-seven pages, written entirely by himself from the materials he had before him, will furnish under different heads several chapters, the full interest of which remains as important in this day as it was when it first appeared forty-four years ago.

CHAPTER II.

THE registered mortality from all specified diseases in England and Wales was, during the year 1838, 282,940, or 18 per thousand of the population. These deaths are exclusive of the deaths from old age, which amounted to 35,564; the deaths from violence, which amounted to 12,055; the deaths from causes not specified 11,970. The total amount of deaths was 342,529 for that year. In the year following, the total deaths were 338,979, of which the registered deaths from old age were 35,063, and the deaths from violence 11,980. The proportion of deaths for the whole population was 21 per thousand.

A conception may be formed of the aggregate effects of the several causes of mortality from the fact, that of the deaths caused during one year in England and Wales by epidemic, endemic, and contagious diseases, including fever, typhus, and scarlatina, amounting to 56,461, the great proportion of which are proved to be preventible, it may be said that the effect is as if the whole county of Westmoreland, then containing 56,469 souls, or the whole county of Huntingdonshire, or any other equivalent district, were entirely depopulated annually, and

were only occupied again by the growth of a new
and feeble population living under the fears of a
similar visitation.

The annual death-rate in England and Wales from
preventible causes of typhus, which attacked persons
in the vigour of life, appeared to be double the
amount of what was suffered. by the allied armies
in the battle of Waterloo. It was shown that
diseases such as those which prevailed on land
did, within the experience of persons still living,
formerly prevail to a great extent at sea, and have
since been prevented by sanitary regulations; and
that where they did so prevail in ships of war, the
deaths from them were more than double in amount
of the deaths in battle. But the number of persons
who die is to be taken also as the indication of the
much greater number of persons who fall sick, and
who, although they escape, are subjected to the
suffering and loss occasioned by attacks of disease.
Thus it was found on the original inquiry in the
metropolis, that the deaths from fever amounted to
1 in 10 of the number attacked. If this proportion had
held equally throughout the country, then a quarter
of a million of persons would have been subjected to
loss and suffering from an attack of fever during the
year; and in so far as the proportion of attacks to
deaths was diminished, so, it appears from the reports, the intensity and suffering from the disease,
generally, was increased. It appeared that the
extremes of mortality at the small-pox hospital in
London, amongst those attacked, had been 15 per
cent. and 42 per cent. But if, according to other
statements, the average mortality were taken at 1
in 5, or 20 per cent., the number of persons attacked

in England and Wales during the year of the return amounted to upwards of 16,000 persons killed, with more than 80,000 persons subjected to the sufferings of disease, including, in the case of the labouring classes, the loss of labour and long-continued debility. And, in respect to all classes, often permanent disfigurement, and occasionally the loss of sight.

It was to reduce in some substantial manner the evils above enumerated that our pioneer of modern sanitation started on his way. He had foreseen that if certain leading principles of action could be brought into play, certain great results for prevention of disease and many untold miseries incident to disease would be realised with certainty of success.

CHAPTER III.

DEFECTS IN SANITATION, AND LEADING REMEDIES.

" THE defects which are the most important, and which come most immediately within practical legislative and administrative control, are those chiefly *external* to the dwellings of the population, and which principally arise from the neglect of drainage. The remedies include the means for drainage simply, *i.e.*, the means for the removal of an excess of moisture; and the means for the removal of the noxious refuse of houses, streets, and roads, by sewerage, by supplies of water, and by the service of scavengers and sweepers.

STREET AND ROAD CLEANSING: ROAD PAVEMENTS.

" The local arrangements for the cleansing and the drainage of towns generally present instances only of varieties of grievous defects from incompleteness, and from the want of science or combination of means for the attainment of the requisite ends. Thus the local reports abound with instances of expensive main-drains, which from ignorant construction as to the levels, do not perform their office, but do accumulate pestilential refuse; other drains have proper levels, but from the want of proper supplies of water do not act; others act only partially or by surface drainage, in consequence of the neglect of communication from the houses to the drains; others, where there are drains communicating from the houses, but where the house drains do not act, or only act in spreading the surface of the matter from cesspools, increase the fœtid exhalations in consequence of the want of supplies of water; others again, as in some of the best quarters of the metropolis, where the supplies of water are adequate, and where the drains carry the refuse from the house, from want of moderate scientific knowledge or care in their construction, act like the necks of large retorts, and serve to introduce into the house the subtle gas which spreads disease after its accumulation in the sewers.

"There are districts where structural arrangements may be quite completed, water supplied, and the under drainage in action, and yet pestilential accumulations may be found spread before the doors of the population in consequence of the defective construction, and the neglect of the surface cleansing of the streets and roads. A remonstrance was made to an active and able member of a Commission of Sewers, for taking no steps to extend the drainage in a wretched district of the metropolis. The reply was a statement, that a drain had been cut through a portion of the district, but had done no good; and the remonstrant was invited to inspect the district himself, and judge whether, with streets that were unpaved and uncleansed, wet and miry, with deep holes full of refuse, it were possible,

by any under drainage, to remove the evil complained of.   Other districts there were in which
the Road Commissioners, or the Paving Board,
appeared to have done their duty; but the benefit
was prevented, and the road was kept continually
out of repair by the neglect of the service of
scavengers.

"All these local defects again are carried back to
the defective construction of the Acts of Parliament,
which generally either presume that no science, no
skill, is requisite for the attainment of the objects,
or presume both to be universal, or which in some
instances actually prohibit the only effectual mode
of drainage, namely, that from the houses into the
main-drains, prescribe cleansing by house - drains
without supplies of water, the construction of roads
independently of drains, and the execution of only
part of the necessary means, leaving essential parts
to the discretion of individuals.

"Between a town population similarly situated in
general condition, one part inhabiting streets which
are unpaved, and another inhabiting streets that
are paved, a general difference of health is observed.
The town of Portsmouth is built upon a low portion of the marshy island of Portsea.   It was
formerly subjected to intermittent fever, but since
the town was paved, in 1769, it was noticed by
Sir Gilbert Blane that this disorder no longer prevailed; whilst Kilsea and the other parts of the
island retained the aguish disposition until 1793,
when a drainage was made which subdued its
force.

"In the consideration of the evidence submitted
as to the condition of the streets on the external

condition of the residences of the labouring classes, it should be borne in mind that the external condition of the dwelling powerfully and immediately affects its internal cleanliness and general economy.

"Such is the absence of civic economy in some of our towns that their condition in respect to cleanliness is almost as bad as that of an encamped horde, or an undisciplined soldiery. Mr. Baker applied to Leeds the observations made by Sir John Pringle in his treatise on the Diseases of the Army, but they were equally applicable to the districts occupied by the labouring classes wherever the inquiry has been carried.

"The towns whose population never change their encampment have no due care, and whilst the houses, streets, courts, lanes, and streams are polluted and rendered pestilential, the civic officers have generally contented themselves with the most barbarous expedients, sitting still amidst the pollution with the resignation of Turkish fatalists, under the supposed destiny of the prevalent ignorance, sloth, and filth.

"Whilst such neglects are visited by the scourge of a regularly recurring pestilence and ravages of death more severe than a war, it may be confidently stated that the exercise of attention, care, and industry, directed by science in their removal, will not only be attended by exemptions from the pains of the visitation, but with exemptions from pecuniary burdens, and with promise even of the . profits of increased production to the community.

"This will appear from an examination of the present mode of removing the refuse from towns,

and contrasting it with improved methods, and
first with relation to the refuse of the houses.

"It is proved that the mode of retaining refuse
in the house in cesspools and privies is injurious
to the health and often extremely dangerous. The
process of emptying these reservoirs by hand labour,
and removing the contents by cartage, is very offensive, and often the occasion of serious accidents.
The expense of this mode also operates, as the
reports from the large towns show, as a complete
barrier to all cleanliness in this respect in the
dwellings or streets occupied by the labouring
classes."

CHAPTER IV.

"IT might have been expected from the value of the refuse known as manure that the great demand for it would have afforded a price which might have returned, in some degree, the expense and charge of cleansing. But this appears not to be the case in the Metropolis. It was stated that, with the exception of coal ashes, which are indispensable for making bricks, some description of lees, and a few other inconsiderable exceptions, no refuse in London pays half the expense of removal by cartage. The cost of removal, or of the labour and cartage, limited the general use or deposit of the refuse within a radius which did not exceed three miles beyond the line of the district-post of the Metropolis, that is, about six miles. It was stated that partly from the nature of the holdings, and from other circumstances within this limited district, agricultural improvements were not so good as might be expected where the facilities were so easy for obtaining any quantity of manure. Some idea may be formed of the loss of value of this manure from the Metropolis, occasioned by the expense of its collection and removal, from the evidence of a considerable contractor for scavengering, who said, with respect to the most productive manure, " I have given away thousands of loads of it; we knew not what to do with it."

" In the parts of some towns adjacent to the rural districts the cesspools were emptied gratuitously for the sake of the manure, but only when there was a considerable accumulation, and any accumulation of any decomposing material which offended the smell. For the saving of cartage, as well as the convenience of use, accumulations of refuse were frequently allowed to remain, and decompose, and dry amidst the habitations of the poorer classes.

" The comparatively recent mode of , cleansing adopted in the wealthy and newly-built districts, by the use of water closets and the discharge of all refuse at once from the house through the drain into the sewers, saved the delay and the previous accumulation, and it also saved the expense of the old means of removal. It was most applicable to the poorer districts, because really the most economical, when they are properly sewered and supplied with water. The cost of cheap and appropriate apparatus, and of water for cleansing, it was proved, was a reduction of the mere cost of cleansing in the old method, independently of the cost incurred by the decay of woodwork and deterioration of the tenement which commonly took place. The chief objection to the extension of this system was the pollution of the water of the river into which the sewers are discharged. Admitting the expediency of avoiding the pollution, it was nevertheless proved to be an evil of almost inappreciable magnitude in comparison with the ill health occasioned by the constant retention of several hundred thousand accumulations of pollution in the most densely peopled districts.

"There was much evidence, however, to prove that it was possible to remove the refuse in such a mode as to avoid the pollution of the river, and at the same time avoid the culpable waste of the most important manure.

"A practical example of the money value which lies in the refuse of a town, when removed in the cheapest manner, and applied in the form best adapted to production, viz., by a system of cleansing by water, was afforded in connection with the city of Edinburgh. In the course of the sanitary inquiry in that city the particular attention of Dr. Arnott and myself was directed to the effects of some offensive irrigation of the land which had taken place in the immediate vicinity of that city. It appeared that the contents of a large proportion of the sinks, drains, and privies of that city were conveyed in covered sewers to the eastern suburb of the town, where they were emptied into a stream, called the Foul Burn, which passed ultimately into the sea. The stream was thus made into a large uncovered sewer or drain. Several years ago some of the occupiers of the land in the immediate vicinity of this stream diverted parts of it, and collected the soil which it contained in tanks for use as manure. After this practice had been adopted for a long period, the farmers in the vicinity gradually found that the most beneficial mode of applying the manure was in the liquid form, and they conducted the stream over their meadows by irrigation. Others, perceiving the extraordinary fertility thus obtained, followed the example, and by degrees about 300 acres of meadow, chiefly in the eastern parts of that city, but all in its immediate vicinity, and the greater part of it in the neighbourhood of the palace of Holyrood, had been systematically irrigated with the contents of the common sewer. From some of this land so irrigated, four or five crops a year were obtained, and land once worth from 40s. to 50s. per acre let for very high sums.

"This use of irrigation followed so gradually, that the time of its commencement seems not accurately ascertained, but is known to have been usual near the beginning of the present century. The tanks are still to a certain extent used. The irrigation proceeds from the beginning of April to the middle of September, and it is supposed that the deposits in the tanks are in the interval increased by the quantity of soil not employed in irrigation.

"The practice was strongly objected to by the inhabitants as an offensive and injurious nuisance. To Dr. Arnott, who surveyed the district, the process appeared to be, like most offensive processes, unfitted for the vicinity of a town. The miasma from the preparation of the large accumulations of manure in open receptacles near places of public resort or crowded habitations would probably affect the public health injuriously to a greater or less degree. In particular states of the weather it could scarcely fail to engender disease. In the decomposition of substances for manure, deleterious gases are evolved, which in particular states of the atmosphere will act with powerful effects on animals within their reach.

But it is at the same time stated, the process of applying manure by irrigation, that is, separated and diluted with water, is considered to be productive of less deleterious gas, and of less injurious effects, than by spreading it over fields in a solid form, and allowing it to remain until it is decomposed and separated by the atmosphere and conveyed into the soil by rain. Liebig, the greatest living authority on agricultural chemistry, states that night soil loses in drying half its valuable products, that is, half its "nitrogen," for the "ammonia" escapes into the atmosphere. By irrigation, by the diffusion and conveyance of the manure to the plant in the medium of water, the escape of the valuable substance as a noxious and injurious gas is diminished. Whatever extent of loss there is from manures by decomposition when placed on the land in a solid form, and when exposed to the action of the atmosphere, it is stated that there is proportionate gain by holding the material in suspension in water. The simple offensiveness, it may be assumed, is a sufficient ground of exclusion of any process from amidst the habitations of a town population. But at a reasonable distance the use of dung or any other manure would not be forbidden; and the process which is the least injurious, the irrigative, is entitled therefore to a preference. Effective drainage must make way for the conveyance of diluted manures, and consequently for effective irrigation.

"The comparative economy of conveyance of fluid in pipes has been but little observed, and has only recently perhaps been applied for the purpose of cleansing. The following is an instance of the application of the principle:—A contract was about to be entered into by the West Middlesex Water

Company for hauling out from their reservoir at Kensington the deposit of eight or ten years' silt, which had accumulated to the depth of three or four feet. The contractor offered to remove this quantity, which covered nearly an acre of surface, for the sum of £400, in three or four weeks. The reservoir was emptied in order to be inspected by the engineer and directors before the contract was accepted. It occurred to one of the officers that the cleansing might be accomplished more readily by merely stirring up the silt to mix it with the water; and then if a cut or outlet were made in the main pipe used for conveying the water to London, it might be washed out. He accordingly got thirty or forty men to work in stirring up the deposit, and accomplished the work at a cost of £40 or £50, and three or four days' labour, instead of so many weeks; and when the directors went to see the basin, to decide upon the contract, the reservoir was as free from any deposit as a house-floor. Since the discovery thus made, the silt has been regularly cleansed out into the common sewers. It is to be observed, in respect to the relative cheapness of the two modes, that the contractor would only have removed the silt to the nearest convenient place of deposit in the immediate vicinity of the reservoir, whereas, in the fluid state, it might be carried, at the actual cost of conveying water, as far as it is at present conveyed, and sold with a profit, twelve or fourteen miles, and raised to heights of 150 feet, at $2\frac{1}{2}d.$ per ton.

"By the application of capital and machinery, the cost of conveyance of substances in suspension in a fluid, even at the water companies' prices, may be rendered thirty and even more than forty times as cheap as collection by hand labour and removal by cartage. In the Metropolis, where the persons who water the roads may obtain water gratuitously from pumps, the water supplied from stand-pipes by some of the water companies at £1 per 100 tons is found to be twice as cheap as the mere labour of pumping the water into the cart. By proper hydraulic arrangements heavy solid substances may be swept away through the iron pipes.

" Though the refuse of the poorer districts is often taken and sold, the immediate objection to the extension of the services of the scavenger to them is the increase of the immediate expense, which it is practically necessary to consider in detail, although if there were no compensation by the sale of any coal-ashes or house refuse, and if the occupants were required to pay for the cleansing at the rate of one of the opulent parishes in the metropolis, that is at the rate of 4s. per house per annum, which would be less than a penny per tenement for the weekly street cleansing; or, in the poorer districts, where there are mostly two families to a tenement, a charge of less than one halfpenny per week for cleansing, would be found to be good economy, as one means of diminishing the existing heavy charge of sickness, not to speak of the wear and tear of clothes.

" The sewerage of the Metropolis, though it is a frequent subject of boast to those who have not examined its operations or effects, will be found to be a vast monument of defective administration, of lavish expenditure, and extremely defective execution. The general defect of these works is, that they are so constructed as to accumulate deposits within them;

that the accumulations remain for years, and are at last only removed at a great expense, and in an offensive manner, by hand labour and cartage. The effect is to generate and retain in large quantities before the houses the gases which it is the object of cleansing to remove. In the course of the present inquiry instances have been frequently presented of fevers and deaths occasioned by the escapes of gas from the sewers into the streets and houses. In the evidence given before the Committee of the House of Commons, which received evidence on the subject in 1834, one medical witness stated, that of all cases of severe typhus that he had seen, eight-tenths were either in houses of which the drains from the sewers were untrapped, or which, being trapped, were situated opposite gully-holes; and he mentioned instances where servants sleeping in the lower rooms of houses were invariably attacked with fever. It was proposed as a remedy, to prevent the escape of the noxious effluvia by trapping the drains; but this was refused on account of the danger to the men, who must enter the sewers to clean them, from the confined gas. In one of the circulars the reason assigned for allowing the escape of the gas into the streets was that if it were confined to the sewers it might impede the flow of the water. It was then proposed to allow the escape of the noxious gases through chimneys constructed at certain distances. But this was decided to be an experiment, and the Committee did not feel themselves authorised to make experiments. Instances were adduced where it had been found necessary either to trap or to remove gully-holes in the vicinity of butchers' shops, to avoid the injurious effects of the effluvium upon the meat. Similarly mischievous effects of the defective construction and management of the sewers are commonly displayed in the medical reports from the provincial towns, and they have been incidentally noticed in the passages already cited.

"It may be mentioned as another instance of the absence of appropriate knowledge that has governed these structural arrangements, that a large proportion of the most expensive sewers are constructed with flat bottoms. In proportion as the water is spread the flow is impeded, and the deposit of matter it may hold in suspension increased. Mr. Roe, a civil engineer, who, much to the honour of the Holborn and Finsbury district of sewers, has been appointed to the care of their sewers, and is perhaps the only officer having the experience and qualifications of a civil engineer, states that, as compared with sewers or drains with bottoms of a semi-circular form, those with flat bottoms invariably occasion a larger amount of deposit; and with the same flow of water, the difference of construction occasions a difference of more than one-half in the deposit which is left. By the common and most expensive form, the drains are apt to be choked up with noxious accumulations; by being built with flat sides (instead of with curved sides, which give the strength of an arch), they are apt, in clayey and slippery ground, to be forced in.

CHAPTER V.

"THE bad condition of the streets in many of our towns is very generally ascribable to pavement being commonly regarded as requisite solely for cart or carriage conveyance, and not as a means of cleanliness. The pavement has, therefore, been usually confined to the chief streets in which the carriage traffic is considerable. Some of the principal streets, even in the Metropolis, almost justify the description of being 'streams of mud and filth in winter,' and 'seas of dust' in summer. But attention has of late been directed to the cleansing of the road as a means of removing damp and dirt or dust, which are each found to be injurious. So far as various experiments have yet proceeded in the Metropolis, they are stated to be highly favourable to the use of wood as a substance for paving the streets, though perhaps in forms different from those at present in use, with improvements which further experience will suggest. Wood, when pinned together and laid on a firm substratum, appears to be less retentive of wet than most forms of stone pavement, and to possess very considerable advantages over the macadamised roads for crowded thoroughfares. If it be brought into general use it will have an advantage in removing the granite dust, which medical authorities believe to be much more prejudicial to health, in exciting or aggravating lung diseases, than the public have been aware of. When there is much dust in the working of close quarries, the effects of it are almost as destructive to the lungs of the operatives as the knife-grinding to the operatives of Sheffield who do not guard against the steel dust. 'It is scarcely conceivable,' Dr. Arnott states, 'that the immense quantities of granite dust pounded by one or two hundred thousand pairs of wheels working on macadamised streets, should not greatly injure the public health. In houses bordering such streets or roads, it is found that, notwithstanding the practice of watering, the furniture is often covered with dust even more than once in the day, so that writing on it with the finger becomes legible, and the lungs and air-tubes of the inhabitants, with a moist lining to detain the dust, are constantly pumping the same atmosphere. The passengers by a stage coach in dry weather, when the wind is moving with them so as to keep them enveloped in the cloud of dust raised by the horses' feet and the wheels of the coach, have their clothes soon saturated to whiteness with the dust, and their lungs, of course, are charged in a corresponding degree. A gentleman who rode only twenty miles in this way, had afterwards to cough and expectorate for ten days to clear his chest again.' The imperfection of road cleansing in paved streets at the same time deteriorates the salubrity of the towns, the value of the refuse for production, and the streets themselves. The farmers find that the refuse of the streets, of which horse-dung and other excrementitious substances form so important a part, is valuable in proportion as it is 'fresh.' On a proposition to sweep the streets of a town district oftener, it was stated by some farmers that they would, in that case, give more for the refuse. It is with this description of refuse, as stated with respect to the night soil—in proportion as it is allowed to remain in the streets to dry, it loses the gas which gives it value ; and the gas which is lost frequently gives to streets the offensive smell perceptible to strangers who have not been familiarised to it, and makes a deleterious addition to the compounds by which the health of the town population is injured. The complete and rapid cleansing of the roads has also its effects on the draught. It is proved experimentally that, ' calling the draught on a broken stone road 5, that on the same road covered with dust is 8, and that on the same road wet and muddy is 10.' A road should be cleansed 'from time to time, so as never to have half an inch of mud upon it. This is particularly necessary to be attended to where the materials are weak, for if the surface is not kept clean, so as to admit of its becoming dry in the intervals between showers of rain, it will be rapidly worn away.' With the even surface obtainable from the use of wood as a pavement, it is stated that the streets which are now kept wet and dirty whilst the process of cleansing is slowly carried on by the hand, may be rapidly and cheaply swept by sweeping machines drawn by horses. With the advantage of such a system of sewerage as that described by Mr. Roe, the surface refuse, which continues exposed during a whole week, may be removed every morning before the hours of traffic from all the principal thoroughfares. In the main streets of the towns of considerable traffic, a smooth and firm surface for the

carriage way would ensure the advantages of a rail-
road, in addition to those to the public health, from
cleanliness. The experience on several portions of
smooth road shows that single horses with lighter
and less expensive vehicles would suffice where two
horses are now required on the common roads; and
where strong stone pavements are required to resist
the shock of heavy vehicles, and heavy vehicles pro-
pelled with double power to resist the battering of
strong pavements, and the grinding and wear and
tear of heavy and dirty roads.

" The cleansing of the streets, and the removal
of the impurities from the habitations, appears to
have been the subject of considerable attention
at Paris of late years. An individual proposed to
the Administration of that city a mode of cleansing
the streets and pavements, by sweeping into the
sewers which are discharged into the Seine, all the
refuse that had hitherto been daily gathered into
heaps, and carted away beyond the precincts. The
Minister of Police thought it advisable to take the
opinion of the Institute on the proposal. The
superiority of the proposed mode of street cleansing
was admitted, but the members of the Institute, to
whom the subject was referred, having ascertained
the quantity of rubbish which was daily collected in
Paris, and also the quantity of water which flowed
in the Seine during the summer time, found
that this volume of water was 9,000 times greater
than the greatest quantity of filth and rubbish
collected in the same length of time from the streets
of Paris; and they reported as their conclusion,
that 'the quantity of dirt which would be thrown
into the Seine, compared with the volume of water

in the river, would be found to be so extremely
small as to be absolutely inappreciable; that it was
not from the consideration therefore of insalubrity
that the project for cleansing the streets as proposed should be negatived, but solely because by
that means there would be lost a quantity of most
valuable manure, which was quite indispensable to
the agriculture around Paris, and consequently to
Paris itself.'

"Mr. Roe has furnished a calculation made from
the flow of water in the Thames, at a neap tide;
taking the ebb, and comparing it with the quantity
of deposit in the water running from the sewers from
the whole of the Metropolis (assuming that the
sewerage bears the same proportion as the Holborn
and Finsbury division), that the proportion of impurities to the volume of water of the Thames is as
1 to 10,100. If the surface cleansing of the streets
were added to the ordinary mass of impurity, he
calculates that the proportion held in suspension
would then be about 1 to 5,069. To this must be
added the impurities from land-floods, and those from
vessels in the river. The amount of impurity discharged from the sewers was calculated from the
amount of deposit known to have been formed in
several of them. The amount of impurity in the
Thames would therefore be, at the least, double the
amount of that calculated for the Seine.

"If the evils of the pollution of such a stream
were much greater, they would still be found inconsiderable as compared with the perpetual pollution
of the air by the retention of ordures and refuse
amidst large masses of the population. What has
been stated as to the practicability of extending

threefold the cleansing of towns, by dispensing with cartage, and using the sewers for the removal of the refuse of the streets, is stated as an advantage, even on the supposition that no use is made of the refuse, and that it is entirely thrown away. But it were a reproach to stop at the advance to this far lesser evil, and to add to the pollution of the streams of the towns, which throughout the country form the chief common sewers, by throwing into them everything that is vile in the towns, *i.e.*, everything that is most valuable for increasing the surrounding fertility.

"On a full examination of the evidence adduced and of the evidence indicated, it will, I trust, be found to be satisfactorily established, that the houses of towns may be constantly and rapidly cleansed of noxious refuse by adaptation of drains and public sewers; and that with such an adaptation, for one street or one district cleansed at the present expense, three may be cleansed by the proposed mode; that the natural streams flowing near towns may be preserved from the pollution caused by the influx of the contents of the public sewers, by the conveyance of all refuse through covered pipes; and, that the existing cost of conveyance, by which use for production is restricted, may be reduced to less than one-fortieth or fiftieth of the present expense of removal by hand labour and cartage. These bounties on cleanliness and salubrity on the one hand, and beneficial production on the other, are dependent on skilful and appropriate administrative arrangements. But for the attainment of these objects, and the relief of the worst-conditioned districts, another provision appears to be requisite, namely, appropriate supplies of water."

CHAPTER VI.

WATER AND HEALTH.

"BESIDES reports from towns in which a large proportion of salubrity is attributed to a natural drainage, from the porosity of the soil, or from the undulations of the surface being favourable to the discharge of moisture, other reports ascribed a large proportion of the comparative health of the population to advantageous circumstances, in respect to the supplies of water. It will be manifest that for an efficient system of house cleansing and sewerage, it is indispensable that proper supplies of pure water should be provided, and be laid on in the houses in towns of every size, and, it might be added, in all conceivable rural villages. No previous investigations had led any author to conceive the great extent to which the labouring classes are subjected to privations, not only of water for the purpose of ablution, house-cleansing, and sewerage, but of wholesome water for drinking and culinary purposes.

"On various reports from the medical officers and others in England as well as in Scotland, in which it is stated that 'a plentiful supply of water *may* be had from the street wells, and also from a burn which runs close to the town,' it is to be observed that the economy of a town, or of any considerable collection of habitations, appears to be essentially defective, in so far as it leaves a large proportion of the inhabitants dependent on such a mode of supply.

"Supplies of water obtained from wells by the labour of fetching and carrying it in buckets or vessels do not answer the purpose of regular supplies of water brought into the house without such labour, and kept ready in cisterns for the various purposes of cleanliness. The interposition of the labour of going out and bringing home water from a distance acts as an obstacle to the formation of better habits; and it is an important principle to be borne in mind, that in the actual condition of the lower classes, conveniences of this description must precede and form the habits. It is in vain to expect of the great majority of them that the dispositions, still less the habits, will precede or create the conveniences.

"Even with persons of a higher condition, the habits are greatly dependent on the conveniences, and it is observed that when the supplies of water into the houses of persons of the middle class are cut off by the pipes being frozen, and when it is necessary to send for water to a distance, the house cleansings and washings are diminished by the inconvenience. Every presumption is thus afforded that if it were at all times requisite for them to send to a distance for water, and in all weathers, their habits of household cleanliness would be deteriorated. In towns where the middle classes have not the advantage of supplies of water brought into the houses, the general habits of household and personal cleanliness are inferior to those of the inhabitants of towns who do enjoy the advantage. The families of the labouring

man in the manufacturing towns rise early, before
daylight in winter time, to go to their work; they
toil hard, and they return to their homes late at
night.　It is a serious inconvenience, as well as
discomfort to them, to have to fetch water at a
distance out of doors from the pump or the river
on every occasion that it may be wanted, whether
it may be in cold, in rain, or in snow.　The minor
comforts of cleanliness are, of course, foregone, to
avoid the immediate and greater discomforts of having
to fetch the water.ꞏ In general, it has appeared in
the course of the present inquiry that the state of
the conveniences gives, at the same time, a very fair
indication of the state of the habits of the population
in respect to household and even personal cleanliness.

" In most towns, and certainly in the larger manufacturing towns, those members of a family who
are of strength to fetch water, are usually of
strength to be employed in profitable industry, and
the mere value of their time expended in the labour
of fetching water is always much higher than the
cost of regular supplies of water, even at the charge
made by the water companies.

" The experience of the water companies tends to
show that the distribution of water directly into the
houses where it is wanted would be good economy
of the water.　When the supply of water into the
houses is stopped by frost, and cocks are, on that
occasion, opened in the streets, the supply of water
required is one-third greater than usual; as great,
indeed, as it is in the heat of summer, when there is
a large additional consumption for watering gardens
and roads.　I would here suggest that it is essential
that the water should be charged on the owners of

all the small weekly tenements, because, where the owner finds it necessary to collect the rent weekly, the smaller collection of rates for longer periods would often be impracticable, and the expense of the collection alone of such small rates weekly ($1\frac{1}{4}d$. per week) would be more than the amount collected.

"The mode of supplying water by private companies for the sake of a profit is not, however, available for the supply of a population, where the numbers are too small to defray the expense of obtaining a private Act of Parliament, or the expense of management by a board of directors, or to produce profits to shareholders; it is, therefore, a mode not available to the population of the country who do not reside in the chief towns.

"Although there is little probability that regular supplies of water would ever have been obtained without the inducement of salaries to the managers, and of returns of interest to the capitalists; although the cost of most of the supplies at the highest is much lower than the labour of fetching water from a pump close to the house, and no valid objection appears against compulsory provisions for water being laid on (*i.e.*, for existing charges of labour being reduced) in the tenements of the labouring classes in towns, at the common charge of the water companies; still the appearance of a profit and dividends on the supply of a natural commodity does, in the new districts at least, furnish pretexts for the objection of the poorer owners and ignorant occupiers to the supposed expense of the improvement which consists in an immediate outlay. Apart from such objections, however, it is a mode of obtaining supplies attended with great inconveniences, which it is desirable to have considered with respect to new improvements. The payment of a dividend for an improved supply of such a commodity will be found as imperfect a measure, even of its pecuniary value, as it would be of the pecuniary value of a good and abundant supply of air and of the light of day. There are indirect effects of the use of such a commodity, of which a pecuniary estimate cannot conveniently be made, as against an immediate outlay. For example, there is little ground left for doubt that the effect of street and house cleansing by means of the supplies of water needed in the worst ·districts, would occasion considerable reductions in the pecuniary charge of sickness on the poor's rates, but it would be extremely difficult to obtain these results in money to make up, with any pretence to accuracy, a profit and loss account as an undertaking for the outlay. The evidence afforded by the creation and success of a private company proves only that a certain class of persons so far appreciate the advantages of the supply as to be willing to incur such an immediate expense as will cover the cost, and yield a profit to the undertakers; it proves nothing as to the intrinsic value of the service or the commodity, which may be immense to the bulk of the community, and yet not one be found ready to volunteer to defray a portion of the expense. But the expense of the machinery of water companies, as already stated, is disproportioned to the means of the smaller towns, and to a large part of the country; and generations may pass away amidst filth and pestilence before the scientific means and the economy of prevention can be appreciated by them.

" There are further objections made in towns

to the mode of supply itself. One is, that it
creates strong interest against all improvements in
the quality or the supplies of water, for every
considerable improvement creates expense, which
is felt in diminution of the dividends of the private shareholders; and so long as a majority of
the ratepayers are content with bad water, or deem
it hopeless to seek to obtain water of a superior
quality, so long as any public clamour will not
endanger the dividends, it appears that no amendment entailing considerable expense can be expected.
Even where there are convenient unappropriated
streams, and a wide field is afforded for competition by
a very populous district, the competition of different
companies does not necessarily furnish to the individual consumer any choice or amendment of the
supplies.

"The competition frequently absorbs the profit on
the funds that might be available to the competing
parties (supposing them disposed to carry out any
plans other than those which have for their object
the cheapest supply that can be procured); and does
not reduce the charge of the supply of water to the
public. At one time there were three sets of water-
pipes belonging to three different companies passing
through the same streets of a large proportion of the
Metropolis. This wasteful competition of three immense capitals sunk in the supply of one district,
for which the expenditure of one capital and one
establishment would have sufficed, ended in an
agreement between the competing companies to
confine themselves to particular districts. The
dividends at present obtained by the shareholders
of the chief companies in the Metropolis on the

capital now employed appears, however, to be
only 4, 5, or 6 per cent., but this is on several
expensive establishments and sets of officers, which
appear to admit of consolidation. The committee
of the House of Commons which investigated the
subject of the supplies of water in 1821, concluded
by recommending a consolidation of the several
trusts; but excepting that the competition between
them has abated, the expense and waste of separate
establishments is still continued, and beyond this
the expense of the fixed capital and establishment,
charged upon perhaps one-third of the proper supply
of water.

" The private companies are also complained of
as being practically irresponsible and arbitrary, and
unaccommodating towards individuals. It is a
further subject of complaint, as respects supplies
by such companies, that they are directed almost
exclusively to the supplies of such private houses as
can pay water rates; that they are not arranged for
the important objects of cleansing the streets or
drains, or of supplying water in case of fire.

" There appears to be no reason to doubt that the
mode of supplying water to Bath, and gas to the
town of Manchester, might be generally adopted in
supplying water to the population. In order to get
an efficient water supply, powers would be required
to enter into the lands adjacent to towns, on a
reasonable compensation to the owners, to obtain
supplies of water; and, as the management of water-
works requires appropriate skill, it would be necessary to appoint an officer with special qualifications
for their superintendence. Ordinary service may be
obtained for the public, if recourse be had to the

ordinary motives by which such service is engaged
in private companies. It is not mentioned invi-
diously, but as a matter of fact, that the majority,
not to say the whole, of such undertakings, by joint
stock companies, are, in the first instance, moved by
a solicitor, or engineer, or other person, for the sake
of the office of manager of the works, and that the
directors and shareholders, and the inducement of
profit to them, through the benefit undoubtedly to
the public, are only the machinery to the attainment
of the object for which the undertaking is primarily
moved. If competent officers be appointed, and
adequately remunerated for the service, there can
be little doubt that the public may be saved the
expense of the management by the occasional
attendance of unskilled directors, and that they
may save the expense of dividends, or apply the
profits to public improvements, and moreover avoid
the inconveniences and obstructions undoubtedly
belonging to the supply of a commodity so essential
to the public health, comfort, and economy by a
private monopoly. Bad supplies of water would
generally be less tolerated by the influential inhabitants of all places from a public municipal agency
than from a private company.

"The queries transmitted to the medical officers
were directed to ascertain the sufficiency of the
supplies for the purpose of cleansing, but the returns frequently advert to the bad effect of inferior
supplies upon the health of the population: and it is
scarcely conceivable to what filthy water, by custom,
reconciles the people. Yet water containing animal
matter, which is the most feared, appears to be less
frequently injurious than that which is the clearest,

namely, spring water, from the latter being oftener impregnated with mineral substances; but there are instances of ill-health produced by both descriptions of water. The beneficial effects derived from care as to the qualities of the water is now proved in the navy, where fatal dysentery formerly prevailed to an immense extent, in consequence of the impure and putrid state of the supplies; and care is now generally exercised on the subject by the medical officers of the army.

"In the Metropolis the public owes the analysis of the supplies of water, and some improvement of supplies not in their nature essentially bad, chiefly to the stirring of speculators in rival companies. But the population of the rural districts, and of the smaller towns, afford no means for the payment of companies, still less any field for pecuniary competition.

"The middle classes are exposed to the like inconveniences, and put up with very inferior water, whilst supplies of a salubrious quality might be obtained by extended public arrangements for the common benefit.

"It will not be deemed necessary to attempt to develop all the considerations applicable to the subject; but there is wide foundation for the complaint that proper supplies of water to large portions of the community are extensively wanting; that those obtained are frequently of inferior quality—that they are commonly obtained at the greatest expense when obtained by hand labour—that the supplies by private companies, though cheaper and better, are defective, and chiefly restricted to the use of the higher and middle classes, unless in such inconvenient modes (*i.e.*, by cocks in courts), as seriously to impede the growth of habits of cleanliness among the working classes. To which may be added, as the expression of an opinion founded on communications from all parts of the kingdom, that as a highly important sanitary measure connected with any general building regulations, whether for villages or for any class of towns, arrangements should be made for all houses to be supplied with good water, and should be prescribed as being as essential to cleanliness and health as the possession of a roof or of due space; that for this purpose, and in places where the supplies are not at present satisfactory, power should be vested in the most eligible local administrative body, which will generally be found to be that having charge of cleansing and structural arrangements, to procure proper supplies for the cleansing of the streets, for sewerage, for protection against fires, as well as for domestic use."

By recent legislation some of the suggestions contained in this chapter on " Water and Health " have been carried out. But although the chapter was written over forty years ago, it stands at this very hour a reproach and a lesson.

CHAPTER VII.

LAND DRAINAGE AND HEALTH.

"IN considering the circumstances external to the residence which affect the sanitary condition of the population, the importance of a general land drainage is developed by the inquiries as to the causes of the prevalent diseases to a magnitude of which no conception had been formed at the commencement of the investigation. Its importance is manifested by the severe consequences of its neglect in every part of the country, as well as by its advantages in the increasing salubrity and productiveness wherever the drainage has been skilful and effectual. The following instance is presented in a report from *Mr. John Marshall, junr.*, the clerk to the union in the Isle of Ely:—

"'It has been shown that the Isle of Ely was at one period in a desolate state, being frequently inundated by the upland waters, and destitute of adequate means of drainage; the lower parts became a wilderness of stagnant pools, the exhalations from which loaded the air with pestiferous vapours and fogs; now, by the improvements which have from time to time been made, and particularly within the last fifty years, an alteration has taken place which may appear to be the effect of magic. By the labour, spirit, and industry of the inhabitants, a forlorn waste has been converted into pleasant and fertile pastures, and they themselves have been rewarded by bounteous harvests. Drainage, embankments, engines, and enclosures have given stability to the soil (which in its nature is as rich as the Delta of Egypt) as well as salubrity to the air. These very considerable improvements, though carried on at a great expense, have at last turned to a double account, both in reclaiming much ground and improving the rest, and in contributing to the healthiness of the inhabitants. Works of modern refinement have given a totally different face and character to this once neglected spot; much has been performed, much yet remains to be accomplished by the rising generation. The demand for labour produced by drainage is incalculable, but when it is stated that where sedge and rushes grew but a few years since we now have fields of waving oats and even wheat, it must be evident that it is very great.'

"Mr. George Elgar, another of the medical officers of the Eastry Union, observes that;—'The parishes forming the fifth district of the Eastry Union are, with one or two exceptions, close to marshes separating the Isle of Thanet from this portion of East Kent, and consequently, during the spring and autumn, the inhabitants are exposed to the malaria therefrom; but for these last few years, owing to the excellent plan of draining, very few diseases have occurred (in my opinion) that can be said to be produced by malaria. There is very little ague, scarcely any continued fevers, and a case of typhus, I believe, has not been known along the borders of the marshes for the last three or four years. Some years back a great portion of the parishes adjoining these marshes was under water from the end of autumn to the early part of the following spring; then agues and fevers of all characters prevailed to a very great extent. Although the malaria does not produce diseases of any *decided character*, yet, during a wet spring or autumn, there are always cases of inflammation of the lungs or bowels, and rheumatism, both·in acute and chronic forms.   The houses in general are good, well drained and well ventilated, having one or two sitting rooms, as many bedrooms, sometimes more, scullery, and some convenient receptacles for refuse and fuel.   The cottages generally are *extremely cleanly*, though of course there must be some exceptions, where the occupiers would not be clean and careful under any circumstances.'

" In the course of inquiries as to what have been the effects of land drainage upon health, one frequent piece of information received has been that the rural population had not observed the effects on their own health, but they had marked the effects of drainage on the health and improvement of the stock.   Thus the less frequent losses of stock from epidemics are beginning to be perceived as accompanying the benefits of drainage in addition to those of increased vegetable production.

" *Dr. Edward Harrison*, in a paper in which he points out the connection between the rot in sheep and other animals, and some important disorders in the human constitution, observed :—' The connection between humidity and the rot is universally admitted by experienced graziers ; and it is a matter of observation that since the brooks and rivulets in the county of Lincoln have been better managed, and the system of laying ground dry, by open ditches and under draining, has been more judiciously practised, the rot is become far less prevalent. Sir John Pringle informs us, that persons have maintained themselves in good health, during sickly seasons, by inhabiting the upper stories of their houses; and I have reason to believe that, merely by confining sheep on high grounds through the night, they have escaped the rot.'

"A grazier has for many years occupied a large portion of an unenclosed fen, in which was a shallow piece of water that covered about an acre and a half of land. To recover it for pasturage, he cut in it several open ditches to let off the water, and obtained an imperfect drainage. His sheep immediately afterwards became liable to the rot, and in most years he lost some of them. In 1792 the drains failed so entirely, from the wetness of the season, that he got another pond of living water, and sustained in that season no loss of his flock. For a few succeeding years he was generally visited with the rot; but having satisfied himself by experience that whenever the pit was, from the weather, either completely dry or completely under water, his flock was free from the disorder, he attempted a more perfect drainage, and succeeded in making the land dry at all times. Since that period he has lost no sheep from the rot, though, till within the last two years, he continued to occupy the fen.

"The late Mr. Bakewell was of opinion that, after May-day, he could communicate the rot at pleasure, by flooding and afterwards stocking his closes, while they were drenched and saturated with moisture. In summer, rivers and brooks are often suddenly swollen by thunder storms, so as to pass over their banks, and cover the adjacent low lands. In this state no injury is sustained during the inundation, but when the water returns to its former channel, copious exhalations are produced from the swamps and low lands, which are exceedingly dangerous to the human constitution, and to several other animals as well as sheep.

" A medical officer of one of the unions who came to town for the transaction of some business before the Board, begged to be favoured by the immediate despatch of his business, inasmuch as from a change of weather which had taken place since his departure, he was certain that he should have a number of cases waiting for him. On being asked to explain the circumstances from which he inferred the occurrence of disease with so much certainty, he stated that within his district there was a reservoir to feed a canal ; that they had let out the water as they were accustomed to do in spring time for the purpose of cleansing it, and that whenever such weather occurred as then prevailed during the process, he was sure to have a great number of fever cases amongst the labourers in the village which immediately adjoined the reservoir.

" The sanitary effects of road cleansing, to which house drainage and road drainage is auxiliary, it appears is not confined to the streets in towns and the roads in villages, but extends over the roads at a distance from habitations on which there is traffic. Dr. Harrison, who gave valuable testimony on the subject of the analogy of the diseases of animals to those which affect the human constitution, in treating of the prevention of fever or the rot

amongst sheep, warns the shepherd that, after
providing drained pasture and avoiding 'rotting
places' in the fields, all his care may be frustrated
if he do not avoid, with equal care, leading the sheep
over wet and miry roads with stagnant ditches, which
are as pernicious as the places in the fields designated
as 'rotting places.' He is solicitous to impress the
fact that the rot has been contracted in ten minutes,
that sheep can at 'any time be tainted in a quarter
of an hour, while the land retains its moisture and
the weather is hot and sultry.' He gives the following instance, amongst others, of the danger of
traversing badly drained roads :—'A gentleman
removed ninety sheep from a considerable distance
to his own residence. On coming near to a bridge,
which is thrown over the Barling's river, one of the
drove fell into a ditch and fractured its leg. The
shepherd immediately took it in his arms to a neighbouring house, and set the limb. During this time,
which did not occupy more than one hour, the re-
mainder were left to graze in the ditches and lane.
The flock were then driven home, and a month afterwards the other sheep joined its companions. The
shepherd soon discovered that all had contracted the
rot except the lame sheep ; and as they were never
separated on any other occasion, it is reasonable to
conclude that the disorder was acquired by feeding
in the road and ditch bottoms.' The precautions
applicable to the sheep and cattle will be deemed
equally applicable to the labouring population who
traverse such roads.

" The condition of large and rural districts in the
immediate vicinity of the towns, and of the poorest
districts of the towns themselves, presents a singular

contrast in the nature of the agencies by which the health of the inhabitants is impaired. Within the towns we find the houses and streets filthy, the air fœtid, disease, typhus, and other epidemics rife amongst the population, bringing, in the train, destitution and the need of pecuniary as well as medical relief; all mainly arising from the presence of the richest materials of production, the complete absence of which would, in a great measure, restore health, avert the recurrence of disease, and, if properly applied, would promote abundance, cheapen food, and increase the demand for beneficial labour. Outside the afflicted districts, and at a short distance from them, as in the adjacent rural districts, we find the aspect of the country poor and thinly clad with vegetation, except rushes and plants favoured by a superabundance of moisture, the crops meagre, the labouring agricultural population few, and afflicted with rheumatism and other maladies. These bad effects arise from damp and excess of water, which, if removed, would relieve the people from a cause of disease, the land from an impediment to production, and if conveyed for the use of the town population, would give that population the element of which they stand in peculiar need, as a means to raise them from that which is their own cause of depression, and return it for use on the land as a means of the highest fertility.

"The fact of the existence of these evils, and that they are removable, is not more certain than that their removal would be attended by reductions of existing burdens, and might be rendered productive of general advantage, if due means, guided by science, and applied by properly qualified officers, be resorted to. The impediments arising from the existing state of the law, and of its local administration, form a subject for separate representation."

Through the labours of modern helminthologists, and by none more than those of the late distinguished Dr. Spencer Cobbold, the parasitic origin of sheep rot has been made most clear, and the suspicion expressed in the old saying that "sheep eat the rot" has been completely proved. But a better sanitary chapter on this subject was never produced than the chapter above written, nor a better chapter generally on land drainage and disease. Seizing on the most salient points with a diagnostic skill that amounts to genius, its author puts the question of drainage and health in a position so simply to be understood, that he who runs may read.

CHAPTER VIII.

VENTILATION AND WORK.

"THE evils arising from the bad ventilation of places of work will probably be most distinctly brought to view by the consideration of the evidences as to its effects on one particular class of workpeople.

"The frequency of the cases of early deaths, and orphanage, and widowhood amongst one class of labourers, the journeymen tailors, led to some inquiries as to the causes affecting these classes; and evidence for peculiar consideration, as an illustration of the operation of one predominant cause, viz., bad ventilation or overcrowding. The consequences of this original cause—bad ventilation—on the moral habits, in the loss of healthful existence and happiness to the labourer; the loss of profit to the employer and of produce to the community; and the loss in expenditure for the relief of destitution—which we have high scientific authority for stating to be easily and economically controllable losses—were brought also under observation.

"Thomas Brownlow, a tailor, aged 52, stated that:—'he had always worked at the largest places in London; one part of the time at Messrs. Allen's, of Old Bond Street, where he worked eight years;

another part of the time at Messrs. Stultze's, in
Clifford Street, where he worked four years. At
Messrs. Allen's they had then from 80 to 100 men
at work; at Messrs. Stultze's about 250 men.

"'The place in which they used to work at
Messrs. Allen's was a room where eighty men worked
together. It was a room about 16 or 18 yards long,
and 7 or 8 yards wide, lighted with skylights; the
men were close together, nearly knee to knee. In
summer time the heat of the men, and the heat of
the irons, made the room twenty or thirty degrees
higher than the heat outside; the heat was then
most suffocating, especially after the candles were
lighted. Young men, tailors from the country, have
fainted away in the shop from the excessive heat
and closeness. Other working men, coming into
the shop to see some of the men, used to complain
of the heat, and also of the smell, as ntolerable;
the smell occasioned by the heat of the irons, and
the various breaths of the men, really was at times
intolerable. · The men sat as loosely as they possibly
could, and the perspiration ran from them, owing
to the heat and the closeness. It is of frequent
occurrence in such workshops that light suits of
clothes were spoiled from the perspiration of the
hand, and the dust and flue which arise darkening
the work. There has been £40 to £50 worth of
work spoiled in the course of the summer from
this cause.

"'The men were more unhealthy in winter, as the
heat from the candles and the closeness was much
greater. Any cold currents of air which came in
gave annoyance to those sitting near the draught.
There was continued squabbling as to the windows

being opened; those who were near the windows, and who did not feel the heat so much as the men near the stoves, objecting to their being opened. The oldest, who had been inured to the heat, did not like the cold, and generally prevailed in keeping out the cold or the fresh air. Such has been the state of the atmosphere, that in the very coldest nights large thick tallow candles (quarter of a pound candles) have melted and fallen over from the heat.

" ' The workplace had a very depressing effect on the energies of the workmen; that was the general complaint of those who came into it. Many could not stay out the hours, and went away earlier. Those who were not accustomed to the places generally lost appetite. The natural effect of the depression was, that they had recourse to drink as a stimulant. They went into the shop at six o'clock in the morning; but at seven o'clock, when orders for the breakfast were called for, gin was brought in, and the common allowance was half a-quartern. The younger hands did not begin with gin. The breakfast was very light; those who took gin generally took only half-a-pint of tea and half a twopenny loaf as breakfast. Liquor was again brought in at eleven o'clock. Some took beer, some took gin again. In a general way they took a pint of porter at eleven o'clock. It was seldom the men took more than a half-quartern of gin.

" ' At three o'clock some took beer and some gin, just the same as in the morning. At five o'clock the beer and gin came in again, and was usually taken in the same quantities. At seven o'clock the shop was closed.

"'After work nearly all the young men, and some of the others, went to the public-house.

"'The wages they received were 6*d.* per hour, which, at the full work, made 6*s.* a-day, or 36*s.* a-week. Very few had anything for themselves at the end of the week.

"'The habit of drinking was produced by the state of the workplace, or the greater part of it; because when men work by themselves, or only two or three together, in cooler and less close places, there is scarcely any drinking between times. Nearly all the drinking proceeds from the large shops, where the men are crowded together in close rooms; it is the same in the shops in the country, as well as those in the town. In a rural place, the tailor, where he works by himself, or with only two or three together, takes very little of the fermented liquor or spirits which the men feel themselves under a sort of necessity for doing in towns. The closer the ventilation of the place of work, the worse are the habits of the men working in them.

"'The general effect of this state of things upon the health of the men exposed to them is that great numbers of them die of consumption. "A decline," is the general disease of which they die. By their own rules, a man at fifty years of age is superannuated, and is thought not to be fit to do a full day's work. The average of the ages of the men at work at such shops was thirty-two or thereabouts, with very few above fifty years of age. Amongst the tailors employed in the shops, there were not ten men in the hundred above fifty years of age, and when they died no provision was made for the families; nothing is heard of them, and if they could not provide for themselves, they must go upon the parish.'

"On being asked: Are these habits created by the closeness of the rooms, attended by carelessness as to the mode of living elsewhere? Brownlow answered:—

"'I think not as to their lodgings. The English and Scotch tailors are more careful as to their places of lodging; and prefer sleeping in an open place. The men, however, who take their pint of porter and their pipe of tobacco in a public-house after their hours of work, take it at a place which is sometimes as crowded as a shop. Here the single men will stay until bed-time. Gin and beer were then not the only stimulants taken in consequence of the want of ventilation, and the state of the place of work when crowded. Snuff was very much taken as a stimulant; the men thought snuff had a beneficial effect on the eyes. After going into those close shops from the open air, the first sensation experienced was frequently a sensation of drowsiness, then a sort of itching or uneasiness at the eye, then a dimness of the sight. Some men of the strongest sight complain of this dimness; all eyes are affected much in a similar manner. Snuff is much used as a stimulant to awaken them up; smoking in the shops is not approved of, though it is attempted; and the journeymen tailors of the large shops are in general great smokers at the public-houses. The tailors from the villages neither take so much snuff nor tobacco, nor so much of any of the stimulants, as are taken by the workmen in the crowded shops of the towns.

"'With the tailors, the eye fails first; after long hours of work the first thing complained of by the

tailors is that the sight becomes dim, and a sort
of mist comes between them and their work.'

"In further evidence Mr. Brownlow said:—'That
in an uncrowded, or well-ventilated room, a man
would do his twelve hours' work in the twelve hours;
whereas in the close crowded room he would not
do more than ten hours' work in the twelve.'

"Thus, of two men beginning at twenty years
of age, the difference in extent of labour performed
by them in town, or in the country, would be, that
a man who had begun at twenty in these crowded
shops would not be so good a man at forty as a
man working to fifty in a country village; of the
two, the country tailor would be in the best condition in health and strength; in point of fact he
is so. The difference may be set down as a gain
of ten years' good labour. There are very few who
can stand such work as the town shops twenty
years. After forty-five years of age the eyes begin
to fail, and the man cannot do a full day's work.

"Supposing a workman to work in a well-ventilated
room, and to be freed from the nervous exhaustion,
consequent on the state of the place, might he not
save at least all that he drinks in the times between
his meals, or be enabled to apply it better, if he
were so disposed; and, perhaps gain the value of
the two hours' extra work in the twelve, when he
is working piece-work?

"'Yes, certainly he might. For, taking the average loss by nervous exhaustion and bad habits to
be two hours' work for twenty years, and twelve
hours' daily work for ten years in addition, and supposing a man to be employed full time, it would be
a loss of the value of 50,000 hours of productive

labour (of the value at 6*d*. per hour, £1,250) ; or,
if he were only in work half a year, at a loss of
25,000 hours ; so that if he were employed the half
time at the full wages, or full time at the half
wages, such workman would have lost the means of
putting by a sum of not less than £600 to maintain
him in comfort when he is no longer able to work ?
Very few do save ; but some save considerable sums.
One man, of the name of John Hale, saved about
£600. He was not one of the most sober men,
but he was in constant employment, sometimes
at Allen's and sometimes at Weston's, and he was
very careful ; but he died when he was about forty-
five. Another man, whose name was Philip Gray,
used to prefer the smaller shops. He was a man
of very good constitution, and he lived until he was
about seventy. He was a journeyman all his life,
and he had, when he died, more than £1,500, all
saved by London journeywork. He used to live at
a baker's shop in Silver-street, Golden-square. He
associated less with the men than others, and they
knew little about him. He was dressed much the
same as the rest, but he was much more clean in his
person ; he was remarkable for his cleanliness, and
he was very neat in his person. Both he and Hale
were single men.'

"The evidence of several master tailors on the effects
of work in crowded or badly ventilated rooms was also
collected. Some were inclined to ascribe more of the
ill-health to the habits of the journeymen in drinking
at public-houses, to the state of the journeymen
at public-houses, and to the state of their private
dwellings ; but in the main results the loss of daily
power, *i.e.*, the loss of at least one-third of the in-

dustrial capabilities enjoyed by men working under advantageous circumstances—the nervous exhaustion attendant on work in crowds, and the consequent temptation to resort continually to stimulants, which in their turn increased the exhaustion, were fully proved, and, indeed, generally admitted.

"The mortuary registers do not distinguish the masters from the journeymen, there are no ready means of distinguishing those of the deceased who have been employed in the larger shops, and it is stated that many who come to work in town, and become diseased, return and die in the villages. But in the registered causes of death of 233 persons entered during the year 1839 in the eastern and western unions of the Metropolis, under the general head ' tailor,' no less than 123 are registered as having died of disease of the respiratory organs, of whom 92 died of consumption ; 16 of diseases of the nervous system, of whom 8 died of apoplexy; 16 of epidemic or contagious diseases, of whom 11 died of typhus; 23 as having died of uncertain diseases,—diseases of ' uncertain seat,'—of whom 13 fell victims of dropsy ; 8 died of diseases of the digestive organs, and 6 of ' heart disease.' Of the whole number of 233 only 29 died of old age ; and of these, if they could be traced, we may pronounce confidently that the greater propor tion of them would be found to be not journeymen, of whom not 2 or 3 per cent. attain old age, but masters. On comparing the mortuary registers in the Metropolis with the registers in the north-western and the south-western parts of England, where we may expect a larger proportion of men working separately, it was found that whilst 53 per cent. of the men died of diseases of the respiratory organs in the Metropolis, only 39 per cent. died of these diseases in the remote districts; that whilst 5 per cent. died of typhus in London, only 1 per cent. fell victims to it in the country; that whilst in London only 12 in the 100 attained old age, 25 in the 100 are registered as having attained it in the remote districts.

"Of that which in these instances appears to be the main cause of premature disease and death, defective ventilation, it is to be remarked that until very lately little had been observed or understood, even by professional men or men of science. It is only when the public health is made a matter of public care by a responsible public agency that what is understood can be expected to be generally and effectually applied for the public protection. Vitiated air not being seen, and air which is pure in winter being cold, the cold is felt, and the air is excluded by the workmen. The great desideratum hitherto has been to obtain a circulation of air which was warm as well as fresh. This desideratum has been attained, after much trial, in the House of Commons; but there is reason to believe that, by various means, at an expense within the reach certainly of large places of work, a ventilation equally good might be secured with mutual advantage.

"The effects of bad ventilation, it need not be pointed out, are chiefly manifested in consumption, the disease by which the greatest slaughter is committed. The causes of fever are comparatively few and prominent, but they appear to have a concurrent effect in producing consumption. The investigation of the whole of the contributary causes to the production of the immense mass of mortality occasioned by that disease, would be beyond the time or means

allowed for the present inquiry ; but defective ventilation, and defective management in respect to
changes of temperature, are causes everywhere
apparent amongst the labouring classes.

" The reports of some hospitals present similar and
generally corroborative experience. In the space of
four years, ending in 1784, in a badly-ventilated
house, the Lying-in hospital in Dublin, there died
2,944 children out of 7,650; but after freer ventilation, the deaths in the same period of time, and in
a like number of children, amounted only to 279.

" One effect of the attention given to the condition
of the workers in the factories has been, that ventilation has been extensively introduced, and with
marked effects on the condition of the workpeople.
At Glasgow a striking instance was pointed out of
the beneficial effects of ventilation when applied to
the dwellings of the working-classes connected with
such establishments. It was stated that there was
in that city an assemblage of dwellings for the workpeople, called, from its mode of construction and the
crowd collected in it, the Barracks. This building
contained 500 persons; every room contained one
family. The consequences of this crowding of the
apartments, which were badly ventilated, and the filth,
were, that fever was scarcely ever absent from the
building. There were sometimes as many as seven
cases in one day, and in the last two months of 1831
there were fifty-seven cases in the building. All
attempts to induce the inmates to ventilate their
rooms were ineffectual, and the proprietors of the
works, on the recommendation of Mr. Fleming, a
surgeon of the district, fixed a simple tin tube of two
inches in diameter into the ceiling of each room, and

these tubes led into one general tube, the extremity
of which was inserted into the chimney of the factory
furnace. By the perpetual draught thus produced
upon the atmosphere of each room the inmates were
compelled, whether they would or not, to breathe pure
air. The effect was that, during the ensuing eight
years, fever was scarcely known in the place. The
process was apparently defective only in not providing for the appropriate warmth of the air introduced. The cost of remedies previously applied in
the public hospitals to the fever cases, continually
produced as described in the Barracks, were stated
by Dr. Cowan to have afforded a striking contrast to
the cost of the means of prevention.

" Similar defective ventilation and overcrowding in
rooms of work, with the addition of the deterioration
of the air by the use of candles or gas-lamps at night
work, produce similar effects on the milliners and
dressmakers employed at the large workshops of the
Metropolis.

" It is not doubted by medical witnesses that in
this class of cases, as in the case of the tailors, one-
third at least of the healthful duration of adult life
will be found to have been destroyed by ignorance
of the question of ventilation."

CHAPTER IX.

OVERCROWDING IN PRIVATE HOUSES.

"THE reports from the great majority of the Poor Law Unions presented evidence of the severe overcrowding of the cottages in the rural districts, and the tenements occupied by the working classes in towns.

"From the returns as laid before the public from the commissioners appointed to take the census, it would appear, however, that the number of houses had more than kept pace with the increase of the population.

"From these returns it would appear that the increase of houses even in Scotland had more than kept pace with the increase of population. But this result was so much at variance with the reports and communications from all parts of the country relating to the dwellings of the labouring classes, that if any increase of the proportions of houses to the population had taken place, it must have been in the houses of the middle and higher classes of the community.

"In the Scotch towns, and in many of the English towns, where it is the custom to let off as separate tenements the flats or floors under the same roof, there appeared to have been,—as compared with the numbers in the last census, when the buildings and not their subdivisions were returned,—an increase of accommodation, when, in reality, there might only have been an increased subdivision of the population. The evidence received from every part of the country, from rural districts as well as from towns, attested that the dwellings of large numbers of the labouring population were overcrowded, and from many districts that the overcrowding had increased.

" It would require much time and various opportunities of observation to attempt to make an exact analysis of the combined causes, and an estimate of the effect of each separate cause which operates to produce the masses of moral and physical wretchedness met with in the investigation of the condition of the lowest population. But it became evident, in the progress of the inquiry, that several separate circumstances had each its separate moral as well as physical influence. Thus tenements of inferior construction had manifestly an injurious operation on the moral as well as on the sanitary condition, independently of any overcrowding. For example, it appeared to be matter of common observation, in the instance of migrant families of workpeople, who are obliged to occupy inferior tenements, that their habits soon become 'of a piece' with the dwelling. A gentleman who had observed closely the condition of the workpeople in the south of Cheshire and the north of Lancashire, men of similar race and education, working at the same description of work, namely, as cotton spinners, —mill hands,—and earning nearly the same amount of wages, stated that the workmen of the north of Lancashire are obviously inferior to those in the south of Cheshire, in health and habits of personal cleanliness and general condition. The difference is traced mainly to the circumstance that the labourers in the north of Lancashire inhabit stone houses of a description that absorbs moisture, the dampness of which affects the health, and causes personal uncleanliness, induced by the difficulty of keeping a clean house. The operation of the same deteriorating influences were also observable in Scotland, and may be illustrated by several instances met with in the course of inquiries.

" One of the circumstances most favourable to the condition of an artisan or an agricultural labourer, is his obtaining as a wife a female who has a good industrial training in the well-regulated household of persons of a higher condition. The following instance of the effect of the dwelling itself on the condition of female servants when married was brought to notice by a member of the family in which they had been brought up. One was of a young woman who had been taught the habits of neatness, order, and cleanliness most thoroughly as household work.

" ' Her attention to personal neatness,' says a lady, who was the informant, 'was very great; her face seemed always as if it were just washed, and with her bright hair neatly combed underneath her snow-white cap, a smooth white apron, and her gown and handkerchief carefully put on, she used to look very comely. After a year or two she married the serving man, who, as he was retained in his situation, was obliged to take a house as near his place as possible. The cottages in the neighbourhood were of the most wretched kind, mere hovels built of rough stones and covered with ragged thatch; there were few even of these, so there was no choice, and they were obliged

to be content with the first that was vacant, which
was in the most retired situation. After they had
been married about two years, I happened to be
walking past one of these miserable cottages, and as
the door was open, I had the curiosity to enter. I
found it was the home of the servant I have been
describing. But what a change had come over her!
Her face was dirty, and her tangled hair hung over
her eyes. Her cap, though of good materials, was ill-
washed and slovenly put on. Her whole dress, though
apparently good and serviceable, was very untidy
and looked dirty and slatternly; everything indeed
about her seemed wretched and neglected (except
her little child), and she appeared very discontented.
She seemed aware of the change there must be in
her appearance since I had last seen her, for she
immediately began to complain of her house. The
wet came in at the door of the *only room*, and when
it rained, through every part of the roof also, except
just over the hearthstone; large drops fell upon her
as she lay in bed, or as she was working at the
window; in short, she had found it impossible to
keep things in order, so had gradually ceased to
make any exertions. Her condition had been borne
down by the condition of the house. Then her hus-
band was dissatisfied with his home and with her;
his visits became less frequent, and if he had been a
day labourer, and there had been a beer-shop or a
public-house, the preference of that to his home
would have been inevitable, and would have presented in this one instance an example of a multitude
of cases.

" ' She was afterwards, however, removed to a new
cottage, which was water-tight, and had some con-

veniences, and was built close to the road, which her former mistress and all her friends must constantly pass along. She soon resumed, in a great degree, her former good habits, but still there was a little of the *dawdle* left about her; the remains of the dispiritedness caused by her former very unfavourable circumstances.'

" In some other dwellings not far from the one above described, another instance of a female who had been brought up as a servant in a well-ordered house, and who, for her station, had received a very excellent religious and moral education, presented itself. Before her marriage she had been distinguished for the refinement with which she sung national airs, and for her knowledge of the Bible and of the doctrines of her Church. Her personal condition had become of ' a piece' with the wretched stone undrained hovel, with a pigsty before it, into which she had been taken. She was found with rings of dirt about her neck, and turning over with dirty hands Brown's Dictionary, to see whether the newly-elected minister was 'sound' in his doctrine. In this case, no moral lapse was obvious, but the children were apparently brought up under great disadvantages.

" There, however, as in most cases, the internal economy of the houses was primarily affected by the defective internal and surrounding drainage that produced damp and wet, and thence the dirt against which the inmates had ceased to contend. On inquiry of the male labourers in the district, it appeared that almost every third man was subjected to rheumatism; and with them, it was evident that the prevalence of damp and marsh miasma from the

want of drainage, if it did not necessitate, formed
a strong temptation to, the use of ardent spirits.
With them as with the females, the wretched condition of the tenement formed a strong barrier against
personal cleanliness and the use of decent clothes.
In the rural districts the very defects of the cottages
which let in the fresh air, in spite of all the efforts of
the inmates to exclude it, often obviate the effects of
the overcrowding and defective ventilation.   It has
been observed, that while the labouring population
of several districts have had no shelter but huts,
similar to those described by Dr. Gilly, as the
habitations of the border peasantry, which afforded
a free passage for currents of air, they were not
subject to fevers, though they were to rheumatism;
but when, through the good intentions of the proprietors, such habitations were provided as were
deemed more comfortable from excluding the weather
effectually, but which from the neglect of ventilation
afforded recesses for stagnating air and impurities
which they had not the means, or had not a sufficient
love of cleanliness, to remove, though rheumatism
was excluded, febrile infection was generated.   In
the towns the access of the wind is impeded by the
closeness of the surrounding habitations, and the
internal construction of the dwellings tends to exclude the air still more effectually.   Were the closed
windows opened, it would be frequently only to
admit a worse compound, the air from neglected
privies, and the miasma from the wet and undrained
court or street.

   " The close pent up air in these abodes has, undoubtedly, a depressing effect on the nervous energies, and this again, with the uneducated, and indeed

with many of the educated workpeople, has an effect
on the moral habits by acting as a strong and often
irresistible provocative to the use of fermented liquors
and ardent spirits. Much may be due to the incite-
ment of association of greater numbers of people,
but it is a common fact that the same workpeople
indulge more in drink when living in the close courts
and lanes of the town than when living in the
country, and that the residence in the different
places is attended with a difference of effects similar
to those described in respect to the tailors working
in crowded rooms in towns, and the tailors working
separately or in the country. The workpeople who
have fallen into habits of drinking, strenuously allege
the impossibility of avoiding the practice in such
places; they do, however, drink in greater quantities
in such places and give increased effect to the
noxious miasma by which they are surrounded.

"Some inquiries from Mr. Liddle, the medical
officer of the Whitechapel Union, as to the condition
of the workpeople he visited in such places as he has
described, brought to notice another indirect effect
of the external as well as the internal condition of
the dwelling on their domestic economy and general
condition.

"It appeared that the persons whom he visited
for the purpose of administering medical relief were
men earning, when in work, from sixteen to twenty
shillings per week, the women earning proportionably.
Yet whenever they were subjected to the frequent
attacks of sickness which prevailed amongst them,
they were in the most wretched destitution; the
house was bare of everything; they had no provisions
and no credit, and their need for relief was most

imminent. In answer to the inquiry how this was
to be accounted for, inasmuch as with agricultural
labourers who earned little more than half that sum
and paid nearly as much for their food, in visiting their cottages with their ministers, there was
commonly some store of provisions to be observed,
Mr. Liddle stated that in such places as those in
his district, in such atmospheres, a store of provisions would not keep; everything decayed rapidly,
and the workpeople consequently lived 'from hand
to mouth.' On inquiring as to this fact from a
respectable butcher, accustomed to selling meat to
persons living in such situations, he stated that
'meat sold on a Saturday night, in hot weather, to
poor people, who have only one close room, in which
they sleep, and live, and cook, will certainly turn
before the Sunday morning; when, if it were kept in
the butcher's shop, or in a well-ventilated place, it
would be in as good a condition on the Monday
morning. There is a great deal of loss of meat in
consequence of the want of ventilation and bad condition of the dwellings of the poorer classes. The
butter kept in such places sooner becomes rancid,
and the bread dry and disagreeable.'

"Here, then, we have from the one agent, a close
and polluted atmosphere, two different sets of
effects; the one set engendering improvidence, expense, and waste; the other, the depressing effects
of external and internal miasma on the nervous
system, tending to incite the habitual use of ardent
spirits; and both tending to precipitate this population into disease and misery.

" The familiarity with the sickness and death constantly present in the crowded and unwholesome

districts, appears to react as another concurrent cause in aggravation of the wretchedness and vice in which the poor are plunged. Seeing the apparent uncertainty of the morrow, the inhabitants really take no heed of it, and abandon themselves with the recklessness and avidity of common soldiers in a war to whatever gross enjoyment comes within their reach. All the districts visited, where the rate of sickness and mortality was high, presented, as might be expected, a proportionate amount of severe cases of destitute orphanage and widowhood, and the same places were marked by excessive recklessness of the labouring population. In Dumfries, for example, it is estimated that the cholera swept away one-eleventh part of the population. Until recently, the town had not recovered the severe effects of the visitation, and the condition of the orphans was most deplorable. Amongst young artisans, who were earning from sixteen to eighteen shillings a week, there were very few who made any reserves against the casualties of sickness. The provost was asked what number of bakers' shops there were? 'Twelve,' was his answer. And what number of whisky-shops may the town possess? 'Seventy-nine,' was the reply. If we might rely on the inquiries made of working men in the wynds of Edinburgh, their consumption of spirits bore almost the like proportion to the consumption of wholesome food.

"Captain Stuart, the superintendent of the police, stated that a man had been executed at Edinburgh for the murder of his wife in a fit of passion, in the very room the commissioners had accidentally entered, and where they were led to make the observations. At a short distance from that spot,

and amidst others of this class of habitation, were
those which had been the scenes of the murders
by Burke and Hare. Yet amidst these were the
residences of working men engaged in regular industry.

"The indiscriminate mixture of workpeople and
their children in the immediate vicinity and often
in the same rooms with persons whose character
was denoted by the question and answer more than
once exchanged, 'When were you last washed?'
'When I was last in prison,' was only one mark
of the entire degradation to which they had been
brought. The working classes living in these districts
were equally marked by the abandonment of every
civil or social regulation. Asking some children in
one of the rooms of the wynds in which they swarmed
in Glasgow, what were their names, they hesitated
to answer, when one of the inmates said, they called
them ——, mentioning some nicknames.

"'The fact is,' observed Captain Miller, superintendent of police, 'they really have no names.'
Within this range of buildings I have no doubt I
should have been able to find a thousand children
who have no names whatever, or only nicknames,
like dogs. There were found, amidst the occupants,
labourers earning wages undoubtedly sufficient to
have paid for comfortable tenements, men and women
who were intelligent, and, so far as could be ascertained, had received the ordinary education which
should have given better tastes, and led to better
habits. My own observations have been confirmed
by the statement of Mr. Sheriff Alison, of Glasgow,*
that in the manufacturing towns of Scotland, 'in the

* Afterwards Sir Archibald Alison, Bart.

contest with whisky, in their crowded population, education has been entirely overthrown.' The ministers make similar reports from the rural districts.

" ' On observation of other districts, and comparison of the habits of the same workmen in the town and country, it will be seen that I consider that the use of the whisky and the prostration of the education and moral habits for which the Scottish labourers have been distinguished, is, to a considerable extent, attributable to the surrounding physical circumstances, including the effects of the bad ventilation. The labourers presented to our notice in the condition described were almost all Scotch. It is common to ascribe the extreme of misery and vice wholly to the Irish portion of the population of the towns in Scotland. A short inspection on the spot would correct this error. Mr. Baird, in his report on the sanitary condition of the poor of Glasgow, observes that "the bad name of the poor Irish had been too long attached to them.' "

" Dr. Cowan, of Glasgow, stated that ' from ample opportunities of observation, the Irish appeared to him to exhibit much less of that squalid misery and addiction to the use of ardent spirits than the Scotch of the same grade.' Instances were indeed stated where the Irish were preferred for employment from their superior steadiness and docility; and Mr. Stuart, the Factory Inspector for Scotland, stated that ' instances are now occurring of a preference being given to them as workers in the flax factories on account of their regular habits, and that very significant hints have been given by extensive factory owners, that Irish workmen will be selected unless the natives of the place, and other persons employed by them, relinquish the prevailing habits of intemperance.' Dr. Scott Alison, in his report on Tranent, has described the population in receipt of high wages, but living under similar influences, as prone to passionate excitement, and as apt instruments for political discontents; their moral perceptions appeared to have been obliterated, and they may be said to be characterised by a ' ferocious indocility which makes them prompt to wrong and violence, destroys their social nature, and transforms them into something little better than wild beasts.' It is to be regretted that the coincidence of pestilence and moral disorder is not confined to one part of the island, nor to any one race of the population. The overcrowding and the removal of what may be termed the architectural barriers or protections of decency and propriety, and the causes of physical deterioration in connection with moral deterioration, are also fearfully manifest in the districts in England, which, at the time to which the evidence refers, were in a state of prosperity."

CHAPTER X.

INTEMPERANCE AND BAD HEALTH.

"NO education as yet commonly given appears to have availed against such demoralising circumstances as those above described; but the cases of moral improvement of a population by cleansing, draining, and the improvement of the internal and external conditions of the dwellings, of which instances will be presented, are more numerous and decided, though there still occur instances of persons in whom the love of ardent spirits has gained such entire possession as to have withstood all such means of retrieving them. The most experienced public officers acquainted with the condition of the inferior population of the towns would agree in giving the first place in efficiency and importance to the removal of what may be termed the physical barriers to improvement, and that against such barriers moral agencies have but a remote chance of success.

"A gentleman who had considerable experience in the management of large numbers of the manufacturing population stated, that in every case of personal and moral improvement the successful step was made by the removal of the person from the ill-conditioned neighbourhood in which he had been brought up. When a young workman married, he interfered to get him a better residence apart from the rest; and when this was done, important alterations followed; but if he took up his abode in the old neighbourhood, the condition of the wife was soon brought down to the common level, and the marriage became a source of wretchedness.

"Benevolent persons, viewing the bare aspect of some of the most afflicted neighbourhoods, have raised subscriptions for the purchase of furniture, bedding, and blankets, for the relief of the inmates, but by this pecuniary aid they have only added fuel to the flame; that is, they enabled the inmates to purchase more ardent spirits. The force of the habit, which is aggravated by misdirected charity, is indicated in the following instance, mentioned by the Rev. Whitwell Elwin :—

"'I was lately informed by a master tailor of Bath, that one of his men, who had earned three pounds a week at piece-work for years, had never within his knowledge possessed table, chairs, or bedding. I found the statement on examination to be strictly true. Some straw on which he slept, a square block of wood, a low three-legged stool, and an old tea caddy, were the complete inventory of the articles of a room, the occupier of which, with only himself and his wife to maintain, was wealthier than many in the station of gentlemen. He had frequently excited lively compassion in benevolent individuals, who, supposing that he was struggling for very existence, furnished him with a variety of household goods, which were regularly pawned before a week was out, and afforded to the superficial observer fresh evidence of the extremity of his distress. The cause of all this is quickly told; the wife was to be seen going to and fro several times a day with a cream-jug of gin, and to gratify this appetite they had voluntarily reduced themselves to the condition of savages.'

"'Those,' adds Mr. Elwin, 'who think that labourers will work for themselves a reform in their habitations very much underrate the effects of habit. A person accustomed to fresh air, and all the comforts of civilised life, goes into a miserable room, dirty, bare, and, above all, sickening from the smell. Judging from his own sensations, he conceives that nothing but the most abject poverty could have produced such a state of things, and he can imagine nothing necessary to a cure but a way for escape. A very simple experiment will correct these erroneous impressions. Let him remain a short time in the room, and the perception of closeness will so entirely vanish that he will almost fancy that the atmosphere has been purified since his entrance. There are few who are not familiar with this fact; and if such are the effects of an hour in blunting our refined sensations, and rendering them insensible to noxious exhalations, what must be the influence of years on the coarser perceptions of the working man?

"'All who know the lower classes will testify that the last want felt by the dirty is cleanliness, that their last expenditure is upon the comforts of their home. Two winters ago, a painter, whose bed was without blankets, whose room was without furniture, who was destitute even of the ordinary utensils of civilised life, whose floor was covered with worse filth than that of the streets, was found at dinner, with a roast loin of pork, stuffed with onions, a

Yorkshire pudding, a large jug of ale, cheese, and
a salad. I will undertake to say that half the
gentlemen in Bath did not sit down on that Sunday
to so good a dinner.'

"A number of communications simply assigned
'intemperance' as the cause of fever, and of the
prevalent mortality. Of most of these communications, which it were unnecessary to recite, it may
be observed that when intemperance is mentioned
as the cause of disease, as being the immediate
antecedent, on carrying investigation a little further
back, discomfort is found to be the immediate antecedent to the intemperance; and where the external
causes of positive discomfort do not prevail in the
towns, the workpeople are generally found to have
few or no rival pleasures to wean them from habits
of intemperance, and to have come from districts
subject to the discomforts likely to engender them.
In one of the returns from Scotland it is observed
that with the people, whether for a fever, a cold,
or consumption, or a pleurisy, whisky is the universal
antidote. The popular belief that fermented liquors
or ardent spirits are proper antidotes to the effects
of damp or cold has been universal, and has not
wanted even medical sanction. Outdoor allowances
of beer have been prescribed by some medical officers
in marshy and undrained districts as the proper
preservatives against ague or rheumatism.

" We are now in a position to urge the importance
of facilitating drainage as a means for the protection
of the population by the prevention of disease and
the inducement to pernicious habits, as well as a
source of profitable industry. But it is now also
to be observed that in several dangerous occupations

temperance is the best means of withstanding the effects of the noxious agencies which the workers have to encounter. Amongst the painters, for example, the men who are temperate and cleanly suffer little from the occupation, but if any one of them becomes intemperate, the noxious causes take effect with a certainty and rapidity proportioned to the relaxed domestic habits. The inquiry presents many instances of the beneficial effects of the changes of the popular habit of having recourse to fermented liquors or to spirits as necessary protective stimulants. In several of the mining districts, for example, it is an extensive practice to provide for the accommodation of the miners out of the hot mines a room in which they may drink beer as a preservative against the effects of the change to the cold and damp air to which they are about to expose themselves. Dr. Barham, in his report to the commissioners appointed to inquire into the employment of young persons in mines and manufactories, notices an admirable example within the province of voluntary exertion, and the beneficial effects produced by it, in the Dolcoath copper and tin mine, Camborne, Cornwall. There the proprietors, besides establishing other easy and preventive arrangements, provide a warm room for the miners to change their dresses and take hot meat-soup, which is cheaper probably than beer. 'And these men' (says a witness) 'say they never feel cold when they take it. We conceive that there have been much fewer cases of consumption on the club since this practice has been adopted.' "

CHAPTER XI.

"VERY dangerous errors arise from statistical returns and insurance tables of the mean chances of life made up from gross returns of the mortality prevalent amongst large classes, who differ widely in their circumstances. Thus we find, on inquiry into the sanitary condition of the population of different districts, that the average chances of life of the people of one class in one street will be fifteen years, and of another class in a street immediately adjacent, sixty years. In one district of the same town, on the examination of the registers, the mortality was only one out of every fifty-seven of the population; while in another district one out of every twenty-eight died annually. A return of the average or the mean of the chances of life, or the proportions of death in either instance, would and does lead to very dangerous errors, to serious misapprehensions as to the condition of the inferior districts, and to false inferences as to the proper rates of insurance.

"With the view of arriving at some estimate of the comparative extent of the operation of the chief causes of sickness and mortality proved to be prevalent, amidst the different classes of society, in the towns where the sanitary inquiries have been made, returns were obtained from the clerks of the several unions acting as superintendent registrars. These returns were, as far as practicable, corrected by particular local inquiry, and submitted as the best approximations. that could readily be obtained. In all districts, and especially in the manufacturing districts, there was some migration of labourers which would, for the obtainment of perfect accuracy as to the chances of life in particular localities, have rendered necessary an examination of every individual case enumerated. This extent of labour has been considered unnecessary. In the returns from single towns, the numbers of deaths of persons of the first class were too small not to be affected by accidental disturbances, but when large numbers of the like class were taken, the uniform operation of the like circumstances was shown in the like results. It is a general defect of the important head of information, 'the occupation of the deceased,' that the deaths of masters are not carefully distinguished from the deaths of journeymen. So far as this error prevails, it will tend to raise the apparent chances of life amongst the labouring classes.

"In some instances the occupations of the deceased, or of the parents of the deceased, in the case of children, are not described in the registers. With these, and possibly with other defects that may have escaped notice, these returns will be received as corroborative of the reports of the medical officers and physicians who have attended and observed many of the individual cases themselves, though not enumerated by them. Had

the mortality prevalent amongst workpeople of particular trades and their families been taken, instead
of the mean chances of persons of all occupations deriving subsistence from weekly wages, the
case of classes with still lower chances would have
been presented; but these would have appeared to
suggest particular remedies. Such returns of the
effects of common evils were, therefore, taken as
appeared applicable to the consideration of common
or general means of prevention.

"In Truro the number of deaths of professional
persons or gentry, and their families, was thirty-three,
and the average age of the deceased forty years. Of
persons engaged in trade, or similarly circumstanced,
and their families, the deaths were one hundred and
thirty-eight, and the average age of the deceased
thirty-three. Of labourers, artisans, and others
similarly circumstanced, and their families, the
deaths were four hundred and forty-seven, and the
average age of the deceased twenty-eight.

"In Derby the proportions appeared to be :—Of
professional persons or gentry the deaths were
ten, and the average age of the deceased forty-nine
years; of tradesmen the deaths were one hundred
and twenty-five, and the average age of the deceased
thirty-eight years; of labourers and artisans the
deaths were seven hundred and fifty-two, and the
average age of the deceased twenty-one years.

"To compare the chances of life between a crowded
manufacturing population and a less crowded rural
population, the county of Rutland was taken, because
it had been selected as an average agricultural
district for a comparison as to its general condition
by the members of the Statistical Society of Man-

chester, and they deputed their agent, Mr. J. R. Wood, to make inquiries on an examination from house to house.

"The rents of the houses in Rutlandshire would appear to have been very low compared with those in large manufacturing towns. Not only was the average cost of the former less than half of the latter, but for that diminished cost the dimensions of the houses were double those in large towns, with comforts and conveniences which the latter never can possess.

"But moral causes, inducing habits of sobriety, seemed from the report of the Manchester society to contribute to the general result of the superior condition of the Rutland population, in which the duration of life amongst the lowest classes was nearly as high as amongst the highest classes in Manchester. Wages in Lancashire, it must be premised, were then (in 1837), and, as was stated from the payers of several thousand labourers, at least double what they were in Rutlandshire.

"In comparison with Manchester it was shown that while in Manchester the average age of death, among professional persons and gentry, and their families, was thirty-eight years, and in Rutland fifty-two years, among tradesmen and their families (in Rutlandshire farmers and graziers are included with shopkeepers) the average age of death in Manchester was twenty, and in Rutland forty-one. Among mechanics, labourers, and their families the average age of death in Manchester was seventeen, and in Rutlandshire thirty-eight.

"In Leeds Borough the number of deaths among gentlemen and persons engaged in professions, and their families, was seventy-nine, and the average age of deceased persons forty-five years. Of tradesmen, farmers, and their families, the number of deaths was eight hundred and twenty-four, and the average age of the deceased was twenty-seven. Of operatives, labourers, and their families the number of deaths was three thousand three hundred and ninety-five, and the average age of deceased persons nineteen.

"But in Liverpool (which is a commercial and not a manufacturing town), where, however, the conditions of the dwellings were reported to be the worst, where, according to the report of Dr. Duncan, forty thousand of the population lived in cellars, where one in twenty-five of the population were annually attacked with fever, there the mean chances of life appeared from the returns to the Registrar-General to be still lower than in Manchester, Leeds, or amongst the silk weavers in Bethnal Green. During the year 1840, the deaths, distinguishable in classes, were as follows :—

" In Liverpool the number of deaths among gentry and professional persons was one hundred and thirty-seven, and the average age of deceased thirty-five years. Of tradesmen and their families the number of deaths was one thousand seven hundred and thirty-eight, and the average age of deceased persons twenty-two years. Of labourers, mechanics, and servants, the number of deaths was five thousand five hundred and ninety-seven, and the average age of the deceased was fifteen years.

" Of the deaths which occurred amongst the labouring classes, it appeared that no less than 62 per cent. of the total number were deaths under five years of age. Even amongst those entered as shopkeepers and tradesmen, no less than 50 per cent. died before they attained that period. The proportion of mortality for Birmingham, where there were many insalubrious manufactories, but where the drainage of the town and the general condition was comparatively good, was in 1838 one in forty; whilst in Liverpool it was one in thirty-one."

In this research the now well-known sanitary map made its first appearance. It was supplied originally with the view of showing the proportions in which the mortality from epidemic diseases and diseases affected by localities fell on different classes of tenements during the same year. The localities in which the marks of death were most crowded were the poorest and the worst of the district; where the marks were few and widely spread, the houses and streets, and all the conditions of the population, were better. By the inspection of a map of Leeds, which Mr. Baker prepared at the request of our author to show the localities of epidemic diseases, it was perceived that these diseases fell similarly on the uncleansed and close streets and wards occupied by the labouring classes, and that the course of the cholera was nearly identical with the course of fever. It was also observed that in the badly cleansed and badly drained wards to the right of the map, the proportional mortality was nearly double that which prevailed in the better conditioned districts to the left.

" The remarkable result obtained from the examination of the mortuary registers of the county of Rutland was an inducement to have them examined for different periods. They were accordingly examined for three complete years, 1838, 1839, and 1840, and it was found that the same general law of mortality obtained with little variation for each period.

" As the climate or soil of that county might possess some peculiarities, an examination was made of the average periods of death amongst the agricultural population of all the unions in the county of Wilts during 1840. In this examination the registers of deaths in the towns were excluded, and only those of persons included who were described as agricultural labourers or as farmers and graziers, or as gentry and professional persons resident in the rural districts. The results of this examination were as follows :—

" In unions in the county of Wilts the number of deaths of gentlemen and persons engaged in professions and their families was one hundred and nineteen, and the average age of deceased persons fifty years. Of farmers and their families the number of deaths was two hundred and eighteen, and the average age of the deceased forty-eight. Of agricultural labourers and their families the number of deaths was two thousand and sixty-one, and the average age of deceased thirty-three.

" The further results of such returns of mortality as had been made for quinquennial and decennial periods, from an examination of upwards of twenty-five thousand cases, were shown. They exhibited in the mean ratios for large numbers of the like class the steady influence of the different circumstances under which each class was placed. The labouring classes became old the soonest, and the effect of the unfavourable influences in the adolescent and adult stages was shown in the smaller proportions who attained extreme old age, and also in the periods of the deaths of heads of families of this class, by which widowhood was produced.

"The difference between males and females in the same locality was also tested. The female is most in the house, she is most regular and temperate in her habits; the male is subject to the influence of his place of occupation,—the operative to his workshop, the clerk to the counting-house, and the merchant to crowded places of business. In the following returns made up by Dr. W. Farr, and in others, the mortality prevalent amongst the females was given separately, as probably indicating most correctly the operation of the noxious influences connected with the place of residence.

"The mean annual mortality of females in metropolitan districts in the two years and a half ending 31st of December, 1839, was in :—

Hackney, one death in	57·87.
St. George, Hanover Square, one death in	57·05.
Camberwell, one death in	55·84.
Islington, one death in	50·08.
Rotherhithe, one death in	88·58.
Clerkenwell, one death in	06·54.
St. Luke, one death in	88·49.
Greenwich, one death in	88·42.
St. George Southwark, one death in	38·77.
East and West London, one death in	83·50.
St. Giles and St. George, one death in	88·46.
Whitechapel, one death in	28·15.

Yet it is to be observed that the best and the worst districts presented striking instances of extremes of condition in the residences and the inhabitants. In the Bethnal Green and the Whitechapel Unions, in

which were found some of the worst conditioned
masses of population in the Metropolis, were also
found good mansions, well-drained and protected,
inhabited by persons in the most favourable circumstances.   Immediately behind rows of the best
constructed houses in the fashionable districts of
London were some of the worst dwellings, into which
the working classes are crowded; and these dwellings,
by the noxious influences described, were the foci of
disease.

" These returns were all from large parishes, containing the mean results from all classes. If it
had been practicable to give correctly the average
rate of mortality prevalent in different classes of
streets, the variation of results from the variations
of circumstances would, it is to be presumed, have
been much greater.   Since the character of the
residences of many of the labouring classes, and the
condition of their places of work and their habits
are known, it is to be considered that where the
occupations are duly registered, returns, on the
principle of those we have first given of the average
age at death amongst particular classes, will afford
the most close approximation to accuracy, or the
best indications of the extent of the operation of
the noxious circumstances under which each of
these classes is placed.

" An impression is often prevalent that a heavy
mortality is an unavoidable condition of all large
towns, and of a town population in general.   It
has, however, been shown that groups of cottages
on a high hill, exposed to the most salubrious
breezes, when cleanliness is neglected, are often the.
nests of fever and disease, as intense as the most

crowded districts. The mortuary returns of particular districts (in the essentials of drainage, cleansing, and ventilation), to which it is practicable to
make other districts approximate, and that too with
reduction of existing charges, prove that a high
degree of mortality does not invariably belong to
the population of all towns, and probably not
necessarily to any, even where the population is
engaged in manufactures. The proportion of deaths
appears in some of the suburbs of the Metropolis (as
at Hackney) and of Manchester and Leeds, to be
lower than amongst the highest classes in two of the
agricultural counties.

"In comparison with the very high state of the
chances of life in the county of Wilts, the city of
Bath presents an example confirmatory of this view.
The Rev. Whitwell Elwin supplied the following
return of the chances of life amongst the different
classes in that city, which was generally considered
remarkable for its salubrity.

"Of gentlemen, professional persons, and their
families, the number of deaths was one hundred and
forty-six, and the average age of the deceased fifty-
five.   Of tradesmen and their families the number
of deaths was two hundred and forty-four, and
the average age of the deceased thirty-seven.   Of
mechanics, labourers, and their families, the number
of deaths was eight hundred and ninety-six, and the
average age of the deceased twenty-five.

"The very high average chances of life amongst
the middle classes, which was nearly the same as
that of the farmers, and of the agricultural districts,
was the fact adduced as most strongly proving the
salubrity of the place.

" ' In making these returns,' said Mr. Elwin, ' I have thrown out all visitors and occasional residents, and my knowledge of the locality, with the assistance of the clerk of the union, has enabled me to attain complete accuracy with respect to the gentry, and a close approximation to it in the remaining cases. The difference in the ages of these several classes presents to my mind a tolerably exact scale of the difference of their abodes. The large houses, the broad streets, looking almost invariably on one side or other upon parks or gardens or open country, the spacious squares, the crescents built upon the brows of the hills without a single obstruction to the pure air of heaven, give the gentry of Bath that superiority over other grades and other cities which their longevity indicates. And herein, it appears to me, consists the value of the return. It shows that the congregation of men is not of necessity unhealthy; nay, that towns, possessing as they do superior medical skill and readier access to advice, may, under favourable circumstances, have an advantage over the country. The situation of the tradesmen of Bath, inferior as it is to that of the gentry, is better than that of their own station in other places. The streets they chiefly inhabit, though with many exceptions, are wide, and swept by free currents of air, with houses large and well ventilated. The condition of the poor is worse than would be anticipated from the other portions of the town. The poor are chiefly located in low districts at the bottom of the valley, and narrow alleys and confined courts are very numerous. Yet even here we have an unquestionable advantage over most large towns. It was only yesterday that I was expressing my horror to a medical gentleman at some portions of the habitations of the poor, when he replied that it excited little attention, because they were so much better than what was to be seen in other parts of the kingdom.

"'Whatever influence occupation and other circumstances may have upon mortality, no one can inspect the registers without being struck by the deteriorated value of life in inferior localities, even where the inhabitants were the same in condition with those who lived longer in better situations. The average age of death among the gentlemen was as high as sixty, till I came, at the conclusion, to a small but damp district, in which numerous cases of fever brought down the average to fifty-four. So again with the shopkeepers, the average was reduced two by the returns from streets which, though inhabited by respectable men, were narrow in front and shut in at the back. The average among the labourers was greatly diminished by the returns from some notorious courts, and raised again in a still higher proportion by districts, which appertained rather to the country than to the town. Of three cases of centenarians, one of whom had attained the vast age of one hundred and six, two belonged to this favoured situation. Not that but great ages were to be found in the worst parts as in the best, or that particular streets did not, in a measure, run counter to the rule. Still, wherever I brought into opposition districts of considerable extent, I found the law more or less to obtain. Bath is a favourable town to institute the comparison, from its presenting such marked contrasts in its houses, and the inquiry being little complicated by the presence of noxious trades, which in some towns would necessarily disturb every calculation of the kind. Even here a colony of shoemakers would bring down the average of its healthiest spot to the age of childhood. My attention was called to this circumstance by the clerk incidentally remarking that more shoemakers were married at his office, and were uniformly more dirty and ill-dressed, than any other class of persons. The proneness to marriage or concubinage in proportion to the degradation of the parties is notorious, and I anticipated from the fact an abundant offspring, afterwards to be carried off by premature disease. Accordingly I went with this view through several of the registers; and the result was, that, while the average of death among the families of labourers and artisans in general was twenty-four and twenty-five, that of shoemakers was only fourteen. Had the shoemakers been excluded from the former average, as for the purpose of this comparison they should have been, the disproportion would be some years greater.

" ' The deaths from fever and contagious diseases were found to be almost exclusively confined to the worst parts of the town. An epidemic small-pox raged at the end of the year 1837, and carried off upwards of 300 persons; yet, of all this number I do not think there was a single gentleman, and not above two or three tradesmen. The residences of the labouring classes were pretty equally visited, disease showing here and there a predilection for particular spots, and settling with full virulence in Avon Street and its offsets. I went through the registers from the commencement, and observed that, whatever contagious or epidemic diseases prevailed—fever, small-pox, influenza—this was the scene of its principal ravages; and it is the very place of which every person ac-

quainted with Bath would have predicted this result.
Everything vile and offensive is congregated there.
All the scum of Bath—its low prostitutes, its thieves,
its beggars—are piled up in the dens, rather than
houses, of which the street consists. Its population
is the most disproportioned to the accommodation of
any I have ever heard; and, to aggravate the mischief, the refuse is commonly thrown under the stair-
case, and water is more scarce than in any quarter of
the town. It would hardly be an hyperbole to say
that there is less water consumed than beer; and
altogether it would be more difficult to exaggerate
the description of this dreadful spot than to convey
an adequate notion to those who have never seen it.
A prominent feature in the midst of this mass of
physical and moral evils is the extraordinary number
of illegitimate children, the offspring of persons who
in all respects live together as man and wife. Without the slightest objection to the legal obligation,
the moral degradation is such that marriage is accounted a superfluous ceremony, not worth the
payment of necessary fees; and on one occasion,
when it was given out that these would be dispensed
with, upwards of fifty persons from Avon Street, who
had lived together for years, voluntarily came forward
to enter into a union. And thus it invariably happens
in crowded haunts of sin and filth, where principle is
obliterated, and where public opinion, which so often
operates in the place of principle, is never heard, and
where, to say truth, virtue is treated with the scorn
which, in better society, is accorded to vice. I have
been rendered familiar with these places by holding
a curacy in the midst of them for upwards of a year,
and my duty as chaplain to the Union, in visiting the

friends of paupers or discharged paupers themselves, keeps up the knowledge I then contracted.

"'I think these facts supply us with important conclusions. Whether we compare one part of Bath with another, or Bath with other towns, we find health rising in proportion to the improvement of the residences; we find morality, in at least a great measure, following the same law, and both these inestimable blessings within the reach of the legislature to secure. When viewed in this light, these investigations, so often distressing and disgusting, acquire dignity and importance.'

"If we could ascertain the rates of mortality formerly prevalent in the separate districts of each large town, it is probable we should find that the improvement in the average chances of life of the whole town has been raised, principally by the improved chances in the districts where the streets have been widened, paved, and cleansed, and the houses enlarged and drained; and that the amount of sickness and chances of life in the inferior districts are as little altered as their general physical condition. The present condition of those parts of London where the average mortality is one in twenty-eight annually, appears to be not dissimilar to the general condition of the whole Metropolis about a century ago, which was said to be about one in twenty, a rate still to be found in some of the most neglected streets.

"An impression of an undefined optimism is frequently entertained by persons who are aware of the wretched condition of a large portion of the labouring population; and, this impression is more frequently entertained than expressed, as the ground of inaction for the relief of the prevalent misery from disease,—

viz., that its ravages form the natural or positive check, or, as Dr. Short terms it, 'the terrible corrective,' to the pressure of population on the means of subsistence.

"In the most crowded districts which have been the subject of inquiry, the facts do not justify this impression; they show that the theory is inapplicable to the present circumstances of the population. How erroneous the inferences are in their unrestrained generality, which assume that the poverty, or the privation which is sometimes the consequence, is always the cause of the disease, will have been seen from such evidence as that adduced from Glasgow and Spitalfields, proving that the greater proportion of those attacked by disease are in full work at the time; and from the evidence of the fever hospitals, that the greatest proportion of the patients are received in high bodily condition.

"If wages be taken as the test of the means of subsistence, how are such facts to be reconciled as these, that at a time when wages in Manchester were ten shillings per head weekly on all employed in the manufactories, including children or young persons in the average, so that if three or four members of a family were employed, the wages of the family would be thirty or forty shillings weekly, the average chances of life to all of the labouring classes were only seventeen years; whilst in the whole of Rutlandshire, where the wages were certainly not one half that amount, the mean chances of life to every individual of the lowest class were actually thirty-seven years? Or, to take another instance, that whilst in Leeds, where, according to Mr. Baker's report, the wages of the families of the worst-conditioned workers were upwards of twenty-one shillings per week, and the chances of life amongst the whole labouring population of the borough were only nineteen years; in the county of Wilts, where the labourer's family would not receive much more than half that amount of wages in money, and perhaps not two-thirds of money's worth in money and produce together, we find the average chances of life to the labouring class thirty-two years?

"If, in the most crowded districts, the inference is found to be erroneous, that the extent of sickness and mortality is indicative of the pressure of population on the means of subsistence, so is the inference that the ravages act to the extent supposed as a positive check to the increase of the numbers of the population. In such districts the fact is observable, that where the mortality is the highest, the number of births are more than sufficient to replace the deaths, however numerous they may be.

"The proportion of mortality in the several townships denotes, with little variation, the state of the streets and houses and the condition of the inhabitants. Thus the township of Broughton is inhabited almost exclusively by the upper classes, who are connected with Manchester. The houses are new, spacious, and well built; the site is elevated, and offers great facilities for drainage. The township of Cheetham and Crumpsall is also inhabited for the most part by the upper classes, who live in peculiarly good houses, with a superior natural drainage. There is a proportion of the working population resident in this district, whose houses are well built and also favourably situated for drainage. The condition of the inhabitants of a large proportion of the labouring population in Manchester has already been described.

"It will be observed also that the moral as well as the sanitary influences have a coincidence in the larger proportion of the illegitimate births in the worst-conditioned districts. In the best-conditioned districts the great majority of illegitimate births belong almost exclusively to the more dissipated of the labouring classes who inhabit them.

"In the ten registration districts of Leeds the mortality prevalent in them varied coincidently with their physical condition, and the recklessness and immorality, as shown in the proportion of illegitimate births, increased in a greater proportion than the mortality; and in this instance also, as in most others, if the registrations were more accurate, the proportion of both legitimate and illegitimate births would be still closer to the deaths in the worst-conditioned districts.

"In the lowest districts of Manchester, of 1,000 children born more than 570 will have died before they attain the fifth year of their age. In the lowest districts of Leeds the infant mortality is similar. This proportion of mortality M. Mallet would designate as the case of a population but little advanced in civilisation, ravaged by epidemics,—a population in which the 'influences on the lower ages are murderous, but where the great mortality in infancy is compensated by a high degree of fecundity. It is the case of the population in many large towns, especially in past ages.' But whilst in Manchester, where one twenty-eighth of the whole population is annually swept away, the births registered amount to twenty-six of the population; in the county of

Rutland, the proportion of births, as shown by an average of three years—and by a registration which I apprehend is more complete than in the lower districts of Manchester—is only one to three of the population."

CHAPTER XII.

MORTALITY AND POPULATION.

"THE increase of births after a pestilence has been long observed; the coincidence of an increase of births in a proportion to the high rate of mortality in the worst districts has frequently been noted on the Continent. M. Quetelet has observed the fact in several countries, and gives instances from which the following are selected :—

"Department of Arne, 52·4 for one death; 147·5 for one marriage; 44·8 for one birth. Department of Finisterre, 30·4 for one death; 113·9 for one marriage; 26·0 for one birth. Province of Namur, 51·8 for one death; 141·0 for one marriage; 30·1 for one birth. Province of Zealand, 28·5 for one death; 113·2 for one marriage; 21·9 for one birth.

"M. Quetelet's returns show that, as far as the present state of information can be relied upon, the same law is observed in general action, not only in provinces, but in whole countries throughout Europe. It is confirmed by extensive experience occurring in the New World. The trustworthiness of the registration of births and deaths in Mexico is attested by the examination and use of them by Humboldt, and has been the subject of legislative proceedings. The ratios of

births and deaths in the province of Guanaxuata have
been referred to by Sir F. d'Ivernois, in illustration
of the position that pestilence does not check the
progress of population. A large proportion of the
inferior Mexican population are reported to 'have
converted the gifts of Heaven to the sustenance of
disgusting misery.' It is reported of this populace
that it is 'half-clothed, idle, stained all over with
vices;' in a word, hideous, and known under the
name of *leperos* (lepers), on account of the malady to
which their filth and bad diet subject them. Nothing can exceed the state of brutality and super-
stition to which they have been subjected.

" The fecundity of this population, sunk in the
lowest vice and misery amidst the means of the
highest abundance, was greater than amidst any other
whole population in Christendom. They stood in 1825
and 1826 as :—deaths, 1 in 19·70; births, 1 in 16·08.
They are much mistaken who imagine that a similarly-
conditioned population is not to be found in this
country; it is found in parts of the population of
every large town; the description of the Mexican
populace will recall features characteristic of the
wretched population in the worst parts of Glasgow,
Edinburgh, London, and Bath, and the lodging-
houses throughout the country.

" Seeing that the banana—with the plantain, or
maize—is the chief food of the inferior Mexican
populace, their degraded condition has been ascribed
to the fertility of that plant, as the degradation of a
large proportion of our population has been ascribed
to the use of the potato, whereas a closer examination would have shown the fact of large classes
living industriously and virtuously chiefly on simple

food, and preferring saving money to better living; and if a high and various meat diet were the cause of health, industry, and morality, those virtues should stand highest amongst the population of the lodging-houses, for more meat and varied food is consumed in those abodes of pestilence than amongst the industrious population of the village. In Manchester, where we have seen that the chances of life are only seventeen years, the proportions and varieties of meat consumed by the labouring classes are as their greater amount of wages compared with the meat consumed by the labouring classes in Rutland-shire, whose mean chances of life are thirty-eight years. But I apprehend that the superior health in Rutlandshire is as little ascribable to their simpler food as the greater amount of disease amidst the town population is ascribable to the greater propor-tion of meat which is there consumed. It is probable, indeed, that the standard of vitality in Rutlandshire might be raised still higher by improvements in the quality of their food. There are abundant reasons to render it desirable that the food of the population should be varied, but it is shown that banishing the potato, or discouraging its use, or introducing any other food, will not banish disease.

"By means of the census of 1841, and the year's completed registration of deaths and births in Eng-land in 1841, it was found that there had been an increase of the population from births alone in those parts of the country where the proportionate mor-tality is the greatest.

"The estimated increase of population in England in the year 1840, as compared with 1839, was 190,460. In the same period the births exceeded

the deaths by 143,178. The difference between these
two amounts, or 47,282, may be considered as the
extent of immigration to England, together with the
cases of births not registered. To whatever extent
emigration takes place from England, there must, of
course, have been a proportionate immigration from
other places to make up the increase of population
beyond the apparent increase from births.

" It is observed in some of the worst conditioned of
the town districts that the positive number of the
natives of the aboriginal stock continually diminishes,
and that the vacancy, as well as the increase, is made
up by immigration from the healthier districts. In a
late enumeration of the settled inhabitants of the
labouring classes in the lower parts of Westminster,
it appeared that not more than one-third of them
were natives of London. If inquiry had been made
as to whether their parents were natives, it would probably have been found that still fewer had inhabited
the district for more than one generation.

"The important general fact of the proportion of
adult physical strength to the increased duration of
life or improved sanitary condition of the individuals
is verified by the examinations of the individuals of
different classes. M. Villermé states that the difference of strength between classes such as those in
which we have seen that the value of life differs, is
well known to the officers engaged in recruiting the
army, but no one had collected the facts to determine the precise difference. The time allowed to
M. Villermé only enabled him to do so at Amiens.
The result was, that the men of from twenty to
twenty-one years of age were found the more frequently unfit for the trade of arms from their stature,

constitution, and health, as they belonged to the
poorer classes of the manufacturing labourers. In
order to obtain 100 men fit for military service, it
was necessary to have as many as 343 men of the
poorer classes, while 193 conscripts sufficed of the
classes in better circumstances. Analogous facts
were observed in the greater part of the towns in
France in which he conducted his official investigations.

"In the evidence of recruiting officers, collected
under the Factory Commission of Inquiry, it was
shown that fewer recruits of the proper strength
and stature for military service are obtainable now
than heretofore from Manchester. Of those
labourers now employed in the most important
manufactories, whether natives or migrants to that
town, the sons who are employed at the same work
are generally inferior in stature to their parents.
Sir James McGrigor, the Director-General of the
Army Medical Board, stated the fact, that, 'a
corps levied from the agricultural districts in Wales,
or the northern counties of England, will last longer
than one recruited from the manufacturing towns,
—from Birmingham, Manchester, or near the
Metropolis.' Indeed, so great and permanent is
the deterioration, that out of 613 men enlisted,
almost all of whom came from Birmingham and
five other neighbouring towns, only 223 were
approved for service.

"The chances of life of the labouring classes of
Spitalfields are amongst the lowest met with, and
there it is observed of weavers, though not originally
a large race, that they have become still more
diminutive under the noxious influences to which

they are subject. Dr. Mitchell, in his report on the condition of the hand-loom weavers, adduces evidence on this point. One witness, well-acquainted with the class, states, 'They are decayed in their bodies; the whole race of them is rapidly descending to the size of Liliputians. You could not raise a grenadier company amongst them all. The old men have better complexions than the young.' Another witness who says there were once men as well made in the weaver trade as any other, 'recollects the Bethnal Green and Spitalfields regiment of volunteers during the war as good-looking bodies of men; but doubts if such could be raised now.' Mr. Duce concurs in the fact of the deterioration of their size and appearance within the last thirty years, and attributes it to bad air, bad lodging, bad food; 'which causes the children to grow up an enfeebled and diminutive race of men.'

" This depressing effect of adverse sanitary circumstances on the labouring strength of the population, and on its duration, is to be viewed with the greatest concern, as it is a depressing effect on that which most distinguishes the British people, and which it were a truism to say constitutes the chief strength of the nation—the bodily strength of the individuals of the labouring class. The greater portion of the wealth of the nation is derived from the labour obtained by the application of this strength, and it is only those who have had practically the means of comparing it with that of the population of other countries who are aware how far the labouring population of this country is naturally distinguished above others. There is much practical evidence to show that this is not a mere illusion of national vanity, and in proof of this might be adduced the testimony of some of the most eminent employers of large numbers of labourers, whose conclusions are founded on experience in directing the work of labourers from the chief countries in Europe,—*e.g.*, Mr. William Lindley, the civil engineer, who, engaged in the superintendence of the formation of the new railway between Hamburg and Berlin, found it expedient to import as the foremost labourers for the execution of that work a number of the class of English labourers called navigators or navvies. These were employed in pile-driving, at wages of five shillings per diem, or more than double the amount of wages paid to the German labourers. The German directors were surprised, and remonstrated at the enormously high wages paid to the English labourers; when the engineer directed their attention to the quantity of work performed by them within a given time, and showed that the wages produced more than among the native labourers. English labourers of the same class have been imported to take the foremost labour in the execution of the railways in France, from Havre to Paris, their work at very high wages being found cheaper than the work even of Norman labourers. Skill and personal strength are combined in an unusually high degree in this class of workmen, but the most eminent employers of labour agree that it is strength of body, combined with strength of will, that gives steadiness and value to the artisan and common English labourer."

CHAPTER XIII.

THE COST OF NOXIOUS AGENCIES AND ACCIDENTS.

"THE more closely the subject of the evils affecting the sanitary condition of the labouring population is investigated, the more widely do their effects appear to be ramified. The pecuniary cost of noxious agencies is measured by data within the province of the actuary, by the charges attendant on the reduced duration of life, and the reduction of the periods of working ability or production by sickness. The cost would include also much of the public charge of attendant vice and crime, which come within the province of the police, as well as the destitution which comes within the province of the administrators of relief. Of the pecuniary effects, including the cost of maintenance during the preventible sickness, any estimate approximating to exactness could only be obtained by very great labour, which does not appear to be necessary.

"To whatever extent the probable duration of the life of the working man is diminished by noxious agencies, I repeat a truism in stating to some extent so much productive power is lost; and in the case of destitute widowhood and orphanage, burdens are created and cast either on the industrious survivors belonging to the family, or on the contributors to

the poor's rates during the whole of the period
of the failure of such ability. With the view to
judge of the extent to which such burdens are
at present cast upon the poor's rates, I have
endeavoured to ascertain the average age at which
death befell the heads of those families of children
who with the mothers have been relieved on the
ground of destitution, in eight of the unions where
the average age of the mortality prevalent amongst
the several classes of the community has been
ascertained.

" The workmen who belong to sick-clubs and benefit
societies generally fix the period of their own
superannuation allowances at from 60 to 65 years of
age. I see no reason to doubt that by the removal
of noxious agencies not essential to their trades, by
sanitary measures affecting their dwellings, combined with improvements in their own habits, the
period of ability for productive labour might be
extended to the whole of the labouring class.

" The actual duration of the ability for labour will
vary with the nature of the work, though there can
be little doubt that the variations under proper
precautions would be much less than those which
now take place. From the information received in
respect to the employment of tailors in large numbers,
it is evident that the average period of the working
ability of that class might be extended at least ten
years by improvements as to the places of work alone.
The experience which might serve to indicate the
extent of practicable improvement is at present
narrow and scattered. The chief English insurance
tables, such as the Northampton and Carlisle tables,
are made up apparently from the experience of a

population subject probably to a greater or less extent to the noxious influences which are shown to be removable. By the Carlisle table, however, the probability of life to every person who has attained the age of twenty-one—the age for marriage—would be 40 years, or 40·75. By the Swedish tables, which are frequently applied to the insurance of the labouring classes, it would be 38.0. The observations that have been made on the subject show that marriage improves rather than diminishes the probability of life. Where the duration of life is reduced by the nature of the employment below the average, by so much the widowhood may be considered as increased, as also the orphanage of the children. As labouring men generally marry early in life, their wives have ceased to bear children before they have reached fifty, so that the great mass of orphanage may be assigned to the consequence of premature death.

" Premature widowhood and orphanage is the source of the most painful descriptions of pauperism—the most difficult to deal with ; it is the source of a constant influx of the independent into the pauperised and permanently dependent classes. The widow, where there are children, generally remains a permanent charge ; re-marriages amongst those who have children are very rare ; in some unions they do not exceed one case in twenty or thirty. By the time the children are fit for labour and cease to require the parents' attention, the mothers frequently become unfit for earning their own livelihood, or habituated to dependence, and without care to emerge from it. Even where the children are, by good training and education, fitted for productive industry, when they marry, the early familiarity with the parochial relief makes them improvident, and they fall back upon the poor's rates on the lying-in of their wives, on their sickness, and for aid on every emergency. In every district the poor's rolls form the pedigrees of generations of families thus pauperised. The total number of orphan children on account of whose destitution relief was given from the poor's rates in the year ended Lady Day, 1840, was 112,000. The numbers of widows chargeable to the poor's rates was, in those unions, at that period, 43,000.

"Instances have frequently been presented in the course of this inquiry of the moral degradation of the children of workpeople, and of the workpeople themselves, who have once been in moral condition; but the cases taken from the pauper roll of the union will serve to show that even a good education will not, of itself, sustain such a body of workmen against the physical causes of depression. The group of cases of widowhood, when considered, will serve to show that the causes in question create the evils of which they are supposed to be natural correctives.

"With an educated class of workmen, the obtainment of a place and the wages of an adult must be the necessary preliminary to a marriage, and unless such place or wages were obtained, the young workman would either remain single or seek employment further afield. But we will suppose, for illustration, that a casualty occurs, such as the last death on the list, J. M., where a young miner who has married, and has a wife and two children, is prematurely swept away by an epidemic at 21 years of age, leaving a widow and two destitute orphan children dependent on poor relations, or on the ratepayers. The first mentioned, say S. H., then takes the vacant place of work, marries, and is killed at 34 years of age by "an accident in the mine," leaving a widow and seven orphan children. The third vacancy in the place of work is occupied by another miner, H. Y., who marries and works until he is 45, when he is killed by "consumption," leaving a widow and five children. Such casualties do not of course actually so fall on any one place of work, but the vacancies so created in different places at the younger periods of life must be and are supplied by new hands coming into the employment, and marrying as a consequence of that employment, and the succession will fairly represent the mode in which the vacancies created by the various causes of death displayed in the last table and in the other tables of the causes of premature widowhood and orphanage occur.

"In works where the average period of working ability is extended to the natural period of super-annuation, which the evidence shows that a combination of internal and external sanitary measures may be expected to give, namely, an average of full sixty years, the account for one place would be one superannuated workman and one widow, and a family of four or five well-grown children, who, having received parental care during that period, will probably all have obtained, before its termination, the means of independent self-support. Whereas with a population of only fifteen or twenty years of working ability, the same place of work may during the same period have been filled by two generations and one-fourth of workpeople, not one of which has brought all the children dependent on it to maturity or a condition for self-support; and the place of

work shows three widows instead of one, and three
sets of stunted and unhealthy children dependent for
such various periods, as those above specified, and
competing for employment at the same place, instead
of one set of healthy children arrived at the age of
working ability for self-support. The occupation of
the places of work by a comparatively young and
procreative population, brought forward by the premature removal of the middle-aged and the aged
workers, by the various causes of premature deaths—
the acceleration of births by premature deaths in
infancy as stated in a preceding note—will, I apprehend, sufficiently clearly account for the generally
increased proportions of births in those districts where
the rate of mortality is high ; and it will scarcely be
necessary to give further illustrations of the dreadful fallacy which tends to an acquiescence in the
continuance of the causes of pestilence and premature mortality as ' correctives of the pressure of
population.'

"Though the deaths from accidents bear only a
small proportion to the deaths from disease, yet
registries show that the scattered deaths from
various descriptions of violence amount to an average
of about 12,000 yearly, in England and Wales alone,
or more than aroused the national attention in the
late massacre of the troops of the empire during the
war in India. The position which this class of
causes occupy, in the production of destitute orphanage and widowhood, does not comprehend the whole
of the effects ; another class of which appear on
examining the causes of pauperism ; namely, the
injuries which occasion permanent disablement.

"On examining the individual cases of deaths that

are classed as incident to the pursuit of the chief
branches of mining or manufacturing industry, or in
transport whether by land or water, it has always
been satisfactory to find that for the future, by care,
the greater proportion of them are preventible.   In
the case of the mining accidents, one part of them
appears preventible by care of the superior managers
of the mines—in arrangements over which the individual workman has no control; the other portion, by
intelligence and care on the part of the workmen; and
this last class of cases again reverts back to the power,
and therefore to the means of imposing responsibility
on the employers in the selection of educated and intelligent workmen of habits of sobriety and care, to
qualify them for works of danger.   But at present they
are, in a great measure, relieved from responsibility by
the charge incurred by the want of care being thrown
on other funds raised from persons who have as yet
no practicable means of protection or prevention.

" When continued and dreadful losses of life
take place, in the face of examples of successful
prevention such as might be collected from every
part of the country, it is impossible to avoid the
conclusion that if the branch of industry were
charged with the pecuniary consequences of the
losses assumed to be necessarily incident to it,
generations would not be allowed to pass away in
fear, recklessness, and misery, without the early
adoption of those means of prevention which self-
interest would then stimulate."

CHAPTER XIV.

FINANCIAL SANITATION BY REPRESENTATIVES OF LABOUR.

"ON viewing the evidence, which shows that in most situations higher chances of life belong to the middle and higher classes of the population, an impression may be created that the higher standards of health are essentially connected with expensive modes of living. The highest medical authorities agree, however, that the more important means for the protection and advance of the health of those classes must be in still further reductions than those which it is the present tendency in the higher classes of society to make of the use of highly stimulating food. The evidence already adduced with respect to the labouring classes in the rural districts and those living on high wages in towns, will have gone some way to remove the erroneous impression with regard to them, and it admits of proof that a higher standard of health and comfort is attainable for them even at a less expense than that in which they now live in disease and misery. The experience of the effect of sanitary measures in the royal navy may be adduced as evidence of the practicable standards of health consistent with great labour and exposure to weather, obtained at a cost not higher than that within the wages of ordinary labourers. The experience of the effects of sanitary measures in banishing spontaneous disease from crowded prisons offers further evidence of the health obtainable by simple means, under circumstances still more unfavourable.

" The prisons were formerly distinguished for their filth and their bad ventilation; but the descriptions given by Howard of the worst prisons he visited in England (which he states were amongst the worst he had seen in Europe), were exceeded in every wynd in Edinburgh and Glasgow inspected by Dr. Arnott and myself, in company with the municipal officers of those cities. More filth, worse physical suffering and moral disorder than Howard describes as affecting the prisoners are to be found amongst the cellar population of the working people of Liverpool, Manchester, or Leeds, and in large portions of the Metropolis.

" Since Howard succeeded in gaining national attention to the condition of prisoners, the evils of prison management have been removed. A large proportion of the prison population is taken from the worst regulated and most confined neighbourhoods, which have been the subject of examination; and, with the view to judge what might be effected by sanitary regulations, I have made frequent inquiries as to the effects of sanitary measures on the worst class of persons, the larger proportion of whom are taken from the worst neighbourhoods, that is, as to the effects of living in the same atmosphere on a less expensive diet than that of the general labouring population, but provided with clean and tolerably well-ventilated places of work and sleeping rooms, and where they are required to be cleanly in their persons.

" The medical practitioners, who are well acquainted

with the general state of health of the population surrounding the prisons, concur in vouching to the fact, upon their own knowledge, that the health of the prisoners is in general much higher than the health almost of any part of the surrounding population; that the prisoners, as a class, are below the average of health when they enter the prisons; that they come from the worst neighbourhoods; that many of them come from the lodging-houses, which, in those towns, as will be shown, are the constant seats of disease; that they are mostly persons of intemperate habits; that many of them come in in a state of disease from intemperance and bad habits; and notwithstanding the depressing influence of imprisonment, the effect of cleanliness, dryness, better ventilation, temperance, and simple food, is almost sufficient to prevent disease arising within the prison, and to put the prisoners in a better working condition at the termination than at the commencement of their imprisonment. At the Glasgow Bridewell the prisoners are weighed on their entrance and at their discharge, and it is found that, on the average, they have gained in weight by their imprisonment. At Edinburgh, there were instances of poor persons in a state of disease committed from motives of humanity to the prison, that they might be taken care of and cured. The facts are to be taken as showing imperfectly the comparative effects of the different circumstances, because when a labourer is obliged to leave work he loses wages; and it is known of large classes of them that they often work improvidently and injuriously to their chances of recovery by continuing at work in impaired health too long; the prisoner, on the contrary, by absence on the sick list,

gains ease and exemption from slave labour, and the
officers have constantly to contend against feigned
sickness to avoid task work and punishment. It
should also be noted that a large proportion of the
sickness of the prisoners is of a character that is
excluded from all tables of insurance, from the
benefit societies as being specially excluded from
their benefits.

" The experience of the effect of sanitary measures
proves the possibility of the reduction of sickness in
the worse districts to at least one-third of the existing amount. Amidst classes somewhat better situated
it were possible to reduce the sickness to less than
one-third ; it were an under-estimate to take the probable reduction at one-half. Taking it, however, at
one-half, by the new payment of $1\frac{1}{2}d.$, or say $2d.$,weekly
for drainage, the occupants of the tenements will
save $7\frac{1}{2}d.$ of the weekly contribution for an allowance
of $10s.$ per week each during sickness. But the allowance insured to be paid during sickness only replaces
the earnings ; the sickness, besides its own misery,
entails the expense of medical attendance, which, at
the usual rate of insurance in medical clubs, would
be $5s.$ or $6s.$ per annum for such a family. This
would also be reduced one-half, making the total
family saving at the least $9d.$ weekly. But the single
payment for structural alterations is to be regarded
as general, and as a means of effecting the whole of
the objects for the whole of the population. For this
$2d.$ each tenement, or $1d.$ each family, then, they will
not only save double the weekly amount, but they
will save in the wear and tear of shoes and clothes,
from having a well-drained and well-cleansed instead
of a wet and miry district to traverse ; they will also

save the sickness itself, and each individual will gain a proportionate extension of a more healthy life. In a district where the wages are not one-half the amount above stated, the expenditure for efficient means of prevention would still leave a surplus of gain to the labourer.

"These are the chief gains on the side of the labourer; but in general every labourer, over and above what he consumes himself, produces enough to repay the interest on capital and cost of superintendence, or the profits of the employer. The loss of this extra production is the loss of the community during the whole time the services of the labourer are abridged by sickness or death. To this loss is to be added, where the labourer has made no reserve, the loss of the cost of his unproductive maintenance as a pauper, and of medical attendance during sickness.

"The existing insurance charge, then, represents the existing charge on the labouring classes from the loss of wages consequent on sickness; to which charge might be added the existing additional charge denoted by the insurance on account of the abridged duration of life and more frequent deaths. The aggregate charge for structural improvements, though amounting to so many millions as a first outlay, is still, for the reasons above stated, only a means of obtaining an incalculably greater gain. But it will be shown that the attainment of that gain is dependent on securities for the application of science to the efficient execution of the combined structural means of prevention. If these were to be no better than those in use in the greater part of the Metropolis and the towns throughout the country, and the outlay for drainage were to be an outlay for receptacles to serve as the means of accumulating decomposing deposits, and as latent magazines of pestilential gases, to be themselves cleansed from time to time of the accumulations at a great expense, or to be discharged to pollute the natural streams of the country, then the aggregate expenditure would, to the amount of the inefficiency, be an aggregate of so many millions of money spent in waste.

" The *immediate* cost of sickness and loss of employment falls differently in different parts of the country, but on whatsoever fund it does fall, it will be a gain to apply to the means of prevention that fund which is, and must needs otherwise continue to be, more largely applied to meet the charge of maintenance and remedies. Admitting, however, as a fact the misconception intended to be obviated, that the necessary expense of structural arrangements will be an immediate charge instead of an immediate means of relief to the labouring classes,—in proof that they have, in ordinary times, not only the means of defraying increased public rates, but increased rents, —I refer to the fact that the amount expended in ardent spirits (exclusive of wines), tobacco, snuff, beer, etc., consumed chiefly by them, cannot be much less than from £45,000,000 to £50,000,000 per annum in the United Kingdom. By an estimate, which I obtained from an eminent spirit merchant, of the cost to the consumer of the British spirits on which duty is paid, the annual expenditure on them alone, chiefly by the labouring classes, cannot be less than £24,000,000 per annum. If visible evidence of the means of payment were needed, I would point to every gin-palace in the Metropolis, or to a similar place throughout the country, as a place chiefly supported from the expenditure of the class of persons who are overcrowded and lodged most wretchedly, while its duty-paying building materials represent a portion of the money available as rent for abodes of comparative comfort. The cost of one dram per week would nearly defray the expense of the structural arrangements of drainage, by which some of the strongest provocatives to the habit of drunkenness would be removed.

"Any measures must commend themselves to public support that would effect, in the application of the immense fund expended in ardent spirits alone, a change for assured physical comforts and undoubted moral advantages of the highest order. Admitting the validity of statements often made and seldom proved in ordinary times, but which nevertheless may occur, of classes of labourers reduced to the minimum of subsistence, that their wages will not admit of any change of application, then another set of considerations would arise, namely, whether the increased charges for new tenements, or for improvement of the existing tenements, will not compel an advance of wages, and thence be charged in the cost of the commodity produced? And whether, if the trade will not allow such advanced wages, the amount of misery of the labouring classes is not really increased by exemptions or legislative facilities, which allow the trade to be carried on only at the expense of the health, the morality, and the comfort of the labourers engaged in it, and also at the expense of the ratepayers in providing against the casualties of sickness and mortality?

"These, however, are questions that appear to be less likely to occur practically to any important extent than may be supposed. The general difficulty would apparently be with the habits of the adults, who will, to use the illustration presented in a portion of evidence previously cited, 'prefer the gin' to the best accommodation that can be offered to them.

"Whilst there is such evidence as that cited above to show that there is in ordinary time no real need, there is much evidence to show the impolicy of any exemptions from the payment of properly distributed charges for the requisite public improvement. In general, labourers have been losers by exemptions from charges on their tenements, and scarcely in any instance have gained even by exemptions from the payment of their contributions to the poor's rates."

CHAPTER XV.

"THE effect of administrative proceedings on the condition of the dwellings of large portions of the labouring classes, and thence on the condition of the labourers, was, under varied circumstances, adverted to in the local reports on their sanitary condition, and it is shown that the former parochial administration had operated mischievously in degrading the habitations of the labouring classes, or in checking tendencies to improvement.

" The mode by which the condition of the dwellings of the labouring classes has been most extensively deteriorated in England has been by the facility afforded to owners of cottage tenements, usually when acting as administrators of the poor law, to get their own tenants excused from the payment of rates. The legal ground for exemption was, not the value of the tenement, but the destitution or inability of the tenant to pay; but inasmuch as the occupation of a well-conditioned tenement, or of a tenement in advance of others, would be popularly considered *prima facie* evidence of ability to pay rates, the cottage speculator would not be at the expense to present evidence against the exemption by which he would gain. The general tenor of the evidence is, that the exempted tenements were of a very inferior order, and that the rents collected for them are exorbitant, and such as ought to have ensured tenements of a higher quality.

" Such residences appear to come in competition very rarely, and, viewed with reference to the place of work, the habitations of the labouring classes in the manufacturing towns extensively partake of the nature of monopolies, and hence the landlord is enabled to exact a price for position, independently of the character or quality of the building, or of the extent of outlay upon it. Where there is any choice, the labouring classes are generally attracted to these tenements by the promise of exemption from the payment of poor's rates, and are deluded into the payment of a proportionately higher rent.

" The mischievous effect of exemptions from rating on the ground of poverty, in bringing down buildings to the exempted scale, and in preventing advances beyond it, was strikingly displayed in Ireland, where all houses not exceeding the value of five pounds were exempted from contribution to the county cess. The general consequence was that the farmers' residences throughout the country are kept down to the level of mere cottages or inconvenient hovels, to avoid passing the line of contribution, and only pass it by indulgent or evasive valuations. But the supposed exemption (which, if it be not often made up by increased rent, is a circumstance peculiar to the smaller holdings in that country), an exemption which no doubt was procured as a boon, was productive of further ill effects to the parties intended to be benefited. Being kept by the immediate expense and the fear of their share of the tax to

thatched roofs, these thatched roofs afforded facilities
to incendiarism, since any one might put a cinder in
the thatch, and run away without detection; hence
it has placed the inmates so far under continued
terror in disturbed times, that it would frequently
have been worth the expense of putting on a
slate roof as a measure of preventive policy. The
depression of the tenement is practically a depression
of the habits and condition of the inhabitants.

"I may assume that it has been proved that the
labouring classes do possess the means of purchasing
the comforts of superior dwellings, and also that they
are not benefited by exemptions from the immediate
charges wherever requisite to defray the expense of
those superior comforts.

"I shall now show how little it is in the power of
these classes voluntarily to obtain these improvements, setting aside entirely the consideration of the
obstacles arising from depraved habits already formed.

"The workman's 'location,' as it is termed, is
generally governed by his work, near which he
must reside. The sort of house, and often the
particular house, may be said to be, and usually
is, a monopoly. On arriving at manhood in a
crowded neighbourhood, if he wishes to have a
house, he must avail himself of the first vacancy that
presents itself; if there happen to be more houses
vacant than one, the houses being usually of the
same class, little range of choice is thereby presented
to him. In particular neighbourhoods near Manchester and in other parts of the county of Lancaster,
in some other manufacturing and in some rural
districts, instances occur of the erection of improved
ranges of larger and better-constructed houses for

the labouring classes; and, making deduction for
the occasional misuse of the increased space by
subdividing them and overcrowding them with
lodgers, the extent to which these improved tenements are sought, and the manner in which an
improved rent is paid, afford gratifying evidence of
an increasing disposition prevalent amongst artisans
to avail themselves of such improvements. These
opportunities, however, are comparatively few, and
occur in districts where multitudes continue in the
most depressed condition, apparently without any
power of emerging from it.

" The individual labourer has little or no power
over the internal structure and economy of the dwelling which has fallen to his lot. If the water be not
laid on in the other houses in the street, or if the
house be unprovided with proper receptacles for refuse,
it is not in the power of any individual workman who
may perceive the advantages of such accommodations
to procure them. He has as little control over the
external economy of his residence as of the structure
of the street before it, whether it shall be paved or
unpaved, drained or undrained. It may be said that
he might cleanse the street before his own door.
By some local Acts the obligation to do so is imposed
on the individual inhabitants. By those inhabitants
who have servants this duty may be and is performed,
but the labourer has no servant; all of his family who
are capable of labour are out afield, or in the manufactory or the workshop, at daybreak, and return only
at nightfall, and this regulation therefore is unavoid-
ably neglected. Under the slavery of the existing
habits of labourers, it is found that the faculty of perceiving the advantage of a change is so obliterated as

to render them incapable of using, or indifferent to the use of, the means of improvement which may happen to come within their reach. The sense of smell, for instance, which generally gives certain warning of the presence of malaria or gases noxious to the health, appears often to be obliterated in the labourer by his employment. He appears to be insensible to anything but changes of temperature, and there is scarcely any stench which is not endured to avoid slight cold.

" It would have been matter of sincere congratulation to have met with more extensive evidence of spontaneous improvement amongst the classes in receipt of high wages, but nearly all the beneficial changes found in progress throughout the country are changes that have arisen from the efforts of persons of the superior class. Inquiries have been made for plans of improved tenements, but none have been found which can be presented as improvements originating with the class intended to be accommodated. In the rural districts, the worst of the new cottages are those erected on the borders of commons by the labourers themselves. In the manufacturing districts, the tenements erected by building clubs and by speculating builders of the class of workmen are frequently the subject of complaint, as being the least substantial and the most destitute of proper accommodation. The only conspicuous instances of improved residences of the labouring classes found in rural districts are those which have been erected by opulent and benevolent landlords, and in the manufacturing districts those erected by wealthy manufacturers for the accommodation of their own workpeople.

" Preparatory to the exposition of the means of protection of the public health provided by the existing law, and of the modifications that appear to be requisite for the attainment of the object in question, I would submit for consideration practical examples of its partial attainment by means of improved dwellings, combined with examples of other improvements effected in the moral condition of the labouring classes by the judicious exercise of the influence possessed by their superiors in condition.

" Throughout the country examples are found of a desire, on the part of persons of the higher class, to improve the condition of the poorer classes by the erection of dwellings of a superior order for their accommodation. These, however, are generally at a cost beyond any return to be expected, in the present state of the habits of the people, in the shape of rent, or any return in money for an outlay on an ordinary investment of capital. But the instances about to be noticed, though generally originating in benevolence, and without the expectation of a return, do, in the results, prove that in money and money's worth, the erection of good tenements affords the inducement of a fair remuneration to the employers of labour to provide improved accommodation for their own labourers.

" Wherever it has been brought under observation, the connection of the labourer's residence with his employment as part of the farm, or of the estate, or of the manufactory on which he is employed, and as part of the inducement to service, appears to be mutually advantageous to the employer and the employed.

" The first advantages are to the person employed.

" He everywhere finds (in contradiction to statements frequently made in popular declamations) that the labourer gains by his connection with large capital: in the instances presented in the course of this inquiry, of residences held from the employer, we find that the labourer gains by the expenditure for the external appearance of that which is known to be part of the property,—an expenditure that is generally accompanied by corresponding internal comforts; he gains by all the surrounding advantages of good roads and drainage, and by more sustained and powerful care to maintain them; he gains by the closer proximity to his work attendant on such an arrangement, and he thus avoids all the attacks of disease occasioned by exposure to wet and cold, and the additional fatigue in traversing long distances to and from his home in the damp of early morning or of nightfall. The exposure to weather, after leaving the place of work, is one prolific cause of disease, especially to the young. When the home is near to the place of work, the labourer is enabled to take his dinner with his family instead of at the beershop.

" The wife and family generally gain, by proximity to the employer or the employer's family, in motives to neatness and cleanliness by their being known and being under observation. As a general rule, the whole economy of the cottages in bye-lanes and out-of-the-way places appears to be below those exposed to observation. In connection with property or large capital, the labourer gains in the stability of employment and the regularity of income incidental to operations on a large scale; there is a mutual benefit also in the wages for service being given in the

shape of buildings or permanent and assured comforts, that is in what would be the best application of
wages, rather than wholly in money wages.   In the
manufacturing districts there is a mutual and large
gain by the diminution of the labour of the collection
of rents, the avoidance of the risk of non-payment,
and also in the power of control for the prevention of
disturbances and the removal of tenants of bad
character and conduct.

" Surprise is frequently expressed at the enormous
rents, ranging up to and beyond twenty per cent. on
outlay, exacted by the building speculators in the
towns.   But when the experience of these descriptions of tenements is examined, it is found that
the labour of collecting the rents and the labour
of protecting the property itself against waste from
unprincipled tenants is such as to prove that accommodation given to the disorderly and vicious is scarcely
remunerative at any price.   The tenants are loosely
attached, large numbers migratory, and partly from
the nature of their work, and having little or no goods
and furniture, they have no obstacles to removal ;
they frequently, before absconding, commit every
description of waste; they often burn shelves and cup-
board doors, and the house door itself, and all timber
that can be got at for the purpose.   An objection
frequently made against laying on the water in
houses inhabited by a population addicted to drinking
is, that they would sell the receptacles, and destroy
the pipe, and let the water run to waste, for the sake
of the lead.   The expense and delay of legal remedies
preclude redress for such injuries.

" In some of the worst neighbourhoods of Manchester, the whole population of a street have risen to

resist the service of legal process by the civil officers. In the course of the constabulary inquiry I was informed by the superintendent of the old police of that town, that one of the most dangerous services for a small force was attending to enforce ejectments. This they had often to do, cutlass in hand, and were frequently driven off by showers of bricks from the mobs. The collection of the rents weekly in such neighbourhoods is always a disagreeable service, requiring high payment. This, and the frequent running away of the tenant, and the waste, greatly reduce the apparently enormous rent obtainable from this poorer class of tenants. For all these vices, risks, and defaults of others, the frugal and well-conducted workman, who has no choice of habitation, is compelled to pay in the shape of an increased rent; he is most largely taxed in the increased rent, necessary as an insurance for the risks and losses occasioned by the defective state of legal remedies.

" All these risks the employer is enabled to diminish or avoid by selecting his own tenants, and he has the best means of doing so ; by reservations of rent on the payment of wages, he saves the labour and risks of collection ; nor will the vicious workman so readily commit waste in the house belonging to his employer as in one belonging to a poorer and unconnected owner. The employer has, moreover, the most direct interest in the health and strength of his workpeople.

" It is not supposed that these are arrangements which can be universal, or readily made the subject of legislation. At the commencement of some manufactures, the additional outlay may not be practicable.

But those manufacturers have generally had the greatest success where good accommodation for the workpeople was comprehended in the first arrangements. When, however, a manufactory has been once established and brought into systematic operation, when the first uncertainties have been overcome, and the employer has time to look about him, there appears to be no position from which so extensive and certain a beneficial influence may be exercised as that of the capitalist who stands in the double relation of landlord and employer. He will find, that whilst an unhealthy and vicious population is an expensive as well as a dangerous one, all improvements in the condition of the population have their compensation."

CHAPTER XVI.

PUBLIC WALKS FOR THE PEOPLE.

"WHILST separation rather than aggregation, more especially for families, is the course of policy suggested by experience for the places of residence of the working classes, accommodation is called for from every part of the country for public walks or places of recreation.

"Much evidence might be adduced from the experience of the effects of the parks and other places of public resort in the Metropolis to prove the importance of such provision for recreation, not less for the pleasure they afford in themselves, than for their rivalry to pleasures that are expensive, demoralising, and injurious to the health. A benevolent gentleman near Cambridge, who wished to arrest the debauchery and demoralisation promoted by a fair, and, if possible, to put an end to the fair itself, instituted, on the days when it was held, and at a distance from it, a grand ploughing match, at which all persons of respectability were invited to attend. This brought from the fair all the young men whom it was desired to lead from it to a regulated and a rational and beneficial entertainment, and thus, without force and at a very trivial expense, the fair was suppressed by the quiet mode of drawing away its profit.

" On the holiday given at Manchester in celebration
of Her Majesty's marriage, extensive arrangements
were made for holding a Chartist meeting, and for
getting up what was called a demonstration of the
working classes, which greatly alarmed the municipal
magistrates. Sir Charles Shaw, the Chief Commissioner of Police, induced the mayor to get the
Botanical Gardens, Zoological Gardens, and Museum
of that town, and other institutions, thrown open to
the working classes at the hour they were urgently
invited to attend the Chartist meeting. The mayor
undertook to be personally answerable for any damage
that occurred from throwing open the gardens and
institutions to the classes who had never before entered them. The effect was that not more than two
or three hundred people attended the political meeting,
which entirely failed, and scarcely five shillings' worth
of damage was done in the gardens or in the public
institutions by the workpeople, who were highly
pleased. A further effect produced was, that the
charges before the police of drunkenness and riot were
on that day less than the average of cases on ordinary
days.

" I have been informed of other instances of similar
effects produced by the spread of temperate pleasures
on ordinary occasions, and their rivalry to habits of
drunkenness and gross excitement, whether mental
or sensual.

" But want of open spaces for recreation is not confined to the town population. In the rural districts
the children and young persons of the villages have
frequently no other places for recreation than the
dusty road before their houses or the narrow and dirty
lanes, and accidents frequently take place from the

playing of children on the public highways. If they go into the fields, they are trespassers, and injure the farmer. The want of proper spaces as playgrounds for children is detrimental to the morals as well as to the health of the towns, and it probably is so generally. The very scanty spaces which the children both of the middle and the lower classes, the ill as well as the respectably educated, can obtain, force all into one company, to the detriment of the better children, for it is the rude and boisterous who obtain predominance.

"In the course of some investigations which I had occasion to make into the causes of juvenile delinquency, there appeared several cases of children of honest and industrious parents who had been entrapped by boys of bad character. I inquired how the more respectable children became acquainted with the depraved, when it was shown that, in the present state of many crowded neighbourhoods, all the children of a court or of a street were forced to play, if they had any play whatsoever, on such scraps of ground as they could get, and all were brought into acquaintanceship, and the range of influence of the depraved was extended. The condition of the children in large districts where there are no squares, no gardens attached to the houses, and no playgrounds even to their day-schools, and where they are of a condition in life to be withheld from playing in the streets, is pronounced to be a condition very injurious to their bodily development. The progress of the evil in the rural districts has been, to some extent, arrested by a beneficent standing order of the House of Commons, that all the Enclosure Bills shall include provision for a reserve of land for the public use for recreation.

For children, however, the most important reservations would be those which could be made for playgrounds in front of their homes, on plots where they may be under the eye of their mothers or their neighbours. The separate or distant playgrounds have many inconveniences besides their being out of sight; and where they are far distant, they are comparatively useless. I have great pleasure in being enabled to testify that the instances are frequent where the regulated resort to private pleasure-grounds and parks has been indulgently given for the recreation of the labouring population."

CHAPTER XVII.

" IN reports and communications, the institution of district boards of health was frequently recommended, but in general terms, and they nowhere specify what shall be their powers, how they shall seek out information or receive it, and how act upon it. The recommendation was also sanctioned by the committee which sat to inquire into the health of large towns; and the committee stated that 'the principal duty and objects of these boards of health should be precautionary and preventive, so as to turn the public attention to the causes of illness, and to suggest means by which the sources of contagion might be removed.' Such boards would probably have a clerk, paid for his services, whose duty it would be to make minutes of the proceedings, and give such returns in a short tabular form as might be useful for reference, and important as affording easy information on a subject of such vital interest to the people.

" The action of a board of health upon such evils as those in question must depend upon the arrangements for bringing under its notice the evils to be remedied. A body of gentlemen sitting in a room will find themselves with few means of action if there be no agency to bring the subject matters before them. And, an inquiring agency to seek out the evils from house to house, wherever those evils may be found, following on the footsteps of the private medical practitioner, would be apparently attended with much practical difficulty.

"The statements of the condition of considerable proportions of the labouring population of the towns into which the present inquiries have been carried have been received with surprise by persons of the wealthier classes living in the immediate vicinity, to whom the facts were as strange as if they related to foreigners or the natives of an unknown country. When Dr. Arnott with myself and others were examining the abodes of the poorest classes in Glasgow and Edinburgh, we were regarded with astonishment; and it was frequently declared by the inmates, that they had never for many years witnessed the approach or the presence of persons of that condition near them. We have found that the inhabitants of the front houses in many of the main streets of those towns and of the Metropolis have never entered the adjoining courts, or seen the interior of any of the tenements, situated at the backs of their own houses, in which their own workpeople or dependants reside.

"The duty of visiting loathsome abodes, amidst close atmospheres compounded of smoke and offensive odours, and everything to revolt the senses, is a duty which can only be expected to be regularly performed under much stronger motives than can commonly be imposed on honorary officers, and cannot be depended upon even from paid officers where they are not subjected to strong checks. The examination of loathsome prisons has gained one individual a national and European celebrity. Yet we have seen that there are whole streets of houses composing some of the wynds of Glasgow and Edinburgh, and great numbers of the courts in London and the older towns in England, in which the condition of every inhabited room and the physical condition of the inmates is even more horrible than the worst of the dungeons that Howard ever visited.

" It has only been under the strong pressure of professional duties by the physicians and paid medical men and relieving officers responsible for visiting the abodes of the persons reduced to destitution by disease that the condition of those abodes in the Metropolis has of late been known; and I believe that it is only under continued pressure and strong responsibilities and interests in prevention that investigation will be carried into such places, and the extensive physical causes of disease be effectually eradicated.

" Whilst experience gives little promise even of inquiries from such a body as boards of health without responsibilities, still less of any important results from the mere representations of such bodies separated from executive authority, I would submit for consideration what appears to me a more advantageous application of medical science, viz., uniting it with boards having executive authority.

" The claim to relief on the ground of destitution created by sickness, which carries the medical officer of the union to the interior of the abode of the sufferer, appears to be the means of carrying investigation precisely to the place where the evil is most rife, and where the public intervention is most called for. In the Metropolis the number of cases of fever alone on which the medical officers were required to visit the applicants for relief at their own residences amounted during one year to nearly 14,000. The number of medical officers attached to the new unions throughout the country, and engaged in visiting the claimants to relief on account of sickness, is at this time about 2,300.

"Were it practicable to attach as numerous a body of paid officers to any local boards of health that would be established, it would scarcely be practicable to ensure as certain and well-directed an examination of the residences of the labouring classes as I conceive may be ensured from the medical officers of the unions.

"From the consideration of such practical evidence, it will be seen that the ordinary duties of the relieving officer in the first instance, and of the medical officer afterwards, ensure domiciliary inspection of large districts to an extent and with a degree of certainty that could scarcely be ensured or expected of any agents or members of a board of health unconnected with positive administrative duties. The inspection of these officers of the boards of guardians more than supplies the external inspection of inquests or of the leets; and it is submitted that in their position these boards may most beneficially exercise the functions of the leet in reclaiming the execution of the law as against acts of omission and of commission, by which the poorest of the labouring classes are injured and the ratepayers burdened.

"It may, therefore, be submitted as an eligible preliminary general arrangement, that it shall be required of the medical officer as an extra duty,

for the due performance of which he should be fairly
remunerated, that on visiting any person at that
person's dwelling on an order for medical relief, he
shall, after having given such needful immediate
relief as the case may require, examine or cause to
be examined any such physical and removable causes
as may have produced disease or acted as a predisposing cause to it; and, that he shall make out a
particular statement of them, wherein he shall specify
any things that may be and are urgently required to
be immediately removed. This statement should be
given to the relieving officer, who should thereupon
take measures for the removal of the nuisance at the
expense of the owner of the tenement, unless he,
upon notice which shall be given to him, forthwith
proceed to direct its removal.

"Except in the way of appeal by the owner against
the proceedings, or where a higher expense than five
pounds, or a year's rent of the tenement, is involved
by the alterations directed by the medical officer, it
appears to be recommended that no application to
the Board of Guardians or the magistrates should be
required in the first instance, as it frequently happens
that the delay of a day in the adoption of measures
may occasion the loss of life and the wide spread of
contagious disease, and an application to the Board
of Guardians or to the petty sessions would usually
incur the delay of a week or a fortnight. To repeat
words of Blackstone, 'the security of human lives
and property may sometimes require so speedy a
remedy, as not to allow time to call on the person
on whose property the mischief has arisen to
remedy it.' When any tenement is in a condition
to endanger life from disease, as it comes within the

principle of the law, so it should be included within its provisions, and should be placed in the same condition as a tenement condemned as being ruinous and endangering life from falling.

"Cases of difficulty requiring superior medical experience and skill occur frequently amongst the paupers. For general supervision, as well as for the elucidation of particular questions, the board have proved the practicability of obtaining for the public service the highest medical skill and science. They have availed themselves of more various acquirements than would be found in any standing *conseil de salubrité.*

"But the results of such occasional visits appear to prove the necessity and economy of an increase of the permanent local medical service, and to establish a case for the appointment of a superior medical man for a wider district than an ordinary medical officer for the special aid and supervision of the established medical relief.

"But besides the medical treatment of the inmates of the workhouses and prisons, there are other cases within most districts which need the preventive service of a superior medical officer for the protection of the public health.

"First, in the cases where the poorer classes are assembled in such numbers as to make the assemblages *quasi*-public, and afford facilities for medical inspection, as in schools.

"Secondly, also in places of work and in workmen's lodging-houses. The occasional visits of a district officer for the prevention of disease would lead to the maintenance of due ventilation, and to the protection of the workpeople on such points as are already

specified as injurious to health, and that arise simply
from ignorance, and are not essential to the processes.
An examination of such places, if only quarterly,
would lead to the most beneficial results.

"So far as I have observed the working of the
Factory Act, it appears to me that the duties now
performed by the sub-inspectors of factories might
be more advantageously performed by superior medical
officers, of the rank of army surgeons, who are independent of private practice.

"Having suggested the registration of the causes
of death (under medical superintendence), a head of
information not contained in the original draft of
the Deaths' Registration Bill, I would guard against
an over-estimate of the importance of that provision ;
but I feel confident it would be found, when properly
enforced, one of the most important means of guiding
preventive services in an efficient direction. For
example, wherever, on the examination of these
registries, deaths from fever or other epidemics were
found to recur regularly, and in numbers closely
clustered together, there will be found, on examination, to be some common and generally removable
cause in active operation within the locality. Amongst
whatsoever class of persons engaged in the same
occupation deaths from one disease occur in dispro-
portionately high numbers or at low ages, the cause
of that disease will generally be found to be removable, and not essential to the occupation itself. The
cases of the tailors, miners, and dressmakers, and
the removable circumstances which are found to
govern the prevalence of consumption amongst them,
I adduce as examples of the importance of the
practical suggestions to be gained from correct and

trustworthy registries of the causes of death occurring in particular occupations, as well as in particular places. When a death from fever or consumption occurs in a single family, in the state of isolation in which much of the population live in crowded neighbourhoods, they have rarely any means of knowing that it is not a death arising from some cause peculiar to the individual. Even medical practitioners who are not in very extensive practice may have only a few cases, and may be equally unable to see in them, in connection with others, the operation of an extensive cause or a serious epidemic. The registration of the causes of death, however, presents to view the extent to which deaths from the same disease are common at the same age, at the same time, or at the same place, or in the same occupation.

" One of the most important services, therefore, of a superior medical officer of a district would be to ensure the entries of the causes of death, with the care proportioned to the important uses to be derived from them. The public should be taught to regard correct registration as being frequently of as much importance for the protection of the survivors as a post-mortem examination is often found to be.

" The mortuary registries and the registration of the causes of death are not only valuable as necessary initiatives to the investigation of particular cases, but as checks for the performance of the duty. The system of registration in use at Geneva, combining the certificate and explanation of the private practitioner and the district physician, corresponds with a recommendation originally made for the organisation of the mortuary registries in England, and the experience of that country might, perhaps, be advantageously consulted.

" It would be found that the appointment of a superior medical officer, independent of private practice, to superintend these various duties, would also be a measure of sound pecuniary economy.

" The experience of the navy, and the army, and the prisons may be referred to for exemplifications of the economy in money, as well as in health and life, of such an arrangement. A portion only of the saving from an expensive and oppressive collection of the local rates would abundantly suffice to ensure for the public protection against common evils, the science of a district physician as well as the science of a district engineer. Indeed, the money now spent in comparatively fragmentitious and unsystematised local medical service for the public would, if combined, as it might be, without disturbance on the occurrence of vacancies, afford advantages at each step of the combination. We have in the same towns public medical officers as inspectors of prisons, medical officers for the inspection of lunatic asylums, medical officers of the new unions, medical inspectors of recruits, medical service for the granting certificates for children under the provisions of the Factory Act, medical service for the post-mortem examinations of bodies the subject of coroners' inquests, which, it appears from the mortuary registries of violent deaths in England, amount to between 11,000 and 12,000 annually, for which a fee of a guinea each is given. These and other services are divided in such portions as only to afford remuneration in such sums as £40, £50, or £60, or £80 each, and many smaller and few larger amounts.

" Whatever may be yet required for placing the union medical officers on a completely satisfactory footing, the combination of the services of several parish doctors in the service of fewer union medical officers will be found to be advances in a beneficial direction. The multiplication or the maintenance of such fragmentitious professional services is injurious to the public and the profession. It is injurious to the profession by multiplying poor, ill-paid, and ill-conditioned professional men. Although each may be highly paid in comparison with the service rendered, the portions of service do not suffice for the maintenance of an officer without the aid of private practice; they only suffice, therefore, to sustain needy competitors for practice in narrow fields. Out of such competition the public derive no improvements in medical science, for science comes out of wide opportunities of knowledge and study, which are inconsistent with the study to make interests and the hunt for business in poor neighbourhoods.

" A medical man who is restricted to the observation of only one establishment may be said to be excluded from an efficient knowledge even of that one. Medical men so restricted are generally found to possess an accurate knowledge of the morbid appearances or of the effects amongst the people of the one establishment, but they are frequently found to be destitute of any knowledge of the pervading cause in which they are themselves enveloped, and of which they have by familiarity lost the perception. Thus it was formerly in the navy that medical officers on board ship, amidst the causes of disease—the filth, and bad ventilation, and bad diet—were referring all the epidemic disease experienced exclusively to contagion from some one of the crew who was discovered to have been in a prison. We have seen that local reports present similar examples of similar conclusions from the observation of single establishments in towns, in which reports, effects are attributed as essential to labour, of which effects that same labour is entirely divested in establishments in the county, or under other circumstances which the practitioners have had no means of observing and estimating. The various contradictory opinions on diet, and the older views on the innocuousness of miasma, are commonly referable to the circumstances under which the medical observers were placed; and examples abound in every district of the errors incidental to narrow ranges of observation in cases perplexed by idiosyncracies, and by numerous and varying antecedents. It should be understood by the public that the value of hospital and dispensary practice consists in the range of observation they give; and that the extent of observation or opportunities of medical knowledge are influenced or governed by administrative arrangements. In several of the medical schools of the Metropolis, however, the opportunities of knowledge are dependent on the cases which may chance to arise there.

"Fortunate administrative arrangements have in Paris greatly advanced medical knowledge by bringing large classes of cases under single observation. The most important discoveries made with respect to consumption, those made by M. Louis, were based on the results of the post-mortem examinations of nearly 1,300 cases by that one practitioner. Nearly all the important conclusions deduced from this extensive range of observations were at variance with his own previous opinions and the opinions that had prevailed for centuries. The later and better knowledge of the real nature of fever cases has been obtained by a similar range of observations gained from the cases in fever hospitals. Applications have been several times made to the commissioners by medical men engaged in particular researches to aid them in the removal of the impediments to extended inquiry, by collecting the information to be derived from the sick-wards of the workhouses and the outdoor medical relief lists.

"The highest medical authorities would agree that whatsoever administrative arrangements sustain narrow districts and narrow practice also sustain, at a great public expense, barriers against the extension of knowledge by which the public would benefit and that any arrangements by which such district or confined practice is newly created will aggravate existing evils. An examination of the state of medical practice divided amongst poor practitioners in the thinly populated districts shows that but for the examinations, imperfect though they be, as arrangements which sustain skill and respectability, a large part of the population would be in the hands of ignorant bone-setters.

"On a full examination of the duties which are suggested for a district physician or officer of public health, that which will appear to be most serious is, not the extent of new duties suggested, but the extent of the neglect of duties existing. The wants, however, which it is a duty to represent and repeat, as the most immediate and pressing, for the relief of the labouring population, are those of drainage, cleansing, and the exercise of the business of an engineer, connected with commissions of sewer, to

which the services of a board of health would be
auxiliary. The business of a district physician con-
nects him more immediately with the boards of
guardians, which, as having the distribution of
medical relief and the services of medical officers, I
would submit, may be made, with additional aid, to
do more than can be done by any local boards of
health of the description given, separated from any
executive authority or self-acting means of bringing
information before them.

"I have submitted the chief grounds on which
it appears to me that whatever additional force may
be needed for the protection of the public health,
it would everywhere be obtained more economically,
with unity and efficiency and promptitude, by a
single securely qualified and well-appointed responsible local officer, than by any new establishment
applied in the creation of new local boards. Including as sanitary measures those for drainage and
cleansing and supplies of water as well as medical
appliances, I would cite the remarks on provisions
for the protection of public health made by Dr.
Wilson at the conclusion of a report on the sanitary
condition of the labouring population of Kelso.
After having noted some particular improvements
which had taken place, as it were, by chance, and
independently of any particular aids of science
directed to their furtherance, he remarks that ' it is
impossible to avoid the conclusion that much more
might still be accomplished could we be induced to
profit by a gradually extending knowledge, so as to
found upon it a more widely directed practice. When
man shall be brought to acknowledge (as truth must
finally constrain him to acknowledge) that it is by his

own hand, through his neglect of a few obvious rules,
that the seeds of disease are most lavishly sown
within his frame, and diffused over communities ;
when he shall have required of medical science to
occupy itself rather with the prevention of maladies
than with their cure ; when Governments shall be induced to consider the preservation of a nation's health
an object as important as the promotion of its commerce or the maintenance of its conquests, we may
hope then to see the approach of those times when,
after a life spent almost without sickness, we shall
close the term of an unharassed existence by a
peaceful euthanasia.' "

CHAPTER XVIII.

" TOWN may be highly advanced in its own internal administration; its general drainage, and its arrangements for house and street cleansing may be perfect, and in complete action, and yet if the inspection of the common lodging-houses be neglected, they will be liable to the continued importation, if not the generation, of epidemic disease by the vagrant population who frequent them. The evidence respecting these deserves, therefore, separate consideration, because they ought to be considered independently of the administrative arrangements which affect the resident population of the labouring classes.

" From almost every town from whence sanitary reports have been received that have been the results of careful examinations, the common lodging-houses are pointed out as *foci* of contagious disease within the district. These houses are stages for the various orders of tramps and mendicants who traverse the country from one end to the other, and spread physical pestilence, as well as moral depravation. The evidence everywhere received distinguishes them prominently as the subjects of immediate and decidedly strong legislative interference for the public protection.

"The injury done to the health of the public in general, and to the health of portions of the operative classes, by the generation or propagation of diseases in such places, forms only one part of the evils which call for interference by preventive measures. These evils appear to require for their correction powers to be put in operation by the concurrent exertions of the officers charged with sanitary measures for the prevention of disease, of the officers charged with the administration of relief to destitution and the prevention of mendicity, and of the officers charged with the protection of the public peace and the prevention of crime. Further, to complete the view of the chief evils arising from these receptacles, we may refer to the report and evidence on the state of them, collected by my colleagues and myself, on the inquiry as to the state of crime, under the Constabulary Force Commission, as expressed in the next paragraph.

" We found only few of the magisterial divisions from which we obtained information that were not seriously afflicted by the existence of such receptacles, and in any arrangements for the prevention of crime within the rural districts the means of suppressing or controlling the common lodging-house must have a prominent place   The tramper's lodging-house is distinct from the beershop or the public-house, or any licensed place of public accommodation : it is not only the place of resort of the mendicant, but of the common thief ; it is the ' flash-house ' of the rural district ; it is the receiving-house for stolen goods ; it is the most extensively established school for juvenile delinquency, and commonly, at the same time, the most infamous brothel in the district.

" On the several grounds of public expediency for the care and preservation of the public health, and for the preservation of the public peace, all common lodging-houses,—all places which are open for the reception of strangers, travellers, and wayfarers by the night, and laid out and provided for numbers of lodgers — should be subjected to regulations for the protection of the inmates as well as the public at large. This appears, indeed, to be consistent with the ancient police of the country. By narrowing the definition of the places for which licences were rendered necessary to those where spirits or fermented liquors are sold to be drunk on the premises (as if a revenue were the only proper object of their government), it appears that there has been a mischievous dereliction of the ancient and sound policy of the law which subjects the ' victualler ' as well as the keeper of the hotel, inn, or lodging-house to responsibilities for the protection of the inmates and the convenience of the inhabitants in the neighbourhood where such houses may be situate. The common lodging-house-keeper is, in fact, an inferior victualler, but evading the licence and the responsibilities of the victualler by sending out for the fermented liquors which are consumed by the lodgers.

" It seems, from various portions of evidence, that the occupation of a lodging-house-keeper is a profitable one : instances are given from various parts of the country where the keepers of such houses have accumulated property ; and whilst the keepers of public-houses, however small, or of beershops, are subjected to the necessity of taking out licences, there is no apparent reason for the exemption of lodging-house-keepers from that charge by reason of poverty; neither should I consider that it would be a disadvantage, but the contrary, if the proper regulation of such houses were effected at some increase of the price of the lodgings. On examination of the description of persons accommodated in such houses (whilst there is a public provision for those who are really in a state of destitution, and means are provided for removing such to their places of settlement when it is necessary), I find no class whose migration is entitled to any encouragement by any diminution of the charge of providing proper lodgings.

"Another topic of consideration in connection with houses of this class is the tendency of the degraded accommodation to degrade the classes of the population who have recourse to it. I would therefore submit for consideration whether all common lodging-houses should not be required by law to take out licences in the same manner as public-houses; and that, as the condition of holding such licences, they be subjected to inspection by the medical officer of the union (or the district medical officer), and bound to conform to such sanitary regulations in respect to cleanliness, ventilation, and numbers, proportioned to the space, as he may be authorised to prescribe for the protection of the health of the inmates. And, also that all such lodging-houses shall be subjected to the regulations of the magistrates, and shall be open to visits and inspection of the police, for the enforcement of duly authorised regulations, without any search-warrant or other authority than that necessary for their entrance into any house belonging to a licensed victualler.

"It may further be submitted for consideration that, by the beneficial progress made in the habits of temperance in some districts, the disuse of spirituous or fermented liquors may enable the proprietors of houses of a higher order of resort than those in question to convert them into coffee-houses or victualling houses, and at the same time dispense with the expense of the public-house which the law has attached to licensed houses of resort for travellers.

"From the reports received from the more populous towns, it would appear that there are few houses which are let for the accommodation of large numbers of regular lodgers which might not be benefited by the inspection of a medical officer. I believe it would be more beneficial to the public to extend than to narrow the definition of the places which should be subjected to regulations as lodging-houses, and that a discretion as to the description of house which shall be included might be safely confided to the magistrates who have local charge of the public peace and the public economy of the towns."

The result of these recommendations respecting common lodging-houses has been most important. Practically the whole of the suggestions have been carried out, and now the common lodging-house, under the systematic inspection to which it is subjected, is freed almost entirely from the charge of being a focus of contagious disease.

CHAPTER XIX.

" FTER as careful an examination of the evidence collected as I have been enabled to make, I beg leave to recapitulate the chief conclusions which that evidence appears to me to establish.

" *First, as to the extent and operation of the evils which are the subject of the inquiry :—*

" That the various forms of epidemic, endemic, and other disease, caused, or aggravated, or propagated chiefly amongst the labouring classes by atmospheric impurities produced by decomposing animal and vegetable substances, by damp and filth and close and overcrowded dwellings, prevail amongst the population in every part of the kingdom, whether dwelling in separate houses, in rural villages, in small towns, or in the large towns, as they have been found to prevail in the lowest districts of the metropolis.

" That such disease, wherever its attacks are frequent, is always found in connection with the physical circumstances above specified, and that where those circumstances are removed by drainage, proper cleansing, better ventilation, and other means of diminishing atmospheric impurity, the frequency and intensity of such disease are abated ; and where the removal of the noxious agencies appears to be complete, such disease almost entirely disappears.

" That high prosperity in respect to employment and wages and various and abundant food has afforded to the labouring classes no exemptions from attacks of epidemic disease, which have been as frequent and as fatal in periods of commercial and manufacturing prosperity as in any others.

" That the formation of all habits of cleanliness is obstructed by defective supplies of water.

" That the annual loss of life from filth and bad ventilation is greater than the loss from death or wounds in any wars in which the country has been enaged in modern times.

" That of the 43,000 cases of widowhood and 112,000 cases of destitute orphanage relieved from the poor's rates in England and Wales alone, it appears that the greatest proportion of deaths of the heads of families occurred from the above-specified and other removable causes ; that their ages were under forty-five years ; that is to say, thirteen years below the natural probabilities of life, as shown by the experience of the whole population of Sweden.

" That the public loss from the premature deaths of the heads of families is greater than can be represented by any enumeration of the pecuniary burdens consequent upon their sickness and death.

" That measuring the loss of working ability amongst large classes by the instances of gain even after incomplete arrangements for the removal of noxious influences from places of work or from residences this loss cannot be less than eight or ten years.

" That the ravages of epidemics and other diseases

do not diminish, but tend to increase the pressure of population.

" That in the districts where the mortality is the greatest the births are not only sufficient to replace the numbers removed by death, but to add to the population.

" That the younger population, bred up under noxious physical agencies, is inferior in physical organisation and general health to a population preserved from the presence of such agencies.

" That the population so exposed is less susceptible to moral influences, and that the effects of education are more transient than in a healthy population.

" That these adverse circumstances tend to produce an adult population short-lived, improvident, reckless, and intemperate, and with habitual avidity for sensual gratifications.

" That these habits lead to the abandonment of all the conveniences and decencies of life, and especially lead to the overcrowding of their homes, which is destructive to the morality as well as the health of large classes of both sexes.

" That defective town-cleansing fosters habits of the most abject degradation, and tends to the demoralisation of large numbers of human beings, who subsist by means of what they find amidst the noxious filth accumulated in neglected streets and bye-places.

" That the expenses of local public works are in general unequally and unfairly assessed, oppressively and uneconomically collected, by separate collections, wastefully expended in separate and inefficient operations by unskilled and practically irresponsible officers.

" That the existing law for the protection of the public health and the constitutional machinery for reclaiming its execution, such as the courts leet, have fallen into desuetude, and are in the state indicated by the prevalence of the evils they were intended to prevent.

"*Secondly, as to the means by which the present sanitary condition of the labouring classes may be improved :*—

"The primary and most important measures, and at the same time the most practicable, and within the recognised province of public administration, are drainage, the removal of all refuse of habitations, streets, and roads, and the improvement of the supplies of water.

"That the chief obstacles to the immediate removal of decomposing refuse of towns and habitations have been the expense and annoyance of the hand labour and cartage requisite for the purpose.

"That this expense may be reduced to one-twentieth or to one-thirtieth, or rendered inconsiderable, by the use of water and self-acting means of removal by improved and cheaper sewers and drains.

"That refuse when thus held in suspension in water may be most cheaply and innoxiously conveyed to any distance out of towns, and also in the best form for productive use, and that the loss and injury by the pollution of natural streams may be avoided.

"That for all these purposes, as well as for domestic use, better supplies of water are absolutely necessary.

"That for successful and economical drainage the adoption of geological areas as the basis of operations is requisite.

"That appropriate scientific arrangements for

public drainage would afford important facilities for private land-drainage, which is as important for the health as for the sustenance of the labouring classes.

" That the expense of public drainage, of the supplies of water laid on in houses, and of means of improved cleansing would be a pecuniary gain, by diminishing the existing charges attendant on sickness and premature mortality.

" That for the protection of the labouring classes and of the ratepayers against inefficiency and waste in all new structural arrangements for the protection of the public health, and to ensure public confidence that the expenditure will be beneficial, securities should be taken that all new local public works are devised and conducted by responsible officers qualified by the possession of the science and skill of civil engineers.

" That the oppressiveness and injustice of levies for the whole immediate outlay on such works upon persons who have only short interests in the benefits may be avoided by care in spreading the expense over periods coincident with the benefits.

" That by appropriate arrangements, ten or fifteen per cent. on the ordinary outlay for drainage might be saved, which, on an estimate of the expense of the necessary structural alterations of one-third only of the existing tenements, would be a saving of one million and a half sterling, besides the reduction of the future expenses of management.

" That for the prevention of the disease occasioned by defective ventilation and other causes of impurity in places of work and in all places where large numbers are assembled, and for the general promotion of the means necessary to prevent disease, it would be good economy to appoint a district medical officer independent of private practice, and with the securities of special qualifications and responsibilities, to initiate sanitary measures and reclaim the execution of the law.

"That by the combinations of all these arrangements, it is probable that the full insurable period of life indicated by the Swedish tables, that is an increase of thirteen years at least, may be extended to the whole of the labouring classes.

"That the attainment of these and the other collateral advantages of reducing existing charges and expenditure is within the power of the legislature, and is dependent mainly on the securities taken for the application of practical science, skill, and economy in the direction of local public works.

"And, that the removal of noxious physical circumstances, and the promotion of civic, household, and personal cleanliness, is necessary to the improvement of the moral condition of the population; since sound morality and refinement in manners and health are not long found co-existent with filthy habits amongst any class of the community.

"I beg leave further to suggest, that the principles of amendment deduced from the inquiry will be found as applicable to Scotland as to England; and if so, it may be submitted for attention whether it might not be represented that the structural arrangements for drainage would be most conveniently carried out in the same form as in England, that is by commissions, of the nature of commissions of sewers, adapted, as regards jurisdiction, to natural or geological areas, and including in them the chief elected officers of municipalities, and other authorities now charged with the care of the streets and roads or connected with local public works.   The advantages of uniformity in legislation and in the executive machinery, and of doing the same things in the same way, always choosing the best, and calling the same officers, proceedings, and things by the same names, will only be appreciated by those who have observed the extensive public loss occasioned by that legislation for towns which makes them independent of beneficent, or of what perhaps might have been deemed formerly, aggressive legislation."

With this chapter I finish the abstracts derived from the Report on the Sanitary Condition of the Labouring Classes, and pass on to later and different sanitary labours with which the name of our author is connected.

CHAPTER XX.

THE DISPOSAL OF THE DEAD, AND THE FORMATION OF PUBLIC CEMETERIES.

AS supplementary to the important work on the sanitary condition of the labouring classes, Mr. Chadwick in 1843 presented to Sir James Graham, Principal Secretary of State for the Home Department, an elaborate treatise on the practice of interment in towns as a result of a special inquiry into the whole of that subject.

This supplementary labour forms of itself matter for a considerable volume, and, although the argument set forth in it, derived from an enormous mass of evidence, has served its purpose and is now of little interest to the general reader, it presents to the historian such a remarkable picture of the social life of England half a century ago, in one particular phase of social life, that he will, I am sure, be grateful to me, should his eye fall on this passage, for directing his attention to it; albeit it is a formal Book, presented to both Houses of Parliament by command of Her Majesty.

In the present chapter we must rest content with an abstract of the work and of the results which sprang from it.

Exposition of Existing Evils.

Our author set forth by indicating that the emanations from human remains were of a nature to produce disease, and to depress the general health of all who were exposed to them. He maintained that interments in the vaults of churches, and in graveyards surrounded by inhabited houses, contributed to atmospheric impurities by which the general health and the average duration of life were diminished.

He argued that the places of burial in towns and crowded districts were destitute of proper seclusion and means for the performance of impressive religious service; that feelings of aversion were manifest at the increasing removal or abandonment of family vaults and places of burial; and that the greatest injury was done to the health and feelings of the labouring classes in many populous districts from the long retention of the body, before interment, in the single rooms in which the families of those classes live, sleep, and have their meals, and where the deaths in the greater number of instances have taken place.

He showed, on the most convincing evidence, that the system he condemned often led to extravagant expenditure for funerals,—an expenditure which could not be less than between six and seven hundred thousand pounds for London, and between four and five millions for the whole of England.

Suggested Remedies.

After describing the general means for the abatement of the evils of interments by sanitary measures

which diminish the proportionate numbers of deaths
and funerals, and increase the duration of life, the
author passed on to explain, on several special
grounds, moral, religious, physical, and the best
usages and authorities of primitive Christianity, that
the practice of interments in towns, in burial places
amidst the habitations of the living, and the practice
of interment in churches, ought for the future, and
without any exception of places or acceptation of
persons, to be entirely prohibited.

He held also that the necessities of no class of the
population in respect to burial ought to be subjected
to commercial associations for emolument; but that
national cemeteries of a suitable description should be
provided and maintained, as to the material arrangements, under the direction of officers duly qualified
for the care of the public health.

He contended that for the avoidance of pain and
of moral and physical evil arising from prolonged
detention of the dead in rooms occupied by the
living, and for removing the painful apprehensions of
premature interments, houses ought to be instituted
in every town, for the use of all classes of the community, for the immediate reception and respectful
and appropriate care of the dead under superior and
responsible officers.

In another part of the work he dealt with the
abatement of excessive charges for funereal materials,
decorations, and services, suggesting that provision
should be made, by the officers having charge of the
national cemeteries, for the supply of the requisite
material and services for securing to all classes, but
especially to the poor, the means of respectable interment at reduced and moderate prices, suitable to

the station of the deceased and the condition of the survivors.

For the sake of abating the apprehensions of premature interment, and for bringing responsible aid, counsel and protection within the reach of the most destitute survivors, as well as for protecting the people against continued exposure to ascertained and preventible causes of disease and death, he proposed a revival on the principle of the early appointment of searchers, and that no interment whatever should be allowed to take place without the verification of the fact and cause of death by the Medical Officer of Health.

In all clear and well-ascertained causes of death from immediately removable causes of disease and death, he proposed that officers of health should be invested with summary powers, and be responsible for exercising them for the removal of such causes and for the protection of strangers from exposure and danger from them.

On Payments for Interments on the New System.

Some carefully-considered propositions were made for the repayment of principal and interest incident to the introduction of the new system as part of the reduced expenses for future interments. Burial fees and existing dues should be collected, it was urged, upon interment, and should form a fund from whence should be paid the compensations which Parliament might award to such existing interests as it may be necessary to disturb, and for the erection of new cemeteries; and that any surplus that might hereafter accrue should be applied to means for improving the health of the living. With the assistance of independent medical officers of health the service of interments in national cemeteries might, it was calculated, be so improved that, with the funeral service better solemnised, the expense of funerals, in the metropolis at least, would be reduced to one half the then existing amount, with full compensation to all who might have legitimate claims for compensation for losses arising from the alteration of existing practice.

ADVANTAGES FROM THE SUGGESTED CHANGE.

The advantages which the measures proposed offered to the classes were thus recapitulated by the author in his final summary.

" To take the poorest class : the labouring man would (in common with the middle and higher classes) gain, on the occasion of his demise, protection for his widow and surviving children, that is to say :—

> " Protection from the physical evil occasioned by the necessity of the prolonged retention of his remains in the living and sleeping room.
> " Protection against extortionate charges for interment, and against the impositions of unnecessary, expensive, and unseemly funereal customs, maintained against the wishes of private individuals and families.
> " Protection and redress to his survivors or the living against any unfair or illegal practices, should any such have led to the death.

"Protection against any discoverable causes of
    ill-health, should any have attached to his
    abode or to his place of work.

"Protection from the painful idea (by arrange-
    ments preventive of the possibility) of a
    premature interment.

"Protection of the remains from profanation,
    either before or after interment.

"Protection such as may be afforded by the
    information and advice of a responsible
    officer, of knowledge and station in the
    various unforeseen contingencies that occur
    to perplex and mislead the prostrate and
    desolate survivors on such occasions.

"Added to these would be the relief from the
prospect of interment in a common graveyard or
charnel, by the substitution of a public national
cemetery, on which the mind may dwell with com-
placency as a place in which sepulture may be made
an honour and a privilege.

"The advantages derivable to the public at large
have already been specified, in the removal of causes
of pain to the feelings of the living connected with
the common burial places; they would also gain
in the several measures for protection against the
causes of disease specified as within the province of
an officer of the public health to remove; and they
would also gain in the steps towards the creation of
a science of the prevention of disease, and in a better
registration of the fact and the causes of death.

"To use the words of a great Christian writer, that
all this, which constitutes the last office of the living,
'to compose the body to burial,' should be done, and

that it should be done well and 'gravely, decently, and charitably, we have the example of all civilised nations to engage us, and of all ages of the world to warrant, so that it is against common honesty and public fame and reputation not to do this office.'"

Such were the recommendations of Mr. Chadwick in relation to interments in 1842. The subjoined extracts contain an exposition of his views in 1885. '

" There is a further topic to which I beg to advert, because it bears on the present burning question of the overcrowding of the poorest of the population— namely, the measures proposed for the discontinuance of the practice of intramural interment. I was charged by the Government to examine the subject, and after making a large collection of experiences, presented a report upon it in a supplement to my report in 1842 on the sanitary condition of the labouring classes. Under our first General Board of Health we renewed inquiries into the subject, and presented a second report on it in 1850. The most horrible evil requiring to be dealt with was the prolonged retention of the dead amidst the living in the family's single room—a retention for days, and even for weeks, until money could be obtained to defray the expenses of the funeral. Besides the physical evils resulting from this practice in the spread of infectious diseases, there were also the moral evils arising from the disrespect for life which it produced, and still produces, for it continues to this day unnoticed. I prepared a plan of an executive machinery, such as has been applied beneficially in some of the Continental cities, for ensuring the presence of an

officer of health immediately on the spot, charged to
examine the cause as well as the fact of death, and
empowered to give orders for the immediate removal
of the body to a suitable mortuary, to be duly provided, and when the exciting cause of death was
removable, to take measures for the protection of
the survivors.   When the cause was the unsanitary
condition of the house, the inquiry would have frequently led to the condemnation of that house as
unfit for habitation.   The plan I proposed would
necessarily have occasioned an examination into the
conditions of between twenty and thirty thousand
deaths which happen annually in the Metropolis from
preventible causes, and ought to have led to some
efficient action for relief.   It required provision for
mortuaries and cemeteries, and for services under
unity of a character befitting an elevated community,
and created, I trust, impressions of moral influences
which now are frittered away in the establishments
under the vestral disunity.

"The proper removal of between one and two thousand dead weekly from the midst of the living, their
removal with individual care, and their interment
with propriety, appeared to be a task which could
only be accomplished by a superior executive service
under unity of administration, of which there was
then no immediate prospect.   I submitted my views
in the following terms:—'I would, in conclusion,
beg leave to repeat and represent urgently that Her
Majesty's Government should only set hands to this
great work when invested with full powers to effect it
completely; for at present there appears to be no alternative between doing it well or ill; between simply
shifting the evil from the centre of the populous dis-

tricts to the suburbs and deteriorating them; fixing the sites of interments at inconvenient distances; forming numerous, separate, and weak, and yet enormously expensive, establishments; aggravating the expense and the physical and moral evils of the delay of interment; diminishing the solemnities of sepulture; scattering away the elements of moral and religious improvement; and increasing the duration and sum of the existing evils. There appears to be no distinct or practicable alternative between these results and effecting such a change as, if zealously carried out, will soothe and elevate the feelings of the great bulk of the population, abate the apprehensions of the dying, influence the voluntary adoption of beneficial changes in the practice of obsequies, occasion an earlier removal of the dead from amidst the living to await interment and ensure the impressiveness of the funeral service, give additional securities against attempts on life and trustworthy evidence of the fact of death, with the means of advancing the protection of the living against the attacks of disease, and, at a reduced expense, provide in well-arranged national cemeteries places for public monuments, becoming the position of the empire amongst civilised nations.'

" A second report was called for from our General Board of Health, and with a view to a commencement, one of the trading companies' cemeteries was purchased, but the practical difficulties were found to be so great under the existing conditions of disunity, that further proceedings in that line of amendment were abandoned. Deep-seated evils thus remain as they were, especially the prolonged retention of the dead amidst single chambered families, who, in many

districts, comprise sixty per cent. of the population.
The attainment of complete unity in the metropolitan
administration would open up prospects of grievously-
needed relief in this respect."

In the modern cemetery we have in these days
one practical outcome of some of the original propositions, by and through which the " gardens of the
dead" were instituted. It had been well for the
country if some of the other propositions had been
as wisely and as widely brought into action. Two
of these, as Mr. Chadwick again reminds us, call
for special attention as still waiting for application ;
namely, the erection of houses for the reception of
the dead in crowded localities, and the appointment
of efficient officers for the verification of the fact and
cause of death amongst all classes of the people.

CHAPTER XXI.

SANITARY DWELLINGS FOR THE WAGE CLASSES.

THE following important and suggestive essay was written as an outline for the competition in sanitation for a prize offered by the King of the Belgians to the International Congress, 1877. It was originally printed for circulation by order of the Council of the Society of Arts.

"It is proper to submit to those who are interested in the subject of the improvement of the sanitary condition of the population, that the great prize offered by His Majesty the King of the Belgians, to be awarded at the next International Sanitary Congress, is, in principle, of the highest importance for the direction of sanitary effort, by bringing together, for competent examination, different results, obtained under varied conditions, in different places. Such comparisons cannot fail to advance and popularise sanitary science and economy.

"Hitherto sanitary science has had no place in architectural art and practice. No reference is made to it in architectural treatises. Houses of the first class have the advantage of ventilation by large space; with them economy of fuel for warming is comparatively of little concern. Convenience of living and agreeableness of aspect are the primary objects of the architect. The habitations of the poor are, however, of necessity of restricted space; commonly overcrowded, to the vitiation of the air; damp, ill-warmed, and ill-ventilated; and with them, though of the greatest importance, sanitary science has hitherto commonly been the least regarded. His Majesty's prize concentrates attention on the deficiency or the sufficiency of the primary elements of sanitation in the habitations of the wage classes, as measured by results in the death-rates.

"The improvements that have been made in England by so-called model dwellings for the wage classes have been commonly made under the influence of the expensive habits of construction of the higher classes of houses. In the new dwellings for the wage classes increased space is commonly given at increased expense. This expense is with them the most serious obstacle to the progress of improvement. His Majesty's prize directs attention to the economical element as a primary one for progress.

"For the removal of obstacles which may be expected to stand in the way of efforts towards the attainment of the objects in question, the following statement of the results obtained in Great Britain may be of service.

HOUSE-RATE AND DEATH-RATE.

"The measure of results by the death-rate of the number of deaths per thousand is, as a single test, confessedly open to many objections. Nevertheless, rudimentary as it is, it would have sufficed, within certain limits, to have awarded a prize for past efforts in Great Britain. Thus, in a district in Glasgow, where the death-rate in the houses occupied by the wage classes had been about 42 in 1,000, it was reduced to 28 in 1,000 in new dwellings for them on the same site. But this effort is surpassed by others in London, where, starting in some instances from as high a death-rate, the reductions effected were to 17 or 18 per 1,000. The difficulty of decision and the interest of the competition would be very great between several where the death-rates are nearly the same; but two would be first put out by the expense, as yielding an interest under three per cent., whilst the others yield five or six per cent. The measure of the single death-rate of the proportion per 1,000 of the population is, however, open to the objection that the residents of the model dwellings do not all die in them, and that some die in hospitals or elsewhere; but it is to be taken into account that the occupants of the dwellings displaced died in far larger proportions in public institutions. It may, however, be submitted that a special statistical return by death-rates under several headings may be found necessary for the satisfactory adjudication of the prize. The heads of the return for this purpose might be submitted to the consideration of a special committee of statists or medical officers of several nationalities, conversant with this class of statistics.

"The adoption of such a common form of return would be of value, moreover, not alone for the immediate object, but as leading to the improvement of the general returns, so as to show more clearly the extent of the positive and comparative prevalence of preventible causes of death amongst different classes in different cities. A death-rate which is a mean of the death-rate of the whole population of a city is almost invariably a pernicious misrepresentation. Thus we have part of a sub-district in London, comprising houses in good condition, where the death-rate does not exceed 11·3 in 1,000, whilst there are adjacent dwellings within the same sub-district where the death-rate rises to the extent of 38 in 1,000 from year to year. A mean of the two is a misrepresentation of the condition of both. It is now reported that there are particular localities in London, where the death-rates are from year to year upwards of 50 per 1,000, overwhelmed and overlooked in the great general mean, which heavy death-rates are now primary objects for attention and relief.

"One elementary test of the condition of any class of houses is the extent of the prevalence of the diseases agreed to be classed as the foul air diseases, or of diseases of the epidemic, endemic, or zymotic class. Another primary test is that of the infantile mortality, the first of which is the proportion of the deaths of infants under one year to the births of infants within that same year. This has been chosen as a primary test, because infants are to the least degree affected from fluctuations from changes of residences, because they are to the least extent affected by occupations, because they are most of their time in the house, and because infant life is most affected by vitiated air. Where the death-rates of all classes, adults included, have a range of from one to two, the death-rates of children have, in England, a range of from one to three, or more. We may extend this test usefully to the infantile deaths below five and below ten years of age."

"Of the most useful death-rates as a measure is the comparative death-rate from the foul air diseases prevalent amongst the large classes of society, especially the wage classes, because these are classes found to denote most largely the comparative influence of the different conditions of habitations. One provision for this object is that of the mean age of death of each class as denoting the number of years of life actually attained by those who have died—a form of return which is not perplexed by the comparison of deaths beyond it, and which does not include that other living population which is usually a shifting population, not easily to be got at, if at all. An illustration of the value of the different forms of returns is given in those obtained by the Sanitary Commission for the Metropolis in 1843. In that year the general death-rate, the common test of the population, was 24 per 1,000. A study of the common form of return of the proportion of deaths to the living of all classes will show how little useful information was to be got from it, in comparison with the return for the same year given in the subjoined footnote.*

	Proportions per cent. of deaths from epidemics to total deaths of each class.	*Proportions of deaths of children under 1 year to births within that year.	Proportions per cent. of deaths of children under ten years to total deaths of each class.	Mean age of death of all who have died, men, women, and children.	Mean age of all who died above twenty-one.
				Years.	Years.
Gentry, professional persons, and their families	6·5	1 to 10	24·7	44	61
Tradesmen, shopkeepers, and their families	20·6	1 to 6	52·4	23	50
Wage classes, artisans, labourers, and their families.	22·2	1 to 4	54·5	22	49

* This return as to infantile mortality was not included with the others as to the classes, but is given here by way of illustration from proximate data. This table comprises the elements of mortality alone, in a form which is the more reliable, as being clear and distinct from the element of vitality, or any reference to the proportions of the living population.

" The deaths amongst each class indicate largely
the localising conditions—chiefly of the dwellings—
of each class. The statistics might be inferred from
an examination of the relative local conditions of the
habitations, and may be taken as measures in great
part of the influence of these conditions. Thus the
known differences of the foul air conditions are attended by corresponding differences of the foul air
diseases amongst the higher and lower classes, of
more than three to one, or 6·5 to 22·2. These conditions affect most powerfully infant life, and the
relative amounts are displayed in the proportions of
deaths under ten years of age, of 24·7 to 54·6. The
conditions mainly shorten adult life in the proportions of 49 years to 61 years of the respective classes
in urban districts. In model dwellings the death-
rates of children under ten years are brought up
nearly to a level with the death-rates of children of
the highest class, and are nearly one-half the general
average of the children's death-rates of those years. .

" In a special return for the wage class for the purpose of the competition as test points, it is submitted
that there should be included returns of the infant
mortality for the one year, and that the deaths from
the foul air diseases and other forms, ought perhaps
to be ascertained by competent house-to-house inquiry.

" The power of sanitation by means of the house
alone, it may be observed, is shown in England by
the effect of the proceedings of the police of the
Metropolis and other cities in respect to the common
lodging-houses, which, from having been the seats of
the worst epidemic diseases, have now a comparative
immunity from those foul air diseases which, in the

proportions as displayed in the above table, ravage the residences of the wage classes. London is talked of as a healthy city by those who know little of the subject—a healthy city where the deaths from such diseases amount to upwards of 20,000 yearly, and where the infant mortality is double

"The questions next to be considered are, In what time and in respect to what number of population may the results of improved dwellings be determined by means of such death-rates?

"In the British metropolis, with new villa residences of the middle classes, which are sometimes, by inadvertence or the omission of forewarning, occupied immediately after the construction has been completed, excessive disease is manifested in a new row of houses within a month after their complete occupation. Nine months is the period during which it is deemed unsafe to occupy even new first-class houses in London; nine months might therefore be taken as a period of trial. The period may be taken determinable for the purpose in question chiefly by the absorbency or the non-absorbency of the materials of which the walls are constructed, and by the time required to dry the walls completely.

MATERIALS FOR SANITARY CONSTRUCTION.

"In some of the houses of the wage classes, the materials are of so absorbent a quality that they are scarcely ever completely dried. The perfection of sanitary construction is with material of a non-absorbent quality, and with walling of glazed and impermeable surfaces. Houses of such construction, and with dry timber, may be safely occupied imme-

diately after completion. Good concrete, made of
Portland cement and gravel, has not one-fourth of
the absorbency of the common bricks or building
stones; and the proportion of moisture which it gives
off is so much less, in effect, that from a fortnight to
one month is assigned as the period of comparative
safety. But this material and a combination of lime
and clay invented by the late General Scott, called
selenite,—which, if properly compounded, may be
regarded as a moulded stone of double the strength of
the ordinary brick and of one-half more strength than
the common building stones,—admits of hollow floors
and of hollow walls, with channels for the permea-
tion of warm air, as invented by Mr. Pope, the architect, after the Roman method of construction. The
warmth and dryness for secure occupancy may then
be almost immediate. These concrete constructions
are, moreover, generally one-third less in expense
than the common brick constructions. General
Scott's selenite, indeed, if boiled in gas tar, is rendered properly non-absorbent, stronger and at a less
price than Portland concrete. On the whole, in
British experience, about one year may be assigned
as a full period for the determination of well-ascertained, positive, and comparative results for the
adjudication of a prize. As between improved constructions, the comparative merits may, however,
be determinable with good observation in much less
time.

NUMERICAL SANITATION.

"The next question to be dealt with would be as
to the number of houses requisite to obtain deter-
minate results. Observation on this point is as yet

very imperfect. The most recent observation is that
some forty or fifty houses or families, or from two
to three hundred of population on each side, well
observed, will form a sufficient basis for determination. But we have had no observation of the comparative amount of sickness in the new dwellings,
which may therefore only be guessed at from the
death-rates. On the opening of the first block of
model dwellings in London, an apothecary set up
a shop opposite to them, on the calculation that
such a population would fully require his services.
But he soon discovered that he was out of his
calculations, and that they did not require his
drugs to any such extent as to enable him to live,
so he managed to sell his business to another,
who speedily ascertained the same result, and
abandoned the premises, which were taken by
a provision dealer, who obtained a satisfactory
trade. As good house-drainage and complete sanitary work has proceeded, house by house, in old
houses, low headaches have been discontinued, and
the digestion has been improved, but there has not
been sufficient observation as to the time of the
alteration of the death-rates to ascertain the nar-
rowest basis as to numbers.

"The best proximate observation as to the effects
of sanitation, in time, on limited numbers, would
perhaps have been derived from passengers in
emigrant ships, from whom distinct death-rates
might have been obtained within the period of a
voyage to Australia. Between two ships, alike
in all respects, but the one ship constructed of
new and green timber, and the other of old and
dry timber, there was a forewarned marked differ-

ence of the death-rate within the voyage. In the
first voyages, from ignorance of sanitation, from
overcrowding, from filth and bad ventilation, the
death-rates were fearfully severe, and as many as a
third of the passengers died, and were thrown over-
board, before the termination of the voyage. At
last, by a simple alteration of the terms of the contract with the shippers, which had the effect of a
perpetual prize of the nature of that now proposed,
in awaking attention to sanitary appliances, and
making interest coincident with duty, the state of
things was wholly altered. The alteration was in
not paying, as heretofore, on the number of emigrants embarked, no matter what became of them,
but in contracting to pay only for those landed alive.
The shippers, of their own accord, engaged officers of
health to take charge of the passengers, and paid
those officers of health also only for those landed
alive. By these contracts we ensured to every poor
passenger affectionate attendance, and at least one
sincere mourner if anything happened to him. The
general result was, in a little time, an extraordinary
manifestation of the power of sanitation, and lower
death-rates by one-half than had prevailed amongst
the same classes of passengers when living on shore.

" If the interests in sanitation could be effectually
combined with duty, which it will be one effect of
the prize to promote, the most important results
might be obtained. Between one institution and
another for the reception and care of destitute
children, between prison and prison, data for safe
comparisons are generally obtainable; and the like
may, by better observation of the children's death-
rate, and the foul air diseases, and others, be ob-

tainable between one block of model dwellings and another.

"It may then be taken as the general conclusion, that a population of some forty or fifty families, with a death-rate comprising the infant mortality, as stated, and with the proportion of deaths from the foul air diseases, would, if well observed, form within a year a safe basis for comparison, for the adjudication of the proposed prize.

"A valuable improvement on the display of the course and seats of epidemic disease, which I gave by maps in the report on the sanitary condition of the labouring population of Great Britain of 1842, has been made by Dr. Janssens, of Brussels, by regularly marking the sites of such disease with coloured pins on a town map, in the same way as the position and progress of campaigns is marked by coloured pins on military maps. This expedient may be well adopted by local authorities. It will display to them at once the positions and courses of the enemies against whom they have to contend.

"With these preliminaries settled, the attention of competitors may be directed to what are the chief objective points of sanitation in the construction and arrangements of habitations, to which they may best apply their attention according to local conditions."

CHAPTER XXII.

BASES FOR THE CONSTRUCTION OF SANITARY DWELLINGS.

"ROM observation in the course of my official service in England, the bases for the construction of sanitary dwellings would be as follows:—

SITES.

" First, to begin at the beginning—the sites for the foundations of houses.

" It was an early direction of that very able army sanitarian, Sir John Pringle, noted in his work on ' Diseases of the Army,' that for the selection of sites for encampments, observation should be made of the height of water in wells near the surface; for he said he had always remarked of the places where the water in wells was near the surface, that they were bad camping grounds.

"The soundness of this observation has been proved of late times in towns newly drained under the Public Health Act, where the drainage works when properly executed have lowered the subsoil water, and lowered the water in wells. The result has been a considerable reduction of the diseases of the respiratory organs. For various reasons the first item proposed, therefore, for a sanitary specification should be,—

" That the water table of the site of the house and the adjacent uncovered land should be lowered by subsoil drainage to not less than three feet from the surface.

" In some instances, no doubt, the object is only to be accomplished on a wide field by the work, not of the architect, but of the engineer. However that may be, it may be pronounced absolutely that the land which is water-logged, land with water close to the surface, land which in Sir John Pringle's experience is 'bad camping ground,' is also bad building ground, and should be excluded as unfit by the sanitary law and specification, until by proper work it is made fit.

FLOORINGS AND WALLS.

" Assuming that this first condition of the sanitary specification has been complied with, the habitation, even upon a clean, well-dried gravel foundation, should be protected from rising wet or damp, or from earth exhalations, by another provision, viz. :—

" The flooring of the house shall be constructed of a material which is impermeable to wet, and so laid as to exclude ascending moisture or damp, and all earth exhalations."

" This ought absolutely to be provided for, and it may be accomplished by several means, as by a Portland cement concrete, or most completely by an asphalte covering, or by vitreous tiles laid upon a good concrete.

" On the next question, 'the wall question,' it may be stated that those medical officers who visit the common crowded dwellings of the wage classes in

our towns, even when they are unoccupied, are aware
that the walls have a peculiar depressing, musty, or
fœtid smell.   On visits after severe epidemic attacks
in some of the dwellings a peculiar offensive smell
has been perceived, and on inquiry what that could
possibly be from, the answer has been that it was the
'dead man's smell,' the dead body having been kept
too long near the wall in a state of decomposition
before it could be removed for interment, and the
fœtor still adhering to the wall.

"In the course of the first service under the Public
Health Act in England, in cases where the occupiers
were all struck with fever, in some instances all the
occupiers were ordered to be removed, and the walls
and ceilings to be lime-washed.   But it occurred that
the performance of this service was obstructed or
neglected with respect to particular houses, and in
those uncleansed houses, and in those alone, and
with fresh occupants, the fever has broken out again
—thus demonstrating the condition of the 'leprous
house,' the walls of which were required to be scraped
all round, and in which the work of purification was
insufficient.   Walls lathed, plastered, and papered are
even worse for such tenements.   The laths rot, the
size of the paper decomposes, and the paper itself
harbours vermin.   The condition of some of the
houses of this construction is horrible.   To admit
of the cleansing of the walls by lime-washing in
various modern dwellings, the walls have not been
plastered or papered.   In some instances, the sanitary orders are that the walls should be lime-washed
twice, and in other instances as many as four washings a year are deemed necessary.

"The conclusions in respect to 'washable walls'

are opposed to extensive observation of the higher and middle-class dwellings, which have soft, permeable walls, with lath and plaster, papered, and which do not smell. But the cubic space in the better class houses is usually four times greater, occupied partially instead of constantly, whilst the lower class houses are occupied, night as well as day, by double the number of persons. In the first class of houses, however, on the occurrence of cases of scarlatina or the like, it is prescribed as necessary to re-paper the walls. Moreover, in larger rooms of the first-class houses it is found that illness is at times occasioned by the decomposition of the size used for papering, and by arsenical and other materials used for paper.

" The condensation of moisture on painted walls, or on walls faced with quick conducting materials, in unoccupied rooms, is often confounded with transuding wet, and objected to as a cause of damp; but washable interior wall-facings have been provided for cottages which are not exposed to this inconvenience.

" The occupiers greatly dislike the bare brick walls provided in some model dwellings. In hospitals the evil is in great measure prevented by facing the interior wall with some hard and smooth surface, generally of the best non-absorbent and washable cement. As a principle, then, the surfaces of all interior cottage walls should be washable.

" Besides the evils arising from the absorbency of the animalised gases by walls of the ordinary construction, there is the common evil of the absorbency and retentiveness of water or damp. In England the common bricks absorb as much as a pint or pound of water. Supposing the external walls of an ordinary cottage to be one brick thick, and to consist of 12,000 bricks, they will be capable of holding 1,500 gallons, or 6½ tons of water when saturated. To evaporate this amount of water would require nearly a ton of coal, well applied. A medium brick holds 12½ oz. of water; a piece of well-made cement of the same size only half an ounce, or a twenty-fifth part as much. Yet new constructions are made in ignorance or disregard of such comparative conditions; as also of relative economies, to the extent of 6*d.* per cubic foot of space for cottages that are dry, as compared with 1*s.* per cubic foot of space for ornate cottages that are damp. The softer and more workable stones are of various degrees of absorbency, and are often more retentive of moisture than common brick.

"Professor Ansted states that the facility with which sandstone absorbs water is illustrated by the quantity it contains both in its ordinary state and when saturated. He states that even granite always contains a certain percentage of water, and in the dry state is rarely without a pint and a-half in every cubic foot. Sandstone, however, even that deemed fit for building purposes, may contain half a gallon per cubic foot, and loose sand at least two gallons. When water presents itself in any part of such material, it readily diffuses itself by the power of capillary attraction, by which, as it was observed on some walls in Paris, it ascends thirty-two feet from the foundations.

"Walls of absorbent construction are subject to rising wet by capillary attraction, as well as to the wet of rain or storm. To guard against the driving wet on the coast, expensive external coverings, "weather slate," are used. But these do not stay the rising wet. Impermeable string courses are put in some walls to stay the rising wet, but they do not stay driving wet. This wet having to be evaporated lowers temperature. Damp walls of houses cause rheumatism, lower strength, and expose the human system to other passing conditions of disease. The majority of the bent figures in our villages are due to infliction of rheumatism from damp. An experienced traveller in England laid down a rule to avoid bedrooms with northern aspects, which having less sun upon them were, when unoccupied, the most damp, and if the bed touched the wall, there was the most danger of a damp bed. To keep out the damp an extra quantity of fuel is necessary. The evil is the greater with the poor, who are often obliged to leave their rooms without the fires which the more wealthy are enabled to keep up.

" The first lesson set in the model cottages erected by Prince Albert was that an improved sanitary construction with hollow brick, or pot walls, with glazed and impermeable and washable surfaces, should be adhered to. It is, therefore, proposed as the terms of a sanitary specification in respect to the wall including the ceiling :—

" *That it shall be constructed of a material of the first order as a non-conductor of heat.*
That it shall be impermeable to water and to gas.
That it shall be washable inside and out.
That it shall be of a material that shall not harbour animalcules.

" To which may be added this :—

" *That the facing shall be of a light agreeable colour.*

WINDOWS AND LIGHTS.

"In considering the complete sanitary construction of the house, the window has to be taken into account.

"It is of sanitary importance to increase the light and sun warmth, by increasing the window space in houses, and especially in cottage dwellings. But if we do that with thin window-glass, we diminish warmth, and to that extent diminish the effect and the value of house shelter in cold weather. It is, therefore, suggested—

> "*That the windows shall be of such thickness and arrangement, that the retaining power, or the non-conducting power of heat, shall be equivalent in cold weather to the non-conducting power of the outer walls.*

"It has been a frequent question put in Scotland, 'Why do you make the windows so small, now the window-tax is removed?' The answer is, 'Because, if we make them large in our climate, the rooms will be so cold in winter.' It is commonly overlooked, in respect to this class of dwelling, how rapidly large windows radiate heat. As a rule, under the old constructions, about one-third of the warming powers was in cold weather radiated through their windows; but a double window, with the stratum of air between, makes the window-space about equal to the common wall-space in non-conducting power, while very thick plate-glass approximates, in proportion to its thickness, to the double windows. By one experiment in winter time it was found that the difference in radiation (the thermometer being at 20° F.) between a thin window and one of thick plate-glass is about

8°. To bring this home to the case of labouring class dwellings. If a man pays a shilling a week, as he generally does in London, for his coal for warming his one room in winter, nearly one-third, or fourpence, would be wasted through a thin window. Now, this waste of heating-power would compensate for getting a thick glass or double one. Moreover, a very thick window is very difficult to cut or break through, and may, with a curtain, save the expense of shutters. .

VENTILATION.

"But having got the house weather-tight, and damp-proof, and miasma-proof, with washable and non-absorbent walls, we shall, nevertheless, if we have them closed almost hermetically, have only placed the population in small crowded rooms, under a set of inverted receivers of vitiated and phthisis-producing air and—if the crowding is intense—fever-producing air. It is, therefore, proposed, as most important heads of sanitary specification for ventilation, that the construction shall be such :—

"1. *As to change the air of each living and sitting-room completely, not less frequently than three times an hour.*

2. *As to change the vitiated air for air that is warm as well as fresh.*

3. *As to save more than one-third of the chimney heat, seven-eighths of which in the common constructions now passes away unapplied.*

4. *As still to apply advantageously the radiant heat of the open fireplace.*

"Those requirements are now attainable by simple

yet inexpensive means, through a perfected invention
of Captain Douglas Galton.

"The principle of the invention consists in
surrounding a smoke flue, which may be of stoneware
or of iron, with a fresh-air flue, the fresh air being
taken from the outer air.   The heat of the smoke
flue expands the air in the fresh-air flue, and causes
it to rise in a current, which is discharged—warmed
—near the ceiling of the room, across which it
spreads.   It then descends and mixes with the
colder and heavier air beneath, is carried with the
current into the open fireplace, and is thence discharged as vitiated air through the smoke flue.   The
smoke flue, surrounded by a fresh-air flue, constitutes
a pump, pumping into the room warmed fresh air in
quantities proportioned to the warming power of the
smoke flue and the adjustment of the size and length
of the fresh-air flue.

"There are objections to ventilating with dry heated
air, but the late Dr. Parkes, of Netley, has made
experiments, which show that, at the rate at which
air passes through the fresh-air flue, and the short
time of its contact with the heated surface, it is
carried into the room with its hygrometric condition
very little altered.

"Another effect produced by the invention is the
maintenance of an equable temperature in all parts
of a room, and the prevention of draughts.   The
soldiers in the barrack-rooms where it has been
introduced say that they are better warmed; and
that they are not now roasted in front whilst they
are frozen behind, as they were with the old grates.

"It prevents smoky chimneys, by the ample supply
of warmed air to the room, and by the draught created

in the neck of the chimney, by the peculiar form of fire grate which Captain Galton adapts to the smoke and air flues. It also largely economises fuel, by making use of the spare heat which would otherwise be carried up the chimney. There are no patents for these contrivances, and the expense of the .new apparatus is inconsiderable as compared with the economy produced. It is claimed for an improved ventilating grate, with a large warming surface for fresh air admitted into the room, invented by M. Chas. Joly, the writer of what I consider the best treatise on warming and ventilating, that it attains conveniently and cheaply the object of the chimney ventilating.

GAS.

"A minor provision—having relation to ventilation—where gas is introduced into dwellings, is :—

"*That for every gas burner introduced into any part of the house a separate channel shall be introduced for carrying away the products of combustion.*

" This is an important sanitary provision, urgently advised by gas managers, who well know the nature of those products, but it is difficult and dangerous to carry away those hot air flues through the common timber floorings. Through floorings of concrete such channels may be conducted on first construction, with comparative convenience and without danger.

WATER SUPPLY AND SEWERS.

" On the water supply of dwellings for the wage classes it should be required that :—

" *Water supplies shall be carried to every floor by pipes
which, if of lead, shall be protected in the interior by
composition preventive of any action of the metal upon
the water.*

" *On each floor or landing there shall be provided a sink with
a waste or return pipe, communicating with the house
drain, and each such sink or waste pipe shall be so
trapped as to prevent the escape of any vitiated air
from the house drain or the sewer, into the premises.*

*The house shall be provided with a water closet, on the
syphon principle, so shaped and provided with water
as to be effectually self-cleansing, and connected with
a house drain of such form, size, and inclination,
as to be effectually self-cleansing throughout, and to
remove everything at once from beneath the premises ;
—to be so trapped as to prevent the ingress of vitiated
air from the sewer, in the event of accidental stoppages ;
and to be at all times free from foul smells.*

" Accidental stoppages only are required, under
proper instructions, to be provided for by flushing,
inasmuch as where sewers are properly constructed,
they are self-cleansing, and are free from deposit ;
there is no decomposition of stagnant matter ; no
need of flushing, and but little need of trapping,
except to ward off the consequences of accidental
stoppages.

Summary Respecting the House.

" *The complete construction of the house must be such that if
it be left clean, and unoccupied for any time, it shall
remain dry, free from any close, musty, or foul smell,
and shall be immediately habitable, without the need of
fires, or of any special preparations for safe occupancy
in winter or in summer.*

" For the completion of the rudimentary sanitary

provisions connected with dwellings, it is necessary to add other specifications to be made, not to architects or to house builders, but to the local authorities having charge of the local drainage works, viz. :—

> " *That the sewers for the reception of all house drainage shall be constructed of such form, size, and inclination as to be completely self-cleansing; to remove constantly, and without leaving any deposit, the refuse discharged into the sewers; and, without occasioning any need of flushing except for accidents.*
>
> " *That all animal or vegetable matter removed from beneath the sites of houses, streets, and towns, in suspension in water, shall be deposited on soil appropriated for its reception for vegetable production, and shall be deposited and applied usually within the day of its production, or before it can enter into any noxious stages of decomposition, or give off any noxious emanations.*

" All this may now with competent sanitary scientific engineering be accomplished.

Streets and Footpaths.

" In respect to the surfaces of the footpaths and streets of towns, it ought to be provided that :—

> " *Both the foot-ways and the carriage-ways shall be covered with a surface impermeable to water and washable.*
>
> " *Both foot-ways and carriage-ways shall be regularly washed at stated intervals and at such times, daily or weekly, as the state of the traffic may require.*

" This may be done with an economy of clothes, as well as of furniture and goods, in houses and shops, under competent sanitary administration.

"The same is conducive to the dryness of the urban atmosphere, to the purity of the air by the prevention of puddles of decomposing refuse of all sorts, and to the cleanliness of the person, clothes, and furniture of the inhabitants. Where towns are well administered, the water ought to be carried into the lower-class habitations at a rate of three-halfpence a-week; the waste water should be carried away, with all excreta, for about a penny a-week, and the streets washed for another penny per week per house.

PROMISES OF RESULTS.

" With external as well as internal provisions duly made under their direction, experienced officers of health will agree that we should make a large alteration in the sickness and death-rates, and in the moral as well as the physical condition of the people. With these new conditions, in cities, inhabited by an educated population competent to apply them, the sickness and death-rates might be reduced greatly beyond those in the public institutions which show the lowest mortality, where they are yet applied only in an incomplete manner.

"The foregoing elementary heads of sanitary specification, it is recommended should, with any other that the locality may specially need, be placed before competing architects for their accomplishment, and the opinion of the officers of health should be taken on the comparative efficiency of the means.

" The primary merits or defaults of sanitary science and art construction of dwellings may be confidently tested after occupation by the smell, by dryness and freshness of smell when the occupants are out; by the absence of the bad drain smell, of mustiness, of damp, and of the foul wall smell,—'the dead man's smell'—on the walls of rooms where there has been a prolonged retention of the dead; and by warmth in winter, with coolness in summer. According to these primary qualities, so will there be, in a great degree, sickness-rates and death-rates, especially amongst children and those who are much in the house."

CHAPTER XXIII.

HOUSE DRAINAGE.

IN a previous chapter—Chapter VII. of this volume—the author's views on land drainage are explained. In the present chapter, which forms a good continuation of the preceding one, on dwellings for the wage classes, he treats on the subject of house drainage as a distinctive sanitary study.

This essay formed the matter of an address delivered before the members of the Association of Public Sanitary Inspectors, at a general meeting held on October 4th, 1884. Prepared for gentlemen whose daily business consists in inspection of houses, and in enquiry into every detail that bears on good and bad house drainage, it is very practical and useful; for which reason, except in regard to some slight repetitions, it is here published entire.

INTRODUCTION.

"Since we last met, you will have observed with grief the heavy blows inflicted on the people of Italy and of France by the visitation of the special pestilence of cholera, which it is your office and sanitary service to aid in withstanding for the protection of the people of this country. You may have observed that in Italy the visitation has already slain some ten thousand people and wounded as many more; and it has done this, we may confidently declare, for the greatest part by the neglect of those defences which sanitary science has provided; although to the efficiency of that science the physician of the Czar bore testimony at the Sanitary Congress at Brussels, when he stated that more than twenty thousand people were killed at each visitation of the cholera at St. Petersburg, until they adopted the sanitary principles of defence prepared by the first General Board of Health of England; and that when they did so the losses were reduced to a fifth or a sixth of what they had been before. With the forewarning of the advance made upon Egypt, and, as stated, the occurrence of premonitory symptoms before the attack came in force, there was no house-to-house visitation, and no examination and preparation of persons, and no examination and cleansing of the places by sanitary inspectors, but an entire absence of any efficient or proper central service, for aid of a local service, such as we now have here for the protection of the people. The state of ignorance in which the people had been kept was shown by their riots and the attacks of their defenders, the physicians, as if they were their murderers. It may be that an advance in their intelligence hereafter may lead them to turn their hostility in a more just direction—on those politicians by whose ignorance and defaults in the neglect of the forewarnings of sanitary scientists, greater sufferings and losses have been inflicted on the population than could have been inflicted in

these times by the swords of the most savage
enemies. Reserving observations, which may be
made hereafter, on the wasteful policy of exhausting
expenditure, on the excessive unproductive barracked
forces of militarianism;—and on the folly of ignoring
economies of productive force, effected by sani-
tarianism, by the removal of the conditions which
sustain the utmost misery and the continuance of the
'unfittest,' I would call attention to some administrative details by which such economies are obtained.

HOUSE DRAINAGE IN BOSTON CITY.

" I have a report from the city of Boston, United
States, where, as respects the general system of
town sewerage, the citizens have fallen into the
enormously wasteful error of the combined system,
such as has befallen this metropolis and other places,
and of throwing the sewage, and, it may be added,
the milk from some forty thousand cows, into the
sea. Nevertheless, chiefly by sanitary house inspection, and the action of such a service as that of the
members of this Institution, an important advance
has been made; and a former death-rate of 31·80 per
1,000 has been reduced to 23·53, and in 1879 to 20·83
per 1,000.

"The *Times* has rendered important sanitary service
by calling attention to the first object of urban
sanitation—the drainage of the house. I wish to
present the example of the way in which the Board
of Health of Boston acted against that defect.
They state in their last report: 'In 1877 we commenced examining houses from door to door, without any reference to any complaint or supposed

defect in the sanitary arrangements; taking every house in the block and selecting the blocks in different sections of the city.' Let this course of action be noted.

"Our practice is now of urging the occupiers of houses to send for some private specialist to examine their houses, and, of course, pay him a fee. But the danger is not unfrequently in the next house, and, therefore, not traced out by the inspection. I nevertheless considered even the expense of the visit of the specialist, and also of the separate works he may recommend, to be means of important economy. I mention the expense, however, as a potent obstruction. It appears that in the first year of the operations in Boston the percentage of defective house drains was 55, and of defective trapping 78. In the last year the percentage of bad house drains was reduced to 34, and defective trapping to 28 only. I believe that similar results would be obtained by the like inspections in London.

"I note as an example of the working of the house-to-house examination in Boston, that out of 306 houses, examined by the inspectors last year, bad odours were found in 180; defective drains in 166; defective trapping in 174; water-closets in 295; offensive water-closets in 47; privy vaults in 43; 'air-boxes' in 167; air-boxes improperly arranged, 4; offensive vaults, 21; damp or unclean yards, 8.

House Drainage in London.

" This enumeration of defects, according to recent evidence, would represent the common hazards,— in great part entirely unknown to him or the owner,

—in which, as a tenant, a man would take a house in a large part of London. It has been declared upon examination, that not above one out of three first-class houses have been found to be safely drained. Fevers amongst servants and bad drainage have prevailed in Belgravia as well as Bethnal Green. The people of Boston appear to regard the good sanitary condition of each other's houses and the prevention of the pollution of the common air as a subject of a common interest to be provided for under common contract; and, in doing so, I can state that they will get the work done at once, and done responsibly, and maintained in good condition, generally at one-third the cost that it is or can be done separately by the private householder who employs his own plumber or architect. This is opposed to trading interests, which local boards here commonly think it their duty to protect. I may, however, question the right of plumbers to sanitary work. Constant supplies of water, water-closets, and tubular drains are, I expect, not to be found in 'Old London.' The plumbers will possibly, however, have large and new work offered to them by common contracts, on competition for districts.

"The board at Boston recite as their work for last year nine thousand pieces of work of the sanitation of houses, including the reparation of nearly three thousand private house drains. They state in their report that the subject of house draining has been pursued by the board during the last year with the same interest as heretofore, and they have been greatly encouraged by the active interest shown in it by the people. They further observe :—'A very decided change of opinion is manifested everywhere on this subject, and it becomes easier every year to convince people and obtain the desired improvements in house drainage.'

"The immediate removal of excreta, and putrescible excreta, before putrefaction commences, which is usually in one, two, or three days, is a primary condition of sanitation. The practical effect of the immediate removal from within the house of sewage before it enters into putrefactive decomposition is shown in this: that when such sewage arrives at outfalls into streams it feeds fishes, whereas in putrefactive stages it kills them. Putrefaction means infection; and the immediate discharge by water carriage is disinfection. But the condition of stagnation and the putridity of sewage is now commonly assumed to be a constant unavoidable condition; and hence immensely expensive schemes of disinfection continue to be propounded. My friend, the late General Scott, estimated that he could disinfect the sewage of the Metropolis for £100,000 per annum. I doubt if he could have done it for that, but if he could, that sum capitalised at the usual rate would suffice for the provision of self-cleansing drains for all the houses needing them, and for preventing the noxious condition of putridity. Moreover, putridity is a waste of manure, which disinfectants do little to prevent.

"Where you meet foul smells, you may say, 'Here is waste of precious manure.' At our Board of Health we got a consolidation of the eight separate Sewers Commissions under unity for the whole of the metropolis. We then got from that consolidated commission—what no separate commission could have got—an Ordnance Survey for the whole of the Metropolis, on such a scale as to admit of the course of the capillaries, or house drains, within the houses to be seen for the purpose of inspection. I was then enabled to get, what the separate commissions would not have got, even if they had sufficient sanitary science to move them thereto, an elaborate set of trial works to determine the sizes of house drains and sewers that would be self-cleansing.

" I can state that were the complete sanitation of houses by constant supplies of water, and removal of fouled water and fæcal matter by water carriage effected, the former expenses under the First Board of Health could have been greatly below the minimum charges against preventible disease. Those expenses did not, when properly executed, exceed threepence-halfpenny per week, payable not by the owner, but by the occupier, who received the benefit, which was equal to a reduction of a weekly insurance charge of one shilling and sixpence per week off an allowance of ten shillings a week during sickness. The cost of labour in works since then may have advanced, but, nevertheless, the complete works will be found to effect an important reduction of insurance charges, to the occupier, as well as a reduction of other charges to the owner.

SIZE OF SEWERS.

" The result of these trials was that if tubular earthenware pipes were made perfectly true as is a gun-barrel, drains of 3 in. of diameter, with a fall of little more than 1 in 60, would be self-cleansing. As to sewers, a pipe of 15 in. in diameter was placed in an old sewer with a sectional area of 15 ft. to receive storm water, and the drainage from 1,200 average-sized houses. In that sewer the deposit accumulated at the rate of 6,000 cubic feet per month, but through the sewer pipe of 15 in. in diameter, with somewhat less inclination, placed along the bottom, it was found that by the accelerated flow it was kept perfectly clear of deposit. Bricks and rats were swept out of it by the force of the flow. It was found, moreover, that the separate house-drainage—apart from that of rain or storm water—would have passed through a 5 in. tube, that is to say, of not one-third the minimum size of a single house drain, which had up to that time and upon the advice of architects been declared to be necessary for a single house, namely, one of not less than nine inches in diameter. Taking the sewer of one street as a fair example, Mr. Thomas Lovick, one of our engineers—now one of the chief engineers of the Metropolitan Board of Works—estimated that the whole of the separate house drainage of the metropolis—then of three hundred and forty thousand houses—might have been carried away in a sewer of three feet in diameter.

"In the United States one sanitary engineer at least, Colonel Waring, has paid attention to the sizes of sewers for self-cleansing action, and he has given one instance, that at the Grand Union Hotel at Saratoga, in which with nineteen hundred people and some hundreds of water-closets, and the water supply as copious as possible, the amount of the full flow of sewage measured $4\frac{1}{2}$ inches in sectional area, and might have been discharged through a $2\frac{1}{2}$ inch pipe. The observations of the inspectors may be well directed to the conditions of the self-cleansing power of these channels.

"One condition has been subsequently shown,

namely, that in a sewer of a proper capacity for
the ordinary flow of house drainage alone the friction
of the flow of water carries the air along with it—
as Mr. Pilbrow has shown particularly at Totten-
ham—with a force sufficient to blow out a candle
at the outlet. Instead of any emanations going up
into the houses from that sewer, there is really a
down-draft from the houses. The sewage being discharged constantly by self-cleansing drains from the
houses, before putrefaction can commence, surveyors
in the towns so drained have declared to me that
there is no smell of putrefaction created or perceptible, and that there is really no need of trapping
except to guard against occasional stoppages, which
do not amount to more than a dozen in a thousand
houses.

"For the sake of the owners as well as of the
occupiers, the result of the house drainage work may
be tested by the sanitary inspector by the smoke
test, or by the turpentine test; and, for the whole
town, by seeing whether marked substances, like
split turnips, put in the closets at the upper part,
and timed, duly arrive at the outfall. Provision for
flushing is needed to guard against accidents; provision for habitual flushing means habitual stagnation; rough brick drains and stone drains have now
generally been superseded by smooth tubular pot
drains, but commonly with compromises of principle.
'Not to go to extremes,' larger than correct sizes are
frequently used, to the extent of double, four, five,
and six-inch drains, by which accidental stoppages
are made frequent, the frictional area increased,
and the flow retarded, where it ought to be most
carefully accelerated, in the house drains. The ovoid

form, which is proved to accelerate small flows, and is the best, has not yet got into proper use for all tubular drainage. The machine-made pipes are deficient in taper.

Tests of Good House Drainage.

"My question on visiting a town which had been completely house-drained and sewered on principle has generally been :—'Are the houses clear from smell?' The answer was usually, 'Yes.' 'Are your sewers clear from smell?' 'Yes.' But I have met with some qualifications as to houses. There is one quarter which was not clear from smells. 'How is that?' I asked. 'Why, in that block the contractor did not do his work properly, and hence the failures and smells.' In another place there was an exception of this sort—the contractor failed to execute his work properly; he jointed his pipes with clay instead of cement, and there the sewage escaped, with foul smells, and, consequently, fever. In one instance, I was informed, even by an engineer, that it was absolutely necessary that provision should be made for the trapping and flushing, for the sewers undoubtedly emitted foul smells. I had enquiries made into the instance he gave me, when it turned out that the new pipe sewers had been connected with a set of old sewers of deposit, which the local board had not thought it worth while to replace by self-cleansing sewers, and the new and small sewers certainly carried from the old ones their gases of stagnation and putrefaction.

"In my own neighbourhood, a general of great distinction, a very robust person, died suddenly. My

physician, who attended him, was confident that the
death had occurred from an exposure to sewer gas.
He examined the house, and found that such gas
permeated a hollow wall close to the head of the
bed. A new pipe sewer had been laid down, and
by a drain connected with the house at the top
of the hill, where it had diffused foul smells never
experienced there before, which had been led from
a connection made with the bad sewers of deposit
and connections with old and badly-drained houses
of a lower district. A proper sanitary inspection
would have protected that and other houses, by
trapping, from such lethal conditions, which the
ignorant and dangerous local authority allowed to
continue. Here there was certainly an augmentation
of private insurance charges, which complete work
would have reduced.

"I might adduce varied examples of the need of
an appeal to a central authority to enforce the representations of the local officers for the protection of
the people against the consequences of the ignorance
of the local authorities. It may be stated, as a
general sanitary rule, that the local administration,
as well as the general administration, may be tested
by the nose. The economical effect of all these
experiences was that three houses and three towns
might be drained well at the cost incurred for
draining one house or one town ill. This general
economic conclusion excited furious opposition in
the House of Commons, and obstruction to the re-
newal of the First Board of Health.

Dealing with Drain Products.

" The common course, un-superintended and unsystematised by administrative principle, appears to
be that of dealing with diminished effect with separate
parts of a system, as if they were properly independent ;—of dealing with sewers, independently of the
houses; of houses as if they were independent of the
sewers; and of both, as if they were independent of
the river or its purity ; and of the direct application
of fresh sewage, instead of inferior and putrid sewage,
in a way to create marsh surfaces on the land. This
separate treatment is, nevertheless, attended with
some advantage, though vastly inferior to the
collective treatment. Thus Boston, by improvement
in the house drainage, appears to have made an
advance from the present common death-rate of
the Italian cities of thirty in a thousand, to twenty
in a thousand, or one-third. But it may be confidently affirmed that by a better self-government and
administration of our more complete plan, it might
gain another third, as at Croydon, where the death-
rate, which was twenty-eight in a thousand, is now
thirteen. And, with the gain, from the application
of the fresh manure direct to the land, the milk of
five cows instead of one cow per acre."

CHAPTER XXIV.

IN Chapter IV. the primary views held by Mr. Chadwick on the disposal of sewage are supplied. They were the views of forty-four years ago. Since then great and important changes of view have been made in which he has taken on one side the leading part. It may be well at this point to glance at the nature of these changes, and of his bearing in respect to them.

The effect of the report on the sanitary condition of the labouring classes was to direct public attention closely to the subject of drainage of large towns, and especially to the drainage of the Metropolis. In the controversies which followed, the disputants were divided into two great camps. .One of these declared in favour of a system of drainage which allowed the water from the heavens to mix in a common stream with the sewage from the houses, under what has been styled the "combined system." The other declared in favour of the plan expressed in the saying, "The sewage to the land, the rain to the river," by which was meant that the storm water of a town or city should be separated from the sewage; in other words, that by a "separate system for each," the two fluids should have a distinct course.

As time went on, from the period of his first studies on these questions, Mr. Chadwick made up his mind entirely for the separate system, of which system he has been for many years the consistent and persistent advocate.

In respect to London the battle that was waged, when it became certain that an entire reconstruction of the system of sewage must be carried out, was lost to the prime mover of the separate system and to all of us who took his view.   The great new system carried out by the Metropolitan Board of Works was the combined system, costly beyond necessity, we believed, unscientific, ineffective.   To this Mr. Chadwick has held tooth and nail, and many of his best essays are to be found in defence of his side of the debate.   To what extent his views have advanced is best shown in his essay on " Circulation or Stagnation " published in 1881, in which the direct application of the sewage to the land is carefully recast in the subjoined extracts.

" Persons who only know of sewage by their experience of its emanations, under the common conditions of stagnation and putrefaction, very naturally object to its application in the vicinity of their residences, and would do so with much reason if those conditions were essential.   Violent opposition is made to the discharge of sewers into rivers, on the score of pollution.   Whilst sewage, however, in the common condition of putrefaction, kills fish, sewage in another condition, that is to say, in circulation—fresh, or before putrefaction—feeds fish.   But on the score of waste I object to its discharge into the rivers, or anywhere except on the land.   People do not object to the cultivation of land, as market garden land, close to their dwellings or to towns. Nevertheless, culture and high farming is frequently conducted in a manner productive of noxious emanations that are injurious to health, and make the culture there a nuisance. This is done by heavy top dressings of what is called ' town manure,' in the solid form, in which condition it remains stagnating until it is disintegrated by decomposition, by which decomposition its fertilising power is diminished, and it is then carried down into the soil by the rain. The complete remedy of this evil is to liquefy the manure at once—to put it in solution, and apply it to the soil in doses proportioned to the soil's receptivity—in fact, to apply it as sewage, by which means one load of stable manure may be made to do the work of more than two. I was advised, when I looked into the subject, that the waste of the farmyard manures and other manures, by the methods the farmers used, was in extensive districts equivalent to another rental. On the other hand, it was pointed out in our instructions that applications of plain water in excess, by the method of submersion, creating marsh surfaces and marsh miasma, were often conducive to the rot in sheep and ague in men ; and, of course, that the distribution of sewage in the like manner would be productive of still worse results. At the irrigations at Paris, as I am informed, this danger has been incurred, through excessive submersion, by the unskilfulness of the small farmers to whom the sewage has been given, and that sewage, not in the fresh state, but as sewage of a bad quality, as nearly all there is.

" The facts should be known that for sanitation it is

a work of skill to avoid the supersaturation of the soil, and that for cultivation it is a work of skill to avoid supersaturation, and to adapt the supply of the liquid manure to the 'hygroscopicity' of the soil, according to the periods of the growth of the plant for root, for wood, for leaf, or for fruit. For the avoidance of stagnation and waste, and the expense of storage tanks, it is a work of skill to place every day's supply from the town on one part of the land or another, whatever be the weather, in frost or snow. In frost this has been accomplished at Dantzig by distribution under the ice.

"Sewage farming is an art foreign to common agricultural practice, and is confined to a high order of horticulturists, growers of prize fruit, to whom its application on a large scale should be confided. Nevertheless, in some hundred of sewage farms, now conducted throughout the country by all sorts of rudimentary methods, with bad sewage from ill-drained towns as well as good, and by various rudimentary workings, the superior productive power of the liquefied manure has been established, not only in the bulk, but in the quality of the produce; and, as to the bulk, whilst the average yield of agriculture in England may be taken to be as one, and the market-gardening as about three and a half, the sewage-farm produce has been as five. It is found that, as a rule, the sewage of more than a hundred of population may be utilised in an acre.

"As to the sanitary effect of sewage farming, the judges of the competition for prizes issued by the Royal Agricultural Society,—of which Mr. Baldwin Latham, Mr. Clare Sewell Read, and Mr. Thursfield were judges,—made particular inquiries about the

sanitary results upon those engaged in the work,
and they display these in a table of the death-rates.
They state that the rate of mortality on an average
of the number of years which these farms have
been in operation (ten) does not exceed more than
three per thousand per annum; that is to say, on
a population of 380 men living on or working on
the farms, and 137 children. From the difference
of working under insanitary conditions amidst stable-
dung and farm-yard manures,—which are attended
with fevers amongst families — and the working
amidst liquefied manures, I should have expected a
marked difference, but not so great as this, which
must be about fourfold.

" In order to secure the best results from the application of sewage to the land, its dilution must be no
greater than actually necessary. The amount of
water requisite for its carriage gives, in this climate
at least, a fully sufficient dilution. Storm and
subsoil water should therefore be excluded from the
sewers, and should be provided for separately. Storm
water is specially prejudical to irrigation, as it always
presents itself at the time when it is least wanted :
during very wet weather. Moreover, the admission
of storm and subsoil water greatly increases the
difficulty of conveying the sewage to suitable land,
by augmenting, in an irregular and uncontrollable
manner, the bulk to be carried. Hence, to avoid
the expense of pumping a greatly increased and
varying amount of sewage, attempts to apply it
have often been limited to areas to which it could
flow by gravitation, or nearly so, where the soil
and situation were unfavourable, or where, on
account of its contiguity to the town, or from

other causes, the cost of land has been excessive, and where, therefore, the extent of ground has been prejudicially restricted.

" By limiting the quantity to be dealt with to the sewage proper, the choice of site for its application, both as to position and extent, is greatly increased. It should be remembered that the cost of raising a given quantity of water does not increase directly as the height to which it is lifted, the efficiency of pumping machinery for high lifts being generally greater than of that for low lifts. In favourable cases, as in large waterworks' steam-engines, 80,000 gallons can be pumped to a height of 100 feet for one shilling. When, therefore, a calculable and comparatively constant quantity of sewage has to be raised, as will be the case where storm and subsoil water is excluded, the cost of pumping need not be feared, when by its means favourable sites for sewage application may be commanded.

" A competent administration will utilise the ground allotted to, or contiguous to, public institutions, such as union houses, prisons, and others, and develop models of liquefied manure cultivation.

" On the difficulty which presented itself for the completion of the system of circulation by the disposal of town sewage by surface irrigation near towns, particularly of sewage in the condition of putridity, in which all was then only to be met with, I was led to consider subsoil or subterranean irrigation, and I got several friends who had gardens to try it, and the trials were very promising. Sir Joseph Paxton promised to try it systematically. But it was tried independently and systematically on a large scale by M. Charpentier, a French vine-grower, near Bordeaux, with whom I had correspondence on the subject. His trials were not with town sewage, but with liquefied manure, and included the old Italian method of distribution by regurgitation, and certainly the results he obtained with vines and fruits, as well as with market garden produce, were most satisfactory. He contended for its superiority over surface irrigation, but it required great skill, and more capital than the ordinary surface irrigations. The early successes with surface distributions, however, withdrew my attention from it ; but the method has been revived with success by Mr. Rogers Field in the disposal of the sewage of some villages ; and his flushing tank greatly facilitates distribution by that subterranean method. It has also been carried out, as reported, with success by Colonel Waring, of Newport, in America. Experiences show that for high culture, for model gardens near towns, for deep-feeding plants, for fruit-trees, and for arboriculture generally and in hot climates, the method in skilful hands will be productive of very great results.

" It is yet, however, to be stated distinctly and kept in view, that advances in administrative knowledge and advances in legislative science and art, are needed, as well as in mechanical and agricultural science and art, for the advancement of sanitary science and its application for the relief of populations."

CHAPTER XXV.

IN a later essay (1885),—a comment on the late report of the Royal Commission on Metropolitan Sewage Discharge,—Mr. Chadwick pursues the subject of the last chapter in a form as original as it is practical.

"From one end to the other of the report there is only one condition of sewage recognised—putrid sewage, the product of stagnation, and the residue of decomposition. It denotes the present low state of sanitary information, that none of the papers read at the Healtheries by chemists and professed sanitary engineers, except that communicated by Mr. Rogers Field, recognised any other condition than that of putrid sewage. We might have been informed that fresh sewage, from self-cleansing house-drains and self-cleansing sewers, is of at least one-third higher productive power than when in a state of decomposition. A sewage farmer took from a corporation the sewage of a town on the presumption that the whole town was drained, as part of it then was, with self-cleansing drains. But he justly complained of the admixture of putrid sewage from the ill-drained portions, and claimed compensation; and I believe he would have maintained his claim for a depreciation of more than one-third by the incomplete drainage, had he gone into court. I was interested in the results of an effort made for a sewage farm at the camp at Aldershot, the sand there being so dense that it appeared to be like an effort to irrigate paving stones. On going to the farm, I at once pronounced that the camp was ill-drained. Had I seen the plan of drainage, I was asked. No, but I knew that it was ill-drained from the smell of putridity at the outfall. The farmer at once affirmed as much, and complained that he was perplexed and damaged by the flushes of stagnant and putrid sewage instead of fresh sewage, a damage which justified his claim to an allowance on its account from the War Office, which I believe him to have applied for and obtained.

"I beg to state that my view on this subject (of sewage application) has been based on the dictum and practical experiences of the greatest vegetable physiologist of the century, De Candolle, who declared it as an axiom that the future of agriculture would depend on giving food and water to plants at the same time. Mr. Smith, of Deanston, the author of thorough drainage, one of the greatest practical agriculturists of our time, and one of the first Assistant Sanitary Commissioners, declared to me that the waste of farm-yard manures in Scotland by putrefaction was equal to another rental.

"Right honourable gentlemen serving at the Local Government Board, who have been driven to restrict their attendance there, and do as much as they can at home, from experience of the foul sewer gases pervading the offices of that department, such as it is, of the Local Government Board; and also members of Parliament, who have been assailed by the foul

smells which they have experienced near the seat
of legislation, which are proved on examination
to come from the stagnant deposit in the large sewers
—may be informed that what they experience is the
escape of the finest materials of production, to the
extent of millions of tons of guano, lost to agriculture,
with an increase of heavy sickness and death to the
population. The most immediate means for purifying
the river is by works for the purification of the
sewage flowing into it, which would be earlier available than the distant works of intermittent filtration
that have been proposed, and are more pressingly due
to the relief of the population. Of their relative
economy I shall speak hereafter.

" The case of Craigenteny meadows at Edinburgh is
presented as the leading case on which the 'separate
system' rests. It was never so used by me. In the
first place, it was on the old method of distribution
by submersion over levelled planes. In our minutes
of information it was objected that irrigations by this
method with plain water were creative of marsh surface, and productive of rot in sheep, and of ague and
rheumatism in men. In the case of the Craigenteny
methods these consequences are avoided by the general
circulation of the sewage, and a very constant sweeping
breeze from the sea. But we objected to the plan on
account of the enormous quantity of sewage used and
wasted—sixty inches in the year—to do that which,
by other methods, might be better accomplished by
one-fifth of that quantity properly applied. In consequence of the enormous quantity of the dilution, it
appeared that the value of the manure distributed in
those meadows was only a halfpenny a ton. The
sewage there is worked by gravitation alone; and

then it is asked, how can it be supposed that it
will pay to lift and move the enormous quantity
of the sewage of the Metropolis at a mere halfpenny a ton. Will it pay at that price? Certainly
not; but it would not be, necessary to lift one-
sixth of the quantity, and the value of the manure
to be lifted would, by avoiding the waste, be
some eight times greater than is assumed by the
objectors.

"I take it, as it may generally be taken, that the
cost of removal, and of the external distribution of
fouled water to every part of a field, need not exceed
the cost of the removal and external distribution of
pure water into the highest common varying heights
of the field of distribution in a town and urban area
like the Metropolis. But I have found even engineers
of water-companies unaware of what that cost is. In
London, the cost per diem of bringing water from
some fifteen miles of distance, of filtering it, and all
other expenses, is three-fourths of a farthing for
thirty or thirty-two gallons; and one-third of that
fourth is reducible by the consolidation of the companies, of which the commission has taken no
account. At the time of my service I ascertained
that the working cost for raising 87,000 gallons 100
feet high was a shilling. Since then, by the progress
of improvement, I learn from the Messrs. Quick that
they are proposing to supply Amsterdam by steam
power, which, with not very large engines, raises
150,000 gallons 100 feet high for a shilling. Lifting
liquefied manure to heights may be effected at
a cheaper rate on a larger scale than could be
accomplished if the manure were raised in a solid
form.

"The report treats of the application of liquefied manure by a process of 'irrigation as by the application of ordinary agricultural knowledge,' by which it is admitted it 'was sometimes very effective,' but it appears to be assumed that 'only agricultural knowledge is available to the purpose.'

"Now the 'ordinary agricultural' knowledge is really inapplicable, and is the source of the failures in sewage farming, which it is assumed does not generally pay. But 'the ordinary agricultural knowledge' is founded on the practice of dressings with solid manure, once, or even twice a year.

The most successful practice with liquefied manure is not 'ordinary agricultural practice,' but horticultural practice, the practice of special plant-feedings by dressings, according to the growth of the plant, often given even twice a week. A farmer, a first-rate practical proficient in the ordinary agriculture of Scotland, told me that it took him more than a year to understand the working of a liquefied manure farm ; and then he found that the produce was so great as to be beyond the capacity of his sheds to store it, or of any stock he had got to consume it ; besides, the liquefied process quickened production in mangolds, or in other roots, to unwonted bulks, at a time when there was no market for them, and hence much loss. It is only after much practice that the inconveniences of an immense but untimely production are obviated, and they are not to be expected to be obviated, by any 'ordinary agricultural practice,' but on a large scale, by very special horticultural skill, when such transformations of produce will be effected as horticultural practice has effected in the plants of luxury Our best guides on sewage or liquefied manure farming

were experienced plant-feeders—horticulturists, of
whom Sir Joseph Paxton was the most distinguished.

"In such hands, by horticultural feeding, the carrot
has been made a new plant, with finer saccharine
matter and a new aroma. The celery is most excellent. The rhubarb is made to exceed itself. At Reading ninety tons of mangolds have been obtained to the
acre. At Dantzic such gigantic cabbages have been
produced as have never before been seen in Germany.
At Paris I prevailed upon the late Emperor to order
some trial works to be made with sewage manure,
when the first produce, though the sewage was not
of the best sort, was an enormous amount of grass.
An Academician pronounced it to be gross, and unfit
for the food of cattle. I appealed from the judgment
of the Academician to the judgment of a cow on
the point. A cow was selected, and sewaged and
unsewaged grass was placed before it for its choice.
It preferred the sewaged grass with avidity, and
it yielded its final judgment in superior milk and
butter of increased quantity. It is with such raw
material of production that the superior Legislature
has allowed the vestral local authorities of the
Metropolis to pollute the river ; and it now seeks to
throw into the sea the milk of some two hundred and
fifty thousand cows, or about one cow's supply for
every two houses, for such results have been obtained.

"I may cite an instance of which I have recently
been informed of the application of the sewage of
an educational institution (that of the district school
of Sutton, Surrey, comprising nearly two thousand
inhabitants) delivered fresh, and without the smell
of putridity, to fifteen acres of land, which yields a
net profit of £400 per annum, or nearly £20 per acre.

"With laboriously collected expositions of principles so full and clear, and with such varied practical instances of their application, as will be found in the information circulated in 1852, it is impossible not to express regret at the almost retrograde state in which the administration appears to stagnate. By this time almost every large district institution throughout the country has presented an example and served as a school of advanced agriculture. It is illustrative of the relaxed state of administrative arrangements that this last cited example of economy has gone on for years without attention or instructional pressure for its general adoption ; and that at the very next similar institution, the sewage which might have served on a farm, so valuable for the instruction of the boys in advanced agriculture, is thrown away to the pollution of the next stream. I am informed of greater examples of intelligent administration presented at some of the county lunatic asylums which illustrate the ignorant and weak assertions of engineers, who are not agriculturists, whose declaration is that the highest order of agricultural production, obtained at the lowest working expenses, 'does not pay,' as it certainly is not likely to do in their hands, or in other than of a high order of specialists.

"I have received from the Health Department of the United States, at Washington, the following example worked out by Mr. Benezette Williams,—an engineer there,—of the application of the separate system to a new town called Pulman, of 8,000 population, at a short distance from Chicago. The sewage is discharged fresh from the houses and conveyed by engine power through a pipe three miles long to a sewage farm, where, as it is received, no noxious

odours can be detected from it, and where it is at
once taken up by the soil and the growing vegetation before any decomposition can commence. ‘The
farm produced during the last season 200,000 heads
of cabbages, 18,000 bunches of celery, besides 100
tons of hay and a great deal of other sorts of farm
produce. It has a dairy department stocked with
fine Holstein cattle, and has paid an excellent return
upon the investment.’ The marked effect of the
purification of the houses and the streets by the
separate system is the reduction of the death-rate to
little more than 7 per 1,000, or little more than one
quarter of the death-rates of the American cities.
The community, it is to be observed, is very largely
a temperance community. Altogether, the working
of sanitation under the separate system in the
Pulman city may be commended to close attention, and the widest promulgation in the way of
example."

Referring to the main drainage of London, our
author sums up in the following conclusions :—

" (a) That the state of the river Thames, pronounced by the Royal Commissioners to be in a
condition to be retrieved at any cost, is due to the
measure of proceeding on the combined system—
that is to say, of carrying off rain and storm water
in the same channels as the sewage proper.

" (b) That this has been done at an expense of
upwards of six millions of money, that would, on
the separate system, have sufficed for the purification of the houses and the streets of the greater
part of the Metropolis from the products of stagnant

decomposition, with large reduction of the enormous expenses incident to excessive sickness, loss of work, and premature mortality.

"(c) That further proceeding with the combined system is to continue injurious waste, and to impose aggravated money burthens on the population; —burthens threefold greater than that of the poor's rates.

"(d) That the separate system has been carried out in a number of towns, with variations in the executive details, and that it would be of advantage if these variations were closely examined, with a view to the application of the experience of the best results to the relief of the Metropolis.

"(e) That whether the sewage be destined to feed vegetation or to feed fish, it must be delivered, not in a condition of putridity, but fresh; that it must be delivered fresh on the land to augment its power of agricultural production, and also to avoid the necessity of carrying it to excessive distances, and to avoid the creation of nuisance, and the resistance to the occupation of land as sewage farms on account of the noxious condition of putridity.

"(f) That chemical disinfectants, deodorisers, or intermittent filtrations, are not needed when sewage is discharged fresh, or before the commencement of putrefactive decomposition.

"(g) That the sewage can only be obtained fresh by the separate system, by the self-cleansing house-drains and self-cleansing sewers, as has been done in a number of towns on that system, attended with the reduction of death-rates, and at outlays which reduce largely the expense of preventible sickness and premature mortality.

" (*h*) That the water pumped into the Metropolis by the trading companies is greatly in excess of the actual domestic consumption, an excess estimated at more than three-fifths pumped into injurious waste, at an extra expense for pumping it out, as well as at the extra expense for pumping it in.

" (*i*) That the effect of this waste is to reduce proportionately the value of the sewage as manure, to increase the cost of its distribution, and to reduce the possible returns from sewage farming with it.

" (*j*) That the effective reduction of this waste would reduce nearly wholly the intakes of the supplies from sewage-tainted river sources, and reduce the demands of pure spring sources, also available in the vicinity, to the Metropolis.

" (*k*) That the trading companies have failed to reduce this waste, and that it can only be effectually reduced, as at Manchester and at Liverpool, when the supplies for the Metropolis are put, as there, under unity of management on a public footing, as recommended by various Royal Commissions and Select Committees of Parliament.

" (*l*) That to arrest the course of continued expense, waste, and grievous evil, and to promote efficient means of the improvement of the condition of the population—especially of the wage classes—it is to be urged that the local administration of the Metropolis should be placed with the least delay under complete unity, with securities for the application of special science for the protection of the people."

CHAPTER XXVI.

THE subject-matter of the present and of the following chapter was delivered on Wednesday, December 14th, 1881, in the Dome, Brighton, as the presidential address to Section A, Health of Towns, of the Brighton Health Congress. It is one of the most useful, as well as interesting, of the author's contributions to sanitation. Mr. Chadwick said:—

"I have been requested to give a paper on the health of towns and on the sanitary legislation affecting them. In relation thereto I begin with an account of one special measure of such legislation, involving the sanitary principles of relief and protection against epidemics. I believe I may best do this by a narrative of the measures for a defensive campaign undertaken to withstand the invasion of the extraordinary epidemic of Asiatic cholera in 1848-49, which may probably be new to most people at this time.

"At the First General Board of Health of which I was the chief executive officer we had, in 1848, warning of the approach from India of the enemy, and the threat of a heavier slaughter by thousands than would be affected by visible enemies of the

largest of hostile foreign hosts. Our first council was
as to the nature and state of the former established
defences.

ORIGINAL DEFENCES BY QUARANTINES. WHY DISCARDED.

"Those of the old routine were for the outer
defences by strict quarantines, and, when these
defences were broken through, of hospitals, and a
common treatment of the sick in them—almost of
necessity in the later collapsed stages of the disease.
We had information that the measurable distances of
infection from the specific disease were not greater
than those of our common epidemics; but, as we
showed in a report on quarantines, which was accepted and translated for circulation, the quarantine
service as practised on the Continent as a defence,
would be as an attempt at shutting out the east
wind, and, for reasons which I shall give, utterly
feeble and illusory as a defence.

LOCAL CONDITIONS OF ORDINARY AS WELL AS OF EXTRAORDINARY EPIDEMICS.

"Our conclusions on this head have been affirmed
by subsequent experience, especially by the vastly
quickened international communications, by steam
on sea as well as on land, which bring in and distribute everywhere persons in conditions of latent
incubation of infectious disease, diffusing everywhere,
—according to our information,—sources of infection
that must have aggravated such visitations to an
extent never heretofore experienced. I had shown
that all the mischievous and false securities against

epidemics, of quarantines, and grievous obstructions
to international communication will have to be removed; and it appeared to me and my colleagues,
on examination, that the great impending visitation
would probably advance, as to places, chiefly on the
lines, in local conditions, on which ordinary epidemics now proceed.

"In Poor Law administration, I had been pressed
by medical officers to take business out of its turn,
because, from the state of the weather, they had a
confident expectation that they would have some
visitation of one of the ordinary epidemics to deal
with. Asking one of them,—a medical officer,—
what was the specific disease he apprehended, he
stated that when he arose in the morning and
found the atmosphere warm, moist, and stagnant,
he always found that there would be an increase
of some foul air disease;—it might be typhoid, it
might be scarlatina, it might be measles, it might
be small-pox, but one species or another of eruptive
disease he was sure to have in such weather in his
low-lying and ill-drained districts. I asked a relieving officer of a large district, in order to test his
knowledge of the habitat of such diseases, whether,
if I gave him some half-dozen cabs, he knew where
he could go and fill them with fever cases, just
as a gamekeeper might go and get a bag of game.
He said he certainly could; the cases might not be
all of typhus, but they would be infectious cases of
one sort or another, and he knew where he could
find them.

"It appeared that small-pox follows on much the
same lines as typhus, and so does scarlatina, but with
wider deviations as to classes of cases and conditions

of persons. On passing through a low district I observed, ' Surely this must be a fever nest,' when out came some children with the marks of recent small-pox upon them. I remember that I was once consulted by Dr. Lyon Playfair as to the readiest mode of making a sanitary inspection of an urban district, without the medical officer's or the Registrar-General's returns, which there was not time to get out. I advised him to go into one of the primary schools, and select a group of the most squalid children, get their addresses, and go there. He told me that he had acted on this suggestion ; and that, in the first school, there were two boys with particularly blotched faces, and he had found that their habitations were at the confluence of some putrid sewage. I have indeed myself, on view of the children of different large district schools, made proximate estimates of the comparative death-rates of the districts whence they came ; and it is a large and pregnant fact, attested by experienced teachers, that as the lowest districts have been improved by sanitation, the type of the children received therefrom has also been improved.

" On inquiring as to the course of the Asiatic cholera in its previous visitation, we found that it was very much upon the common fever conditions. It did not visit them all, but such as it did were visited with marked severity. Indeed, medical officers of experience in the former visitation foretold in which streets, and on what sides of streets, and into what houses it would again come ; and their forecast was verified even as to the rooms of some particular houses.

VARIED TYPES OF EPIDEMICS IN COMMON CONDITIONS.

" The variations of the types of these extraordinary visitations, and their repeated attacks on populations in the like local conditions, and the state of the intelligence which continues those conditions, is a matter of profound interest in sanitation. In the City of York we had one classical instance presented of a particular court, called the Hagworm's Nest (the Hagworm is a species of anguis, infesting foul heaps), which by tradition was the first spot visited by 'black death;' the first by the 'great plague;' the first by the 'sweating sickness;' and, as it remained unchanged, inquiry was made whether it was true to its traditions on the visitation of the cholera in 1832, and it was so. We have had analogies to such variation of the types of epidemic visitations on the like local conditions, in more recent times. For example, Dr. John Sutherland, our active sanitary inspector in London and on the Army Sanitary Commission in the Crimea, and Captain Douglas Galton, in their report, as members of the Barrack and Hospital Improvement Commission, on Malta, show that the same localities and houses in Malta which yielded the majority of plague deaths there in 1813, yielded the majority of the deaths in the cholera epidemics of 1839 and 1865; and that in the intervals the same localities yielded the majority of cases of small-pox, fever, and of an anthrax, a very special eruptive epidemic attended by carbuncles. Up to our time, although the occurrence of the epidemics on certain local conditions was noted, the occurrence was accepted as a constant result, and no steps were thought of or taken to change those conditions.

ALTERATIONS FOR PREVENTION.

"The observations derived from previous experiences had pointed out to us that the first objective points of defence against the coming attack were the alteration, as far as might be done within the time, of the conditions of the exposed places, the sites of the ordinary foul-air diseases in their epidemic visitations.

"We sent out instructional notifications to the boards of guardians and the local authorities, to put them on the alert against the extraordinary visitation coming. They were inapt and dilatory. We then sent out our sanitary inspectors to examine and report on the particular measures to be taken for the protection of the population in the most exposed districts in the Metropolis; but it is to be observed, that action by such authorities at intervals of board meetings is slow, and that, for prevention, it must be quick, and by skilled and responsible officers. Much was done in the lower districts there and elsewhere by extra activity in surface cleansing. Parish fire-engines were turned out, and courts and alleys were thoroughly washed down. For covering the excrement-sodden pavements and surfaces in the close courts, such as urban districts, particularly of the Northern towns paved with boulder stones present, we ordered fresh mould to be brought in, and a covering made over them and over dung-heaps, some three inches deep, to serve as an earth-work. The people where this was done declared that they felt themselves in new atmospheres such as they never had before. We ordered pigs to be turned out and the styes to be cleansed. In some of the Scotch towns there was great uproar against this, but our orders were then law, and the pigs were turned out by the thousand, and kept out, until the epidemic had passed. Stagnant ditches were ordered to be drained; but we soon found that, simple as it might appear, the work of ditch cleansing could not be left with safety to the parish authorities, but must be done under skilled superintendence, as to methods and times. Otherwise, the people were apt to spread the putrid contents over the banks and extend the evaporating surface, so as to generate immediate fever. Stable dung we ordered to be removed, and the stables in mews to be cleansed daily, and one experience I gained was, that by proper arrangements this might be done in ordinary times with little extra expense.

Evidence of the Climatorial Character of the Extraordinary Epidemic Visitation.

"But there were places which we found to be in conditions of filth that were irretrievably bad. There our only remedy appeared to be, as the epidemic advanced, to tent out the people. We borrowed tents from the army stores in the Tower, and ordered the people to be tented out in them, at Wolverhampton and other places. One, the small fishing town of Mevagissey in Cornwall, presented when the cholera came an instructive instance of the climatorial character of the epidemic. People in the tents after some days got tired of bivouacking out and returned to their dwellings, where they were re-attacked with premonitory symptoms; they returned to their tents, and were freed from them. They again ventured

back to their homes, and were again attacked. They
returned to the tents, and were freed, and remained
there until the epidemic had passed. I was informed
that members of the bar of the Northern Circuit, on
going to towns where the cholera was advancing,
were many of them subject to premonitory attacks;
on leaving one town were freed until they got into
another affected town, where they were again attacked;
and on leaving it, were again freed.

" During the prevalence of the epidemic Lord
Palmerston sent for me, and told me that the Queen
had been invited to return from Scotland in the direction of one of the towns, and asked whether I thought
it safe for Her Majesty to do so. I advised certainly
not, and I did so from the belief that the epidemic
was climatorial, and on the information of the fact
that passengers staying only for a night in the good
hotels of one of the districts had been subject to
premonitory attacks.

" Instances were noted in India, Russia, and
Germany, as characteristic of the epidemics, that
birds, such as rooks, disappeared on its advance, and
only returned on its departure. Thus Colonel W. K.
Stuart, of the 86th Regiment, in his Memoirs, states
in relation to the cholera at Burantyore :—' Before
proceeding further, I must relate a curious circumstance that occurred, which, in my opinion, establishes
beyond doubt the fact that the cholera is atmospheric.
Every person who has served in India must be aware
of the number of kites, vultures, and other birds of prey
that congregate around the cantonments of a regiment. For some days before the first case of cholera
broke out, all these birds had disappeared ; not one
was to be seen, and they never returned until the

plague was gone. Where they went to nobody knew, but such was the case. Surely they must have been made conscious by the sense of smell, or by some instinct, that there was danger in remaining in that atmosphere.'

"It has been held that the cholera is conveyed only by human intercourse ; and when it advances itself, in the direction of lines of communication, it may appear to be carried in that way. If there had been any affected persons in the houses at Mevagissey, it might have been surmised that the people returning were infected by the persons instead of the places, and the places, many of them, excrement-sodden, the attacks might have been ascribed to the alvine secretions which were probably exciting causes. But troops on the march in India have been attacked on particular open spots, clear of population, and on a change of position as from one hillside to another, have been freed from attack.

"We had neither time nor means to direct the efforts of chemists, to ascertain, if they could, what these aerial conditions were. But be those conditions what they might, they appeared to traverse districts in particular directions. In India there appears to be a law on the subject, the cholera moving along a certain line to the north-west. In the rural districts the people are sedentary, and they scarcely ever move from home. But onward moves the epidemic. At last it arrives on the borders of the desert, where there are no people, and no intercourse, no alvine secretions, and no sewers, yet the statistician sitting in Calcutta can tell almost the day in which the epidemic influence will have crossed the desert. On such facts there appears to be as little ground for speaking of the importation of the infection of cholera by persons, as there would be of the importation of the ' infections of some skin eruptions,' which we know are attendant on the advent of the east winds.

EPIDEMICS INFECTIOUS THOUGH CLIMATORIAL.

" I may here state, that although the evidence points to the fact of great epidemics occurring at long intervals being chiefly climatorial, or affecting particular areas, they may yet be, and, as in the case of the small-pox, they largely are communicable by infection. Permit me to illustrate this by a story told of Beau Brummel. A friend met him with his throat muffled up, and asked what was the matter with him, when Brummel answered that it was owing to that rascal Tom his servant having put him in the same room with a damp stranger! Now a damp stranger might have done this to a highly sensitive person. But a crowd of damp strangers in a room might be really additionally dangerous, although the cause was climatorial, and due to the outside storm which made them damp. When an ordinary epidemic advances, is it ever observed, that there has been no extraordinary corresponding movement of persons, or of society preceding it? We directed an examination of the cholera advance in the Metropolis, and found it did not advance in succession, case after case, but nearly simultaneously in widely scattered instances between which it was impossible to prove communication.

" By the various means I have recited, we got the local defences more extensively prepared than might have been expected, considering the very inadequate central staff we had at our disposal, and the weak local staff. We were greatly aided by reasoned notifications through which we derived much aid from the clergy, and from persons of education.

"But we could not cover all points of defence effectively. There were obviously weak lines through which we must expect that the coming epidemic would break, and that we must provide for a greater or lesser number of sick and wounded. For them the provision of hospital accommodation was heretofore usual and general, on the exclusive system. On this topic we made anxious inquiry. We sent for all the practitioners we could get together, who had been in the thick of previous visitations, and consulted their experiences as to what did do and what did not do in cholera.

Why Large Hospitals for Treatment were Abandoned.

"From the hospitals we gathered this experience; that, in the stages of collapse of the disease, the mere act of lifting up the patients from their beds to remove them frequently killed them ; also that conveyance over rough roads in common cabs, or even in litters delivered many dead at the hospital. In the hospitals, moreover, the mortality, under every form of treatment, was excessive. On the whole, with all defects of their homes, and the difficulties of medical appliances in them, it were better to let the sick remain there than to remove them. The evidence in support of this conclusion was so strong that we were led, as a general rule, to dispense with the provision for

special, or even general, hospitals. We had then to
resort to provisions for home treatment. At this time
we made what was really, as regarded all antecedent
treatment, a discovery.

DISCOVERY OF PREMONITORY SYMPTOMS OF THE EXTRA-ORDINARY EPIDEMIC.

"Through my friend Mr. Hodgson, of the College
of Surgeons, we learned that a Dr. McCann, of
Bilston, had made much observation of the previous
course of the disease, and had ascertained that it had
generally premonitory symptoms of slight diarrhœa,
with rice-water purgings, and that in that stage, if
taken in time, it was amenable to regimen and
medical treatment. This general fact was established
upon the widest information we could collect. We,
upon this, consulted the curative authorities, the
College of Physicians, and obtained from them the
sanction of medical treatment by opiate confection.

HOME TREATMENT OF THE PREMONITORY SYMPTOMS.

"With this we inaugurated a general system of
house-to-house visitation, to inquire as to each person in the family, whether he had experienced
any premonitory symptoms, or observed rice-water
evacuations, and if so, to give the medicines provided, and to accompany such exhibitions with instructions as to precautions in the regimen required
by a weakened stomach. There was at first great
difficulty in finding properly qualified house-to-house
visitors, and getting them into action. Then it was
that we had experience of the evils of the default of
the local administrative organisation, against which I
had from the first remonstrated, and which has yet

to be removed for the effectual reduction of the
ordinary epidemics—the evils, *e.g.*, of allowing the
public health service to be combined with private
medical practice. For at this time, when there was
the greatest pressure for the public service, there was
the conflict of the preponderant private interest, with
the greatest pressure upon the officer for his service
to his private patients. We got the local deficiencies
from this cause supplied as well as we could in the
time, though it was with great inconvenience and
often with loss. On the whole, the house-to-house
visitation and home treatment was eminently successful in meeting the extraordinary epidemic, and it
commends itself for adoption decidedly in dealing
with ordinary epidemics. By it, in this epidemic,
errors in regimen were most easily overcome. An
effect of the visitation reported as observable in
various districts, the causes of which passed without
examination, was to depress vitality, to make it as
if the people were made old and weakly by it, and
to make irregularities and all errors in diet, which
in ordinary times had been heretofore incurred with
impunity, at this time particularly injurious. It
appeared as if some of the common sources of water
supply had been injuriously affected by a passing
cause; so much did this appear to be the case in
some of the rural districts as to create a suspicion
in the minds of the people that their wells had been
poisoned.

ORDINARY COURSE OF THE ATTACK OF THE EPIDEMIC.

" The common course of the attack of the
epidemic on a place undefended by any organisation

was that it began with a large proportion of deaths to the attacks ; one half, even, fell ; then one out of three. As it spread widely the proportion of deaths diminished to one out of four, of five, and of six, and so it went on until the epidemic was exhausted. Its rise was represented by a curve, like a mountain ; the curve then gradually fell in number and in the proportion of attacks, until the epidemic disappeared. At the first onset of the epidemic, no treatment appeared to succeed ; as the epidemic spread, and the force of the attack weakened, and became utterly reduced, almost every sort of medical treatment appeared to succeed, or had the credit of succeeding. By the defensive course taken, of the reduction of the local aerial impurity by the cleansing of the places, the number of the attacks was reduced ; by the house-to-house visitation, and the dietetic and medical treatment, the proportions of the deaths to the attacks were immediately and decidedly reduced. So clearly was this the case, that if from the daily returns to one central office from any place it appeared that the proportion of deaths to the attacks was not reduced,—if the proportion of attacks still went on,—we were clearly of opinion that there must be some default, and that the house-to-house visitation must have been interrupted, or not carried out. In one large place the house-to-house visitation had been arranged and brought into operation, with the proper results. Suddenly the proportion of deaths to the attacks, and the attacks, rose again, on which it was evident to me, at the Central Board, that the house-to-house visitation was interrupted. One of our most efficient assistant commissioners was telegraphed for and sent to the spot, where it was found, as apprehended, that, from some dispute amongst the local authorities, the house-to-house visitation had been stopped. Matters were arranged, the practice was restored, and carried on properly, when the proportions of the attacks, and of the deaths to the attacks, were again reduced, until they entirely ceased.

GENERAL RESULTS OF THE COURSE OF DEALING WITH THE EPIDEMIC, BY ALTERING THE LOCAL CONDITIONS AND BY HOME TREATMENT.

" On a view of the results of this same great epidemic visitation of the cholera in continental countries, where it was met in the old way chiefly by reliance for defence on quarantines, and when it got in, on impromptu hospital accommodation, with general treatment necessarily chiefly in the collapsed stages ; and, on a comparison with the results of the treatment we adopted by the removal, as much as possible, of the predisposing local causes, and by cleansing the places, with a house-to-house visitation and home treatment in the earliest stages, in the place of a general hospital treatment—it was evident that we obtained a gain of full two-thirds by our defensive course. Comparing the rate of mortality with that which prevailed in Sweden, where the ordinary death-rate was then lower than in Great Britain, but where our precautions and the home treatment were not taken, it appeared that we might claim to have saved some fifty thousand lives. But Professor Zedkauer, consulting physician to the Emperor of Russia, supplies decisive testimony of demonstrative facts on this point in a letter written to the last Medical

Congress at Brussels. In that letter he says that
' to England is due the honour of having introduced
on a large scale measures (prophylactiques) against
the contagion of cholera.' He states that during the
cholera epidemics of 1830, 1848, and 1855, there were
not less than from 23,000 to 25,000 deaths, or from
47,000 to 50,000 attacked with cholera in St. Petersburg ; but that in 1866, when they became acquainted
with our practice in the house-to-house visitation and
followed it, out of 15,000 attacks they had only 3,000
deaths. On an independent examination of the work
for the attainment of the end described, I think it
would be evident that if there had been any other
than the ordinary distracted political attention prevailing at the Government ; had there been a Minister
of Health,—such as it is now agreed that a State
organisation requires, with a superior responsibility
and interest in observing the beneficial working of
the temporary administrative power confided to us—
if it had been duly observed how large an amount of
sickness and death was saved by the exercise of that
power during so short a time, it may be submitted
that there would have been an anxiety to make the
authority permanent, to strengthen it, by due public
acknowledgment of the service rendered, and to
extend it. But when the extraordinary epidemic
disappeared, the special organisation and the powers
of prevention were allowed to lapse.

INJURY TO THE PUBLIC BY THE CHANGE OF THE FIRST
SANITARY AUTHORITY.

" Some time after the First Board which had
achieved the results I have named was discontinued,

the visitation of cholera had ceased. The discontinuance of the board was received abroad as a shock and injustice, and was publicly expressed as such by the chief sanitary authority of France. The uninstructed, unaided, and lax local administration reappeared, and with it the causes of the foul air diseases, and also the ordinary epidemic diseases which now cost some hundred thousand of the preventible deaths throughout the kingdom. The visitation of the cholera in 1848-9, which the First General Board of Health dealt with, reappeared in 1854, and had to be dealt with by the department, under the presidency of a political chief. Most beneficial examples had been achieved by the almost entire clearance of the common lodging-houses from the ordinary epidemics, by the application of the principles developed by the First General Board under Lord Shaftesbury's Act, and by the model lodging-houses, house drainage, ventilation, and prevention of overcrowding, initiated by the Prince Consort. The death-rates of the class-occupants had by these means been reduced nearly one-half. But these examples cited in the general report, made for the new president by Dr. John Sutherland, our chief sanitary inspector, had yielded little imitation. It was found on renewed local examination by the officers of the board in the Metropolis, that the local conditions of filth, and of the ordinary epidemic diseases, had reappeared, together with those ordinary epidemics. I may mention, as respects London, that our board had elaborated a plan for placing the water supply of the Metropolis under unity of management on a public footing, such as we had effected in a number

of provincial towns, involving the adoption of the
constant supplies, and the abolition of stagnation
in cisterns which make good supplies bad and bad
supplies worse.

"In the report made by a new inspector, Dr.
Hassall, on the second reappearance of the Asiatic
cholera, he was struck with the continuance of those
evil conditions. He reported, 'I beg to express my
conviction that the water supply of the Metropolis
will never be in a satisfactory condition until the use
of cisterns is abandoned, and the constant method of
supply adopted.'

"But through the greater part of the Metropolis
this vicious system is continued up to this time
(1881), together with the waste of more than three-
fifths of the water pumped in, which waste s fouled
water, and saturates the excrement-sodden sites
with a quantity almost equal to a double rainfall,
the results of which are shown in the supersaturated
lower levels by double attacks of the ordinary
epidemics. This continuance of the old evils as
respects the water supply is accompanied by
augmented charges, sanctioned by Parliament, for
double and threefold separate works, belonging to the
separate trading companies, that would have been
unnecessary under the unity projected on a public
footing, which unity has since continued to be rein-
forced, as a necessity, by commission after commission. Plans had been got out, based on trial works,
and experiences obtained of buildings for carrying
out all the fouled water by self-cleansing house-
drains, and this would have been accomplished
—as was proved by experiences in block buildings, within the expenses incurred for amending

and maintaining the old drains of deposit—at about a third of the expense that must now be incurred by the individual householder who drains his house separately. For the reception of the fouled water tubular sewers were provided chiefly, which by their ordinary dry weather flow were proved to be self-cleansing and to need no flushing. For the lower districts a concentrated flow and a quick discharge by engine power from pumps was prepared. For the relief of the low-lying marsh districts, which are a great source of the fogs of the metropolis, a separate system was in preparation on the principle of the successful drainage of the fen districts of Lincolnshire.

" From the results of the rudimentary applications of the sanitary principles executed in some twenty towns,—as at Croydon,—where the whole of the fouled water is out of the houses and out of the town on the land in some two hours, there can be no doubt that all the matter of putrefaction which now remains in ill-drained houses and the sewers of deposit for months and years would have been removed from the Metropolis within half a day, with the result obtained in those several instances quoted, of a reduction of the general sickness and death-rate by at least one-third.

"But to effect this entire unity over the whole Metropolis it was essential for the combination to be effected by very special science. It would be too long, and beside the present purpose, to state how the sanitary authority which had prepared this was set aside by a surprise-vote against the Government, and by combined adverse interests at a morning sitting; or, how the succeeding political President of the Board

brought in a 'Bill' for the government of metropolitan works, by which all the requisite unity was
destroyed, with the entire omission of the essential
part of the system—the house drainage ; and how a
bill was passed to effect the disunity by placing the
trunk lines of the sewers under one authority and the
branch lines under thirty-six others, and those others,
of all authorities for dealing with a scientific work,
the vestries ! Under such rule the old conditions of
the ordinary epidemics are maintained. On a recent
examination of some mile of trunk sewer, which was
a foot deep with putrid deposit, a line giving off fever
into the public offices was discovered which, combined with bad house drainage and the foul sewage
of the rest of the district, recently occasioned the
loss of Dean Stanley.

"By the change brought about at the Central
Department, officers who had done the most meri-
torious preventive work, calling for acknowledgment,
were put under a cloud, as it were, as if they had
been doing something bad, only excusable by defaults
of their instructions. In the Metropolis the works
were given over chiefly to railway engineers, who had
nowhere done sanitary work or reduced a death-rate
by a percentage. The first objective point for sanitation was the attempt at purification of the river by
intercepting sewers, made great to receive, with the
sewage, extraordinary storm water. Those works are
great blunders, accumulating deposit, and acting as
extended cesspools, giving off noxious products of
decomposition. The expense of these trunk lines of
intercepting sewers would, it is now shown, have
sufficed for the re-drainage of every street, court, and
alley in the Metropolis, with self-cleansing sewers,

and would also have re-drained the worst of the ill-drained houses.

"The great lines of the ordinary epidemics have been left, and every measure which sanitary science had prepared will inevitably have to be restored, to bring up the Metropolis to the sanitary conditions of the places where proper measures have been properly applied. Our subject is then, how, there and elsewhere, to check the spread of the ordinary epidemics coming along those lines which complete sanitary measures will effectually close. I say effectually close, because I could adduce examples where former centres of epidemics have been effectually closed to them, and in which the children's epidemics are effectually banished."

CHAPTER XXVII.

" THE primary schools being common centres of children's epidemics, we framed in the First Board of Health, amongst the rules for the regulation of the duties of the local officers of health, as one of the duties, that the officer should regularly visit and inspect the children of the schools, and that when he detected premonitory symptoms in any child, he should separate it, and go with it to its home, and there give orders for its preventive treatment. The course in the home would be to separate the well from the ill; to give order that the child should be placed by itself in a room in a proper condition, and should have proper attendance and appliances, and that no one else should be admitted until after the disease had passed. It would follow that trained nurses should be appointed to visit the house, and see that the health officer's instructions are properly carried out. We had provided regulations of the duties of the officer of health, which included weekly visits and examinations of children, at the infant and the primary schools. In going over the school with him the schoolmistress would point out to the inspector,

or he would observe, the child with premonitory
symptoms to be looked to—the cold shivers, the pains
in the head—and would separate it from the rest, and
go home with it, examine the state of the habitation,
take order for the separation of the healthy children,
direct the sick ones to be kept alone, and give the
requisite directions for treatment. A trained nurse
would follow with more frequent visits to see that
the directions were complied with.

" The regulations provided for similar visits and
examinations of places of work ; the separation of the
workers, followed by visits to the habitation, and by
the removal, as far as possible, of the injurious conditions found there. Had these regulations which
we had prepared been duly carried out, they would
have carried prevention to a great proportion of the
excess of fifty thousand fatal cases in the school
stages, in addition to the adult stages of life, of the
classes the most scourged, and would have stopped
the wide spread of the ordinary epidemics.

Mode of Staying the Spread of an Ordinary Epidemic.

" Meanwhile, until justice is reclaimed for the
administrative service in behalf of the public, as
much as possible should be called for by appeal for
voluntary effort. Of what this may do in preventing
the spread of the ordinary foul air epidemics, I will
state the experience of a nurse of twenty years'
practice as a specialist in dealing with the most
infectious and dangerous of these contagious fevers.
Her chief practice was the common one in respect
to all cases of the varied epidemics—to isolate the

patient in a single room, the upper room if possible, and let no one else enter it; to so arrange as to keep the door and part of the window open in order to let a current of air pass through the room over the patient; to observe all the details of regulations as to the cleanliness of the patient and the articles of clothing and furniture, and the removal of excreta. As to her own personal protection, her practice was never to drink out of the same vessel that had been used by the patient, to wash from head to foot twice a day with tepid water, and to change her clothes each day. With these precautions, she had never had a single case of the spread of the disease to a member of the family or any one else during the twenty years; nor had she once contracted the disease herself!

"A collective example of the working of the principle provided for preventing the spread of epidemics is supplied by the Sanitary Aid Society, at Hastings, and at St. Leonard's-on-the-Sea, under the direction of a very able and energetic lady, Mrs. Johnston. At Hastings, on the early information of the occurrence of infectious disease, the health officer attends, and she follows and visits from time to time more than he can do, to see that the requirements as to the isolation and treatment of the patient are duly attended to by the mother or the female resident in the house, as it may be. The service is given which would have been rendered, under our regulations, by a trained nurse visiting the patients at their homes instead of at the ward of a hospital. I am assured that the arrangement has the full efficacy we anticipated from our rule. As one example, it is stated that since it has been at work not an instance has taken place there of the breaking up of schools from the outburst of an epidemic. On the nurse's practice of the protection of herself by head-to-foot washing, I may note that two medical officers who had been through the most dire epidemics in the East stated to the Academy of Medicine that they ascribed their immunity to their careful attending to that practice. Presuming that the advocates of what is called the germ theory of disease could sustain their case, it is still believed by many observers, that a predisposition or nidus in the affected person must exist before the exciting influence can take effect. At the International Medical Congress held in London, Virchow's observations were strongly in support of this modified acceptance of what is called the germ theory of disease.

Frequent Bodily Ablutions Protective Against Epidemics.

"If a great epidemic were to occur again, I would proclaim and enforce the active application of soap and water as a preventive. I have had frequent opportunities of observing this plan as a factor of sanitation. I may state that I have received accounts of it, showing its efficacy, such as this. In one orphan institution, where the death-rate was twelve in the thousand, the cleansing of the place, the removal of cesspits and foul drains before the cleansing, effected in the death-rate a reduction to eight in a thousand. Next, a cleansing of the person was effected by a constant ablution with tepid water, and then a reduction by another third, or to four in a thousand, was achieved. Other experiments tend to establish the value of personal cleanliness as a preventive factor at one-third.

EPIDEMICS EXCLUDED FROM INSTITUTIONS IN GOOD SANITARY CONDITIONS.

" It is to be borne in mind that our immediate object is the prevention of the spread of the foul-air-diseases occurring on the lines of the ordinary epidemics. Sanitary Science has now evidence of the primary prevention of their occurrence. In institutions, such as well-managed district schools on the half-time principle, where the children's diseases, as they are called, are, as of primary origin, banished, a case of typhus has not been seen for many years; and in well-administered prisons, the walls of which cannot shut out the epidemics of a climatorial character, whilst they are freed from other contagious epidemics, the surrounding populations are ravaged by them. In staying the spread of the ordinary epidemics by home treatment, or treatment in small refuges, we are saving the sufferers from the vastly increased dangers which statistics demonstrate to be occasioned by collections of sufferers in the best-appointed and the best-managed huge hospitals.

" It may be objected that the intrusion of house-to-house treatment will not be accorded; but as a matter of experience I can state that the house-to-house visitations, which we ordered under a penalty, during the visitation of the cholera, were everywhere well received, and that we did not hear of refusals, or of any case for the infliction of a penalty. All, however, depends upon the manner in which the law is executed, and on the securities taken for the proper qualifications of the officers of health for the performance of the duties set forth in the regulations.   The expense of the personal for the requisite improvement in local organisation may be objected to by those who have still to be informed of the wastefulness of ignorance and of unskilled service. The extension required would be the attribution of some three thousand local health officers, who would be under the control of the Local Government Board, forming part of the greater local administrative force, including that for the relief of destitution, with which the Board is now charged.

"Objections were made locally to the appointment of some seventeen thousand paid local officers, including medical officers, on the principles of administrative organization, set forth in my report of 1833, on the administration of relief to the destitute. But by that expenditure the administration was, with all shortcomings, vastly improved, and an economy effected of more than one-half over the unpaid services of the overseers and of the parish officers; such half amounting to upwards of four millions.   Since then, by error in superior administration, it has been sent back, and the economies of the local taxation have been reduced.   But here again I have the consolation of the vindication of principle by the recent reclamations of the representatives of the new local sanitary authorities (the Boards of Guardians), who have sent petitions to both Houses of Parliament, praying for a return to the more efficient administration of those same principles of 1833.

"By the last returns it appears that the death-rate in the Indian army, which was formerly 69 in a thousand, was during the last decade 20 per 1,000; and that during that decade there has been a saving of life of 28,000 men, and a saving of force from sickness of about the same number,—a total saving of nearly double the British army at Waterloo. But no account is taken of the saving in money. It is an under-estimate at £100 per man, which makes the money-saving during the decade £5,321,700 for that period, an economy which may be commended to the attention of the Chancellor of the Exchequer, and to the House of Parliament, with the assurance that, with a due attention to past sanitary service, and to the improvement of its organisation, and effective position for the future—a yet greater economy may be effected. In further assurance of this, we may recall the partial economies of sanitation—the economies first achieved, as I have recited, by our defences against the extraordinary epidemic with which we had to contend,—when the savings of the expenses of funerals from premature deaths throughout Great Britain must have been about as much as if the whole of the present population of the City of London, 50,000, were saved from being killed and interred separately. We may add to this the pecuniary economy of the saving of force by the saving of the health and lives of the second army in the Crimea, acknowledged to have been achieved mainly by the specialists trained under our Board. Altogether we may, I submit, claim credit for the collective economies of the past for the sake of the future—now especially—in claiming as a source of economy, if properly conducted, the relief of the population from the pecuniary burdens, direct and indirect, inflicted upon them by the continued retention of removable conditions of the ordinary as well as of the extraordinary epidemics.

General Conclusions for the Prevention of the Occurrence and Spread of Epidemics.

"I now beg to recapitulate the chief conclusions which the facts that have been before us in the preceding chapter appear to establish.

I.

"That cases of small pox, of typhus, and of others of the ordinary epidemics, occur in the greatest proportion, on common conditions of foul air from stagnant putrefaction, from bad house drainage, from sewers of deposit, from excrement-sodden sites, from filthy street surfaces, from impure water, and from overcrowding in private houses and in public institutions.

II.

"That the entire removal of such conditions by complete sanitation and by improved dwellings is the effectual preventive of diseases of those species, and of ordinary as well of extraordinary epidemic visitations.

III.

"That where such diseases continue to occur their spread is best prevented by the separation of the unaffected from the affected, by home treatment if possible; if not, by providing small temporary accommodation; in either case obviating the necessity of removing the sick to a distance, and the danger of aggregating epidemic cases in large hospitals—a proceeding liable to augment the death-rates during epidemics.

IV.

" That the skilful and complete works of sanitation and the removal of conditions of stagnancy and putrefactive decomposition are the most efficient means of reducing the expenses of excessive sickness and of death-rates."

CHAPTER XXVIII.

LONDON CENTRALISED FOR HEALTH AND ECONOMY.

"UNITY of government is as advantageous to a city as to a nation, and no better proof of the fact can be afforded than the experience of the evils arising from the want of unity in the Metropolis. It is hard to tell the price London pays for its disunity, which has retarded improvements, diminished efficiency, and increased cost in every branch of local service.

- "To begin with the sanitary administration. The sanitary requirements of an urban district are generally (a) arrangements for subsoil drainage to relieve the supersaturated sites of the suburban lands; (b) arrangements for the general drainage of the houses; and (c) special arrangements for separate sewerage. In the examinations instituted by the Metropolitan Sanitary Commission, of which I was a member, we found that cases of ague and fever always increased among the population with the prevalence of easterly winds blowing over the metropolis from the marshes of Kent and Essex, or of fogs aggravating the effect of the excessive smoke of the city. We found that fevers and diseases of the zymotic class were most frequent on the supersaturated sites of houses on the lower levels, and we found that these houses were generally ill-drained and the sewers, generally, sewers of deposit.

"The duty of providing and maintaining the primary works of sewerage for the whole of the Metropolis was then divided among eight independent commissions (*i.e.*, counting the extensive jurisdiction of the city corporation as equivalent to one), and the functions of these various commissions chiefly consisted in the repair of old sewers, the extension of new ones to new buildings, and the sanctioning of junctions of drains from houses, with whose internal formation, as a system, they had nothing to do. The commissioners were usually tradesmen, or other persons of the social rank to which vestrymen commonly belong. They were never men of any position or note in science themselves; and their chief officers were, with one exception, architects engaged in private practice, to which their public service was very subordinate in importance, and whose knowledge of hydraulics may be seen displayed in their examinations, or in their practice of draining houses by means of drains that were as capacious as factory chimneys, and might each serve for the requirements of several hundred houses.

"Under an administrative organisation of this sort, which distributed the public service among separate and independent commissions, it was utterly impossible for that service to be carried on according to any systematic plan, even if the commissions had been composed of the best materials and provided with a staff of officers of special scientific competency. The several commissions had each its own work to engross its attention, and besides, they could not separately do the general work required for the whole

Metropolis, even if they were so minded. On our recommendation, accordingly, the separate commissions were dissolved and replaced by a single commission for the entire field of service of the metropolis and suburbs. On that commission we obtained the services of Sir Henry de la Beche, the chief of the Ordnance Survey, and several other scientists of distinction. Lord Carlisle, who was at the time President of the General Board of Health and a member of the Cabinet, was our chairman, and bestowed earnest attention on the subject. We secured for our permanent staff of sanitary engineers the best specialists that were to be got, and required them to give their whole time to the work, and to be ready to act at any point where their service was needed. We made a considerable addition to the number of this staff of permanent officials, and in consequence of the unity of organisation that had been introduced, we were able to effect that important addition, not only without any increase of expense, but actually with a material reduction from the expense of the comparatively inferior service under the separate organisations.

"We directed our earliest attention to the attainment of an Ordnance survey of the whole of the Metropolis, on a scale that would enable the lines of drains laid down in future to be registered, so that they might be found when required. The area of the survey was to include also the suburban marsh lands of Kent and Essex, which for the protection of the metropolis needed to be subjected to systematic subsoil drainage. We reversed the common order of procedure with respect to surface drainage of towns; we made the houses the first object of amendment,

the street or the sewer the next, and then the main
trunk outfalls.   I had the first pipe-pot sewer made
that I know of in modern times, to ascertain the rate
at which water moved in a smooth channel, as compared with its rate in the rough brick channels of
which house-drains and sewers were in those days
formed.   We instituted trial works, under careful
supervision, to determine the size, forms, and inclina-
tions at which tubular drains could be made self-
cleansing.   In one of these experiments, in a street,
it was found that a five-inch pipe would force and
carry away the fouled water from 1,200 houses.   This
was apart from any rainfall, and yet the professors of
architecture had declared that a pipe of that size was
necessary to carry off the rainfall from a single house;
and engineers, in order to carry it off from such a
number of houses as we had to do with in that experiment, had provided a flat segmental sewer, three
feet wide, and with a sectional area of fifteen feet,
which accumulated deposit requiring to be cleansed
out by manual labour.   .

" Before applying the new system of self-cleansing
house-drains and self-cleansing sewers to the metropolis generally, we made some carefully-prepared and
carefully-observed trial applications of them to blocks
of houses.   One of these was for the purpose of trying
the plan of what is known as combined back drainage
—that is, the plan of carrying the drains along the
backs of houses, instead of through the houses into
the front streets ; and several of them were made on
houses of the lowest class, or what would be called
slums.   The draining and water-closeting of the
slums were successful in reducing the foul smells,
but the result would have been more satisfactory if

the water arrangements of the front pavement had, at the time, permitted cleansing in front of the houses with the hose and jet. The inmates declared themselves much satisfied with the mode of cleansing adopted, and the experiment was certainly most successful from an administrative point of view, because it showed that the force gained through unity could be directed, even upon the worst parts of the system, with a power and speed that would have been quite impracticable under disunity. It was in fact proved that with a trained staff the work could be done more economically in one-third of the time than any of the separate commissions could do it, if they had the authority. By means of other trial works which we instituted, we were able to establish the receptivity of the soil near the metropolis for the sewage, and thereby to promote utilisation for purposes of agricultural production.

" But important as all these trial works and their results were, when impartially considered—important for the advance of sanitary science generally as well as for the sanitary improvement of the Metropolis—they were regarded with much jealousy by the various vestry interests represented in the House of Commons, and this opposition was seconded in the House by certain civil engineers, chiefly railway engineers. Mr. Robert Stephenson, it must be said, was strongly prejudiced against pipe sewers, and fought vehemently for the continued use of ' man-sized sewers,' which accumulated stagnant deposit and required men to enter them for its removal by manual labour. He expressed his detestation of pipe sewers. I was greatly taken by surprise at this opposition from Mr. Stephenson, who had previously deferred to me by

withdrawing a plan of a hard-water supply which he
had proposed to the Health of Towns Commission,
in favour of the one I proposed,—a soft spring supply
from the Surrey tanks,—and had led me to believe in
his entire concurrence with me in sanitary principles.

" The system of sewerage which we adopted after
much examination, was what is called ' the separate
system,' and it is epitomised in the expression, ' the
rainfall to the river, and the sewage to the soil '
(land). On this system all the clear rainfall and all
the subsoil water from spaces uncovered by houses
was to be conveyed to the river ; whilst all the
fouled water from the houses was to be treated as
sewage. But this separate system was rejected for
the trunk line of sewers under the control of that
general representative body of the vestries, the Board
of Works, and another system was adopted, which
was known as ' the combined system,' because it
combined in the same sewer all the ordinary rainfall
and all the storm water, and threw both away altogether with the sewage into the river, or into the sea
when the sea could be reached.

" The combination of the rainfall with the sewage
proper requires the construction of large tunnel
sewers of sufficient capacity to receive the rain and
storm water. On ' dry days ' the flow is shallow,
and, being spread over wide bottoms, deposit is occasioned, and hence putrid decomposition, and the
necessity of periodical flushing operations by manual
labour to cleanse the sewers. One hundred and
twenty-five men were so employed, at a cost of £14,000
per annum, for work which I declare to be an ignorant and pernicious malfeasance. The cost of the
whole of the lines of outfall sewers completed by the

Board of Works has been five millions. Sir Robert Rawlinson, in a paper which he read at the meeting of the National Association for the Advancement of Social Science held at Liverpool, gives the following estimate of the expense of laying the whole Metropolis with self-cleansing sewers:—'Supposing,' says he, 'a sewer did not exist in the Metropolis; then, according to the cost of the public sewers in other places named in the table hereto appended, the money required to sewer the whole of the Metropolis, to include outlets, should not exceed £1,396,333 6s. 4d.; that is, for instance, 340,000 houses at £3 18s. 8d. each, that being the average of the nine towns named in the table.'

"Had our 'separate system' been adopted the sum of five millions, that has actually been expended in outfall sewers alone on the 'combined system,' would have sufficed for the construction of a complete system of self-cleansing sewers for every court, alley, and street in the metropolis, and for the redraining of all the ill-drained houses, more than two-thirds of which are stated to be still drained on the old system.

"The present system fails to purify the Thames from sewage, for constant complaints are made on the subject; it wastes the sewage itself by dilution, and adds enormously to the expense of its separation by precipitation. But under the separate system as applied to London, with its low levels north and south, the discharge of the sewers as well as of the rainfalls would have been converged, as is done in the flat fen districts of Lincolnshire, into separate 'sumps,' from whence it would have been lifted by steam power. The experiences of the fen system of working by conveyance into sumps warrant the conclusion, that from every part of even the remotest corners of the Metropolis, the sewage of the morning from its half-million of houses would have been on the land by about the middle of the day, not merely in mechanical suspension, but, as at Croydon, in chemical combination.   Fresh sewage is more fertilising by a third than putrid sewage, and a verification would thus have been presented on a grand scale of the maxim of De Candolle, the greatest vegetable physiologist of the last century, that the future of agriculture will be found in giving food and water at the same time.

"An idea prevails that a share in the recent reduction of the death-rate of the Metropolis must be credited to the Board of Works, but the idea is wholly unfounded; for large tunnel sewers, like those of Westminster, which give off emanations from stagnant and putrid deposit, lead to augmentations of the death-rate, and not to its reduction.   The reduction which has actually taken place has been the result of the extensive suppression of nuisances which has been effected in the same period, and which may be found described in the reports of the newly-appointed officers of health and their surveyors and sanitary inspectors.

" To cover all defaults in sanitation in the metropolis, it is put forth that London is the healthiest metropolis in the world.   As compared with those capitals and cities where, in mediæval periods, when sanitary science did not exist, where the pressure of war was felt, and where threefold populations were heaped in what I have often called perpendicular streets, modern London may be justly called the *least* unhealthy.   But, as compared with our own provincial cities, where the death-rate was at one time higher than that of London, and where, even by rudimentary sanitary measures, we were enabled to apply to some extent the principles of sanitary science, London is one of the most unhealthy, by at least one-third.   The excess of deaths in London above those, as yet, in important respects incomplete standards must be, at the least, I estimate, six in a thousand, an annual excess of full twenty-five thousand per annum, chiefly from diseases of the zymotic class ; and, involving an excess in the expenses of funerals and of sickness alone of at least three-quarters of a million of money.

"A strong battle is now being fought for the continuance of detrimental disunity of action ; for the separate administration of a drainage area of one square mile out of one hundred and twenty-five ; for the sanitation of from nine to ten thousand houses out of half a million ; and for a population of less than 51,000 out of nearly five millions, all so heavily death-rated in comparison with the great majority, that no mayors or aldermen, I believe, now venture to reside amongst them as of old, but after visiting the office in the city for a few hours a day, seek refuge with their families in some district with a lower death-rate.   Indeed it appears from an estimate, that by spending a ninth of their time daily going to and from their places of business, they gain a fourth more of life.   In some well-drained suburban districts the death-rate of children is about one-half what it is in the bounds of the Corporation.   Health officers and surgeons are aware that if a serious operation is to be performed, it will be performed at some third more risk in the air of the Corporation's jurisdiction, than if it were performed in the purer air of a good suburban quarter.

"The Corporation has claimed as its subjects all who come into the City from the suburbs to do business at their offices for the smaller part of the day, although they and their families, for the sake of pure air, live and sleep out of the city in quarters where the Corporation cannot and does not render them any service. In the same way Westminster, which has more inhabitants than the City, might claim as its population all who are daily brought in from Brighton and other places where they live with their families. Even by this method of calculation the population under the jurisdiction of the Corporation is only brought up to a sixth part of the whole population of the Metropolis. A late Lord Mayor sought my counsel on a sanitary question of water supply, in which he was interested, but could see no possibility of aid in the sanitary force furnished by disunited administration. The radical change lately proposed will be a change from the piecemeal administration of a third-rate metropolitan parish—a mere sham—to the reality of a united organisation for a population as large as that of the whole of England in the time of Queen Elizabeth and approaching that of Belgium at the present day.

"To return to the work of the first General Board of Health. After consolidating the eight separate Sewers Commissions, our attention was next directed to an examination of the water supplies. It was found that these supplies were in the hands of eight separate companies, who, under the authority of as many separate Acts, had invited shareholders to

advance their money for the introduction of water
into separate districts. The supply generally came
from river sources, at best from the surface washings
of land usually under cultivation, but for the most
part from rivers notoriously polluted with sewage;
although with proper search pure spring supplies
were undoubtedly obtainable in adequate quantities.
We found that extensions from these corrupt sources
had been sanctioned by Parliamentary Committees
after it was proved that at least three-fifths of the
existing supplies were injurious; and we found besides
that the pollution of the sources was not the worst of
the evil, for the house distribution itself was made
by means of butts and cisterns, and such other
methods as produced stagnation, and made good
supplies bad, and bad worse and dangerous to drink.
In our report we prepared a measure for the introduction of unity into our water supply system,
including the payment of compensation to the shareholders of the existing companies, which could then
have been accomplished at less than one-third of
the cost that must admittedly be incurred now for
retrieving the ignorant and mischievous work done
under disunited administration and sanctioned by
successive Parliamentary Private Bill Committees.

"At the Consolidated Commission of Sewers I got
trial works made for ascertaining the quantities of
water that would be required for the regular cleansing
of the streets by water and by the jet. It was proved
that the work could be done by that method, as it
is now done in clean-streeted Paris, in Vienna, and
Madrid, much cheaper than it can be done by the
scavenger's broom, which indeed at best daubs the
surface and leaves much putrescible matter there and

between the interstices of the carriage pavement. By the measures proposed every court, alley, and street would have been made as clean as a courtyard, and the population of the Metropolis would have been relieved from their grievance of seas of mud in winter and clouds of dust in summer; from a great source of aggravation of diseases of the respiratory organs; and, from much injury and loss on clothes and on furniture."

CHAPTER XXIX.

HEALTH VERSUS WAR. A PLEA FOR THE ECONOMY OF PEACE.

ONE of the choicest arguments used by Mr. Chadwick in favour of sanitation is the economy of life-saving methods, compared with those which are devoted to the art of destroying life in bad and useless wars. The essay of most note bearing on this important subject was read before the Association of Public Sanitary Inspectors, as a presidential paper, on Saturday, June 5th, of the year 1886.

In the opening part of this essay the author dwelt on the evils arising from delays in sound sanitary legislation. Then he put in, by way of contrast, the facts which have already appeared in these pages, on the results of good health in schools and prisons. Thence he passed to indicate the saving accomplished by good drainage on the separate system. Finally, he contrasted sanitation with militarianism as follows :—

INFLUENCE OF INTERNATIONAL MORALE.

" Great Britain, in regard to the extent of its population, has the smallest army of any of the Great Powers, and for the demands of that population is the least to be found fault with on the score of militarianism. Let us by contrast look abroad at the working of some bad economical conditions which reduce health and life and strength. Let us look at Italy. Two millions of money were voted for the relief of Naples, by sanitation, from the late visitation of the cholera. But there was a deficit in the treasury, and the Government had not the money to give. The deficit was due to the enormous expenses of *militarianism*—to bloated armaments, and to a fleet of big war ships, some of which ships must have cost, as ours have done, a million of money each. This expenditure was money thrown away, because there is at this time an international *morale* that would prevent the employment of it. If France, with its million of force, were to threaten little Belgium or Holland, it would be met by this *morale*, which *morale* will now be aided by the new guns of precision, that will give one to offence and more than three to defence, and will add to the moral security of the smaller States as well as to the greater States occupied on the work of sanitation.

"A French military writer showed some time ago, in the *Journal des Economistes*, that with the new arms of precision an army of a hundred thousand men, trained to their use, might defend France effectually against invasion, and it may be confidently declared that if at this time Italy had not a regiment of soldiers beyond its requisite police force, or the smallest naval police, that same international *morale* would prevent any one of the great war States from assailing her, or from preventing the peaceful application of her revenue to the works required for the relief of the distressed population, or from lessening her

purchasing power of her best allies. As an example
of the aggression of militarianism to the depression
of the life and strength of civil populations in peace,
I have seen exhortations to the Government of the
United States that they ought to have a fleet of big
war ships corresponding to our big war ships, and
costing a million of money each. The biggest naval
Power to attack her with such big ships would be
our own. But imagine our Queen permitting a shot
from one of them being thrown upon our American
brethren !

A WARSHIP'S WORTH OF SANITATION.

"It may be of use to give an estimate of the
civil life and force that may be gained to sanitation
by the application of a million of money—the cost
of one big ship—if the sum were spent on sanitation. In the towns where water-works were properly
carried out on the separate system by contracts under
the Public Health Act, the cost was a penny a
week for bringing a constant supply of water to the
door, a penny halfpenny per week for the internal
distributory apparatus, including the water-closet
and the kitchen sink and the self-cleansing house
drains, and a penny a week for self-cleansing sewers,
or 15s. per annum. Since the time of our works
on the separate system, the price of labour in
England has been raised by a third. But the
cost of the chief materials has been reduced by
about one-half, so that the estimates I have cited
would stand for England very much as they were.
The expenditure of a million at 5 per cent., the cost
of the big ship, would at this rate be equal to the

sanitation of 66,666 houses, or, at five inhabitants per house (the suburban average with us), it would serve for 333,333 inhabitants. Suppose the expenditure effected a reduction of the death rate by only five per 1,000 (and on the average of the towns under the separate system it is nine per 1,000), the saving of life would be 1,667 per annum.

" To each case of death there are at the least twenty cases of bed-lying sickness of adults, so that there would be a total annual saving of at least 33,330 cases of sickness for the value of each big ship. For one decade the saving would be 16,667 lives, and 333,333 cases of sickness. And be it noted that this accumulation of civil life and force and economy goes on during all the long intervals of peace, whilst in militarianism waste goes on from the deterioration of the appliances of war and the progress of inventions.

MILITARIANISM VERSUS SANITATION.

" The money wasted by the Italian Government on two big war ships would, I estimate, have sufficed to advance the health of the population of Naples in its grand and superior climate up to the normal. The sanitation of Paris is now delayed by the deficit in the municipal funds, and the general Budget of the Republic, and that delay is due to the wasteful expenses of its big and, for defensive purposes, wasteful, armaments. I have had means of estimating the losses of France by militarianism in Algeria, where the needless fortifications of internal towns would have sufficed to put each town in good sanitary condition, to have fitted them as seats of emigrants, and to have given strength as well as revenue. The evident waste by militarianism in Algeria since its occupation by France would have sufficed to have put all the cities and towns of France in a position that in seven years would replace with a stronger and better population, all that France has lost by the cession of Alsace and Lorraine, while it would also, by the extensive preservation of infant life, check the relative depression of the progress of the population of France.

" Let me extend the illustration. I would submit to the examination of my *confrères* of the Institute to consider that we hold all India with a force of some seventy thousand men, and about two hundred thousand of native force, or little more than is employed by the French to hold Algeria, on the pretext of its use as a school of military exercise, in which it has proved to be an egregious failure. In 1865, I obtained permission of Lord Ripon, then Minister of War, to have an examination made of what appeared to me to be an important sanitary norma for application to India which the specialists from India who inquired declared it to be. One of the most eminent of the Indian administrators (the late Mr. Robert Ellis, afterwards member of the Indian Council) stated to me, upon his observation there, that we should certainly hold Algeria effectively with a third of the force used there for France.

" Full two-thirds of the force in Algeria is a dire waste by militarianism at the expense of the most poor and depressed population of France. In some conversation which I had with the late Emperor, I learned that when he visited Algeria he had never heard of the existence of the sanitary norma, which

appeared to be so important, and which showed a
reduced death-rate of the army from eighty to twelve
in a thousand, with a corresponding reduction of the
death-rate of the civil population. It had been
evidently kept out of sight, as leading to the extended application of resources to a new and special
service.

"A year's cost of keeping each soldier unpro-
ductively in camp or cantonment would serve to
drain one hectare or two acres of the marshy or
waterlogged land, so extensive in France. M.
Maurice Block, of the Institut, reckoned the loss of
productive labour occasioned there by the conscrip-
tion at one hundred and thirty-two millions of days,
annually estimated at two francs a day.

"Let me give another example of the wastefulness
of militarism in the State with a large deficit,
occasioned by militarism, and with the most
heavily death-rated population of all Europe. We
English hold all Bengal, which has a population of
upwards of sixty-five millions (the equivalent of all
the old Russia), with about ten thousand of British
force and some twenty thousand of native force.
For holding an equivalent population Russia has a
million of military force. One of the most able
sanitary engineers of our service, in the army sanitary commission of the Crimea, declared to me, as
he was well competent to do, that if the money spent
by Russian militarism in the fortification of
Sebastopol had been applied in opening up the fine
territory thereabouts with roads and such sanitary
works as would fit it for settlement, an amount of
civil population and of force would have been raised
there, that would have withstood the combined

armies of France and England which the fortifications failed to do. Russia, judged by its army (where the death-rate and the loss of force is three times greater and heavier than the death-rate of the German army), appears to be the heaviest death-rated State of all Europe. Towns and villages are destitute of any sanitary provision whatsoever, and are immense cess-pits of putridity, with waste of the manure; while in their wretched fields, according to Lady Verney, the produce is only from two and a half to four and a half of the seed sown, instead of fifteen to twenty, as in England.

"Yet Russia had one sanitary norma from our first Board of Health. At each visitation of Asiatic cholera, St. Petersburg was ravaged with a loss of twenty thousand people killed, until, as a physician of the Czar informed the Sanitary Congress in Holland, they heard of the preventive course taken by our first general Board of Health, and adopted the same, with the result of decreasing the death-rate to one-fourth of what it had previously been. But there has been no recognition or extension of this example. The application of English capital was invited for improvements of the Russian cities; and one of the first waterworks and of sanitary works in Europe was provided by an English company, completed by my son, but the promised payment has not been forthcoming, and English capitalists are warned against further schemes.

" Wheresoever we see a heavily death-rated State we see a State where the sanitary condition of the population is neglected, and we see a troubled and insecure State, and that is the condition of Russia beyond any other State in Europe; where occupation is provided for its excessive army by continued threatened troubles; and where repression by the excessive military force generates and maintains expense.

"Look, again, at the defenceless condition, from want of sanitary knowledge, of the poor people of Spain as shown in the last attack of cholera, when more human beings fell than in the great Peninsular War. Yet, untaught by that terrible experience, I read only this week of a Spanish admiral proposing an expenditure of eleven millions of money on new war ships; which, on our reckoning, would save for a decade 183,335 lives and 3,666,667 cases of sickness. The proposed cost of this fleet expended in sanitation would save in one decade more than a thousand lives, and forty thousand cases of sickness of adult labourers, and more than half the ordinary insurance charges against excessive sickness and mortality.

MILITARY GAINS FROM SANITARY SCIENCE.

"Germany, it is reported, has by the application of sanitary science reduced the army death-rate to five per one thousand annually; that is to say, to less than one-half of the death-rate prevalent amongst the civil population of the same ages. By this reduction, and by physical training, during a short service, it augments the aptitude and productive power of the men for civil service. It is considered that such economy might be effected without so much long barrack detention. Indeed, we have shown that the largest proportion of military exercises may be beneficially transferred from the productive adult stages to the less productive juvenile stages and almost to the infantile stages of life. However, by the application of sanitary science, Germany has gained during little more than ten years as much life and force as was lost during the Franco-German war.

"Professor Sormani, of Pavia, has shown us by an analysis of the death-rates of the armies of Europe the progress of our science. With us it is, of the home army, eight in a thousand (it was once seventeen). In France it is ten in a thousand; in Austria and Italy it is as much as eleven and a half, but in Russia it is more than sixteen in a thousand.

"For ourselves, sanitation has gained for the Indian, as well as the home army, a great extent of the relief we proposed for it. In the Indian army we have obtained a reduction from the old death-rate of sixty-nine to less than twelve in a thousand. During the last decade, when the reduction had been got down to twenty in a thousand, a gain of forty thousand of force, first to last, had been achieved, and a further gain of six millions of money. Our Royal Navy has made advances in sanitation more than double that of the mercantile marine, but it is yet, with a selected class of superior subjects, far behind the sanitation of the prisons, with their lowest class of population in regard to physical condition.

"A sanitary official tells me that he was once sitting with a principal medical officer looking at some artillery practice at sea, when the officer exclaimed, 'There they go! If I could only get the money they waste for a few days I should be able to place my hospital in the best sanitary condition.' We have yet to advance in India and to hold more firmly our dominion by the sanitary improvement of the civil population. In our colonies, where, in the ignorance of sanitation, settlements have been made on undrained and malarious sites, with undrained houses and towns, there has been a great excess of preventable disease. Sanitary defences against these enemies in our colonies are, it may be shown, of primary importance. They will give more strength of life and force than those military defences, so very gratuitously, as I conceive, imagined to be immediately necessary. Mr. Sala, the well-known writer, would, I expect, confirm this view.

" In conclusion, I would say, despite neglects, let us keep our attention on our established sanitary normas and on extending those normas, with confidence that our work will give us a greater future than the world has ever imagined, much less seen. Towards this great future your labours, modest as they are, will contribute their certain and useful quota, if you go on and on, trusting ever in industry, truth, and increasing knowledge."

CHAPTER XXX.

ADMINISTRATIVE UNITY IN SANITATION.

FROM the beginning to the end of his labours Mr. Chadwick has insisted on the importance in sanitation of complete unity of action, so as to do the best thing in the best way, and always in the same manner. In the present chapter—at the risk of a little repetition—I have selected a few passages from his works illustrative of this argument.

RECREATION GROUNDS.

"One of the highest services a local board can render is the provision of means of recreation, such as attractive and well-arranged exercise grounds, for sedentary adults as well as for children. Except in the greater parks, the provision of such playgrounds in the metropolis is the most wretched possible. When I was attending as a juror at the Sanitary Section of the International Exhibition at Paris in 1867, I was requested by the Society of Arts to observe and report upon anything that might be suggested for adoption in the British Metropolis. Two things that struck me particularly were the high and brilliant state of horticulture displayed not only in the public thoroughfares from one end of Paris to

the other, but in the gardens and open spaces in
the most obscure quarters, and the liberal supply
of seats and playgrounds for infants, children, and
adults. But all this would be quite impracticable in
London under its disunited vestral authorities, for it
is only under unity that the highest horticultural and
decorative science would be employed to put its
principles into practice everywhere. It would be a
great advantage of unity that it would secure attention to this subject.

Efficient Lighting.

"On the question of efficient lighting, I have
shown in my sanitary report, from the example of
Manchester, the advantages that would accrue from
placing lighting on a public footing. In the Metropolitan Sanitary Commission we had begun to enter
upon this subject, with much promise of sanitary
advantages, but further progress was prevented by
the obstructive opposition that was raised and by
preoccupation with other topics. In various towns
the example of Manchester has been followed, with
gain to the population, but not so much gain either
in money or sanitation as might have been obtained,
if superior scientific aid and supervision had at the
same time been engaged. Taking, however, the
standards of supplies by a public body; the cost of
gas under unity, in the metropolis, might be, and
would have been, reduced from 3s. to 2s. 4d. per 1,000
cubic feet, with a clear profit of £500,000 per annum
for carrying on improvement works, as has been done
at Manchester. Or the price might be reduced below
2s. per 1,000 cubic feet, leaving a gain of £250,000

per annum in aid of district rates.   Such a reduction
would very largely turn the scale of economy in
favour of gas for cooking and heating as against coal,
and aid the diminution of the great smoke nuisance.
To this must be added, the production of a cheap,
smokeless coke for open fires, and for manufacturers,
and the extended use of gas instead of steam for
power.   In Paris, by bringing eight separate companies under unity, the cost of private lighting
was reduced 30 per cent., and of public lighting
40 per cent., with improved receipts to the shareholders.   But the general supply was left in their
hands as contractors, and the public did not derive
the further advantage obtainable by a responsible
scientific administration.   A recent voluntary amalgamation of the companies in London has been
accomplished by themselves, but I cannot judge how
far their position as respects the public may be
affected by it.

Unity in Road Administration.

" On the subject of road administration, we entered
in 1842 into investigations, which, except as to the
drainage of rural roads as a means of facilitating land
drainage, we were prevented from completing.   I
subsequently continued them, chiefly in relation to
the metropolitan roads, in my position as chairman
of a committee of the Society of Arts, with the aid
of Captain Douglas Galton and other scientists.
The results, may be presented as an example of
waste and injury inflicted by disunity; parts of
a mile of a main line of street were under three
different parochial administrations, and half of one

line of street was divided longitudinally, one half
being paved by one parish in one way, and cleaned
at one time, and the other part paved by another
parish in another way, and scavenged at another
time.

"The modes of cleansing frequently made the
surface 'greasy' and slippery and dangerous to cross,
and the consequence was an increase of street accidents by which between two and three hundred
people are killed every year, and upwards of three
thousand so seriously injured as to be taken charge
of by the police.   In the north-western suburban
district there was an example of a road district
administered under unity by a scientist, Mr. Macadam.
The condition of the roads under unity of administration was said to be so much better than the condition
of those under disunity that you could tell at night
when you got on the parish roads by the lesser
amount of jolting you received.

"The administration of the roads under unity was
formerly supported by turnpike tolls.   Then there
arose a movement against turnpikes, and they were
abolished, but along with them was also abolished
the unity of administration, and the roads formerly
under the united trust were restored to the separate
charge of some twenty parishes and their parish
surveyors, with the result of increased cost to the
ratepayers and general detriment to the traffic from
inferior service.   After trials with the dynamometer
at the Society of Arts the general conclusion arrived
at was that by unity of administration in a road-trust
a saving might be effected of one horse out of three,
besides a reduction of the sanitary evils of bad clean-
ing and foul surfaces, which are so much complained

of for making seas of mud in winter and clouds of
dust in summer.

"The final conclusions at which we have at this
point arrived may be summarised as follows:—

" (a) That the common methods of forming, paving,
maintaining, and cleansing the surfaces of streets
and roads in the metropolis, in respect to the
science and art conclusions, powerfully affect the
health of the population to an extent heretofore
unknown and disregarded, and ought to be brought
within the cognisance of sanitary officers. (b) That
the street and road formation might be so far improved
on a long-tried principle as to reduce the tractive force
needed for traffic by more than one-half, and that a
threefold amount of street cleanliness is obtainable
by improved machinery, without any augmentation
of the usual rate of expense for hand-cleansing.
(c) That the general condition of the streets, filth,
and noise, and disorder, are the reflex of the general
condition of an expensive local administration.
(d) That the common defective conditions of the
greater proportions of the surface, formation, paving,
and cleansing of the streets, with the increasing
traffic of the increasing population of the metropolis,
occasions much filth, consisting chiefly of pulverised
horse-dung and granite dust, to be deposited on the
person, clothes, furniture, and houses of the population.
(e) That the filth so deposited is highly injurious to the
health, to an extent hitherto unregarded, of the children, especially of the wage classes of the population,
as well as the adults of those classes, who have little
means of frequently washing themselves to remove
it. (f) That such aggravations of the conditions of
personal filth and squalor, besides being detrimental

to health, have a pernicious effect in lowering the
self-respect and the moral status of the wage classes
of the population. (g) That the excessive noise
occasioned by vehicular traffic over the common pavements is a cause of suffering to invalids, occasions
doors and windows to be shut to keep it out, and
ventilation to be obstructed. (h) That on an average
upwards of two hundred persons are annually killed,
and upwards of ten times that number maimed or
injured, in the streets of the metropolis, the greatest
proportion of which injuries occurs on what are called
"greasy days," or days of excessive slipperiness,
occasioned by defective cleansing. (i) That such
conditions of bad cleansing and defective methods
and bad paving are the occasion of excessive cruelty,
accidents, and injuries to horses, and fractures to
vehicles. (j) That the best means of preventing such
accidents, by better applications of supplies of water
for cleansing the streets, are the same that are
needed for the better protection of life and property
from fire in houses. (k) That the economical and
efficient application of art and scientific means of
relief is frustrated by the conditions of the fragmentary areas of independent, obscure, and virtually
irresponsible local administrations, under which the
metropolis is placed, which give, for example, one
main thoroughfare from east to west to fourteen
vestries or independent authorities, of which the
Corporation is only one, and another line from north
to south to thirteen parishes, each being charged
with only one mile of the line which divides some
streets longitudinally between different parishes, one
cleansing or paving the street at one time, and one at
another, in a manner detrimental to both. (l) That

the first and essential step to any effective and
economical improvement is to get rid of these disorderly and discreditable administrative conditions—
which exist at the expense of life and limb, and health,
and comfort of the population, and the freedom of
traffic of the Metropolis—and to place the whole
area under unity of administration by a specially
competent and responsible authority. (*m*) Finally,
that unity of administration is the declared object of
the agitation for a metropolitan municipality, which
it may be assumed would include the administration of the roads; that several years, four at the
least, must elapse before that object could be
obtained, and so large a body be got into working
order; but that such delay would be unnecessary
and injurious, under a special provincial commission, or general metropolitan road trust, properly
constituted, and giving its individual attention to
the service, so as to get the streets in good condition
without sacrifice of health, waste of life and property,
perpetual fatigue and annoyance.''

REMOVAL OF DEPOSITS.

Dealing with the deposits from horses and stables,
which are present in the streets of large cities in the
morning, and of the uncleanliness produced by such
deposits, our author estimated that six millions a
year might be saved for London in laundry work,
and similar kind of cleansing, if the streets were
daily kept free of the impurities described. For this
purpose the broom, he considered, was insufficient;
and that nothing effective would be done until
cleansing by water jet was so effectively carried out
that every portion of refuse found in the morning on

the streets was washed into the sewers, and carried
immediately away. The streets might then be like
the cleansed floors of houses, and with uniform
paving would be uniformly wholesome.

UNITY IN POOR-LAW ADMINISTRATION.

"In poor-law administration, the gain from unity
would be very large, and unity was, I know, originally
intended by the reformers of the poor law, but it was
frustrated by metropolitan members in the interests
of the vestries of the districts they represented. I
cannot specify all the improvements in the relief of
suffering which may be effected in the metropolis by
unity under the guidance of science; and I will only
advert to some points of detail to show the disadvantages of disunity under the vestral administration.
In the supply of provisions, for example, there would,
under unity, be great gain in quality as well as in
price through superior responsible superintendence.
The cost of maintenance under the several vestries
has been examined, and it displays wide variations.
Bread is in one place 9s. 4d., in another 16s. 4d., per
cwt.; beef in one place 6s. 5d. per stone, in another
10s. 2½d.; leg of beef in one place 2s. 11d. per stone
of 14 lbs., in another as high as 8s. 2d.; bacon in one
place 56s. 3d. per cwt., in another as much as 102s. 8d.;
butter in one place 72s. per cwt., in another 172s. 8d.;
tea in one place 1s. 2½d. per lb., in another 2s. 4d.;
coffee in one place 105s. per cwt., in another 168s.
In the mind of the examiners these variations denoted
variations in jobbery. By unity a saving of the retail
charges would be effected, and the supplies brought
up to the conditions as to quality as well as economy,

to which those of the army and navy are stated to have been brought through due superintendence. As regards the administration of relief, while in several of the East-end unions creditable progress has been made in the adoption of correct principles and practices, there have been in others relapses to grants in aid of wages and outdoor relief in money, which, it was well known, would have to be spent in payment of the rents of bad tenements owned by many of the guardians, and in expenditure at their shops. Under unity abuses of that kind would be difficult to practise, and the whole system of relief would be improved, especially the relief of the sick; the operation of corrupt influences in large expenditures would be reduced, and the general cost would be brought down to the level of that of the best administered unions, with the effect of reducing the burdens of the rate-payers by one-third, and greatly improving the health of the people.

Schools.

"Schools are the centres of the children's epidemics. We proposed in 1842 that they should be regularly visited and examined by a health officer, charged with the duty of removing any child on whom he detected premonitory symptoms of infectious disease, of going with it to its home, of providing for its treatment there, and, when he found the conditions of the place such as to produce the disease, of taking steps for having it treated elsewhere. This would often have led to the condemnation of places as unfit for habitation, and it must have carried relief far and wide. In Brussels preventive action against disease arising in schools is carried out with encouraging success.

SLAUGHTER HOUSES.

"Under the Metropolitan Sanitary Commission the subject of private or intramural slaughter houses was examined, and their nuisances, their cruelties, the evils of cattle being driven through the streets, the fact that about one-third of every carcase had to be carried from the place of slaughter, mostly in the slums, out of the metropolis, the butcher's two-thirds being all that was usable as food—all these things testified to the superiority of extramural abattoirs, as at Paris. But though the whole question, together with that of the distribution of diseased meat, was partly gone into, under the special lead of our colleague, Professor (now Sir Richard) Owen, no result followed except the removal of Smithfield Market, the conclusion in favour of the manifestly and directly beneficial abattoir system being overruled in the interests of Newgate Market. This left a conviction that any prospect of efficient relief was obtainable only under writs of authorities guided by science.

DRAINAGE UNDER UNITY.

"A late Lord Mayor is reported to have asked, in relation to the proposed measure for the unity of the Metropolis, 'What could a man living at Hampstead know about the drainage of Greenwich?' This he appeared to think was decisive against unity, as if it must be a 'unity of ignorance;' and so it

might be if the man in question were supposed to be,
as the Lord Mayor evidently supposed him to be, a
layman acting under the confused impressions prevalent under disunity at Hampstead.   Such a man
would usually know as little about the drainage of
his own house as he would know about that of a
house at Greenwich.   But under systematised unity
both houses would be examined and tested by an
expert, who would detect the dangers to which they
are exposed from within as well as those from without, arising from the malaria brought by easterly
winds from over the Plumstead or the Essex marshes,
influences from which they would be relieved by the
superior drainage works that would be possible and
certain under administrative unity.   When it is proposed to extend to the wage classes the benefits now
derived from occasional indoor examination by a
sanitary inspector, the landlords of inferior tenements
may be expected to raise against such indoor inspection the cry that 'every Englishman's house is his
castle.'   It may be so, but it is a castle without
defences against raids and slaughter, greater than
those of any wars, by invisible enemies, the foul air
diseases, against which the palace, in spite of all its
safeguards, is no better protected than the cottages,
where from twenty to thirty thousand are now annually slain in the Metropolis.   The effective defence
of 'the castle' must now be conducted by sanitation,
mainly from within, by qualified sanitary inspection,
which the well-to-do may provide for themselves, but
which the poor must have provided for them by a
united local administration.   So far from repelling
this inspection, the poor have been proved to wel-
come it when they get it, and to complain when they

do not. It is fair to mention that the health officers of the Corporation have been enabled to contribute to these defence s by continuing the practice, which we introduced at the cholera period, of washing with hose and jet the pavements and walls of a number of the courts and alleys.

"All the principles of administration I have here laid down for the improvement of the metropolis have been based on varied and carefully examined experience, and have been expounded in reports presented to Parliament. They will all, it may be confidently affirmed, have to be adopted in principle, with, I hope, improvements in detail, for the removal of the vast evils and waste that have been caused by disunity. But they have failed to gain attention. By the vote obtained under the combination of interests I have elsewhere described, the first General Board of Health was dissolved. Instead of rallying against that surprise vote, as might probably have been successfully done; instead of a challenge being given for a statement of the grounds of the vote, and a hearing being claimed for the Board in answer to the allegations made against it, the preparation of a new measure for the local administration of the metropolis was left to the metropolitan member who had led the opposition on behalf of his vestry. By his bill, which was passed, the previous disunity, which had been arrested, so far as drainage was concerned, by the consolidation of the eight separate commissions into one, was aggravated by the distribution of the superintendence of the branch drainage among thirty-five vestries, and by the entrusting of the work of main drainage to a body of representatives from such vestries.

NONFEASANCE, MISFEASANCE, AND MALFEASANCE.

" The faults of the metropolitan local administration may be conveniently grouped under the three old legal categories iuto which transgressions of official responsibility were divided—nonfeasance, misfeasance, and malfeasance.

" The loss from misfeasance in the expenditure on outfall sewers alone, in consequence of adopting an erroneous system of combined works which generates foul gases, and which will have to be replaced by other works on a more correct method, amounts to five millions sterling—a sum that would have sufficed to redrain the whole of the Metropolis with self-cleansing sewers, and to relieve besides most, if not the whole, of the ill-drained houses occupied by the poorest part of the population, houses which there is an imperative necessity for redraining now, and putting into the improved condition of the common lodging-houses.

" A loss from nonfeasance arises from neglecting to repair the evils of disunited organisation by placing the eight separate water companies under a single system and on a public footing, as was recommended by one commission after another. The money loss from this neglect is estimated by Mr. Quick, jun., C.E., at £372,596 per annum. This is exclusive of the assignable loss accruing in the adoption of a system of delivering water to houses by means of butts and cisterns that induce stagnation, make good water bad, and bad worse, and provoke to habitual intemperance in spirituous liquors.

" There is another loss from nonfeasance in not putting the gas supply under a public trust for the whole Metropolis, as has been done in provincial cities. This would have reduced the price of gas below 2*s.* per 1,000 cubic feet, and at the same time produced a profit of £200,000 per annum, which might be applied to public improvements, as, for example, to the erection of improved dwellings for the wage-earning classes.

" Among losses from nonfeasance and misfeasance together are to be included upwards of 25,000 deaths, and more than twenty times that number of cases of sickness; while the money loss from funeral and sick expenses must be more than three-quarters of a million per annum.

" Then there are the losses from malfeasance caused by the obstruction and prevention of measures which were prepared and tried under unity for the effacement of all the slums, and which would have effected that object many years ago.

" The losses from malfeasance in neglecting to place the organisation of the fire service, as is done in Liverpool and Glasgow, in the hands of the police, include the results of three thousand serious fires and three hundred persons burned alive.

" The losses from misfeasance, and often from malfeasance, by reason of the extreme disunity of the road administration, are estimated, on inquiry, at a loss of force of at least one horse out of three, besides the loss of goods and furniture from seas of mud in winter and clouds of dust in summer, and the diseases arising from the same cause.

"All these losses in the past from ill-regulated local administration show the gain that may be derived in the future from skilfully-devised local unity with executive responsibility in the cause of sanitation.

"It may be noted that when the measure of disunity was passed, agitation ceased; all for a time appeared in Parliament to be working satisfactorily, and the author of the measure, entailing all the evil recited, and more, claimed a peerage for what he did, and obtained it. I really believe that neither he nor the parties by whom he was supported could have been aware of the consequences of their action. If the reports presented at that time be examined, it will be seen that an amount of sanitary work had been done, and was proposed to be done, of a character to have required the most earnest support. Independent and competent sanitarians have declared that the effect of that vote in the frustration of work—work laboriously prepared to be done, and which must yet be done in the metropolis, —has been to throw back sanitary progress for a quarter of a century at least."

CHAPTER XXXI.

RESULTS AND PROJECTS IN SANITATION.

PROPOSE to bring to an end this part of our author's work by epitomising in a few short abstracts certain of his projects and advanced studies in sanitation.

Each one of these abstracts might easily, from the matter before me, be extended into a separate chapter; but as they are rather, as the heading of the chapter conveys, fragmentary and incidental communications than completed works, they may, very profitably, be brought together in a concise and ready form for the service of future students and labourers in the field of sanitary science.

SAVINGS BY SANITATION IN ONE CITY.

" Dr. Russell, the health officer of Glasgow, shows that during the last decade there has been a saving in Glasgow of not fewer than ten thousand lives, which saving he ascribes to reductions of overcrowding, more efficient scavenging, and other sanitary work, by which zymotic or foul air diseases have been reduced; so that, out of every ten thousand of the population, there have died of fevers only seven in

place of twenty; only one in place of two of small-
pox; nine in place of thirteen of scarlet fever; seven
in place of eight of measles; twelve in place of
fifteen of whooping cough; five in place of six
of croup and of diphtheria.

"Those acquainted with sanitary science will be
aware that these are but minor advances. Yet the
saving of the expenses of funerals, and of the curative expenses at the same rate as the common rate
in England (of £5 per funeral for all classes, and
£1 per case of sickness), will have been upwards of
£250,000 for the decade—a reduction effected by
the local sanitary service of the money burthen to
Glasgow from preventable disease.

"Now, the reduced death-rate of Glasgow is yet as
high as twenty-six in a thousand; but I apprehend
that there is no tenable reason why the death-rate
there should be higher than the death-rate in Dover
(the first town reported to our Board by Mr. Robert
Rawlinson, our sanitary engineer), where it was
once as high as that in Glasgow; but, since the
works initiated by our first General Board of Health
have been carried out, the Dover death-rate is now
only fourteen in a thousand, which I take to be,
nevertheless, only a passable urban death-rate.

"Hence I take it that the present death-rate in
Glasgow is still in excess by no less than ten in a
thousand. I apprehend that the insurable cost for
funerals and sickness will be found on examination
to be now upwards of £400,000 annually for
its half million of population, or upwards of
£4 per house annually for each of its 100,000
houses. I am not prepared to state what was the
cost of the chief factors of sanitation at Dover, or

whether they were economically executed or not
under the local authorities; but in some twenty
towns in England where the death-rates have been
reduced by more than one-third, the cost of the
works, as executed by the engineers of the first
General Board of Health, were as follows. For a
constant supply of water carried into every house,
for self-cleansing drains that carried away instantly
the foulest water from every house into self-cleansing
sewers, and from them immediately out of the town
by the combined works; the first charge spread over
a period of thirty years, was from 15s. to 17s. per
house per annum, or less than one-fifth of such a
charge as that arising from the preventible sickness
and death-rate in Glasgow. But Glasgow has
already its water supply, and ought to have its preventible sickness and mortality reduced by complete
sanitary works at proportionately less cost. The
economy of such works as those specified depends
on their execution by a common contract for a large
area. Where such work is executed separately by
the individual owner or occupier the cost is usually
three times:-as great, with greater risks of failure.
The expense of labour has been subsequently increased; but I may confidently state that in no case
will the cost of the properly-executed works and
properly distributed charges for those of prevention
be found to be so great as the existing insurable
charges of excessive sickness and mortality.

" It will be found on proper examination that
where there is the greatest amount of work to be
done by sanitation there is the greatest amount of
money to be saved to pay for it. In some of the
depressed districts of Glasgow the death-rates are

threefold greater than in some of the well-to-do districts; but in those same depressed districts it will still be found that there is the greatest amount of money to be saved to pay for the work."

A report on dwellings characterised by cheapness combined with the conditions necessary for health and comfort was contributed by our author upon a visit of inspection to the Paris Exhibition of 1867. Many of the observations here recorded have already appeared in other parts of this volume; but one or two abstracts are so excellent they ought not to be omitted in this place. I select three passages from this work relating to (*a*) detached dwellings; (*b*) utilisation of roof space; (*c*) value of soft water.

Advantages of Detached Dwellings.

"Conceding the economical advantages of the four-tenemented houses over the house rows or the street, I should yet advise to proprietors in rural districts the construction of completely detached dwellings as having considerable social advantage. For the lower we descend in the social scale, the less is the self-restraint, the greater the passion and violence, and the greater the need of a certain extent of separation. In blocks of four contiguous houses, one morose owner, one shrew or ' common scold,' or one set of ill-conditioned children, from whom there is no power of escape, may render the habitation and the ownership of the other three almost valueless. I do not know how this may be or how it is provided against at Mulhouse. But experience in penal administration shows that too close aggregations of ill-trained people frequently work badly in England, and how important is the power of ejection and freedom of change of occupancy. A magistrate's clerk of great experience in the city of London once observed to me that in rebuilding a city, the architect should, for social reasons, be prevented making close courts or alleys with common pumps. When the rooms in close places overlooked the opposite rooms, the female occupiers were apt to put about offensive tales and criticisms on what went on in each other's rooms, which ended in fierce quarrels and assaults. One or two common pumps almost kept two low attorneys, the sequence being this :— A little girl going to fetch water was thrust aside by a big girl, and being saucy was beaten by the big girl; then the mother of the litle girl came out and straightway beat the big girl;—then the mother of the big girl came out and straightway attacked the mother of the little girl;—then the husbands came forth to do battle for their wives and children, and then usually, with the Irish, sides were taken by the other occupiers of the court, and there was a 'battle royal.' Afterwards came prosecutions for assault before the magistrates, and the work for the attorneys. One owner of a close square of buildings told me that he found it necessary to make two entrances to it, so that people in feud might avoid meeting each other. Precautions are necessary to prevent people coming too close to each other, and jostling each other, for if they jostle each other they hate each other. I regret to say that, according to my observation, in our own country, the great Christian precept, 'Love thy neighbour as thyself,' has yet to be made completely prevalent amongst people of high as well as of low degree. As a minor illustration of too close contiguity a proprietor stated to me that he found that he had made a great mistake in building cottages in rows with the doors contiguous to each other, as he observed the women in constant idle gossip with each other. This will be observed in streets with one side of the street with contiguous doors and the other with separate doors. Even middle-class houses, the semi-detached, by which the speculative builder saves a wall and a yard of space between the two houses, are found to be productive of discomfort in other ways than the noise through the walls; the higher rents are given for dwellings with the same internal space, but completely detached."

UTILISATION OF ROOF SPACE.

"Where ground space is dear, as it is with the dwellings of the labouring classes in town, there is good reason for utilising the roof space. It serves as an additional drying-ground. In dry weather it may be used for the children to play on. One example has been set in London, where, in a densely crowded neighbourhood, there being no playground for a boys' school, they have made one for them on the flat roof. If any one will look over the *cité ouvrière* of Mulhouse it will be seen what a large amount of roof space is lost; and yet the cost of the weather-tight flat roof of concrete or hollow brick is nearly a third less in England than the timber-slate, or tile roof. Its greatest convenience or use, however, would be for self-contained dwellings; on them the father of the family may sit in fine weather, and have better air and an extended prospect, and enjoy himself in the Oriental fashion."

VALUE OF SOFT WATER.

"Pure soft water is, I believe, of so much value, that in the chalk districts, or in other districts where it is not to be got, it is worth while to prepare roofs expressly to catch it, and underground tanks to preserve it pure. In Britain it is estimated that the average quantity of rain water which falls on a square yard of surface in a year is 126 gallons. Three yards would give rather more than a gallon a day; or a surface of 100 yards would give 12,600 gallons, or 34 gallons per diem, or about $6\frac{1}{2}$ gallons per head to an average family of five. If this were insufficient for the purpose of the household, it would be worth while reserving it for drinking and for washing the person, and the more special uses. The collection of the rain water is one important use of a flat roof, properly prepared by an impermeable surface of hard tile or other material to which access may be had for cleansing it from soot or birds' dung before any coming rainfall, of which the first should be allowed to run to waste. A deep underground covered tank, —for which concrete faced with impermeable earthen-ware tiles are the best materials—should be prepared to receive it, and keep it cool, and out of the way of any floating cause of impurity. The best trainers of racing horses in England are very careful to do all this for their horses, and even to have water carried with them for the use of the horses at races. I was glad to hear the intelligent foreman engaged in the construction of the Emperor's model cottages, near

Vincennes, point out the absence of any proper
provision for collecting and storing rain-water, as a
serious defect in them.   He had constructed receptacles for the purpose in various parts of France, and
he bore testimony to the high order of their utility to
the poor.   In densely-populated districts such provisions are scarcely practicable, and, under good
public administration, collective arrangements may
be made with greater efficiency as well as vastly
greater economy.   The estimate of one engineer, Mr.
Bateman, for bringing an ample supply of soft water
from the Welsh mountains beyond the Severn to the
Metropolis, is a charge of about 6s. per head per
annum of the population, including even compensation for existing works.   Our estimate at the Board
of Health was much less than that even for bringing
fresh water from Wales.   But we found that upwards
of forty-six millions of gallons of soft perennial spring
water of a superior quality, pure, free from the taint
of peat, and well aërated, or double the then actual
consumption of the Metropolis, might be had, by
proper administrative consolidations, within the
existing charges.   Yet, as a matter of sanitary
economy, a charge of $1\frac{1}{2}d$. per week per head of the
population, for an ample supply of pure soft water,
would be a great saving."

MORTALITY IN THE ELIZABETHAN AND VICTORIAN ERAS.

" Instances of the beauties of mediæval art are
revived and presented which raise associations of the
beautiful with mediæval administrative institutions,
as if all were befittingly beautiful in the conditions
of the people, resulting from the self-government of

their mayors, their aldermen, their guilds, their wards, the securities of their nightly watch, and the beneficence of their parochial administration. Whereas, to use the words of Hobbes, the life of man in general, under the then common conditions, was 'poor, nasty, brutish, and short.' According to John Graunt's reports, from the parish registers, the condition of the whole city, in the time of Queen Elizabeth, was very much that of a 'slum.' The death-rate was, in fact, that of a slum, it was more than forty in a thousand. But now, under some advance towards unity and centralisation, it is about twenty in a thousand, still including upwards of one-third of preventible deaths. The death-rate then largely exceeded the birth-rate, and the lesser population of the city at that time was kept up by immigration from beautiful rural districts; now the reverse is the case. The death-rate of the children under five years was then one-third, or thirty-three per hundred. It is now twenty-seven, and grievously too heavy. The deaths from old age, or the age then called old, of seventy, were 7 per cent.; they are now sadly too low, but even in the city proper they are 18 per cent. It was a boast that the deaths from starvation were not more than one in a thousand, exclusive of a large omission of the deaths of infants. At that rate the deaths from starvation for the whole of the Metropolis would be 1,250 annually. But deaths from actual starvation, the privation of food, are now so rare as not to form a heading in the statistical returns. I got particular inquiries into the rare cases that did occur, and found that they really amounted to cases of suicide in neglecting to make due application for the relief

now provided for the destitute. As to personal
security John Graunt boasted that not more than
one in two thousand was then murdered annually,
which he ascribes to the good local government.
' The post of the government and the guard of the
city being by citizens themselves, and that alter-
nately. No man settling into a trade for that
employment.' 'Whereas in Paris few nights escape
without their tragedy.' At that rate, the numbers
of murders for the whole of the Metropolis would
amount at present to 2,500 annually, whilst under
the metropolitan police they actually amount to an
average of no more than twelve for the whole five
millions of population guarded by that force,—a
population which approaches to that of the whole
kingdom of England and Wales in the time of
Elizabeth."

CIRCULATION OR STAGNATION.

Under this heading Mr. Chadwick published the
following spirited preface to Mr. F. O. Ward's excellent
sanitary essay, in which the principles of sanitation
were illustrated from a comparison of the two streams
of circulating blood in the living body.

"' *Circulation or Stagnation ?* ' Such is the neat
and concise form in which Mr. F. O. Ward and his
colleagues have just put the sanitary question before
the Congress of General Hygiene at Brussels.

" In reproducing under this title the two principal
speeches of this sanitary reformer, we believe that
we shall render a service to all who are interested in
this great cause—the cause of humanity at large.

" *Continuous Circulation* is the fundamental principle of English sanitary reformers. According to their theory, the main conveyance of pure water into towns and its distribution into houses, as well as the removal of foul water by drains from the houses and from the streets into the fields for agricultural production, should go on without cessation and without stagnation either in the houses or the streets.

"Hence they would do away altogether with cisterns and cesspools, which Mr. F. O. Ward designates as 'two congenital forms of pestilential stagnation;' and wherever the double movement of water and sewage is hindered by the flatness of the land, they maintain complete circulation by steam power. It is at this last point especially that, according to Mr. F. O. Ward, the new system of drainage coincides with the general progress of the nineteenth century.

"'*Hygiene* by steam power' (we quote his exact words) 'is at once the logical extension and the necessary complement of *locomotion* by steam power, which has of late been organised throughout the whole of Europe. The steam engine, which has already quadrupled the means of transporting products from one place to another, will now quadruple the produce of the matter transported. This new application of the great invention of Watt will before long effect the same happy and astounding transformation in our domiciliary and agricultural arrangements, as it has already produced in nearly all the other branches of industrial art.'

"As to the method of thus applying steam to the service of public hygiene, it consists chiefly in the establishment of a vast tubular system. Mr. F. O. Ward has given us a rapid sketch of the physiological analogies and material organisation of such a system. In the words of this eminent sanitary reformer, ' The discovery by the immortal Harvey of the circulation which goes on in the individual body has prepared us for the reception of the strictly analogous and fruitful discovery of the circulation in the social body.'

" Conceptions such as these, based as they are on numerous experiments and very positive results, deserve undoubtedly the impartial investigation which Mr. F. O. Ward and his colleagues solicit.

" Let, then, these conceptions, these experiments, and these results be carefully examined ; let the press and the public join in the discussion of them. The scheme proposed to us is no less than the reconstruction, on principles of a very bold nature, and hitherto but little known, of the material bases of civilisation.

" What answer, then, must we give to this question, so concisely formulated, and apparently so simple, but of which the scope is immense :—' Circulation or Stagnation ? ' "

LOCAL SELF-GOVERNMENT IN SANITATION.

Against the errors of local self-government our author can never be too trenchant. In the subjoined paragraphs he gives the inhabitants of his native town, Manchester, the benefit of his criticism.

" Take the common case of a slum with a death-rate of forty in a thousand, and of the expenses it entails on the community. There will be twenty-five funerals at five pounds each, and at least twenty times that number of cases of sickness at one pound each, every fifth case on the average being that of an adult, entailing, on an average, a loss from disability for two and a half weeks at one pound per week, making one thousand eight hundred and seventy-five pounds per annum of expense for one thousand.   Let us make a rough estimate of the immediate loss merely in money, apart from the suffering and misery resulting therefrom, caused by an excess of ten deaths per thousand, the amount by which I maintain the present death-rate could be diminished by good sanitation.   For every thousand of the population, then, we have ten unnecessary funerals, at say five pounds each, or fifty pounds. For every such avoidable death there will be, according to the experience of benefit societies, and much more than that in the experience of the army, twenty cases of sickness, or two hundred in all, at a cost of one pound each, or two hundred pounds.   Of these cases of sickness, according to the experience of friendly societies, about one-fifth will cause a loss of wages for two and a half weeks on the average, or two pounds ten shillings; for forty cases, therefore, one hundred pounds, making in all a total annual loss or unnecessary expenditure of three hundred and fifty pounds for each thousand inhabitants, or seven shillings per inhabitant per annum,—for the population of Manchester, one hundred and forty-eight thousand.   This amounts *annually* to fifty-one thousand eight hundred pounds, or, in other words, to the interest at 5 per cent. on more than one million of money.   It will be in the like proportion for Salford, Prestwich, and other connected districts.

" The proportion of the inhabitants over the whole district appears to be five per house.   In the more heavily death-rated sub-districts, needing the first attention, where there are forty or more deaths per thousand, there are usually to be found one family or more to a single room; but, taking the general average of five to a thousand, it makes the loss or excess of cost to be thirty-five pounds per house per annum, which, at 5 per cent., represents a capital of thirty-five pounds per house. The main works which I have specified were executed under the General Board of Health, at a distributed cost of seventeen shillings per house per annum; and this, capitalised as before at 5 per cent., amounts to seventeen pounds per house. Making every allowance for the increased rates of wages, etc., the cost of the requisite works cannot possibly reach the sum of thirty-five pounds per house, which represents, at a very moderate estimate, in one factor only of the loss due to their absence, namely, the sickness, the loss of labour, and the funerals, to say nothing of the cost of the citizen, not to speak of the misery and pain.

"This, however, is exclusive of the value of the individual life lost, which cannot be less than one hundred pounds. In the United States it is rated at double that sum; but, taking it at the lowest sum, the annual value of life lost will amount to one hundred and forty-eight thousand pounds! There is, moreover, an excessive expense of police and penal administration, which is chiefly occupied with heavily death-rated populations and places.

"It appears to me to be absolutely necessary, upon such experiences, to speak out against the ineffable conceit and ignorance shouted out as to the excellence of our self-government, as if it were the glory of our age and country; whilst really, in its existing condition, it will be found to be, in truth, the worst of

any we have. It is within compass to say that of
every two deaths from typhus, one at the least out
of every three is due here to that same government.
Of the scourge of rheumatism, more than one-half is
now due to it. One result of insanitary conditions,
especially in childhood, is the early disease and loss
of teeth. The odds are, that most raging toothaches
that are endured here may be found to be due to the
conditions of the local misgovernment."

RESULTS OF SANITATION IN INDIA.

The influence of sanitation in the Indian army has
been for many years a subject of close study to Mr.
Chadwick, but perhaps was never better expressed
than in the following quotation from a speech delivered before the Sanitary Congress at Croydon.

" Now let me state the last results, and the economies of sanitation in the Indian army. The former
death-rate per 1,000 of mean force was 69. For the
last decade of the returns, 1869 to 1878, the death-
rate has been 20 to 1 per 1,000 of the aggregate
force of 518,899. The actual deaths during those
ten years was 11,815. The aggregate saving of life
for the decade has, therefore, been 328,805 lives. The
old sick-rate was at least 100 per 1,000; but during
the decade it has been (though still too high) 56·67
per 1,000. There has been an aggregate saving of
sickness during the decade of 25,085. Add the saving
of sickness to the saving of 28,085 from premature
death, and we have a total saving of 53,217 of force,
which at £100 per man makes an aggregate saving
of £5,321,700 for the decade, or £532,170 per
annum.

"Leaving these points let me go on to show the economies of money and of force in the home army. The former death-rate was 18 per 1,000. During the last decade it was 7·769, being an aggregate saving of 7·612. The actual death-rate was 12·51 per 1,000. The sick-rate was about 50 per 1,000 ; during the decade it has been 39·38. The grand total of the saving, to be made known for the examination of the War Minister, has been, for the home army, £1,494,100 for the decade, or an aggregate strength of not less than 878,925 men, or £149,410 per annum.

"Let me conclude with the statement of the savings effected in the army serving in the colonies, of which the aggregate force during the ten years was 240,876 men.

"The former death-rate was about 30 in the 1,000. The aggregate at that rate would have been 7,226. The deaths during the decade were 2,427, or a death-rate of 10·7 per 1,000, and an aggregate saving of 4,839 deaths. The former sickness rate has been estimated at 70 per 1,000 ; the latter at 39·81 per 1,000. The total saving of money has been during the decade on this branch of military administration £1,211,000, or £121,100 per annum.

"The grand total saving, brought to our knowledge and to the consideration of Ministers, and all who are interested in financial questions, is that during the decade there have been no less than eight millions and a quarter, or £822,000 per annum saved, with a saving of force of 40,000 men from death, and more than that from sickness, or of 8,227 men per annum."

SANITATION AS A REMEDY FOR IRISH DISCONTENTS.

In the same address as that from which the above abstract is taken our author made an eloquent appeal for sanitation as a moral and political remedy for discontent, taking "that unfortunate country," Ireland, as a grand field for work for sanitary reformers. On this subject he said :—

"By the combined application of factors, practically demonstrated, I am confident that the death-rate of Dublin may be reduced one-half. For myself, I must say that I consider the Irish working man extremely unfortunate in the misdirection of efforts for his relief. In my collection of experiences of him in England, I found general expressions of respect for him by employers, as respectable and respectful, and as being good in conduct when rightly dealt with, and more loyal than even English workmen. On such testimonies I stood alone for a time in contending for the introduction of the compulsory system of relief for the able-bodied, which has been well justified in Ireland.

"It appears to me that one of the largest political mistakes, leading to the misdirection of effort, is in overlooking the effect of the physical upon the moral conditions of populations. In England I have always found, in local inquiries, that the seats of epidemic disease, the results of bad sanitary conditions, are the seats of irritation and of disturbance, of crime, and the chief sources of the chief occupation of the police in repression. Some time ago I got out evidence of the influence of the physical condition on a large scale in Ireland. I took the four counties where the proportion of mud hovels to the population was the highest, and compared them with the four counties where the proportion was the lowest. The four counties where the proportion of mud hovels, cabins with only one room, was highest, showed 61 per cent. of such hovels. The four counties where the mud hovels were the lowest showed 29 per cent. In these highest the proportion of deaths from epidemics was forty-seven, whilst in the lowest it was thirty-five. In the most mud-hovelled populations the mean age of all born was only twenty-six years and eight months. In the counties of the lowest proportion of mud hovels the mean age of death was thirty-three years and four months. But the mean age of death of the English agricultural labourer was and is fifty and fifty-six years of age, with much for us yet to amend.

"The contrast as to the crimes of violence and passion was, as I had anticipated, greatest in the four counties where the proportion of mud hovels was highest. There the crimes were as seventy-two, whilst in the four counties where the proportion of mud hovels was the lowest, it was as thirty-two. And so it will continue to be where the population is in low physical conditions; as Jeremy Taylor has expressed it, ' Man is kept desperate by a too quick sense of constant infelicity.' Early in my sanitary work I wrote papers to urge a measure of general land drainage as a primary sanitary measure, for the reduction of the diseases of damp and stagnant moisture, as well as for increase of agricultural production. I urged that the permission to drain settled estates should be taken out of the Court of Chancery and placed in the hands of a special authority, with power to regulate the advances of loans and the application of loans for the purpose. So far as that measure has been carried out, it has answered the purpose as a measure of improved agricultural production as well as of sanitation. All round it has paid itself in seven years. Now Ireland is wetter than England; it has more land for productive improvement, as well as for sanitary improvement than England.

"I leave the reader to draw his own inferences as to what might speedily be done through sanitation for the redemption of Ireland from her leading causes of distress, and naturally resulting disturbances."

CHAPTER XXXII.

EMPLOYERS' LIABILITY FOR ACCIDENTS.

ON the question of the liability of employers for accidents to those under their employ, our author has expressed the strongest views. His best exposition of this subject is, I think, afforded in his evidence before the Committee of the House of Commons on railway labourers and labourers on public works, in 1846 :—

" A person who jobs a horse, or set of horses, sustains inconvenience or loss when any one is lamed or knocked up ; yet there is so wide a difference in the treatment of horses when the owner or the employer has to sustain the whole consequences and loss from any accident, that those who let out valuable horses for the season are in the habit of stipulating that they shall send with them their own responsible drivers, or take other precautions to guard against the difference of treatment to the animals, which they know from practical experience will occur under different degrees of responsibility. In the course of our inquiries into labour in mines, it was found, that in a class of mines of a certain depth, fatal accidents were very frequent from the breakage of ropes, which

were pieced with iron clamps, and patched and
pieced again and again, to save the expense of new
ropes. When lives were lost by the breakage of the
ropes in this class of mines, there was *some* loss
and *some* trouble to the owners. But it was observed that in another class of much deeper mines,
where the breakage of the longer rope imposed much
more serious loss, and the stoppage of more important works, there patched ropes were seldom found;
—there they were regularly renewed, and fatal
accidents of that class were comparatively rare. At
present, the contractor intending to adopt the
cheapest method of working, underbids him who in-
tends to adopt precautions entailing any considerable
expense. By this new plan, the cautious and humane
man would save money, the careless one would be
ruined. An eminent gas engineer (Mr. Clegg) was
consulted as to a method of removing gas from a
coal mine, so as to render the formation of an ex-
plosive mixture impossible. The plan was not
adopted, because the expense was thought too much
in proportion to the risk of the proprietor; the risk
to the men was not reckoned. If the proprietor had
been responsible, as I contend he ought to be, for all
the many losses occasioned by his works, for the
support of the maimed, and of the families of the
killed, it would have been good economy to himself
to have incurred the expense. And suppose it had
added a penny per ton to the price of coal, and
suppose it had somewhat lessened the rent of the
coal mine; it would have diminished misery and
destitution, it would have saved lives and limbs, it
would have lowered poor rates, and probably rendered
mine work less dangerous. Further, by sheltering

the men and their families from the destitution
caused by accidents, it would have lowered wages
without producing the ill-effect of lowered wages ;
for it would have diminished the want which wages
have to meet, and there would have been all the
benefit without any sacrifice."

DRINKING WATER FOR THE PEOPLE.

At the Congrès International d'Hygiène, 1879,
Mr. Chadwick, as First Honorary President, chose
for the subject of his address, " Water Supply for the
People," from which I condense the three succeeding passages :—

" The deeper the filtration through natural strata,
such as those of the chalk formation, the more perfect the precipitation. But then the deeper those
sources are, the greater usually are the mineral im-
pregnations drained in the course of the water. Now
every grain of chalk in water reduces its soluble
action on food, as well as for other purposes. We
have had evidence that persons accustomed to soft
water become dyspeptic when removing to hard-
water districts. Animals, horses particularly, are
frequently much affected by the change. But a
process called with us ' Clarke's process,' of adding
lime in order to precipitate lime, has been greatly
improved to an extent to reduce the quantity of suspended chalk from sixteen or eighteen grains, or
degrees of hardness, as it is called, to between two
and four degrees of hardness. The process has been
carried on in some very successful instances, on a
sufficiently large scale to prove its extensive applica-

bility. Mr. Bateman, an engineer, who has conducted some extensive works for bringing in soft water chiefly from the surface washings of granite or strata of the primitive formations, observed to me, that in one instance where he had applied this ' Clarke's process,' he considered the water obtained to be about as good as his Loch Katrine water,—a water of some two degrees of hardness; but I venture to believe that water so softened is better than the Loch Katrine water, delivered with its ' wood lice,' generated in the lake, or than water derived from the surface washings of granite, in times of storm containing infusions of peat, which do not agree with the dyspeptic.

" One attendant evil of the common methods of supply by companies for a trading profit is that they usually have no effectual control or interest in exercising any supervision over the distributary apparatus, or the care of the closets, or the prevention of waste. The consequence is that the waste is immense. In London it amounts to three-fifths of the water distributed. In London the quantity distributed on the intermittent system of supply is thirty-two gallons per head of the population. At Amsterdam the supply is only ten gallons per head, public consumers excepted. It is true only a small part of that city is water-closeted, but if all the houses were so treated it should only add one gallon per head to the existing consumption. There is this result from the waste of water in London, that the surplus fouled water permeates through bad house drains and sewers, and super-saturates the subsoils and creates marshy sites. In instances where the supplies have been placed with the whole of the distributary apparatus on a public footing, and the waste effectually reduced, there has been attendant upon the reduction of the damp in houses, as at Liverpool, a marked reduction of the sickness and death-rates. It has been stated to me that in one town, the wells having become excessively polluted, recourse was had to a pipe-water supply; but as no measures had been taken for the removal of the water and the prevention of waste, and the drawing from the wells—which previously had lowered the water-level beneath the sites—having ceased, the water-level rose, and so with the waste of the new pipe-water supplies, the site was made a swamp, and the whole town was put in a worse sanitary condition than before. The effect of the better potable water was counteracted by the excess of damp from the fouled water.

"On such and other experiences it results as a sanitary axiom, that the duty of carrying fouled water *out* of houses, and *out* of towns, clear of the sites, constantly through self-cleansing channels, should with the duty of carrying water *into* houses, devolve upon one and the same authority, and that such authority should be a competent and responsible public one. We have numerous satisfactory instances, chiefly in small towns, of the working of this principle of sanitary administration, where the service of taking out the water as well as of taking it on to the land, has been extended to the application of the sewage to agricultural production, so that there is no stagnation either of the fresh water, or the fouled water, or the sewage applied to the land. Nature abhors stagnation! Our first great object of getting potable water for villages and towns for the sake of

health and temperance, is indeed combined with the
means of getting well-collected and well-distributed
water—for the great sanitary objects : clean persons,
clean habitations, and clean air.

" I will close with a summary statement of the
general conclusions to which sanitary science has, I
consider, arrived at in England, for the extension of
improved supplies of potable water.   The first is, the
improvement of machinery and methods of distribution, by connecting the house service pipes with the
street mains as parts of *one* system, and that a public
one, responsible for the removal of all conditions of
stagnation, as in cisterns, by which the *best* supplies
are made bad, and *bad* supplies are made worse.
The second is, that the service of carrying in pure
potable water shall be united with the duty of immediately carrying away fouled water, and preventing
its stagnation by its removal, through self-cleansing
drains and sewers, and its application direct to the
land.   The third regards the sources of supply, aban-
doning as soon as possible *river* sources containing,
besides the sewage of towns, the surface washing of
lands, especially highly-manured lands, and substituting, by preference, supplies from *spring* sources,
or sources derived from primitive rocks, or clean surfaces ; or, where good natural springs are not within
reach, by creating artificial ones.   On the controversies
as to the eligible qualities of water, I may say that
observations of the effects of different sorts of water
upon individuals are perplexed by idiosyncrasies.   But
we may clearly see the results on classes of people
under similar conditions.   Thus, in a prison supplied
with the sewer-tainted water of the river Thames,
cases of typhoid fever were frequent.   The sources of

supply were changed to spring sources, and fever almost entirely disappeared, and there was a marked advance in the general health.   In one prison there was an outbreak of diarrhœa, such as prevailed regularly amongst the outside population.   Accidental contamination of the water in the prison cistern with sewage gas was detected.   When that was prevented, health was restored.   In one prison, cases of goitre appeared.   They were suspected to be due to the water.   The water was changed, and cases of goitre ceased.

The most important collective test as to the value of pure water supplies is found on board our steam ships of war.   All these are now supplied with water distilled from sea-water duly aërated.   As compared with the supplies obtained from the common sources of potable water got from shore, this supply is considered greatly superior, and is a great sanitary boon. There is no doubt that the superior quality of the water thus supplied to the Royal Navy is one of the chief factors in contributing to the greater healthiness of the sailors of the Royal Navy over those employed in the mercantile marine."

UTILISATION OF CANALS FOR CONVEYANCE OF SEWAGE.

For the application of sewage to agricultural production, Mr. Chadwick made varied trials.   In one he proposed to utilise canals for irrigation with liquefied manure.   He got a small steam boat of 10 horse power, with a hose a thousand yards long, and carried some night-soil in a tender on the Bridgewater Canal. The liquefied night-soil was pumped through the hose on to the adjacent lands of those who would try it.

The success was complete as to the power of the liquefied manure, and the cheapness of its distribution, by means of hose and jet, as compared with the cost of the distribution of solid manures with the cart. But the farmers who could be got to try the liquid manure were far distant from each other, and the supplies small. The only means of success appeared to be to take a farm adjacent to the canal, and devote the entire service to it. But for that Mr. Chadwick had neither time nor capital to spare. He proposed a plan of taking the horse into the boat and making the horse work it, on a horse-power platform and by a screw propeller. When the boat was stopped the horse-power was to be used for pumping, and for distribution through the hose on to the land. The plan has been proposed for the utilisation of the deserted canals of France for the purpose of irrigation.

SANITARY WORK FOR THE UNEMPLOYED OF LONDON.

In an address delivered in February last to the South-Western Sanitary Inspection Association, the following project for giving work to the unemployed was supplied by our author.

" The condition of legislation is continued at an excessive sacrifice of life and property. At this time there is a pressing demand for work for the unemployed. The provision of work, of useful work, as out-door relief for the unemployed on occasions of large and sudden emergencies of destitution, was one of the principles of the Poor Law Amendment Act. That principle was early and variously applied, generally by road work. Road work was provided on

occasions for Spitalfields weavers and in Lancashire
for cotton weavers. After some temporary soreness
of the hands had been overcome, many of these men
took to the work very well in return for the average
of wages. But the largest provision of work was by
Sir Robert Rawlinson, who made,—as no one else
could have made it at the time,—a provision of
sanitary earthwork for forty thousand unemployed
men, of which provision not much more than seven
thousand men took advantage. What became of the
rest? One social element is overlooked, that, as a
rule, all have connections generally in other occupations. The cotton spinner may have had one who is
an ironworker, whom he visits and lives with, and
who assisted him to find work elsewhere, or to emi-
grate rather than partake of the out-door relief. By
the social aid evoked in one form or another, the
congestion for the greater part was reduced. For
urban sanitation, two-thirds of the main drainage
work is earthwork, which is available for rude
labour under skilled superintendence. For undrained
rural districts, and for suburban districts, like
Wandsworth Common, Wimbledon Common, Barnes
Common, or Sheen Common, earthwork would well
serve the purpose, and would repay itself by a contribution of superior soft and pure water, collected
by subsoil drainage from unmanured surfaces, and
by the contribution to the reduction of the fog
and unwholesome damps of the general site, especially the suburban sites of the Metropolis. As
a Sanitary Commissioner I bestowed great attention on the subject, and put together 'minutes of
information' for the practical working of subsoil
land drainage."

VENTILATION FROM CLOUDLAND.

One of the latest projects put forward by Mr. Chadwick and published by him in January, 1886, is to draw down air, by machinery, from the upper couches or strata of air and distribute it through great cities, like the Metropolis. How the idea arose in his mind he tells us in the succeeding paragraph.

" I believe that provision for the ventilation of public edifices, hospitals, and schools, may be obtained by mechanical means, such as I will now submit for consideration.   On the repeated sight of the great blanket of fog spread over the Metropolis, I discussed the subject with Dr. Neil Arnott, who was a man of distinguished mechanical ability, and our conclusion then was that we might form a Pure Air Company, which would engage to draw the air from a suitable height above the common layers, and distribute it into houses by engine power, or, as gas is distributed, and do it with a profit, at a very low rate, or for some few shillings a year give even a better air than people generally obtain in suburban residences."

He proposes to take advantage of all buildings of great height, and to bring down, from their highest part, pure air; or, even in different parts of a large city like London, to build special towers for the purpose. To what height these towers should reach he supplies a general estimate in the subjoined statements.

"As to the different degrees of purity of air at different altitudes, important experiments are being carried on at Paris by Messieurs Miguel and Davey. So far as they have been carried, they are entirely corroborative of the general results I have stated. Thus, at the lantern of the Pantheon, which is about 310 feet high, the air is found to be twenty times more pure than the street air in the vicinity of the Rue Rivoli. In high altitudes of 2,000 metres no microbes have been found, whilst in the open part of Mont Louris at Paris 7,000 were found in the cubic metre, but in the street of the great Rue Rivoli there were 35,000 in the cubic metre."

THE CLINICAL EXAMINATION OF A SICK TOWN.

The last of the series of projects, but perhaps the most striking of all, is one for the scientific investigation of those towns and cities which require to be thoroughly inspected in regard to their sanitary state. Under the original idea that all towns are unhealthy, Mr. Chadwick suggests that each one should be considered as if it were a sick person, and that the sanitary doctor should inquire in due diagnostic form into its constitutional condition. He would have the sanitary doctor inquire into the state of the intestine or sewerage of the place. Are the great canals properly purged and cleansed? Is the breath of the place sweet and wholesome? Are the environs of the place, the outer surfaces of it, clean and wholesome? Is it free, or is it infested with vermin? Is the circulation of what goes in and what goes out of the town orderly and regular? Is the water with which it is supplied of good and proper quality? Is the food sufficient in regard to quality and quantity? Is the place supplied with pure air, or does mist hang over it morning and evening like a fog? Is the mental condition of the place good? Is it free of discontent, irritation, or excitement? Is the death-rate that of a healthy community, and is the hereditary history of the town of such a character as to be creditable to its constitutional qualties? In a word, is it a town that an insurance company could insure wholesale without weighting it with any excess on the normal premium?

If the answer to all these questions be in the affirmative, then the town may be pronounced healthy. If it fail to give so clean a record, then the sanitary doctor is to prescribe for it sanitarily, as the curative doctor, might in his way, prescribe for a sick man; and, sadly to the injury of the last-named gentleman, is expected to perform the ruinous act of destroying the curative business altogether.

VOLUME II.

PART II.

PREVENTION OF PAUPERISM AND POVERTY.

CHAPTER I.

FIRST WORKS ON POOR LAW REFORM.

I APPROACH now those particular parts of Mr. Chadwick's labours which have reference to the Poor Law and the prevention of poverty. Regarding these labours, public opinion has all through been deeply interested and somewhat divided.

To some thinkers these are the most important labours of our author, as well as the most useful. To other thinkers they are considered minor in comparison with what he has effected in educational and sanitary advancement. To a third, and small class, they have always been, and still are, open to criticism and objection.

There is something offering in itself distinctive proof of great administrative ability in works which have excited so much wide and diverse opinion and sentiment, and I have material before me, — historical, controversial, and personal,—sufficient to fill several volumes on these works alone. Thirty years ago I might have produced from them such volumes, but, alas! the generation that would have been interested in them has largely passed away, and so, I believe, I shall contribute to the general taste most successfully by condensing into some sixty or

seventy pages the salient points, historical and personal, of the subjects in hand.

In 1829, Mr. Chadwick, then looking forward to-
ward a professional career as a barrister, contributed
to the *London Review* two papers, one on the
Public Charities in France, the other on Preventive
Police. Both essays attracted considerable attention,
and may be said to have brought their author immediately into public notice. The essay on Preventive Police will be noticed further on ; the essay on
Public Charities in France requires this notice now,
because it stimulated inquiry into the state of poverty
in England. At the same time it brought its author
forward as one who would prove a good practical
inquirer and administrator on the then vexed question of the English poor, and the mode of legislating
for them in the most advantageous manner for the
nation

Twelve years before this time a Committee of the
House of Commons had stated their opinion that,
" unless some efficacious check were interposed, there
was then every reason to think that the amount of
the assessment would continue to increase until at
a period, more or less remote, according to the progress the evil had already made in different places,
it should have absorbed the profits of the property
on which the rate might have been assessed, producing thereby the neglect and ruin of the land and
the waste or removal of other property, to the utter
subversion of the happy order of society, so long
upheld in these kingdoms."

In consequence of the recommendations of that
Committee, the power of ordering relief through the
magistrates was restricted, and some other changes

were introduced; but matters remained in an un-
settled state until 1832—the year of the passage of
the Reform Bill,—when Lord Grey's government
established a Commission of Inquiry into the operation of the existing Poor Laws in England and Wales,
—laws which had been enforced from the time of
Elizabeth.

The body of Commissioners thus appointed consisted of the Bishop of London (Dr. Blomfield), the
Bishop of Chester (Dr. Longley, afterwards Archbishop of Canterbury), W. Sturges Bourne, Nassau
W. Senior, Henry Bishop, Henry Gawler, and Walter
Coulson, under whom eighteen Assistant Commissioners were appointed, who in the performance of
their duties travelled through different parts of
England, and collected inquiries of the most systematic kind in the districts allotted to them.

At the instance of Mr. Nassau Senior, Mr. Chadwick was appointed as one of the Assistant Commissioners, and the districts of London and Berkshire
were assigned to Mr. Chadwick, whose name finally
appeared, with that of Mr. James Traill, in the
Complete Report of the Commission, published
from Whitehall Yard on the 20th of February,
1834.

The instructions given by the Commissioners to
their Assistant Commissioners suggested inquiry
under four heads :—

I. The form in which parochial relief is given.

II. The persons to whom it is given.

III. The persons by whom it is awarded.

IV. The persons at whose expense it is given.

These were the first four grand divisions ; but it
was intimated that the inquiry would suggest con-

siderable alterations in the existing law. It was also suggested that those alterations might be facilitated by some further measures, such as :—

V. Affording facilities for emigration.

VI. Facilitating the occupation and even the acquisition of land by labourers.

VII. Removing the tax on servants so far as it is found to interfere with their residence under their employers' roof.

VIII. Improving the rural police.

CHAPTER II.

PLAN OF INQUIRY INTO THE STATE OF THE POOR.

THE series of reports on the state of the poor in England, which emanated from the Assistant Commissioners in 1832–3, and which led to the Report of 1834, is one of the most important documents in the history of the century. It depicts with photographic accuracy the England of that day as it appeared to the eyes of a body of men as competent as any it was possible to find for the purpose of the investigation. I commend this report to every historian, as I have ventured to commend the report on the sanitary condition of the labouring classes; but I can only deal with it here in so far as it relates to Mr. Chadwick's labours.

Mr. Chadwick's report sets forth at its opening that, in the course of his inquiries into the practical operation of the Poor Laws in the Metropolis, some points occurred to him which induced him to avail himself of the opportunity of visiting one of the agricultural counties for the purpose of investigating different modes of administration and their effects in the agricultural parishes, and of comparing them with similar operations in some of the larger parishes of London.

This, at the outset, was the intention. But the report is memorable in consequence of the results which spring from it. It may be stated without risk of exaggeration that, whether for good or for evil, the summary of this report included the great change which took place afterwards in Poor Law administration, and was practically the basis of the modern English Poor Law as distinct from the administration which had dated from the days of Elizabeth.

I shall quote at length this important summary in the next chapter; but I think it necessary, at this point, to fix the attention of the reader by one or two examples on the plan of the inquiry. He will in this way see the more readily how the conclusions submitted were derived.

INQUIRY AT WINDSOR.

Mr. Chadwick's inquiry opened at Windsor, where Mr. Charles Hodges, Assistant Overseer to the parish, supplied the information that was desired.

At the time in question the parochial affairs of Windsor were managed by a committee of twelve inhabitants and by the parish officers, the assistant overseer receiving a salary of one hundred pounds. When a poor person applied for permanent relief, the assistant overseer inquired into the circumstances of the case, and reported to the committee. Casualties were relieved by the overseer in pay. There were four overseers, and they each took it in turn for three months to pay all the parochial demands. In summer quarters the average casual relief was about seven pounds weekly; in winter it might by double that amount.

No labour was given to the paupers in Windsor excepting work on the roads. The men worked from six o'clock in the morning until five in the afternoon in summer, in the winter from seven until four. Single men were allowed a shilling a day, married men with two children one shilling and sixpence, men with larger families two shillings. About twelve men with large families had their rents paid by the parish. The parish authorities did not consider that twelve shillings a week was more than sufficient to maintain a labouring man and his family; and as private individuals did not give more than twelve shillings a week to a day labourer, and made no distinction between married and single men, the parish labourers had many advantages over industrious labourers who maintained themselves; they got the same wages, they got their rents paid, they got opportunities of picking up additional shillings, they worked less time, and they were relieved from the burden of looking out for work. If they thought they did not get enough wages, they would run to the magistrates for redress, which was a check to any strictness on the part of the overseers.

Industrious and independent labourers who had large families were reported to be prevented from throwing themselves upon the parish by only one thing, viz., the sense of degradation, and this was diminishing. The characteristic of the wives of paupers and their families was, that the wives were dirty, nasty, and indolent; the children, generally, neglected, immoral, and vagrants.

A striking contrast was obtained as to the condition of the wives and families of independent labourers. The wife and children were clean, and the cottage

tidy. In passing along a row of cottages, the transient observer could tell, in nine instances out of
ten, Mr. Hodges deposed, which were paupers' cottages, and which were the cottages of independent
labourers.

The chances of depauperising any of the paupers
were pronounced practically hopeless unless very
severe measures indeed were adopted. A family once
on the parish was very difficult to get off; and there
were instances of three generations of paupers. If
overseers were severe in putting a stop to the
system, they were open to the censures of the
local magistrates and to the newspapers, so that
in the course of nine years only about four out
of thirty-four overseers were disposed to severity.
Sometimes relief was refused to applicants unless
they went into the workhouse, and as a large proportion declined to go into it, they were got rid of
in that way.

In addition to the above-named advantages to the
parish labourers, other advantages were shown to be
derived from the attention of charitable ladies, who
were cheated by them on all sides.

On the whole, the aspects of pauperism in Windsor,
fifty-five years ago, were gloomy enough. It was
shown in further evidence that applications for rents
to be paid were so numerous, that the Committee
were forced to refuse all new applicants ; that a great
number of artisans and labourers brought into the town
by works carried on at the Palace increased the parochial difficulties; that four mechanics' clubs, which
had greatly relieved the parish, had been broken up in
consequence of the suspicion that the Government
wanted to get hold of their money ; that the savings

bank in the town was, apparently, not very flourish-
ing; that two private funds in two establishments
had relieved the parish, but that such trade clubs
were not generally popular ; and that various ancient
charities led people to settle in the parish for the
purpose of obtaining a share of the produce of those
charities.

INQUIRY AT READING.

From Windsor the research was continued to
Reading, in which town the various parochial officers
were examined, the result of the examination showing
that if several parishes were united they could afford
to pay for the direction of the labour of the paupers
for the whole of them.   It also brought out that
non-parishioners were more useful and of superior
value as labourers than parishioners.   Evidence from
other parishes was adduced to show that non-
parishioners were worth three or four shillings a week
more than parishioners, because the non-parishioners
had not the poor-rate to fly to.   Some conception of
the state of the outdoor poor in some of the agricultural parishes was conveyed by the evidence of the
Rev. Mr. Cherry, of Burghfield, who stated that in
comparing parish and private work many single men
in his parish preferred six shillings a week for working
on the roads or in the gravel pits to seven or eight
shillings for working for the farmer.

Mr. Clift, the Assistant Overseer, gave stronger
instances where men who received six shillings a
week from the parish had refused nine shillings from
the farmer.

This observation as to labour was pursued into

London parishes. If the authorities could get work for their able-bodied outdoor poor so as to make their condition less eligible on the whole than that of the independent labourer, what proportion of those who were chargeable to the parish would remain so, was the question put to the various officials. The answer was unanimous to the effect that, if such labour were instituted, scarcely any working paupers would remain.

In connection with this subject the causes of profusion of expenditure in dispensing parochial relief under the old system were examined, and were traced to be many in number. There was an uncontrollable facility and temptation to fraud in the administration of any out-door relief when not given in the shape of wages for labour. There was the ignorance of the annual officers and the operations of personal interests at variance with their duties. The fraud of parties receiving relief as being out of work when they are in work, or of continuing to receive relief after they have obtained work; of persons receiving out-door relief in money on account of sickness, and continuing to receive that relief after they have recovered; of women receiving relief on the ground that they have been deserted by their husbands while their husbands are living with them; of women receiving relief on pretence that their husbands are in search of work while they are in full work; of persons receiving pensions for relatives or children as if they were alive, while they are dead; of respectable classes of mechanics, whose work and means of living are tolerably good, obtaining outdoor relief.

LAWRENCE WORKHOUSE, READING.

Returning to Reading, the condition of the poor in the workhouses there opens up a very interesting and curious piece of national history.

The workhouse contained from forty to fifty inmates,—men, women, and children,—who consumed seldom less than one hundred and fifty pounds of meat weekly. The bread was good, the table beer pronounced "excellent," with a superior quality of the same beverage two years old and "potent," reserved for the overseers after the performance of a dry day's work. The place was clean, the inmates healthy. One inmate, a hale-looking man of sixty-three, had with his wife been on the parish more than forty years. On the whole the inmates were better off than the labourers, and better off than one-half of the ratepayers of the place out of the House; for they were well fed, had little work, and no responsibility. In the course of his inspection Mr. Chadwick found that the men's rooms were all locked in order that the men might not come in and lie down before bed time; and this, not to escape from work, for there was none, but in order to prevent them coming up "to lollop about and roll about in their beds after dinner, or when they were tired of doing nothing." Naturally enough this kind of life was not unpleasant. There were some who could not bear the regularity and preferred the dog's life of hunger and liberty; but the majority never left, and most of these were undeserving characters who had been reduced to poverty by improvidence or vice.

The male and female paupers were separated in the night, but in the day the young girls and the mothers of illegitimate children, and all classes, might meet and converse together in the yard.

In this same workhouse two old persons who had been in the workhouse the greater part of their lives were the progenitors of three generations of paupers living in the parish at a cost to the ratepayers of over one hundred a year.

The above is the description of one particular workhouse in which the condition of the inmates might be considered as favourable.

We shall find in the next chapter a description of a workhouse much less commendable.

CHAPTER III.

PROFESSOR MASSON, in an extremely able paper on the work performed by Mr. Chadwick during the Poor Law Inquiry, points out that our author extracted from his researches these all-important truths. (*a*) *That the old Poor Law "contributed to make the condition of a pauper throughout more eligible in all material respects than the condition of an independent labourer;"* (*b*) *" The advantage of a large as compared with a system of small areas in the administration of legal relief."*

"Here," continues Professor Masson, " the results of his investigations were completely contradictory to the *à priori* opinion of various economists, including Mr. Macçulloch. By narrowing the areas of relief, Mr. Macculloch held, the burthen of supporting the poor would be brought home more impressively to every man's door, so as to create a general desirousness on the part of all to keep down population, and thus reduce pauperism. According to Mr. Chadwick, facts did not bear out this notion, feasible as it seemed. Thus, in the hundred largest parishes of England, the proportion of paupers to the whole population was found to be 1 in 16, or $6\frac{1}{4}$ per cent. ;

in the hundred intermediate parishes it was 1 in 10,
or 10 per cent.; while in the hundred smallest
parishes it mounted to 1 in 6, or 16½ per cent. So
also, while in the hundred largest parishes, the increase of pauperism during ten years had been at the
rate of 1½ per cent., and in the hundred intermediate
parishes at the rate of 2½ per cent., it had proceeded
in the hundred smallest at the rapid rate of 8½ per
cent. From these and other facts Mr. Chadwick
contended that pauperism was more likely to be kept
down by a system that should group parishes into
large areas. One evident reason of this consisted in
the fact, that in large areas the workhouse mode of
relief could be more easily and rigorously upheld.
Nor was the possibility of thus reducing the mass
of pauperism the only argument in favour of such a
system. As regarded the treatment of the paupers
themselves, he maintained that the system would be
more efficient. This view was supported by a glance
at the state of the existing workhouses in almost all
the smaller parishes of England. Thus, in the words
of the General Report of the Commissioners :—

" ' The first difficulty (in the matter of workhouse
management) arises from the small population of a
large proportion of the parishes. Of the 15,535
parishes (including under that name townships supporting their own poor of England and Wales), there
are 737 in which the population does not exceed 50
persons ; 1,907 in which it does not exceed 100,
and 6,681 in which it does not exceed 300. Few
such parishes could support a workhouse, though
they may have a poorhouse,—a miserable abode,
occupied rent-free by three or four dissolute families
mutually corrupting each other. Even the parishes

which are somewhat more populous,—those containing from 300 to 800 inhabitants, and which amount to 5,353 in number,—in the few cases in which they possess an efficient management, obtain it at a disproportionate expense. In such parishes, when over-burdened with poor, we usually find the building called a workhouse occupied by sixty or eighty paupers, made up of a dozen or more neglected children (under the care, perhaps, of a pauper), about twenty or thirty able-bodied adult paupers of both sexes, and probably an equal number of aged and impotent persons, proper objects of relief. Amidst these, the mothers of bastard children and prostitutes live without shame, and associate freely with the youth, who have also the examples and conversation of the frequent inmates of the county gaol, the poacher, the vagrant, the decayed beggar, and other characters of the worst description. To these may often be added a solitary blind person, one or two idiots, and not unfrequently are heard from among the rest the incessant ravings of some neglected lunatic. In such receptacles the sick poor are often immured.'

"Now, in order to secure the possibility of a proper classification of the objects of relief, and, consequently, of a more careful attention to their individual wants —as regarded the young, to their education; as regarded the sick, idiotic, or lunatic, to their medical treatment, and so on—it was absolutely essential, Mr. Chadwick maintained, that such small parishes should be consolidated, and their paupers undertaken collectively in considerable masses. Other powerful arguments in his estimation, for the same system, were such as these: the comparative freedom from jobbing and sinister influences that would be experienced in large districts; the greater economy that would be possible in management on the large scale; the greater likelihood of procuring efficient officers, and the greater encouragement that could be given to such by gradation of ranks; and the increased skill and experience that would be accumulated.

"A third point elucidated by Mr. Chadwick at great length in his report was the impolicy of the existing Law of Settlement. By a large amount of detailed evidence referring to special localities, it was shown that the Law of Settlement, chaining down masses of labour, as it did, to particular spots, instead of permitting it to circulate freely according to the law of demand and supply, was one of the most efficient instruments that could have been devised for perpetuating pauperism wherever it existed, for creating new masses of pauperism at new places, and for diffusing listlessness and want of energy through the labouring population of a country."

SUMMARY.

These basic principles, so tersely stated by Professor Masson, form an excellent prelude to the summary which Mr. Chadwick presented to his colleagues, and which is here subjoined.

"1. That the existing system of Poor Laws in England is destructive to the industry, forethought, and honesty of the labourers; to the wealth and the morality of the employers of labour, and of the owners of property; and to the mutual good-will and happiness of all: That it collects and chains down the labourers in masses, without any reference to the demand for their labour: That, while it increases their numbers, it impairs the means by which the fund for their subsistence is to be reproduced, and impairs the motives for using those means which it suffers to exist: And that every year and every day these evils are becoming more overwhelming in their magnitude, and less susceptible of cure.

" 2. That of these evils, that which consists merely in the amount of the rates,—an evil great when considered in itself, but trifling when compared with the moral effects which I am deploring,—might be much diminished by the combination of workhouses, and by substituting a rigid administration and contract-management for the existing scenes of neglect, extravagance, jobbing, and fraud.

" 3. That by an alteration, or even, according to the suggestion of many witnesses, an abolition of the Law of Settlement, a great part, or, according to the latter suggestion, the whole of the enormous sums now spent in litigation and removals might be saved; the labourers might be distributed according to the demand for labour; the immigration from Ireland of labourers of inferior habits might be checked; and the oppression and cruelty to which the unmarried labourers, and those who have acquired any property, are now subjected, might, according to the extent of the alteration, be diminished, or utterly put an end to.

" 4. That, if no relief were allowed to be given to the able-bodied, or to their families, except in return for adequate labour, or in a well regulated workhouse, the worst of the existing sources of evil, the allowance-system, would immediately disappear; a broad

line would be drawn between the independent
labourers and the paupers; the number of paupers
would be immediately diminished, in consequence of
the reluctance to accept relief on such terms; and
would be still further diminished in consequence
of the increased fund for the payment of wages
occasioned by the diminution of rates; and would
ultimately, instead of forming a continually-increas-
ing proportion of our whole population, become a
small, well-defined part of it, capable of being provided for at an expense less than one-half of the
present poor-rates.

" 5. That the proposed changes would tend powerfully to promote providence and forethought, not only
in the daily concerns of life, but in the most important of all points—marriage.

" 6. That it is essential to the working of every
one of these improvements, that the administration of the Poor Laws should be entrusted, as
to their general superintendence, to one central
authority with extensive powers, and, as to their
details, to paid officers, acting under the consciousness of constant superintendence and strict
responsibility."

"These facts and recommendations," says Professor Masson, " corroborated as they were by the
independent evidence furnished by the other Assistant Commissioners, the services of many of whom
would deserve special notice, were, with hardly an
exception, embodied in the general report prepared
by the Commissioners themselves, and submitted
to Parliament in February, 1834.

"Altogether the Report of the Commissioners,
whether as a collection of particulars relative to

the state of society, a magazine of illustrations in political economy and the sciences of legislation and administration, or a code of rules and devices for reforming a bad system, was probably as remarkable a publication as had ever been given to the world.

" So evidently Parliament thought; for in the famous Poor Law Amendment Act, passed in August, 1834, the principal recommendations of the report were adopted and formularised. The piece-meal system of management by 15,000 distinct local sovereignties was abolished; and the administration of the whole pauperism of England and Wales placed under the control of a central Board of three paid Commissioners, sitting in London, and directly responsible to the Secretary of State for the Home Department. Under these Commissioners, but appointed by Government, was to be a staff of nine Assistant Commissioners, each assuming the charge of a particular district. The central Board was to have the power of uniting parishes for administrative purposes; and from it all rules and regulations for the direction of the local bodies were to proceed. The administrative local bodies in the various unions were to consist of guardians annually elected by the ratepayers; but the masters of workhouses and other paid officers were to be under the orders of the Commissioners, and removable by them. The system of paying wages, or money in aid of wages, out of the rates was declared abolished; and, except in extraordinary cases, which were to be determined by the Commissioners, relief was to be given to able-bodied paupers only in the workhouse, and there in such manner and way as, while amply sufficient for healthy subsistence, should still be so much less agreeable than the condition of an independent labourer of the lowest class, as not to tempt men unnecessarily to seek it. Finally, the Law of Settlement was modified somewhat after the recommendations contained in the report."

CHAPTER IV.

PRINCIPLES OF ACTION.

MR. CHADWICK by no means entered into the inquiry with confidence as to the adoption of executive measures on sound principles of administration. This want of confidence was occasioned by his view of the low conception of administration prevalent on the subject in Parliament at that time. The commission contained, however, some very eminent men, of whom the chairman, the Bishop of London, Dr. Blomfield, was said to be in judgment a model man for a Prime Minister. Mr. Senior was an eminent political economist, and Mr. Walter Coulson was a Government draftsman. The studies of our author on insurance and the casualties of sickness and mortality, on the administration of medical relief in France, on the urban and rural police force question, placed him in advance of the others in the rapidity with which he got at his points of examination and the readiness of their development.

The depressing forecast he had before him arose from the circumstance that men of high position, as cabinet ministers, were imbued with the doctrine of population introduced by Malthus.

Everywhere the increase of pauperism and of

burthens on the rates appeared to be due to the mal-administration of the legal provisions for compulsory relief, to the imbecility, or to the sinister interests of ignorant local administrators, and to the habits of the recipients of the rates induced by lax administration, rather than to the assumed inevitable pressure of a willing and capable working population, depending upon limited means of subsistence. His colleagues, some of them of strong preconceived opinions, yielded to this evidence, and to the concurrent testimony of other investigators to the like effect, while they, nevertheless, recognised as general conditions, that in all extensive communities, many untoward circumstances will occur in which an individual, by the failure of his ordinary means of subsistence, will be exposed to the danger of perishing; that to refuse relief, and, at the same time, to punish mendicity, when it cannot be proved that the mendicant could have obtained subsistence by labour, is repugnant to the common sentiments of mankind; and that to punish even depredation apparently committed as the only re-source against want is equally repugnant.

Whilst under these conditions the Commissioners adopted as a settled principle that a legal provision of compulsory relief should be made to the able-bodied, they did not propose that it should be extended to more than the relief of indigence—to the state of a person unable to labour, or unable to obtain, in return for his labour, the means of subsistence. They did not propose to extend the provision to the relief of poverty, strictly so-called, that is, the state of one who, in order to obtain a mere subsistence, is forced to have recourse to labour. They did not consider that a compulsory system of relief by the nation was available as a direct means, as some theoretical writers had assumed and had proposed, as a means of elevating the condition of the nation.

But the evidence collected appeared to establish as a conclusion for practical administration that a compulsory provision for the relief of the indigent can generally be administered on a sound and well-defined principle; and that under the operation of this principle the assurance that no one need perish from want, might be rendered complete, and the mendicant and the vagrant repressed by disarming both of their weapons,—the plea of impending starvation.

It was assumed, however, that in the administration of a compulsory system of relief, they were warranted in imposing such conditions on the individual relieved as might be conducive to the benefit either of the individual himself or of the community at large, at whose expense he had to be relieved. One primary condition was, that his situation, on the whole, should not be made really or apparently so eligible as the situation of the independent labourer of the lowest class. Every penny bestowed that tended to render the condition of the pauper more eligible than that of an independent labourer was accepted as a bounty on indolence and on vice.

One further primary condition of a sound system of relief was admitted to be established, viz., that the relief given should be entire—not partial relief. Any partial relief, any relief given in aid of wages, had, as respects the able-bodied labourer, an inevitable tendency to reduce his motives for exertion; to lessen the productive power and value of his labour, to lower wages; to substitute parish doles for wages; and to destroy independence of character. They held that relief must be so given as to draw a clear and visible line between the paupers and the self-supporting classes.

Mr. Chadwick found that, in the administration of their own club funds, the working classes anxiously and laboriously applied this principle in the shape of a rule, that the recipients of relief should be either wholly on, or wholly off, the box, or the sick list. It is not absolutely necessary, however, that in the application of this principle relief should be given, as commonly supposed, in the workhouse. The pauper might be set on out-door work, and might receive out-door relief in return for work, provided that his whole time is occupied in working under proper superintendence, in return for this subsistence. He might be set on out-door work, as many of the able-bodied in Lancashire now are, strictly in compliance with the Statute of Elizabeth, provided it be under proper superintendence and security that his whole time is occupied in working in return for relief. The workhouse is the most convenient means of providing for fluctuating numbers of applicants, on occasions when they are too few to make it worth while to provide out-door work, or to employ special officers to superintend it.

It may be of interest to dispose of this doctrine by stating at once some facts on that law which he met with in the course of his earlier as well as of his later inquiries. In examining the allowance system of relief on account of the number of children in families, he found that in the healthy rural districts, the intervals of birth were generally two years ; so that where there were eight in a family, the eldest would be sixteen, the next fourteen years, the next twelve, and the next ten ; and three, if not four, would be capable of contributing to their own livelihoods. But in the unhealthy urban districts the intervals of the births he found to be much shorter, and not generally to exceed a year. After a sweeping epidemic there was a remarkably quick reproduction. The mother who went on suckling her own child might do so for more than two years, whilst with the mother who lost her child, the conception appears to be immediate. On further and wider observation, especially in India, it appeared that, except in the case of most extraordinary visitations, the ordinary epidemic visitations did not check or really reduce the numbers of the population, which was assumed to be their effect, but only rendered the population weaker and more burthensome.

As to the economic effect of the increase of the population, he soon found evidence that increase, under good industrial condition, must actually diminish the pressure of population. At the time when Malthus wrote his work of alarm on the pressure of the population, the population of England, which is now over twenty-five millions, was ten millions. The example of Lancashire, which was then half a million, and is now two millions and a half of population, may serve as an example of the diminished pressure with the increase of the numbers of the population. It may be premised that the fact of a new comer obtaining wages, shows that over and above the cost of his own subsistence he obtains a surplus that is a return to the wage finder, or work finder,—the capitalist who employs him. The more wages the workman gets, the more means of subsistence he gets, and the less is the pressure on the means of subsistence.

An instance of the progress may be thus stated. At the beginning of the century, the wages divided by a manufacturer near Lancaster, for spinning cotton, was 4s. 6d. per week per head of the working population; divided at that rate amongst a family of three,—man, wife, and one boy or girl,—it was about 14s. per week. Now from that same mill the wages that go to the cottage are 17s. per head, or for the family of three about £2 per week, or a hundred pounds a year. The cost of the sort of cotton spun at the beginning of the century ("shirtings No. 40") was a shilling in the pound. It is now a halfpenny in the pound. This extraordinary reduction is effected by extraordinary improvements in the machinery, putting more and more of capital in single hands requiring more and more of discretion and skill, which is only to be got by more and more of intelligence of interest in the work, which again is only to be got by increased wages, which must be given, whatsoever may be the number of competing hands. The general result is that in the whole of that vast increase of population there is now the lowest cost of production at the highest cost in wages ; and that process is yet going on.

In agriculture, it was positively predicted that, by the operation of a change from the Elizabethan law, wages must inevitably fall largely, and that the only safeguards would be a large provision for emigration. In Norfolk and Suffolk there were thirty thousand men on the pauper rolls in receipt of out-door relief in aid of wages. They were all struck off, whe the pauper dole was soon replaced by wages, and wages rose. They are now about one-third higher than they were then. Two get as much wages as three did then. And with the advance of steam power and more economical production, higher wages yet have been given. Out of a fleet of fifteen vessels provided for emigrants, a number only sufficient for one could be procured, and those were people who would mostly have gone of themselves, without any State provision.

In the common reasoning there went to the pressure of population an expenditure of upwards of six millions per annum in drink. As results of that pressure there were upwards of one hundred thousand cases of preventible deaths, and twenty times that number of cases of preventible sickness; while all the criminal and mendicant population were living, as was proved under the constabulary force inquiry, on twice the earnings obtainable by honest industry.

Mr. Chadwick found as the result of wide examination, that the successful administration of relief to the destitute poor requires a very high order of cultured judgment; in fact, the exercise of as high an order of science as medical science or chemical science; but as yet, and until specially developed, it is rare as a culture. Let the different opportunities be observed of obtaining administrative knowledge, available for local administration with no actuating sinister interest, with no party interest, and with no disposition to act otherwise than fairly on such knowledge as they may obtain by culture, and good administrations will then be found.

Take the case of the elected respectable guardians of a Local Government Board, who are charged with the administration of relief to the destitute poor.

In urban districts this administration does not usually exceed half a day of a scattered attention at the weekly meeting of the Board. If it receive more than half a day's attention, it is accidental. An examination of the state of the knowledge possessed by guardians for the performance of their trust in the administration of the public moneys has led to singular results.

The following are the statements of some of the respondents (clergymen and gentlemen serving parochial offices in the Metropolis) to certain queries addressed to them. What can a family earn, and whether they can live on these earnings and lay by anything?

The answer from Chiswick stated that "a family might earn £49 per annum, on which they might live, but could not save." St. Anne and Agnes and St. Leonard, Foster Lane,—"Family might earn £60, but could not live on it." St. Botolph Without, Aldersgate,—"Family might earn £63 18s., on which they might subsist, but could save nothing." Mile End New Town and St. Mary's, Somerset, City of London,—"Family might earn £65, on which they might live, but could not save anything." St. Leonard, Eastcheap,—"Family might earn £78, but could not save; cannot ascertain whether they could live upon it." St. James, Westminster,—"Man might earn £78, besides material assistance from his wife and children; might live on wholesome food, but

cannot attempt to say whether they could save."
Holy Trinity the Less,—" Family might earn £93;
might live on spare diet; could not save anything."
Mr. Baker, the Coroner and Vestry Clerk of St. Anne's,
Limehouse, stated that " a family might earn £100 on
which they could live but *not* save." Hammersmith,
—" A family might earn £49 8*s.*, which would give
them wholesome food, and they might and *do* save.

Facts such as these led to the concluding words of
his first report, after the recital of the several recommendations, quoted in the last chapter:—

" And lastly, it is essential to the working of every
one of these improvements that the administration
of the Poor Laws should be entrusted, as to their
general superintendence, to one central authority
with extensive powers, and as to their details to paid
officers acting under the consciousness of constant
superintendence and strict responsibility."

The services of the unpaid would be confined to
systematised supervisory duties, similar to those of
the visiting justices to the prisons. But he failed
in attaining this improvement, and the initiative
of relief in the hands of the unpaid was continued.
There have been subsequent reclamations by petitions
to Parliament from Guardians and from Chambers of
Agriculture for the restoration of the rule as laid
down in the report of 1833, and it is now held that
there must be a return to that principle to secure an
advance in administrative efficiency and economy.

Some illustrations may be given for the explanation of the opposite principles of administration. A
guardian—a squire perhaps—says he knows that
poor old body, a widow, and that she must have
relief. He proposes half a crown in money weekly,

which will be economical, for if she is taken into
the house it will cost five shillings weekly. He is
unaware of the immense demand of half crowns or of
the sort of cases that will arise out of the exceptional
contravention of the correct administrative rule. The
last exhortation of the Rev. Thomas Whately, the
brother of Dr. Whately, the Archbishop of Dublin,
and one of the ablest of practical political economists,
was, "Do not flinch at striking off all the out-door
allowances of all widowed and aged persons. I did
so with all the widows and old persons in my parish,
and all round I doubled their allowances by it." This
result was what no one expected. How was it
brought about? This poor old body had a brother
who was a shopkeeper, and he allowed her eighteen-
pence or two shillings a week rather than that she
should go into the house; she had a son in place who
allowed her a shilling a week; she had a daughter in
place who allowed her another shilling; and she had
also a connection who made another contribution.
And so on with the rest; their contributions from
family and friendly connections were all doubled.
The effect of the out-door money relief is, as a rule,
to suppress all such family or other social contributions. It suffices to know that an allowance is made
from the parish, to suppress all others; it suppresses
the claims of relationship and social claims of relationship and known conditions. The guardian is unaware
of these facts, and their existence and operation
will probably be only known or believed to exist by
the intelligent and discreet permanent officer, who
is aware that, as a rule, all of the wage classes of
the population have relations or connections. If
any destitute person has none, if he be truly a lone

person, then the well-regulated Union-house is certainly the best place for him, the most benevolent that can be practically provided.

On the occurrence of the cotton famine, labour, good real labour, sanitary work, earthwork, fairly paid, was provided for forty thousand of the destitute workers, but only seven thousand took to it. But what became of all the rest? The answer must be that they all had either relations or connections. The destitute cotton spinner might have had one brother who was a carpenter, another who was an ironworker, or others with whom he dined and whose aid was evoked until work could be got elsewhere, or until emigration could be provided. One fact was that the death-rate, instead of being augmented, was reduced to an extraordinary extent during that cotton famine.

The administrative maxim propounded by Mr. Chadwick, that the initiative of relief should be with permanent, responsible, and well-qualified paid officers, and that the unpaid officers should only be charged with supervisory functions, such as those of the visiting justices to prisons, has received several sufficient important trials. At many important unions, as at Manchester, Whitechapel, London, and several others, the initiative of the relief has been practically left to the chief paid officer, and the guardians have charged themselves only with the supervisory services as proposed. Manchester, in 1869, had as high a number as 24,000 out-door paupers. In that year the cost of out-relief was £3,000. In September, 1885, the number of the recipients was 943, and the cost of the out-door relief was £61. In the Whitechapel Union the

number of out-door paupers in the sixth week of
the Lady Day quarter of 1870 was 6,758.   The
number in the corresponding week of 1885 was 74,
inclusive of 49 boarded-out children, which for
purposes of comparison should be deducted from
the "out-door" and added to the "indoor," as
they would otherwise be maintained in the District
School.   Deducting these 49 boarded-out children
from 74, we have only 25 out-door paupers.   In the
former period in 1870 the amount expended in
out-relief was £168 17*s.* 4*d.*, whilst in the corresponding week of 1885, it was £4 8*s.* 1*d.*   Added to
Whitechapel is St. George-in-the-East, and also a
rural union, St. Neots.   The mean of the out-door
paupers of these four unions was in 1871, 15,452 ;
in 1884 the number was 1,928, showing a reduction
of 13,524.   If the rule had been prevalent in England,
and the reduction in accordance with it, the total
number of out-door paupers would be now 110,150,
instead of 586,799.

The total expenditure for out-door relief in these
four unions was in 1871, £44,064, and in 1884 it was
£5,677.   The increase of the number of the indoor
paupers with the great reduction of out-door paupers
was inconsiderable.

Hostility might assume that the consequence of
such a large reduction of out-door relief to the
destitute must be a large increase of crime.   On the
contrary, it has been distinctly proved in Whitechapel
that the criminal business of the police offices there
has been reduced by one-half the former amount.   The
vices of pauperism have at every point been reduced
by the operation of the principle.

CHAPTER V.

IT was impossible that so serious a change could take place in the social organisation of England as that which was produced by the new Poor Law, and could pass into operation without severe criticism. The change was sudden, although it extended over what was really a considerable period of time, because the people were not prepared for it; and, as it came out that Mr. Chadwick was the leading spirit in that change, so the feeling against it was directed far more against him than his colleagues.

It is just to explain in these memoirs that if what he designed originally had been carried out in full, no such objection to his methods would have been taken. But changes were made after the labours of his colleagues and of himself were completed, in which changes, most of the most objectionable details of administration, were brought forth.

I have before me at this moment a draft of "Measures proposed with Relation to the Administration of the Poor Laws," which Mr. Chadwick drew up for the Cabinet. It is a singular historical document on many grounds. It contains perhaps the

first use of the word "guardians," as designating
a Board of representatives chosen annually by the
ratepayers of the several parishes united into a union
for the superintendence of the poor, together with
some other definitions of curious interest. The most
important paragraph, however, to which I would
draw particular attention, is the following, in which
the author describes the proposed Union workhouse,
then only a prospective institution.

"The towns comprehending several parishes, and
the rural districts comprehending several parishes, in
each of which there is already a workhouse, admit
of a superior management under an incorporation in
which several workhouses will be combined under one
management. Thus, when a town which contains
four or five parishes, each with its respective workhouse, is incorporated, each house may be exclusively
appropriated to a particular class of paupers. The
old and impotent might be placed in one house by
themselves; the whole of the pauper children may
be placed in another house; the able-bodied females
may be placed in a third of the workhouses; and the
able-bodied males may be placed in the fourth house,
the best adapted for discipline and regulation. Each
class may thus receive an appropriate treatment:
the old may enjoy their comforts, the children may
be educated properly for service, and discipline and
rigour may (not by the Legislature or the Government, but by the Commissioners' regulations) be
concentrated, to stop the influx of pauperism from
the able-bodied. It is found very difficult in one small
workhouse to introduce any system of management
adapted to the various classes maintained within it,
and utterly impossible to maintain any classification;

but, by a combination of workhouses under an incorporation, a classification, to the extent of the number of workhouses included, may be made without any additional expense, with all the economy of extended or wholesale management, and with many advantages which are not obtainable when the whole of the various classes of paupers are brought under one roof."

The course suggested in the above extract was the view of the Commissioners, most strongly of the Chairman of the Commission, Bishop Blomfield. It was believed by the Commission that the amendment of the vestral administration, by the separation of their mischievous admixtures, and by providing for each class separate buildings, would be a great and lasting reformation. For the children it would provide separate schools away from the influence of the depraved paupers; for the old and infirm, institutions of the character of almshouses; for the sick, hospitals; for the lunatics, the blind, and the idiots, proper establishments; and for the able-bodied and the vagrants a distinct suitable building. But all this plan was overborne by one started within the Executive Commission of treating the separate classes in separate wards of the same house, the Union house, under one chief manager. The separate system was the most difficult. It required services of specialists in administration which could not readily be obtained. For the treatment of the pauper children by school teachers on the mixed physical and mental training, the teachers had then all to be trained. For the aggregation of cases for the purpose of segregation and the special treatment of the segregated cases suggested by Mr. Chadwick, undivided individual power was requisite. But he had none. All the Assistant Commissioners—lawyers and soldiers mostly —went in for the Union house, and he was driven to adopt it. But time and arising experiences present increasing vindications of the original principle. In the administrative arrangements for the relief of the sick in the Metropolis, he preferred, from study, those of Paris, with its securities for the superior qualification of officers by the *concours*, and with its system of admission, with the control of all the beds, and the power of directing the application of the highest order of specialists to the relief of the poorest in need. In London the state of departmental knowledge has been displayed in dispensing with the requisite securities for skill in administration. After severe experiences of the injuries done to children by bringing them up in the same building with depraved paupers, efforts were made, chiefly by Mr. E. Tufnell, for their rescue, and powers were obtained, unfortunately clogged by the consents of the guardians, for the formation of districts of unions, to which the orphan children from the Union houses might be taken. Of 30,000 children some 11,000 or 12,000 were rescued, and a foundation laid for that half-time principle of mixed mental and physical training which now promises, on grounds hereinbefore stated, to change the entire system of elementary education.

In time also, lunatics, as well as the solitary blind, were removed from the Union workhouse, and the rooms for the able-bodied were generally kept largely free of occupants.

The services of the unpaid parish overseers have been substituted by paid overseers,—generally, it is true, with imperfect functions, executed under inferior directions. Nevertheless, the economies accruing from the application of paid service cannot be less than some three millions per annum. With the full application of the responsible initiative as displayed in the examples cited of Manchester, Whitechapel, and the other unions, with other collateral economies, further reductions of local burthens under an improved administration on the principle of unity of action, may, it is conceived, from progressive examples, be confidently anticipated for the future.

It is but fair to state these facts in regard to the chief originator of the modern Poor Law system. It was at first said of him as a reproach for his suggestion of separate homes for separate classes, that he would, if he might have his own way, make such an aggregation of idiots from the whole kingdom as to have created an " Idiotopolis." In fact, his plan was to deal even with idiots in such a scientific way that they should learn, according to their limited capacities, some semi-automatic work, that should be at once to them a source of amusement and a source of usefulness. In this suggestion we have the highest humanity combined with the purest science, — a method surely far superior to that which left the idiot in the parish workhouse to be the helpless butt and scorn of those who were just sufficiently above him in intelligence to be his masters and tormentors.

So in regard to the indigent blind. The idea of removing these from the rest of the indigent in their infantile stages of blindness, of placing them in comfortable separate homes, and under medical care by which many of them might be cured of their blindness, and in which again many permanently blind might be taught some useful occupation, was surely an idea deserving of the warmest commendation.

Again, in respect to the lunatics of the United Kingdom belonging to the indigent community, can it be doubted that it was an idea of the greatest mercy to propose to remove them from the crowded workhouse, or from the barns, sties, and huts in which they were too often imprisoned by their families, and to place them in grand asylums where, under scientific supervision, they would be classified and treated in such a manner as to be made happy in themselves, where that was possible, and of some service to others as well as themselves, where that was possible?

Lastly, in respect to the young criminal classes spread out in the thousands of old parish workhouses and parishes, was it not a truly noble as well as philanthropic suggestion that they should be lifted, bodily as it were, out of the environments of iniquity in which they were imprisoned, into the good and active life of the scholastic institution, where mental work, physical work, and healthy play would all combine to transform the most unfortunate representative of our race of children into an intelligent, active, happy, and healthy being?

Indeed, as we survey the change that has taken place in English social life since the leading spirit of the new Poor Law system commenced his arduous task, we see that his ideas have all indirectly come into acknowledged repute as well as operation. The asylums for idiots, for the blind, and for the insane, the industrial schools and the reformatories for the criminal classes, are so many monumental proofs of the correctness of his views and the breadth of his intelligence. They date from the great change of 1834, as distinctly as political advancements date from the Reform Bill of 1832. They have been introduced, no doubt, on a different principle of human action than that by which he was moved. They have sprung rather from educated sentiment than from educated reason, as disjointed efforts, seeming to be a response to a pure voluntary desire to do good— efforts springing from the heart of humanity. Mr. Chadwick's objects were for the same end, projected systematically, and springing from the head not less than the heart. His desire was to do at once by the force of law, and by what may be considered a beneficent tyranny, that which is being done by slow development and sympathetic progression.

Which method is the best is a question which I leave the reader to decide, according to his own taste and judgment.

One word more in closing this chapter. Mr. Chadwick has been severely commented upon for having, it is believed, suggested the separation of married couples in the Union workhouse. It is but justice to him to say, firstly, in respect to this matter, that the majority of his colleagues on the Commission were at one with him; and, secondly, that he was opposed from the first to the separation of those married couples who had passed beyond the period of age in which they would be likely to cause an increase in the numbers of the indigent community. The law which separated younger married couples in the workhouse was suggested by the evils which were too manifest under the old system, by which the workhouse became the birthplace of a great pauper population. And, tender as our sympathies may be for individual liberty, we must, on reflection, feel that the general good was consulted in the enactment, although it has received such severe and sustained criticism.

CHAPTER VI.

IN closing the part of these volumes which treats on the Prevention of Pauperism, I select some passages from various essays bearing on topics to which Mr. Chadwick has drawn attention with special care and precision.

In an article, published in 1837, on the "Principles and Progress of the Poor Law Amendment Act," he illustrated the nature of the central control and improved local administration introduced by the new statute. The article bristles with points of practical interest belonging to the time in which it was written, and in some matters it is even yet instructive as indicating the existence of grave errors that have not as yet been removed. I select a first example, in which it is argued that, by systematising management, unpaid services may be dispensed with, and fitting officers duly paid may be advantageously substituted for unpaid.

PAID SERVICE THE BEST SERVICE.

"As the arts advance, as competition becomes more active—we may say, as society advances—individual attention becomes concentrated, and the leisure of the labouring and middle classes diminishes.

" We deem it an improvement that fewer unculti-
vated people are now idle; although, wherever the
present leisure time of any class is not marked by
sensual excess, we think it desirable that that leisure
should be extended for profitable cultivation. The
leisure of the educated classes diminishes from another
set of causes, namely, from the increasing attraction
of literary and scientific pursuits, and from the increasing demands upon their attention, for the successful performance of the more private duties. Look
at the increasing number of scientific societies, of
public companies yielding profit, each engaging the
attention of numerous active minds! Observe also
the increased attention which is required to discharge properly the business of a landowner, or of the
manager of capital! It will not be denied that public
business also, when properly executed, becomes more
complex and laborious. The sense of its difficulty
too frequently deters those from undertaking it who
are the best qualified; whilst the ignorant, who perceive no requisites, impelled by vanity or the torments
of *ennui*, the disease of unfurnished minds, rush in
and seize the most important trusts. When we have
excepted those who have good fortunes, and who
make public business a study for professional purposes, it may be said that the fact of any one but a
young and untried man having much time to spare
is daily becoming stronger evidence of intellectual
barrenness and inferiority.

" In the case of persons who have no property and
no visible means of livelihood, yet have much spare
time for attention to public business, the presumption
is of a more serious character. These circumstances
which occasion the withdrawal of the educated classes

from the performance of voluntary trusts, leave large
fields of public service open to the ignorant and vain,
or to the unprincipled and rapacious; and the evil is
not confined to the local administration. The local
oligarchies, aggregated of the worst elements, mischievously affect the higher political representation.
Having no perception of elevated principles, and no
use or care for them, except as means of promoting
their personal interests or base gratifications; having
no high social purposes, and no moral dignity themselves, they have little appreciation of it in others.
If we see instances of large constituencies represented
in the supreme legislative assembly by men publicly
tried and convicted, and publicly known to be guilty
of offences of great moral turpitude, we at once
assume that each of these members will be found to
have been brought forward and mainly returned by
means of hands destitute of real character, who have
imposed him, as well as themselves, upon the multitude, who are too much intent upon their individual
business to attend to the business of the community.

" But whether or not we have indicated the proper
causes, which appear to be of an importance requiring
the most careful analysis and exposition, the fact
undeniably is, that the state of things presents a
stronger necessity of economising the demand for all
good unpaid service, and for appointing paid officers
to perform all functions requiring continuous and
well-sustained application. Each individual man can
give to the administration of the affairs of a multitude
of others, no more than casual and, therefore, superficial attention, fraught with error. The best public
policy is, therefore, to economise the demands for
extraordinary merit; and, to concentrate respon-

sibility on those who have the best means of bearing
it; those who give continuous attention to the
performance of their duties, namely, the paid
officers."

In another place he gives the following graphic
description of a very important social change in our
national life.

THE EMANCIPATION OF PAUPERISED AND SERF LABOURERS.

"At the time of the passing of the Reform Bill,
and when the Liberals came into power, the condition of the agricultural labourers was most wretched,
especially in the southern counties. Their wages
were low, and their labour inferior and unproductive,
and relief was given in lieu of wages under a system
which created a large part of the evil to be relieved,
and did not relieve all it created. The labourer who
did little got his dole, and he who did much got
no more. The labourer rarely could get work, if he
sought it, out of his parish; and whilst the labourer
was confined to his parish, and generally to his farm,
the farmer was confined to his labourer. It was
practically a system of serfage or slave labour, and a
capitalist who bought a parish, practically as much
bought the labourers of the parish as he bought the
rabbits of the parish. Improving farmers from the
North have, where they could, generally brought
their labourers with them. When they could not
change the labour, and have been confined to the
pauperised parish labour, they have refused to take
farms in the South, even at greatly reduced rents.

" Out of the conditions then prevalent 'Swing' fires went through the pauperised districts. Conservative statesmen declared that they could do nothing with the evil, and practically acknowledged it to be beyond their legislative capacity. Peel and Wellington both abandoned it.

"Indeed, their conception was that the poor man —the agricultural labourer—'must be poor,' must have a life-long support on parish doles, must have his relief as a parish pauper; that his future was a parish poorhouse, and when he died he must have a parish funeral in a pauper's grave. The condition was admitted to be sad, but one that could not be altered, and the evil must be endured. Any alterations of the common conditions tending to the reduction of parish allowances in aid of wages were, indeed, denounced as cruelties.

"The Liberal Government grappled with the difficulty, and appointed a great commission, which probed the evil to the core; and the Government adopted the principles of legislation and administration elaborated by it, and succeeded in their extensive application as against the main evils affecting the working classes. The labourer was emancipated from the thraldom of the parish pay-table, and from confinement, by the Law of Settlement, to the parish, and of parochial administration.

"He has, indeed, by the operation of law, been made a free man.

"At the same time the relief to the really destitute has been largely improved at every point, and the burthens on the ratepayers have been greatly reduced."

TRAINING OF PAUPER CHILDREN.

We have seen in the essays on education the active part our author has taken in the education of children in the pauper schools. In like manner, as Secretary of the Poor Law Commission, he was busily occupied in framing the outlines of the important report on the training of pauper children, which appeared in 1840. He had already laboriously examined into the position of the English labourers all round,—those belonging to different counties, those connected with agricultural and manufacturing work, Irish and English; soldiers and sailors, educated and uneducated,—in comparison of efficiency with the same classes in foreign countries.

In the report above referred to, the influence of the information he had thus obtained is excellently brought out in the evidence taken by him from Mr. Albert G. Escher, of Zürich, a witness already alluded to in a previous page. In this evidence he extracted from the witness the curious statement, that the natural intelligence of workmen, as distinguished from any intelligence imparted by the labours of the schoolmaster, shone out, first, in the Italians, next, in the French, and, lastly, in the northern nations, including the English. The Italians' quickness of perception, it was said, is shown in rapidly comprehending any new descriptions of labour put into their hands, of quickly comprehending the meaning of their employer, of adapting themselves to new circumstances, much beyond what any other classes have. The French workmen have the like natural characteristics, only in a somewhat lower

degree. The English, Swiss, German, and Dutch
workmen, have all very much slower natural comprehensive faculties..

In further evidence it was adduced that Scotch
workmen abroad got on much better than the English,
for the reason that they were better educated in their
youth ; and this, in short, was the meaning of the
whole inquiry to elicit, as it did, the fact, that the
true way, and the only way, of raising the English
artisan in the social scale is to educate him in his
early youth.

Ideas for Preventing Distress during Periods of Depression.

On September 26th, 1864, Mr. Chadwick delivered
an address at York, as President of the Section of
Economy and Trade of the Social Science Association. The address bore on the cotton famine, the
event of that day; but there are certain parts of it
bearing both on manufactures and on agriculture
which, as they are as worthy of notice now as they
were twenty-three years ago, are herewith subjoined.

Distress in Manufacturing Districts.

" An important subject before us is, What may be
done socially or by legislation for the improvement
of the present manufacturing population ? What
may be done for the population which is coming, to
prevent or mitigate the social and economical evils
attendant upon the past ? And, first, what may be
done to avert or mitigate the periodical recurrence of
distress, and outcries for external sympathy and aid ;

for, although it is to be hoped that nothing so extraordinary may again occur, as that which has arisen
from the large loss of the supply of raw material—
cotton—yet experience warrants the anticipation of
recurring disturbances from over-production, from
under-consumption, from bad harvests, from changes
of fashion, and from improvements in machinery.
Change must, therefore, be regarded as a normal condition of our manufactures to be provided for in the
interests of ratepayers, as well as of the employed.

"In addition to the improvement which is to be
looked for from an extension of several sources of the
supply of the raw produce, as a means of preventing
for the future the violent shocks and inconveniences
occasioned by an almost exclusive dependence on one
supply, there is a lesson of domestic prudence, on the
like principle, the expediency of which, for families
of the wage classes, ought to be strongly impressed
upon them; namely, to avoid, as much as they can,
having all the working members of the same family
engaged in the same manufacture. The intensity
and bitterness of the late suffering in these districts
have been proportionable to the exclusive occupation
of neighbourhoods as well as families with one manufacture. In places where cotton mills were isolated,
or where those engaged in the manufacture have only
formed a minority in the manufacturing population,
members of the same family were more frequently
engaged in different trades. If there was only one
member of a family, or of a circle of relations, out of
three, engaged in the paralysed occupation, he commonly derived aid from the other two of his relations
who were in full work; if not in money, in a share
of their meals. But for such family and friendly

assistance from friends amongst fellow-workmen, the public pressure of the late famine would have been far more severe. I learned from the Continent that the shock had fallen there heavily or lightly in proportion as there had been a mixture of employments. The lesson taught, as to the distribution of members of the same family in different occupations, is in accordance with the common household proverb, 'Not to have all your eggs in one basket.' The expediency of this recommendation is disputed in the interests of manufacture; and there certainly are economical advantages in the aggregation of establishments of the same sort; but if that aggregation be maintained, those interested in it should be called upon to provide against its dangers and evils, or at least to promote actively the measures necessary to avert them. One of these evils is the long-continued congestion of unemployed labourers, on occasions of manufacturing depression. Early training and education, and the development of the intelligence and capacities for ready changes of employment, is one means of reducing these congestions.

" Few who have not had experience in the administration of relief to the destitute in periods of wide distress can be fully sensible of the difference in amount of trouble and chargeability to the ratepayers, between educated and intelligent, and uneducated and unintelligent people of the wage class—the heavy lumpishness of the uneducated, their abject prostration, their liability to misconception, and to wild passion, their frequent moroseness and intractability, and the difficulty in teaching them, as compared with the self-help of the better educated, who can write and inquire for themselves, and find out for themselves new outlets and sources of productive employment, which no one else can find out for them, and who can read for themselves, and act upon written or printed instructions. The really well-trained. educated, and intelligent, are the best to bear distress; they are the last to come upon charitable relief lists, and the first to leave them. They are most easily helped. I remember when we promoted the migration of the surplus southern agricultural labourers to the north, that there were villagers in places who had heard of America and were willing to go there, but had not heard of Lancashire, and could not be got to move there, even on the promise of largely increased wages, until they had sent one of their own people to see what sort of people they were in Lancashire, and return and inform them. The uneducated workmen in Lancashire are more intelligent, but, if we are to believe a story told of some of them, they have been led to America by a recruiting song, the chorus of which was—

"' And we will drink at every ale-house what we do come nigh,
   Until that we get to the North Ameriki.'

"Instead of being kept crowded, as the adult workers recently were, in schools, to remedy the gross defects of elementary education, to teach them reading, and to keep them from hanging about the streets exposed to disorder, they would, if they had already been properly educated, have been abroad seeking occupations for themselves, for which their elementary education might qualify them. On a former occasion some got engaged in the police force, for which reading and writing are necessary. One operative, who could read and write well, left his fustian jacket at home, put on his best Sunday clothes, and went about to inquire for a shopman's place, or a clerk's place, which he succeeded in getting, and did well in. A great deal of the good conduct of the operatives has been owing to the extent to which elementary education in, and the partial application of, the factory half-school time system has leavened the mass of workpeople; difficulties and disturbances have arisen entirely with the ill-educated.

" When I talk of education, I presume an acquaintance with the different sorts of it, from the positively worthless to the better qualities in which the results, practical, moral, and physical, in combination with proper training, are proved to be most satisfactory; from the inferior education in which, I have elsewhere shown, not one in three turn out well, to the superior training, in which there are not more than two per cent. of failures. The general and complete compulsory application of the half-time principle of school teaching by good teachers, combined with early physical training, may be urged as a means of obviating future prolonged chargeability, from manufacturing changes and reverses such as those of the past. I add physical training, because to enable a manual labourer to turn his hand to anything easily, he should be early trained physically to turn his fingers as well as his hands to any work. The future of the wage classes will lie in large manufacturing processes, in which there must be action in concert; for this the military drill has great value by imparting habits of order, prompt attention, and exact obedience to command. Systematised physical training imparts aptitude for every sort of manual occupation,

It is now proved that by it three persons may be fitted to be as effective in ordinary labour as five who are untrained; an economy of force which is of peculiar importance in itself, most especially to these districts, to meet an impending serious scarcity of labour.

"Another course for the prompt and salutary reduction of congestions of labour is the removal of such barriers to the circulation of labour, as those created by the law and practice of apprenticeship, in its arbitrary requirement of a seven years' bondage—for it is a slave labour condition, that is, labour without immediate interest in the work, and at the command of another—inducing slavish and slow habits of work in prolonging for years the learning of processes which might be learned in a few months.

On Agricultural Distress.

Agricultural Associations generally confine themselves to the discussions of questions of progress in agricultural art. The discussion of questions of agricultural economy appears to be deemed out of place there, and even the education of agricultural labourers, which is so important to the progress of agricultural art itself, is little entertained by them. But here the general survey of the whole field of labour and production will be deficient if the great agricultural portion, from which manufactures draw so largely, be passed without examination or notice. The same economical principles pervade the entire fields, though under varied conditions, which it will be advantageous to both to observe. Extensive land agents and successful land improvers who are con-

versant with manufacturing economy are wont to
express their wish that land should be taken in hand
by men of manufacturing habits, which include the
economical principles applied in manufactures.   It
has been confidently declared to me by practical men,
that the application of the like principles would be
eventually attended by the like wages and profits in
agriculture as in manufactures, and I believe it may
be made evident that they would.   In examining
the general condition of agriculture, we cannot fail
to be struck with its comparatively slow rate of
progress.

" The principles of the subsoil drainage of land,
for example, have been demonstrated in practice for
more than a quarter of a century, and I know from
official sources that under all varieties of rude and
imperfect work, such drainage repaid itself in from
four to ten years ; yet of the land requiring drainage,
after all that has been said, not more than some
fifteenth part has yet been drained.   Five years may
now be taken as the average period of repayment
for proper land drainage works.   Manufacturing
economy would not linger long in availing itself of
such results.   In the course of some investigations
to get quickly at the knowledge of the places where
drainage works were most neglected, I once asked a
candle manufacturer in London from whence the
greatest quantity of their rushes were got for rush-
lights.   ' From Lancashire and Cheshire,' was the
answer.   That is, from the vicinity of the great
manufactures.   In an agricultural report it was
declared not long ago, that two-thirds of Cheshire
was too wet to bear sheep.   Land drainage ought
indeed to be pointed out as a great field of most

salutary and suitable work for the employment of
the unemployed in the cotton districts.   In the rural
villages old men and women, bent and withered with
rheumatism from working in wet fields and living in
damp cottages, are considered regular subjects for
the exercise of artistic skill and sympathy.

An outcry has recently been raised, founded upon
official medical examination by Dr. Edward Smith,
on the great need of milk for the use of the town
population, and especially for children.   In our
report of 1842 I stated, with reference to the sewerage of the Metropolis, — which was then equivalent in population to that of all Lancashire—that
taking the rate of production even from the wasteful
method of applying the sewerage of Edinburgh, by
submersion, the refuse now thrown away would serve
to feed no less than 218,000 cows annually.   If the
more economical method of applying liquid manure,
pointed out in the official minutes of information
which I was enabled to prepare in 1851, and which
were laid before Parliament in 1852, by which a
quantity of water or liquid manure equal to a heavy
thunder-shower may be thrown on any sort of culture
at a rate of a shilling an application per acre, and
the formation of sewer marsh surfaces be avoided—a
double production would be obtained.

"Added to the immense waste of the town manures,
there is a general waste (an increasing number of
model farms excepted) of all the liquid farm-yard
manures, as well as of two-thirds of the effect of all
the solid farm-yard manures (as demonstrated in the
minutes to which I have referred), from their application in defective methods.   This general waste of
the farm-yard manures has been estimated by good

agriculturists as equivalent in itself to another rental
of the land.

" Such are the present common conditions of the
fields of agriculture, besides those of manufactures,
for the application of economical principles. One of
the available principles is that which I call of *in-
tensive* as compared with *extensive* production, of
the heaviest amount of produce from high culture on
narrow areas of land as against thin production from
low culture on wide areas. M. Lecouteux corroborated this in his '*Principes de la culture améliorante*,'
that by applying different doses of manures in the
proportion of nine, of fourteen, and of twenty
respectively to the same areas of land, the prime
cost of raising a quarter of wheat was brought down
from 40s. to 32s., and from 32s. to 17s. per quarter,
rent included. Now this reduction in price was
gained by the adoption of the economical principle,
the operation of which I have already described in
manufactures, namely, of distributing the fixed
establishment charges over the greatest amount of
gross produce. Thus, if the acre which only produced twenty bushels hitherto is made to produce
forty, the double quantity will only have half the
fixed charges upon it of rent, rates, roads, hedges,
buildings, etc, But the greatest economical result
to be looked forward to in agriculture is in the increase in the ' intelligent force ' applied to it. The
striking advance of the cotton manufacture is, certainly, due mainly to the great bulk of the labour
being on the piece-work principle, and to the ease
with which it is applied. Cotton manufactures could
not, indeed, be worked as farms are by day work.
An instance has recently been mentioned to me of a

family of agricultural labourers who had become mill
workers, and, of course, trained in piece-work; but
having been thrown out of employment during the
late famine, had offered to, and had been engaged to
do agricultural work, such as getting off crops, as
piece-work, at less than would have been paid for
day work to attain the same object, and were believed
to have paid themselves well. I have been informed
of other instances of the same sort. Agricultural
labourers also, who have joined gangs of navvies, and
have been drilled with them into their energetic
piece-work habits, on returning to farm labour, will
do their tasks of work in half the time of the common
day labourers. Examples of the highest order of
agricultural piece-work, with increased wages, closely
approaching to manufacturing wages, are presented
in market-garden culture near the metropolis.

"A great economical and social improvement
would be consequent on emigration or migration if
farmers could be got to apply the piece-work principle
in each case of the departure of one labourer by
saying to two others: 'Now, Brown is going, and I
propose to put you two, Jones and Robinson, chiefly
on task work, and divide his wages between you, if
you will make it worth my while by also dividing his
work and doing it well between you.' This, with the
younger workers, would meet with a hearty response.
This is a topic for a large economical exposition.
Recently in France, at a model farm for the trial
of sewage manure, situated near to Paris, I had the
advantage of a discussion upon it with the director
of the farm, Professor Moll, the most eminent
scientific agriculturalist perhaps in Europe, and also
with Mr. Amerfoordt, the Mayor of Haarlem, who

conducts the chief model farm in Holland. It was declared by Professor Moll that economical progress in agriculture was only practicable on the piece-work principle. Mr. Amerfoordt concurred, and he gave me the following examples of payments for results, in addition to ordinary wages, which he assured me were working exceedingly well:—The steam-plough is introduced on his model farm, and over and above the regular wages a certain extra payment is made for each hectare which is pronounced to be well ploughed; the payment being divided between the engineman and ploughman and boys in attendance. The horse-keeper, over and above his fixed wages, has a payment for each living foal got from a mare; the cowkeeper has an extra allowance for each living calf got; the shepherd an extra allowance for each lamb sold, or living six weeks after it is born; the poultry keeper an extra allowance upon each hundred eggs delivered to the housekeeper, and upon each cock or hen sold; and the dairymaid an extra allowance for each lot of butter and cheese sold, without reasonable objection to its quality from the purchaser. On this particular farm the cereals are at once worked up into bread for sale. The baker on the establishment has a fixed wage allowance, for which, however, he must sell not less than a given quantity of bread. For all he sells above a given quantity he has a percentage. Fines for irregularities, coming late, or neglecting horses, are put into a common fund, which is every quarter divided equally amongst all the men, so that the punctual and diligent have an interest in looking after the laggards.

" This system, I am assured, works at Haarlem

and elsewhere, as persons conversant with manufactures would expect it to work. The heavy, stolid agricultural action is replaced by a vivacious outlook and intelligence. The food manufacturer is saved the labour and distraction of superintendence and incessant fault-finding for carelessness. With us, the benighted law of partnership would prevent the baker and other servants being made responsible for losses as well as shares in the profit, making them partners, and rendering the employer liable in his whole property for the defaults of each. The amendment of this law would be of especial importance for the gentleman farmers and land improvers, who cannot give that laborious attention to details, and to checking piece-work, on which agricultural success mainly depends, and who must be dependent on farm bailiffs and stewards.

"The increasing emigration to America from Ireland, and the continued flow to our colonies from England, and the demands from the general labour market in towns, have begun to render labour scarce in agriculture in some districts, and under the pressure of inconvenience or distress from that scarcity, to extend the use of labour-saving machines. Steam ploughing has fairly 'turned the corner of profit.' The demand for 'intelligent force' promises to be accompanied by larger demands for 'intelligent directors of force.' Hitherto there has been as much successful labour-saving machinery unused in the agricultural districts, as there is of such machinery used, and mechanical force unused is unused from the want of intelligent directors of it. Even in manufactures intelligence is scarce and deficient for the direction of steam-force. Mr. Fairbairn showed some time ago that as much power was obtained from one pound of coal in Cornwall, where the working of steam-engines is chiefly on the piece-work principle, as in Manchester from five. Improvements have since been made, but the smoke is the outward and visible sign of wasteful work. An intelligent engineman will work a locomotive with half the coal used by one who is unintelligent. In one instance, where the enginemen were put upon the piece-work principle, that is, were paid for the amount of power they obtained out of a given quantity of coal, the reduction of the consumption of coal was from thirty down to seventeen. But, in general, employers are not at the pains to get registries or to attend to them. The application of the piece-work principle would reduce the general consumption of coal enormously. Where the causes of steam boiler explosions are ascertained, they are generally found to have been the result of unintelligent direction. Mr. Fairbairn has long urged the necessity of an augmentation of the intelligence for the direction of force, by improved elementary instruction. If the want of intelligent direction for force be great for manufactures, it is still greater for agriculture. It is well known that steam-engines scarcely ever do the duty in the farmyard that they do in the yard of the maker. I have been informed by a firm which lets out steam-power for agriculture, that it is always conditional that they send men whom they know, and can make responsible for the working of their engines, for they cannot trust their engines in such hands as are at present to be got amongst farm servants.

" To obtain more intelligent forces and directors of

force needed for agriculture, it will be requisite to
provide suitably for them in respect to habitations.
At present in England, from the distances of the
labourers' habitations from the farms, it often happens
that a large proportion of the labourer's force is used
up in walking to and from the field where he is to
apply it. His force and that of his family is further
wasted by the disease consequent on overcrowding,
and by the inferior sanitary condition of his dwelling.
In agriculture as in manufactures, it will be found to
pay to have improved habitations in connection with
places of work, not indeed in direct rent, any more
than farmhouses pay in direct rent apart from the
land, but as practical additions to wages, and as
means of obtaining and keeping a respectable, intelligent, and steady description of labourers.

"The economical principles which I have indicated as evolved by the progress of machinery in
manufactures, may be expected to be attendant
on the extended use of machinery in agriculture.
On impartial examination, on economical grounds,
it will, I conceive, be found, that the fitting intelligence needed to be combined with productive
manual force, as well as to direct mechanical force
needed in agriculture as also in manufactures, must
be obtained by improved elementary instruction in
the schoolroom, combined with the interest which
stimulates intelligence on the half-school time
principle in agriculture. Parents of the wage
classes on the one side, and employers on the other,
have to be informed that by proper training the
value of the young, as intelligent force, may be
augmented by at least one-fifth, and as 'intelligent
directors of force' by more than one-third.

"If the advanced economical principles deducible from the progress of production in manufactures be applied to an improved production in agriculture, as by the reduction of establishment charges, by high cultivation and the extended use of labour-saving machines, whilst in manufactures production will be increased, prices to the consumers will be reduced, wages will be advanced, and the net profits of the capital will be augmented. The concurrent advance of agricultural as well as manufacturing production will be attended on the one hand by improved demands, and on the other by improved supplies between more intelligent populations, with mutual physical, moral, and social elevation."

MEDICAL RELIEF TO THE DESTITUTE POOR.

We have seen that in his original scheme for the amended Poor Laws, Mr. Chadwick proposed what he called the segregation of different classes of the poor in opposition to the principle of aggregation in one large building. That he was correct in this view, the experience of the working of the Act as it was passed has distinctively proved; for in many instances the large union-houses which were erected are sometimes half empty.

Failing in his original purpose, he made an attempt to draw attention, through *Fraser's Magazine*, to the destitute sick of the Metropolis, and to show how, in their particular case, the treatment of their diseases could be most economically and effectively carried out, together with principles of prevention, by one grand and comprehensive scheme.

After defining the powers of the Poor Law Board, and defending the guardians of the poor from the charge of not doing what they had no power to do, our author shadows forth that the 12,400 cases of disease of the poor in the metropolis, 6,000 of which are more or less acute cases, and 6,400 of which are old and infirm, requiring some medical attention, should be put under the most systematic hospital management, so that they may have the best medical attendance and the best possible nursing. Under the present system of workhouse management this, he contended, was impossible. He would, therefore, meet the difficulty again by the segregation principle. He would put cases of a similar kind in one large institution specially adapted for them; he would have well-paid medical officers, who understood preventive as well as curative science, to take charge of these institutions; he would have thoroughly educated nurses, or sisters, as attendants; and he would furnish the institution with baths, lavatories, water-closets, and other provisions for health of the very best kind, so as in each case to ensure the readiest means of relief or cure. In such institutions the best dietaries could be supplied at the least possible expense, and however great the first expenditure might seem, the result would be an economy in the long run.

By a further arrangement these great institutions might obtain for the sick the highest possible medical skill; they might become great schools of clinical medicine, and, by an easy transition, do away altogether with the voluntary hospital system, which, like all purely voluntary efforts, is naturally capricious, and therefore unreliable as a permanent national necessity.

PUBLIC CHARITIES IN FRANCE.

I bring to a close these summaries on Poor Law administration by a notice of one of our author's earliest papers on "Public Charities in France," published in the *London Review* in the year 1829. The paper gives an excellent description of the public charities, the sisters of charity, and the medical schools as they existed in France nearly sixty years ago. The account of the Bureaux de Bienfaisance, so centralised that they all co-operate with the hospitals and other charities with mutual advantage, is exceedingly interesting. "No healthy person," he tells us, "in a state of idleness, is assisted by a Bureau de Bienfaisance; the answer to such an applicant is, Work, and you will gain your livelihood; if you fail in procuring work, we will find it for you; but if you consume your time in idleness and your wages in debauchery, you will get no assistance; if you beg, you will be imprisoned."

Great advantages were obtained, it is pointed out, by centralising the funds in the several establishments for the relief of the poor. In the medical schools he greatly commended the system of the *concours* or public examination of the medical officers for distinguished posts. Of the sisters of charity, as nurses, he gives a doleful account; and on the hospitals of France of that day he was keenly, but not too keenly, severe, in regard to their construction and sanitary arrangements.

Finally, in this early paper we see, as it were, the germ of all that preventive work against disease and poverty which for more than half a century has filled our author's thoughts, words, and acts for the reformation of the communities belonging to his time. It forms, therefore, a fitting close to this part of the present memoirs.

VOLUME II.

—

PART III.

PREVENTION OF CRIME.

.

CHAPTER I.

MR. CHADWICK'S labours for the prevention of crime originated as far back as those which related to the prevention of disease and of poverty. They date from the year 1829, when he published his famous essay on " Preventive Police," in the *London Review.*

As stated in the biographical dissertation, the reading of this essay led Bentham to seek our author's acquaintance. It also led Mr. James Mill, the father of John Stuart Mill, to observe that the essay read like the work of a man of ripe experience ; and it had the effect of removing its author from professional life at the Bar, for which he had been educated, into the course it was his ultimate destiny to follow.

The essay on Preventive Police is still of first rank as an effort of jurisprudence, and, in many important principles, is, perhaps, as much in advance of the present as it was of the time when it first appeared.

Ten years after the appearance of the paper on Preventive Police, our author, with Mr. Charles Shaw Lefevre and Mr. Charles Rowan, signed the first Report of the Commissioners appointed to inquire into the best means of establishing an efficient Constabulary Force in the counties of England and Wales, under which the revision of the Police took place, and the present system was established. Since then, on numerous occasions, the author has reverted to the subject of Police Administration, notably in his essay on the Functions of a General Police Force for the extinction of fires, and on other subjects to be noticed in the succeeding chapters.

CHAPTER II.

PREVENTIVE POLICE.

THE essay on the Preventive Police was fortunate in appearing in the *London Review*, a periodical which, in the year 1829, possessed an influential, if not a very extensive circulation. It was the organ of the thoughtful readers of all classes and of all politics, so that every essay brought forward in it received immediate attention. At the time named also, as our author sets forth by saying, "some conspicuous portion of each day's recorded transactions adds to the impression on the public mind that the introduction of a preventive system of police has become absolutely necessary."

At that moment Sir Robert Peel was framing his famous Act for the introduction of the new body of police in London, and here again, therefore, this essay in the *London Review* came forth opportunely. The essay commences by showing that the then existing system of police consisted of disjointed bodies of men, governed separately under heterogeneous regulations; whereas a good police should be "one well-organised body of men," acting upon a system of precautions to prevent crime and public calamities; to preserve public peace and order; and to perform whatever other useful functions might be comprehended in their duties without hindering the best performances of those of an important nature.

To the few who are interested in the development of the present as it is seen in the history of the past, this essay may be very much commended for study.

But for the many who may read these pages, I have thought it best to ask Mr. Chadwick himself to give what may be called a revised *précis* of it, with some account of the Constabulary report in which he was also engaged. This he has been kind enough to do in the following notes, with a few additions expository of the working of the system in practice.

Précis of Preventive Police revised by Author in 1884.

" I found the parochial police partake to a remarkable extent of the Dogberry and Verges type, very much under the direction of the local Shallows.

" In the organisation of a systematised police force, I tried to deduce principles of action. I directed attention in the first place to the army of systematised depredators who lived by spoil ; who rose in the morning and went out to seek a livelihood by spoil including mendicity and vagrancy, but excluding for the time the crimes of passion and what may be termed the indoor crimes,—fraudulent transactions by persons whom the police could not be set to watch.

" My examinations then led me to suggest an alteration of the treatment of all the out-door criminal class.

" In the court was seen a man on trial for picking a pocket. The public saw no farther than that one offence. The inference was that it might have been committed from want of employment or from sheer poverty. The fact was that it was

one of a long series of offences committed for
a double profit, over that derivable from regular
industry. At that time the wages for rude labour in
the Metropolis did not exceed three shillings a day,
but the pickpocket's earnings did not average less
than six shillings a day; six silk handkerchiefs, which
he sold at a shilling apiece, with the chances of
other prizes, such as pocket-books, with cash in
them; and with the exception of being once or twice
'policed,' his average chances of being at large were
five years. About a fifth of the prison population of
this class I found to be removable by re-commitments
every year. The habitual crime of this class was not
of necessity or of passion, but of calculation of comparative profit. I knew Leon Fouché, a member of
the Institute of France, who took a special interest
in the condition of the prison populations, and I told
him of the results of my investigations as to the
profits of regular depredators, and he repeated my
course in France, of which he gave me this anecdote:
—He found in the prison a returned convict, to
whom he talked. 'Here again! I have thought you
a particularly sensible man. Why will you not reform, and live honestly?' 'Tenez, Monsieur,' was
his answer, 'I keep myself within bounds of modera-
tion: yet, as a thief, I realise eighteen francs a day.
But at my trade as a tailor I only earn three. I put
it to you—would *you* be honest only on that?'

"'Such fellows were noted for their frequent returns
to prison, and for their imposition on religious communities, who visited the prisons to effect reforma-
tions by religious treatment. The practised thieves
entered themselves as Protestants, or sometimes as
Jews, and pretended to have been firmly converted to

true Catholicism by the ministrations they received; which effected great rejoicings. By the influence of the nuns, they obtained extra indulgencies, and mitigation of the duration of their sentences. Some of the thieves were found to have been re-converted several times from the errors of Protestantism or Judaism.'

" The conditions of these classes of depredators suggested to me a new course of action for prevention; not by punishments or varied inflictions, as by flogging, which they disregarded, but by the reductions of the profits of their career, by the direction of the services of a preventive police. But to do this their action would be directed to carry into practice several fundamental axioms.

"First, that every arrangement which renders increased exertion necessary to obtain property illegally is so much gained to the prevention of crime.

" Secondly, that every arrangement which increased the difficulty of converting to the use of the depredators property dishonestly acquired was so much gained in diminution of the motives to commit crime.

" Thirdly, that every arrangement which diminished the chances of the personal escape of the depredator was so much gained in diminution of the motive to commit crime.

" These axioms were comparatively easy to enumerate, but it was very difficult to get the executive particulars comprehended, or to get them acted upon.

" One proper object of a Poor Law service is the reduction of mendicity and vagrancy.

" In 1837 I proposed to Lord John Russell the

appointment of a small Commission for the examination of the provincial constabulary, made up of parish constables, and to examine it with a view to the formation of a general preventive police. He gave me as a colleague Colonel, afterwards Sir Charles, Rowan, and Sir Charles Lefevre, afterwards Lord Eversleigh, as a representative of the county magistrates, but who left us when he became Speaker.

" My previous investigations served me greatly for the immediate prosecution of the inquiry; on one topic especially I went to the prison at Pentonville and examined some prisoners myself as to their past careers. I got very important aid from Mr. Clay, the prison chaplain of the Lancaster County Prison, a man of very distinguished ability, and also from the chaplain of the Lancashire Gaol, and from the governor of the prison at Pentonville. A natural son of George IV. was introduced to me who took up the subject with great ability.

" I got one most important return to show the chances of escape and the wide profits of impunity. It was from the Bank of England, to show the number of forged bank notes presented there, every note distinguishing a distinct detail and a separate offence. It was shown that during the years from 1811 to 1825 there was only one conviction to between three and four hundred offences. In subsequent years the convictions were one in 613 offences.

" The general course of the examinations taken was as to their course of life since they were in honest employment; but many of them never had been, as they had been beggars, vagrants, and thieves from infancy; where they had lived or lodged; to what houses they resorted; who did they meet there;

how and where did they dispose of their spoil. These were not questions as to any offences they had themselves committed. They answered, on the whole, without restraint and satisfactorily. We had no authority to make any promises on the information given, but it appeared very clearly that by an exercise of an authority such as is exercised in relation to offenders who give Queen's evidence, giving to one a mitigation in consideration of information which will lead to the conviction of two or more, or a source of delinquency, a great advance may be made in the work of prevention. The information of one as to the place where he was accustomed to dispose of his stolen goods would be corroborated by others; that of another as to places of resort known as flash houses, would enable the superior officer of the police to direct the service of the police to effect their extinction.

" In corroboration of our view of the effect of arrangements narrowing the hours of escape, instances were given us of burglars and thieves who, on account of the reduced profit of depredation, returned to honest occupations.

" This method of obtaining information, when systematised and regularly conducted by a public prosecutor and a chief of police, would have great advantages over the method of obtaining information through detectives.

" The method of detectives implies communication with thieves and recognition and consorting with them, which is highly objectionable; it implies a tacit recognition of the action of many for the capture of one when he is ' wanted ' on a particular charge.

" I know from Sir C. Rowan and Sir Richard

Maine that they disliked detection on principle, and only yielded to its adoption on what they deemed superior authority.

"The regular examinations of the careers of the delinquents is a means of developing incorrect points or defects in the action of the service, and of making them good, which the detective service fails to do.

"One organisation of the career of a delinquent served to bring under consideration an important application of the first axiom of prevention, viz., that every arrangement which renders increased exertion necessary to get at property illegally is so much gained to prevention.

"On inquiring of a delinquent of the cleverer class —a burglar—his career, and asking him where he next went, he said to Scotland. And what did he do there? Nothing; he only went there on an excursion tour, for nothing worth while was to be done in a Scotch town. He explained that from the number of Scotch banks, and the general habit of banking with them, tradesmen, who got interest on their deposits, were in the habit of taking over to the bank, which was close at hand, their receipts every day; so that, after all the labour of a reconnaissance and of preparation, when a shop was entered at night, only a little loose silver was to be found, which did not pay the expenses. Whilst in England, where the habit of banking had then very little extended to retail tradesmen, the receipts, not only of the day, but of the week or of the month, or even longer, were kept in the till of the counter exposed for depredation. At Mortlake, there have been repeated burglaries at the shopkeepers', and large amounts stolen. There is no branch bank nearer than Richmond. On the system of the Scotch banks there would have been three branches in this place, and perhaps all the losses that have occurred in Mortlake would have been saved. When Mr. Gladstone was Chancellor of the Exchequer, I called his attention to the large differences in crime, under the conditions of the two systems of banking, to which subject he promised his consideration. The murders of lone old people may be said to be invariably for known and suspected hoards of money, from which they would have been saved had it been understood that it was kept, for the interest as well as the security, at the bank.

"The whole of the functions of banking and their returns by Government savings banks, and the pay-ments by cheques and money orders, and the saving of the possession and the transmission of coin, are to be regarded, formulated, and cultivated as an immense source of the prevention of crime, under first axioms.

"Cattle, instead of being, as heretofore, paid for in the market in coin, are generally paid for by ante-dated cheques.

"By these means, and also by the mounted police patrol, the class of highwaymen is now extinct, and also the regular footpads; and, on the whole, by the preventive banking service, so far as it has been carried, it is probable that the predatory population has been reduced to one-half of what it formerly was.

"On another primary axiom, viz., the prevention of those arrangements which diminished the chances of the escape of depredators, as being so much gain for the prevention of crime, the plan adopted on the first institution of the police is still very defective.

"Its chief defect lay in the direction of the rank

and file of the force uniformly to the watching, and to
the place rather than the person. It is on the military system of regular patent, by which it is appointed
that the policeman shall traverse a spot every fifteen
minutes, allowing to the depredators fifteen minutes
of opportunity for crime or for escape,—a chance
adopted systematically by them.

"The arrangement has been characterised as one
of the privy sentinels everywhere to watch and guard
the hen-roosts, while giving the fox a quarter of an
hour's chance, instead of pursuing him exclusively.
The Head Constable of Hull told me that he kept
the town clear of depredators in this way. When a
ticket-of-leave man, or one from the prison, came
into the town, of which he had notice, he despatched
a constable in plain clothes, with the instruction :
Now you are to follow that man constantly, wherever
he goes ! If he goes near a shop you are to go there
too ; if he goes into a public, you are to go there too ;
or into a place of entertainment, you are to be his
shadow so long as he remains in Hull. Hull was
thus cleared of him, under the combined system, a
telegraphic description from police station to police
station, and keeping eyes upon him the whole route,
until he was cleared into honest courses. The rank
and file are of opinion that they ought, as it were,
to be allowed to break step, and to act in plain clothes
at intervals. The objection raised was this, that the
inhabitants liked to see the police in uniform, as it
gave them a sense of security. But the inhabitants
should be properly instructed as to their loss of force
by the present method, and that when a district is
cleared they may be satisfied of the fact by the
instant appearance of the police in uniform."

CHAPTER III.

IN May of 1863 Mr. Chadwick forwarded to me for publication in the *Social Science Review*, of which I was the editor, a very useful and practical paper respecting two executions for murder which had just previously taken place. There are so many valuable suggestions in this short communication, that it is herewith inserted entire, as well worthy of present study. It appeared in the *Review* on May 16th, 1863.

"The case of the murder at Ribchester, in Lancashire, for which two men have recently been executed at Liverpool, is one of a class of murders, which, from not looking at the common causes, and from not removing them where practicable, are of almost regular repetition. I would beseech all persons in position in the press as well as the pulpit, to use every occasion to give serious exhortation to all people, of whatever degree, never to keep hoards of money at home, although they may feel sure that the hoard is unknown to any one but themselves. The recent case to which I refer is thus stated:—' The murdered woman, who was an infirm old woman, seventy-nine years of age, followed the occupation of a beerhouse-keeper and small farmer. She was sole occupant of the premises, situate in a lonely part of the highway ; and as she was of somewhat penurious habits, and did a considerable business, it was generally believed by those who knew her that she was worth money. It was further rumoured that she kept her money in the house. It was known that she had sold a cow for £18 to pay her rent, and this appears to have excited the cupidity of the two culprits and two of their companions. These four men, M'Phail, Woods, Carr, and Hartley, resolved to break into Mrs. Walne's house, and plunder her of the money she possessed. In accordance with this resolution, on the night of the 10th of November they proceeded from Preston to Ribchester, and after some considerable deliberation, and a thorough survey of the premises, they went round to the back of Mrs. Walne's house, removed the lower sash of the window, and all the men entered, Woods leading, Hartley following, and the two others bringing up the rear. A lantern was lighted, and the men went upstairs, Woods still leading. In the bedroom they found the tenant of the house, she having been alarmed by the noise, sitting up in bed ; they demanded to know where she kept her money, and on refusing to tell, she was violently thrown back in bed, the place searched, and a small parcel wrapped in flannel discovered in the room. When this money had been secured, all the men went downstairs again, continuing their search of the premises, and the fatally-injured woman, who had created considerable noise by her cries, continued to scream with much vigour.'

"Now this is one of a class of cases of lone unprotected persons, old women, unprotected females, sometimes lone old men, living by themselves, the known or suspected possessors of secret hoards of money upon their premises; and the fact coming to the knowledge of prowling ruffians, the temptation of the loneliness and the defencelessness of the victims, leads to the commission of the crime to possess the booty. The possession of money or readily convertible valuables on the premises, is the temptation to theft as well as to murder; and the thefts are, of course, more numerous than murders. The possession of a hoard on the premises is a source of painful suspicion to the possessors, and of anxiety which diminishes greatly the value of the property itself. In lone places the possessors of such property can receive little protection from the police, who cannot be expected to be constantly watching out-of-the-way premises, even if they were apprised that there was money or peculiar temptation to robbers in them.

" The real preventive of these murders is simply not to keep money upon the premises, but always to go with it at once to deposit it in a Post Office Savings Bank, or some other well-known place of security. If the poor widow,—widow Walne,—after selling her cow, had gone and placed the £18 in the bank,—and she might with a little arrangement have left it at the bank at the market-town, where perhaps the cow was sold,—she would have slept in security from the robbery, and there would, of course, have been no murder. People should also be informed of the mode of carrying money about them as a preventive of robbery, namely, to get payment when they can, in cheques, dated a day or two after the time of payment.

" Many persons live at a distance from the old
savings banks. To these persons the modes of
paying money into the banks, and of drawing it out
from them, is inconvenient. Many do not wish to
be seen going to deposit money there, or to have it
known by poor relations (and consequently to be
plagued by them to lend) that they have savings.
Many put money into savings banks at a distance to
avoid such persecution, and many are not convinced
of the safety of savings banks. But the new Post
Office Savings Banks are free more or less from all
these objections. They have the highest amount
of security,—that of the nation. They are now so
much more numerous than savings banks, as to be
within reach of most persons in every part of the
country. It need not be known that the visit to the
post office is a visit to deposit money, or that it is
not a visit to inquire about a letter. But I would
urge that every one should be impressed with this
rule, that it is far more safe, far less uncomfortable,
to be known to have money deposited in a bank than
it is to have any hoard kept in the house, though it
is believed to be securely hidden, and the fact of the
hoard unknown to any one else. The income and the
expenditure of a person is known to many, and the
hoarding suspected; and the tortures of the robber
and of the murderer compel the disclosure of the
place where it is secreted. Moreover, poor people
should be impressed with the fact that the money
hoarded, or kept upon the premises, is generally kept
there at a loss. The poor widow would have got
ninepence a month as interest from the bank for
keeping the money. The legal interest paid to the
depositors in the Post Office Savings Bank is a half-

penny per month, or sixpence for the year, for every pound kept; or five shillings for every ten pounds of savings in the year;—a respectable reward for frugality. The habit of banking, as a habit of security and of comfort, and of the prevention of crime, as well as being a habit of frugality, has yet to be made popular amongst the great mass of the population including artisans and the smaller shopkeepers, in most parts of Great Britain, except in Scotland.

"The vast amount of money kept in greater or less sums on the premises by retail dealers, farmers, and others, and hence kept exposed to depredation as well as to the loss of interest, is highly discreditable to the good sense and frugality of the persons who do it. Of this publicans are a common example, and they are frequent victims of depredation. In the course of some investigations of systematic depredation, a police officer stated to me that when the extent of culpable exposure of property was considered, there ought to be little surprise at the extent of habitual depredation. Thus he said he might almost undertake to find blindfold large sums of money kept by publicans as well as by other tradesmen. He would grope his way to the bedroom on the second floor, and he would find a chest of drawers with three large drawers and two small drawers at the top; in the right hand small drawer, which had the commonest lock, one that might be opened by a nail, or by a piece of bent wire, would be found a bowl in which there was silver and gold, and now and then notes, kept for paying the brewer and the distiller. These stores are from time to time swept away by thieves. And so it is frequently with other tradesmen, who keep for months as well as weeks their quarterly collections in the most exposed manner on the premises. One common course of depredation in London is on the Sunday, when a tradesman goes out on a pleasure excursion with his wife and children, leaving a servant girl alone in charge of the house and shop. A young fellow, a thief, pays court to her, and gains admission to the premises, finds out where the money is kept, and in regular course it is stolen. I do not see why some of the more popular banks should not make arrangements for receiving cash boxes with the money collected up to Saturday after banking hours, and save the risk of keeping it on the exposed premises during the Sunday.

The Scotch are much more prudent in this respect. Shops close early on Saturday in Scotland, but the shop-keepers make exertions to clear away everything, and carry it to the banks ; so that on the Sunday they have the satisfaction of reflecting on the balances which they have in safety there.

" The practice of frugality in this respect, besides being a duty to ourselves, is in fact part of the Christian duty towards others : ' Lead us not into temptation.'

" The ancient proverb says it is ' opportunity '— in other words, temptation—' makes the thief.' On every example of the crimes of murder or robbery for money, exhortations as to the duty of prevention ought to be inculcated by judges and by magistrates. It would form an important topic of exhortation from the pulpit by the clergy. The clergy of Devonshire have set an admirable practical example in this respect by constituting themselves a collecting agency for the county savings bank. Many people have not opportunities of carrying small sums to the savings bank, which is at the county town, and the clergy perform that service for them. They take even single shillings, and deposit them regularly in the bank. In doing this, besides powerfully promoting frugality, they practically apply the doctrine, 'lead us not into temptation,' and they certainly do deliver the people from a great deal of evil, including the evil arising from spending money as fast as it is got, of making no reserve for rainy days, and the crimes arising from intemperance.' Of this I can give statistical evidence. In Lancashire the ordinary wages of the families, cotton workers and others, have been on the average double the wages of families of the working classes in Devonshire. In the Exeter Savings Bank there is a large amount of deposits from agricultural labourers, heads of families who received no greater average wages for full work than I am informed is now given as pauper relief to Irish and other labourers, for at most nominal work.

"Frugality, through temperance, in all things, has close connection with sanitary conditions, and I am induced to add to the statistical contrast, as to frugality, that of the duration of life as resulting from sanitary and social states in the two counties, Lancashire and Devonshire.

	In Lancashire.	In Devonshire.
"Amount of saving per head of the population; from deposits in the savings banks	£1 6s. 5½d.	£3 2s. 2½d.
Crimes against property with violence and malice ; proportion to every 10,000 of the population	1·91	0·44
Crimes of violence and passion (chiefly arising from drink)	0·61	0·18
Average age at death of all who die—men, women, and children	22yrs. 10m.	38yrs. 0m.
Average age at death of adults above 20 years	50yrs. 2m.	60yrs. 3m.

" My lamented friend, the late Rev. John Clay, the Chaplain of the House of Correction, made particular inquiries into the causes of crime, which corroborate my view as to the causes of these relative proportions. The excellent institutions, the co-operative stores, and the money invested in them, would, to some extent, but not to a very considerable degree, reduce the extreme disparity of savings as evidence of frugality on the side of Lancashire. The general causes of crime, as shown by such researches as those of Mr. Clay are infrugality, exposure of money, insecurity, and intemperance. He would have agreed with me that if by exertions the first figures as to relative frugality could be reversed, the reversal of most of the lower figures as to crime, as well as some of those as to the relative sanitary condition, must follow.

" I intended to have brought the whole of these facts before my friend and efficient colleague of the Poor Law Commission of Inquiry, the late benevolent Archbishop of Canterbury, and to have submitted to him the expediency of exhortations to extend the application of the example set by the clergy in Devonshire.

" Without depreciating the necessity of measures for efficiency of the police and the certainty of punishment, the course of exertion which I have indicated is one of several others which may be commended in the way of voluntary exertion for the prevention of crime; exertion which will avail where the present means of penal administration fail or are of far inferior efficiency."

CHAPTER IV.

IN the beginning of the year 1881, Mr. Chadwick published a review of the experience he had gained by the work he had done for police organisation on the subject of the suppression of riots, a topic which at that moment was creating almost as much attention as it is at the present hour.

In the passages subjoined a summary of his views is supplied direct from the original essay, the great lesson conveyed throughout being that for all local disturbances the police rather than the military force should be utilised, a principle embodied in the three following propositions.

THE AUTHOR'S PROPOSITIONS.

" 1st. That for the restoration of law and order recourse should be had to a skilled and responsible force, free from local connection and from local feeling and passion.

" 2nd. As against riots, and attacks made with weapons or means that are not deadly, never to use for repression weapons that are deadly.

" 3rd. Not to use the ordinary military force except

in cases of the greatest emergency ; and in those cases of greatest emergency, only against armed and disciplined forces, under skilled commanders.

But in the first instance, of civil force as of the Metropolitan Police Force, it is assumed that there would not be time to effect the organisations requisite to the full application of these conclusions to immediate conditions like those in Ireland. There are grave portents of conditions of insecurity from the ill-educated and ill-trained masses, including large masses of Irish population, and the extending use of arms amongst them, which, it may be submitted, renders an extended organisation of the civil force for use in place of military force a subject for early and serious consideration.

" I expect that if the present commanders of the police were required to act with their force against a mob armed with firearms, but imperfectly trained, they would prefer, in the first instance, to act against them without firearms, or at most with cutlasses, and by personal encounter, and would keep firearms in reserve for the last extremity. There is, however, a pernicious and dangerous change taking place in the extended use of the revolver, which is becoming almost general amongst town populations. These implements are now made in various forms so cheaply that they are getting into unguarded use even by very young boys. The now general use of the revolver in America appears to be a return to the time when all men went about armed with mortal weapons, and is a return to their frequent use on sudden impulses of passion, leading to fatal frays. The police there are sanctioned in their use almost at their discretion, and they do use them almost with impunity, and to an extent which would here excite strong public feeling. In the treatment of serious riots there, military force is more freely used than with us. The militia, which may be considered as the equivalent of our volunteer force, is the force generally used there, and they display little of the weakness which it is there considered we use here.

. "If the Spafields Riot in London had been dealt with as a theatrical riot,—the 'Aston Riot,'—was dealt with in New York—not one, but some hundred of the rioters would have been slain. The Irish riots in New York were suppressed with deadly volleys, and the rioters were slain by scores—probably, it was presumed in defence of liberty, law, and order. The rioters at a recent strike in Lancashire would have been confronted—as large strikes have been by our republican kinsfolk—with an array of infantry, and of cavalry, and of artillery, with grape and canister, which experience had shown would have been used unsparingly for the maintenance of the freedom of trade in service.

"In one case, indeed, of railway trade unionists, the unionists who came forward with arms were met and borne down by the militia with bloodshed, which was sanctioned by public opinion. A distinguished philanthropic republican general has expressed to me his opinion that our volunteer force should be utilised in the same way for the defence of liberty—but, for the reasons stated, it is submitted that even on extraordinary occasions the police force is preferable. Nevertheless, with the increasing use of revolvers in this country, it may be necessary for the due protection of the police itself to allow the ordinary use of them at night and also on special occasions.

" But it should be known that for extraordinary service, or for large military service, a civil police force is capable of conversion into a force that might be, in case of need, more overpowering than any ordinary military force. To support this proposition I must enter into distinct military topics; but I do so with the information derived from discussion with distinguished military officers with whom I have had the honour to be associated in civil service, including my friend the late Field-Marshal Sir John Burgoyne.

" It was a leading axiom of Napoleon, in the organisation of military force, that whilst physique is as one morale is as two.

" The superiority of a properly organised police force is in morale. They are all selected men, having the guarantees of two householders for their moral character, and they have all had an elementary education sufficing for their ordinary duties. A regiment of police officers would be more than a regiment of sappers and miners, who receive about one-third more of pay than an ordinary regiment. General Hay, the Commandant of the School of Musketry, used to say that the shooting he got with the new arms of precision was as the intelligence. It is notorious that in the rifle competitions the fast or the intemperate, though intelligent, go down before the temperate. From their greater aptitude, the recruits of the police attain better drill in weeks than the recruits to the Guards do in months. In after-dinner speeches it is usual to vaunt the valour of the British soldier, which has been very well hitherto; but for the present purposes the strict truth should be carefully regarded, and the declaration of the old Duke should be remembered—that the rank and file with which he had to fight was composed of the dregs of British society, and that they could not bear properly either victory or defeat.

"The progress of science, and the new arms of precision, create grave differences. These have to be estimated with statistics to aid the estimation. In the police-force, on the sound footing on which it is placed, there are no desertions. If any one is tired of the service, or finds anything better to do, it would be detrimental to the morale of the force to retain him. Ninety per cent. of the police are married men. Out of a total force of ten thousand seven hundred and eleven men last year, only eleven constables were charged before magistrates during the year; one was acquitted, three discharged, and six fined and imprisoned, and one held to recognisances. In the army there have been some twenty thousand court-martials, and six thousand imprisonments annually. During the last three years an average of 4,844 deserted, and 1,968 were discharged as bad characters, being a total annual loss of 6,812 from these causes alone, excluding the failures in training, from bad constitution, which are equal to rather more than two brigades of infantry on a war establishment. Now the minimum cost of an English soldier is £100 per man. Hence the direct loss from such sorts of force of low morale may be estimated. The sense of military officers on the morale of the force is denoted by their contention for the power of flogging, and also of branding, or rather of marking, for the restraint of desertions. Mr. Forbes, the able correspondent, contends strongly for the retention of the power of flogging. Such proposals to flog and mark policemen would be deemed an outrage. The popular estimate of the state of the morale of the military force at present is denoted by the resistance made by householders to having any barrack constructed near them.

" The performances of the army in the field with the new arms of precision have been in accordance with the morale in its widest sense, and have excited serious misgivings for consideration as confirmatory of the axiom quoted of the most sagacious warrior of late times. Certainly a force of the intelligence and morale of the police force would not have required forty shots to kill one Zulu with the new arms, the stated average of late military performances. None are admitted into the police force under twenty-five years. Let the value of the temperament of strictness for wielding the arms of precision at that age be estimated as compared with that of a force at an age of only eighteen or nineteen !

" The experience cited, when duly considered, will be found to justify the conclusion that one regiment of the police is worth more than two of the Guards as a protective force, and that (results considered) the police force is the cheaper force.

" This, however, takes into account the relative value of the two descriptions of force for one purpose only, as a military force, for internal or external security—that is to say, if the force of the higher efficiency were kept in barracks, could it remain without detriment to its efficacy, doing nothing. There is to be added to the account of the police force all the value of daily service against crime ; all the administrative services for the regulation of traffic ; all such services as the prevention of loss of life and property by fire, which in the case of the police in provincial towns with proper equipments has amounted to a saving of two-thirds of the previous losses; such social services as the restoration of some eight or nine thousand lost children, and three thousand lost adults, besides the care of three thousand persons from accidents in the Metropolis—these social cares add to the moral force of the police for the extraordinary service in question.

" These beneficent services gain an extent of popular moral support and implicit obedience to the police which excites the admiration of foreigners, who see with admiration, the regulation of the traffic, in which the wave of the hand of the Metropolitan policeman has more effect than the flourish of a sword in the hand of a policeman of Paris. Formerly the instinct of bystanders was to join the assailants of the police. It is now that of all, except the delinquent class, to support them, as M. Taine shows. The expectations and the exigencies of the public as to the qualities of discretion to be exercised by every private of the force are, however, it must be submitted, somewhat excessive. He appears to be expected to have the individual exercise of the acuteness of a high law officer (without any due preparation), the knowledge of the law, and immediate action upon it, with the equanimity of a judge, amidst brutal assaults without any ushers to protect him, and, indeed, with the forbearance of a saint under every provocation. Moreover, the knowledge of a physician or of a surgeon in dealing with the cases of suspended animation, whether from drunkenness or disease, which he has to deal with in the streets. All this is expected for eighteen or twenty shillings a week from every private.

"A review of the experiences cited will reaffirm our conclusions as Constabulary Force Commissioners of the efficiency and economy of a general force, of which a county, including all the towns within it, should be the unit.

Instead of that, only fragmentary forces, in towns and counties, have been adopted, at increased expense, with inferior results at all points, rendering it necessary to keep reserves of inferior military forces at various points in barracks. The separation and isolation of the county forces from each other, and from the borough force within each county, is obstructive of information, and destructive of the efficiency and economy of combined action both of which are essential to the ordinary preventive as well as to the repressive action of a police force. It is very much as a military force would be if it consisted only of separate companies of varying and inferior organisations, each acting independently of every other, without concert, the gradations of organisation, or cohesion of any considerable parts to the whole.

" I was in Lancashire in 1844, in communication through our department with the Home Office, on the occasion of the general turn-out and riotous assemblages threatening manufacturing property. There was a police force of some 600 in Manchester, where very dangerous tumults were threatened. There was a greater force in Liverpool, which, for the time, might have been brought in aid, if Liverpool had been disposed to give aid, which it was not; and there were forces throughout the county so scattered as to be incapable of that concentration which would have rendered any stationary military force unnecessary. Riots have subsequently occurred that, under a competent organised force, would have been rendered hopeless, and property has been destroyed before the military force could be brought up to arrest the destruction and restore order. On the latest occasions the repugnance to, and inconvenience of, manufacturers and large employers of labour acting in the exercise of magisterial functions, and the bitterness of the feelings engendered by it, were manifest in a higher degree than that stated as early manifested in the rural districts.

"The service was of increased danger as well as of increased expense to the locality. Throughout the country there are outcries for the reduction of local taxation, very generally by action on the principles first propounded, chiefly those for the better administration of the poor-rates. I am dealing with the question of the one branch of relief claimed by charging on the Consolidated Fund the whole of the expenditure for the maintenance of the local police forces.

"In the mounted police, which will be augmented by the proper addition of the fire service, the police organisation affords cavalry as well as infantry of a superior order. For security, the artillery of the volunteer forces, and indeed their arms, might be left for security at the police stations safely, in charge of the police. I am well advised that on occasions some thousand men might be detached from the police for several days of distant service. To this force might be added, on occasion, contingents, in like proportion, from the rest of a national police, making up an *élite* of some three thousand men, equal, for reasons stated, to double the number of ordinary military force.

" To such gain on extraordinary occasions, with collateral advantages which I need not specify, is to be added the gain derivable from unity to the ordinary every-day service of a police without any material addition to the ordinary expenditure, whether it were to be continued from the local rates or not. In administration, as in other things, there is nothing so wasteful as ignorance and want of system. It was proved before a committee, by the chief of the Essex Constabulary, Captain (now Admiral) McHardy, that the cost of the county police did not exceed the total cost of the old, and often ostensibly unpaid, separate parish constables, and the parish administrations. The same economic results were displayed by Captain Harris in respect to the county police force for Hampshire. Farmers with land on the border folded their sheep within the area of the police jurisdiction for their better protection, and acknowledged that it gave an additional value to their land. All the additional protection to life and property and new local administrative service, which is now acknowledged to be indispensable, by administrative organisation, was, in fact, given to the inhabitants gratis. It may be confidently averred that the like advances in administration would be made in the boroughs with the like advances in economy, and in efficiency for all purposes, from a superior organised force of some thirty thousand men.

" Uncontrolled or insufficiently controlled subventions made to loose local administrations, frequently augment expenses, and almost always fail to give the full amount of the relief intended for the ratepayers. Since the subventions in aid of the provincial police

the expenses of those forces have been raised above
the rate of expenses of the Metropolitan Police Force.
Under a good general organisation the expense would
be within or below it for an increased service. It is
a characteristic fact that officers, as well as privates
of the Borough Forces, have exchanged, even at
lower pay, into the County Forces, for the sake of
action under superior rule—the rule of the Borough
Forces being comparatively disagreeable to them.
The dislocated jurisdictions, under existing conditions,
occasion gaps, and in a great measure reduce the
immense benefit derivable from electrical communication in directing the attention of the whole force, and
mobilising it, from one end of the kingdom to the
other, to prevent the escape or the action of criminals,
or for use in other ways, for which the unity of the
force would give double efficiency, without increased
expense.

" 'The danger of centralisation' will be repeated
as an outcry, as against that of the police force. An
advancing intelligence will perceive that such centralisation in England will participate of the character
of the centralisation of the postal service, and of
the telegraph service, in a largely augmented,
superior, and more respousible way, at a reduced
cost, or without increased cost. The real danger of
centralisation will be great to professional crime
which is centralised; its evil will be to jobbery which
is localised in the boroughs. No. doubt, however,—
to use the medical aphorism, *Remedia non agunt
in cadaver*,—no sort of evidence will work on minds
closed to it by sinister interest and ignorance.
Nevertheless, though we had compulsory powers we
always preferred to proceed by voluntary adoption of

our measures. But then we did not accept the voice
of the rate expenders as the voice of the ratepayers.
An Assistant Commissioner was sent to examine the
local defects, and expound them by printed reports.
He also, at open public meetings of the inhabitants,
answered objections verbally, by which violent
opposition on the part of the rate expenders was
almost invariably overcome. When it is put to
the ratepayers by a *plebiscitum* or a house-to-house
collection of the votes whether they will vote to
continue paying heavily for a notoriously inferior
service or have a superior service gratis, my experience is that the results of proper expositions may be
confidently anticipated."

CHAPTER V.

THE POLICE AND THE EXTINCTION OF FIRES.

ON a special report made to the Society of Arts in 1876-7, Mr. Chadwick pressed strongly for making the police everywhere, under one uniform system, the practical fire brigades of the country. This was in accord with the recommendations which he had advanced in the essay on Preventive Police in 1828, and with his colleagues in the Constabulary Report of 1839.

The arguments in support of this service by the police were supplied in the following extracts from the paper now in hand.

THE ECONOMY AND EFFICIENCY OF A POLICE FORCE.

"An elementary principle of political economy ruling administrative economy, is the economy of force for the public service—a principle which is displayed in its contravention in the separate arrangements of the functions of the police service and of the fire brigade service of the Metropolis.

"I may claim in an accepted position as a political economist, and in my public service as a Commissioner of inquiry, to have elaborated, with my colleagues, some of the leading administrative principles bearing on the subject-matter in question. These principles were, indeed, expounded in a paper so early as 1828 as grounds for the establishment of a preventive police in the Metropolis, and again in our first report of 1839, as Commissioners of inquiry, as to the state of the local Constabulary, and into the means requisite for the establishment of a provincial police force.

" The appointment of a separate force to deal independently with the work of fire extinction, is an example of the dereliction of the administrative principle there enunciated.

" The Metropolitan Fire Brigade, under the Board of Works, is a force of 400 trained firemen acting under an independent command. It has been declared by the chief officer of the force that it is strained by the ordinary fire service, and that to meet the requirements of the Metropolis it ought to be augmented to a force of 930 men, it being assumed that the general police force will have no more to do with the fire service than they have at present; that is to say, of only waiting, on the occurrence of a fire, until the arrival of the special force, and then maintaining order and preventing obstruction to its action by the crowds.   Our first report served as a text book for the first organisation of provincial police forces, and the principles recited were subsequently generally adopted, together with our further recommendation that the extinction of fires should be a primary service of the police force, and that every police-station should be a fire-station, with engines, hose, fire-ladders, and other apparatus requisite for that service. In our report of 1850, from the General Board of

Health, we recommended for the fire service as well as for the sanitary service that the water supplies should be placed on a public footing, on the constant system at high pressure, and that hydrants with hose, to which the police should have keys, should be placed in all the streets, so that they might apply hose at once for the extinction of fires.

ECONOMY OF THE COMBINED POLICE SERVICE.

" The cities of Manchester, Liverpool, and Glasgow, present examples of the application of these principles. In these cities the entire police force, it may be said, is constituted, with more or less of variation, as a fire force. The greater proportion of the men have been taught the use of the hose, a special body being trained, as a brigade, on the principles elaborated by the late Mr. Braidwood, to the working of steam and hose or of manual engines, under the general command of the chief of the police, supervised by a fire committee.

" The results yielded by these cities show that the cost of protecting life and property, under the existing conditions of the separate brigade force, in the Metropolis is more than double, and approaches to threefold the cost of a combined police force system, with the command of hydrants, on the administrative principles originally propounded. But whilst this separate system of the fire brigade force is thus more than double, or some forty thousand pounds of annual cost to the ratepayers, it has been proved not to have above one-third of the beneficial result in the protection of life and property that it has in

the provincial cities administered in conformity to
principle.

"In those cities the calls for brigade engines
amount only to 3 or 4 per cent. of the cases of fire.
At Glasgow so little have the brigade men to do,
that at the chief brigade station the men are mechanics employed in manufacturing hydrants and
hose, and other apparatus, who are paid about six
shillings a week extra wages, on condition of their
attendance with the engines on the occurrence of
calls for them. Mr. Bryson, the chief of the fire
service, has stated, that if London had a constant
system of water supply at high pressure, about one-
half even of the present number of men of the
Metropolitan Brigade force would suffice for the same
amount of service. Glasgow, he observed, has been
increasing its population at a rate of 10,000 a year,
but the brigade has not been increased under the
present system. On the system of the Metropolis,
Glasgow would have required a fourfold brigade
force, and yet would not have been by any means
so well protected. In the instance of Manchester,
which has been well compared with London, Mr.
Tozer, a distinguished fire brigade officer, states
that in Manchester the losses of life and property are
less than one-third the rate they are in London. He
observes upon the comparative expense: 'In London
and Liverpool a considerable sum is expended in
supporting a salvage corps. We do the work in Manchester with the fire brigade. In fact, in Manchester
we hardly know what it is to have a fire requiring the
work of salvage; 97 per cent. of our fires are confined to the room in which they occur.' The calls
for the Metropolitan Fire Brigade average at present

from four to five per diem.   On correct systems, as
above displayed, of calls in 4 per cent. of the cases of
fire, the calls for the service of the Metropolitan
Brigade would be about one a week.

Superior Efficiency of Small Force Near, to Large Force Distant.

"On the principle we propounded in our report,[*]
that fire extinction, and small appliances near, are
of more importance than great appliances at a distance, we stated that, ' taking the point of actual
ignition, the value of a supply of water diminishes in
a ratio rapidly increasing with the lapse of time
before the arrival of such supply. In the first minute
of the ignition a jugful of water may suffice ; in the
second not a pailful ; in the third not three or four
pailfuls ; and in a few minutes more nothing will
suffice but supplies that can be applied only by
engine-power.' Five minutes was the limit of time
laid down by Braidwood, in his evidence as the
limit of time for relief to be effectual for the protection of life and property. But the runs from the
brigade stations, as maintained by the Board of
Works, average more than a mile and a half, and
are not executed, at the quickest, in less than fifteen
minutes, and their requirement then is 2,000 gallons
a minute—i.e., a thousand pailfuls a minute—according to Captain Shaw's evidence. Very likely, under
the continuance of such a system, when fires have
got ahead ! But in the cities where the service has
been arranged in conformity with the principles here
laid down for the Metropolis, water is applied from

[*] "On the Supply of Water to the Metropolis in 1850," pp. 245 to 261.

the hydrants in little more than three minutes, or in less time than it usually takes to attach horses and start the distant brigade engine, when, in the majority of cases, scarcely a fifth of such a quantity of water is used for the whole time.

SUPERIOR EFFICIENCY OF THE PRESENT METROPOLITAN FIRE POLICE SERVICE.

" Nevertheless, good as these provincial police fire services are, I think it just to the Metropolitan Police Force to state, from information as to what they now do when they have fire services to perform, with the proper appliances of a constant supply and hydrants, as at Woolwich, the Houses of Parliament, and other public establishments—in such instances they have brought jets to bear from hydrants at forty yards' distance in about one minute, and at sixty yards in about two minutes. In the fire drill of the Metropolitan Police at Woolwich, the men usually rig out an engine and get it into play through four forty-feet jets in about one minute and three-quarters of time. On a trial to test speed, on a false alarm of fire by telegram from Plumstead gate to the main gate of Woolwich Arsenal, stating that the Carriage Square saw mills, 700 yards distant from the main gate, were on fire, the police off duty started with fire-hose, reels, and the engine, and they arrived, the first reel in five minutes, the second in five and a half minutes, the third and fourth in six minutes, and the fifth, with the engine, in seven minutes, and they were all ready. But it may be expected that the efficiency of the Metropolitan Police services will be much in the order of the magnitude of the establishments in which they have practice. Portsmouth Dockyards are under the charge of a Metropolitan Police force of 200 men; the Devonport Dockyards, 160 men; Chatham, 150; Woolwich Arsenal, 140; and Pembroke Dockyard, 30 men,—altogether, a trained fire force of 680 men, having charge of manufactories, large workshops, containing combustible materials and property amounting to some millions of money in value, and guarding against the carelessness and recklessness amongst some thousands of workpeople. This force, besides that in charge of the Houses of Parliament, the British Museum, and other public establishments in the Metropolis, is necessarily of superior training, from constant occupation in the work of prevention, as compared with a force which has no such charge of local apparatus, and is engaged only on the work of extinction.

ELECTRIC SCIENCE AVAILABLE FOR FIRE EXTINCTION.

"In fires even seconds of time are precious, and these Metropolitan Police services are the closest of any which we have hitherto had in this country. Electrical science has shortened the time of sending 'calls' to stations; but it has yet to receive a more developed application than it yet has in this country. Upwards of three minutes of time is expended here in getting the horses put to, when the call arrives at the brigade stations. But in Philadelphia and other American cities, by an arrangement of an electric telegraph, the horses at the station are detached from their stalls in an instant, and, being drilled, turn round of their own accord, run each to their

station at the engine, and are hitched on and start
in less than half a minute. Electric communication
is made available there from houses to the police, as
well as from the patrolling police to the fire engine
stations.

Loss of Time from Excessive Distance.

" The fatal excess of distance from relief in the
Metropolis is due to the original and continued
dereliction of settled administrative principle for the
constitution of a police force, by the institution of a
separate force, exclusively, for fire service. By this
arrangement, as shown by Mr. Swanton, the experienced director of the Salvage Corps, the public safety
has not only not been increased, but has been
diminished ; neither, as he asserts, has the progress
of serious fires been arrested, nor can they be
further arrested considerably by the means proposed
by the Metropolitan Board of Works.

" There are now fifty brigade stations which the
Board of Works propose to extend or to enlarge.
But this enlargement, the numbers remaining the
same, will not bring relief nearer to the public, for
the distances apart must remain the same. The
arrangement in accordance with our original principle of administrative organisation, of assigning the
fire service as an integral and primary function of
the police service is verified in practice in the
instance cited of the provincial cities, where the
principle has been applied, and creates more than
double the stations and more than double the security.
As stated by Captain Harris, there are now 152
convertible stations, of which police-stations seventy-

five are within and seventy-seven beyond the boundary of the Metropolitan Board of Works. The police-stations have not, I consider, been arranged systematically, but as circumstances permitted, at the time of the first institution of the force. A re-arrangement for the paramount object of fire service, that might be brought about by a return to correct principles, would be conducive to the improvement of the efficiency of the general force for its ordinary service. It would lead to important improvements in the sanitary construction of the stations. But in respect to the gain from the increase of stations derivable from amalgamation and unity, it may be stated as a rule, that the force of one man for fire service at half a mile is worth four men at three-quarters of a mile, worth six men at a mile, and worth eight men at a mile and a half. How much longer time will it take to get this elementary principle of fire prevention perceived and applied!

" The augmentation of the separate brigade force from 400 to 900 is, then, in contravention of correct principles, and has no support from officers of very long experience in the brigade, such as that fire brigade officer, Mr. Tozer, of Manchester, who has had experience of the working of combined force, which Captain Shaw has not had. The Captain's proposed augmentation of the force at distant stations will not bring them nearer to the fires in the essential point of time. It would, doubtless, bring an increase of the existing force to check the extension of extraordinary fires,—such as the fire at the Pantechnicon,—which only occur once in some twelve months. But the proposed increase of in-dependent brigade force to 900 men would be very inferior to the combined police force, which, as Captain Harris puts it, would be a fire service of 10,000 men.

Reduction of Crime of Incendiarism by Police Service.

"By keeping the police fire service out of the house, the opportunities of immediate observation, and pursuit, and detection of incendiaries has been very much kept from their knowledge. The fire brigade have no crime preventive functions, neither have the salvage corps. It is held by the insurance companies that it is not to their interest to prosecute, even in cases of loss to themselves, and that they only add to their losses by acting as public prosecutors. Under the existing conditions, the practice of incendiarism for insurance money is far more prevalent than the public are aware. It is estimated by officers of extensive experience, that full one-third of the fires in the Metropolis have been not accidental, but by design. In the feeling prevalent upon the subject, but under loose notions of administrative principle, it has been proposed that there shall be some distinct inquiry, by some distinct authority, into the origin of every fire, and a distinct service appointed to conduct it, with distinct means of prosecution.

"The present conditions, maintained by the Board of Works in the Metropolis, of the large brigade stations at a mile and a half distance, gives time for the fire work of the incendiary to get full hold of the building and to obliterate the traces of its preparation. At the time of the promulgation of our

original measures, systematic incendiarism for insurance money was rife at Hamburg.   When those
measures were adopted as they were there, with the
street hydrants under the charge of the police, and
smoke was seen arising from some closed premises,
the door was burst open by the policemen and a jet
of water immediately applied, and the fire was
promptly extinguished; at the same time, an incendiary trail was displayed with which the fire had
not time to communicate.   It takes time to spread a
fire through premises which an application of water
in two or three minutes arrests.   In Manchester
they have rarely any trace of the practice of incendiarism for insurance money.   In Liverpool it
has received a very satisfactory check.

PROTECTION FROM FIRES AND PANICS AT THEATRES,
      AND OTHER PUBLIC ESTABLISHMENTS.

" Securities should be taken, by a public authority,
for protection against these calamities before such
edifices are constructed or opened for the reception
of the public.   All large places of public entertainment and large hotels, many stories high, and for
the accommodation of several hundred persons,
ought to be included in the like provisions for protection.   It was suggested by witnesses before the
Select Committee, that an independent special fire
authority should be appointed for the purpose.   But
this proposal is objectionable in principle, as involving either a separate and weak establishment, or,
if it be a strong one, an excessively expensive one.
On consideration, it will be seen that the most

eligible course will be to charge such duty upon the fire service of the general police force, because, of necessity, it must have the largest amount of experience for its guidance, and the greatest executive force to see to the constant application of that experience in any provision for security that science and practice may suggest. At present the special fire service of the Metropolitan Police has a greater amount of practical experience in fire prevention than any other force in the country. But for a high order of skill, and a vigilant patrolling force, combined with a force of engine power, Portsmouth, and other dockyards, would have been repeatedly destroyed.

"Under the existing arrangements, such provisions as there are for the prevention of fires in the Metropolis fall to district surveyors under the Board of Works—architects in private practice, not of the highest practice, but in practice much needing amendment, as the frequent destruction of property in houses of their construction shows. The work of fire prevention increases in speciality with the magnitude of the building and the numbers of the people to be accommodated and protected, and the speciality of service applicable to the purpose rises above the highest architectural practice. The care against fire necessarily accompanies the elaborate provisions now required in public edifices for warming, for lighting, and ventilation. The new great theatres are becoming elaborations of new practical science. The new Grand Opera at Vienna has some twenty miles of pipe to be regulated for the distribution of warmth, and between five and six thousand jets of gas to be regulated for its lighting, with electric communication from a central office to collect thermometrical conditions of all parts of the theatre. The provisions against fire, in progress when I visited it, were correspondingly elaborate. These developments of science, in the larger constructions, are applicable in their degree to lesser buildings. Provision might, it should be submitted, be most advantageously made for them in connection with the present high practice of the general police service, which might conveniently have such consultative scientific aid as is now provided for the Houses of Parliament for the guidance of the large executive service of rank and file available for the public protection."

CHAPTER VI.

TRICYCLES FOR POLICE.

THE last essay which our author has given to the world—published, in fact, in the present year, 1887—has reference to the use of the tricycle by the police for the prevention of crime.

From the first introduction of the tricycle, Mr. Chadwick has taken the greatest interest in the science and practice of cycling. Not one of our youths interested in the race or the tour on the bicycle or tricycle, has shown more enthusiasm on this matter than he. At the Sanitary Congress at Leamington, ten years ago, over which I had the honour to preside, there was one of the first great exhibitions of cycling machines, in which he took the greatest delight. He considered that the Exhibition was one of the most legitimate as well as the most interesting parts of the Congress, and was full of suggestions to the manufacturers respecting the construction of machines to meet various national necessities.

The value of the tricycle as a means of obtaining healthy exercise, was at once seized by him as a matter of course. But he was not less quick at perceiving and explaining the advantage which the

machine would be to the police, and on the 30th of
November, 1886, he conveyed to the Society of Cyclists
his latest views, in the essay which follows, and which
forms the concluding pages of these volumes.

"Perhaps not one person who is present has any
recollection of the time when the modern policeman
was an officer who had no existence. I am one who
has the most perfect recollection of that time, and
am also the one who took, perhaps, the leading part
in the suggestions which led up to the system of
preventive police which we now possess.

"When I tell you that my first essay on this subject was written in the reign of King William IV., you
will be able to form an opinion how great an interest
I have taken in the body of men to whom we entrust
so much authority and so much responsibility.

"In the early days of which I speak the small
number of officers that belonged to our badly-
organised police establishments performed a far
greater amount of service than the whole of the
officers attached to the parochial establishments of
the country. Of the men belonging to each of the
police offices, five or six of the most active often
performed more duty than all the rest of the men
belonging to the establishment. The best organised
body of officers was that of the Thames Police, which
was formed under the superintendence of Mr. Harriot
and Mr. Colquhoun. It soon put an end to all the
immense extent of systematic depredation which was
formerly committed on property on the river Thames.

"At that same period I ventured to point out that
all testimony and all experience proved that in the
government of a body of men like the police their

pecuniary interests could alone be relied upon as motives of constant and sure operation. 'If,' I said, quoting my own words of fifty years ago, 'if these interests were carefully and skilfully adjusted, they would act with the certainty of gravitation.' I pointed out that in order to determine correctly the reward due to police officers as preventors of crime, their real service in prevention ought to be ascertained, and that to arrive at correctness on this point, the amount of crime committed, then most imperfectly calculated, should be correctly discovered and made known. The service of the police would then be determined by comparing the number of their detections with the returns of crime committed. I had no doubt that by thus giving the officers an interest in diminishing crime, a great and necessary step would be attained towards creating an efficient police.

"I judged also that it would be expedient to place the police on a more respectable footing, to give them an adequate remuneration for valuable and responsible service—cheap service being in a police, as well as in most things where talent is required, uniformly bad service. It was requisite, I contended, to establish among them gradations of rank ; to make their appointments for life, with pensions or superannuation, as in the army ; to make promotion determinable by the amount and value of services ; and, *cæteris paribus*, by seniority ; to concentrate responsibility at each step on individuals ; and, as the best security against improper appointments, to let the officers be chosen in general by magistrates, who should be considered responsible for peace and security within their district.

"I regret to say that many of these original propositions have not been carried out. At the same time, I admit that the general organisation of the police force has been, on the whole, a distinguished success, and that we rely for our protection on a body of men who are every day becoming more conspicuous for their intelligence, activity, respectability, and discipline. The introduction of the drill system has been conducive, not only to their efficiency as a protecting force, but to their own health and regulation of habit and life.

"These few notes bearing on the history of a great national development will not, I hope, be taken amiss as introductory to one or two new suggestions on a subject which is specially germane to the work of a society of cyclists, which has for one of its principal objects the utilisation of the art of cycling for national wants and national necessities—namely, the use of the tricycle by the police.

"I had the pleasure of introducing the attention of your president, Dr. Richardson, to the use of the tricycle as a sanitary exercise at the Leamington Sanitary Congress in 1877; and at that same period I was also led to suggest the employment of the tricycle as a means of additional security by the service of the police forces. With the object of eliciting a few minutes' discussion on a subject so important by a learned society which may be said to make cycling a speciality, I have thrown together a few new notes in continuance of my original suggestion.

"At present in the suburbs of the Metropolis the police patrol singly at the rate of three miles an hour, and the present arrangement as to single patrol is that the policeman shall pass every part of his beat once in a quarter of an hour. The defect of this arrangement is that depredators calculate upon the opportunities afforded to them during this quarter of an hour, and arrange for it; they watch for the approach of the patrol, and may hear his footfall, or may, in the event of pursuit, outrun him, and make their escape. If surprised, they may overmaster the single unarmed policeman, as they have repeatedly done, by murdering him.

"As a Commissioner of inquiry into the organisation of a general force, I have proposed a patrol by a tricycle worked by two men abreast, armed with revolvers. The patrol with the tricycle would be regulated to be worked at eight miles an hour instead of three. There would be no footfall to be heard, and the patrol would be silent for all suburban districts. If there are any men perceived at night with a trap that takes to flight, the tricycle patrol may put on extra speed which will keep them in sight or overtake them, for the tricycle has now attained a possible speed of eighteen miles an hour. The difficulties of the escape from two men would be enormously increased.

"Another great advantage which would spring from this method of following and detecting crime and criminals would be the greater rapidity and certainty of detection. These influences alone are powerfully deterrent, because, when the best is said of him, and the strongest excuses are made for him, the professed criminal is by nature, as a rule, a timorous man at heart. He may be desperate when he is at bay; but he is usually a man of a physical constitution, has an extreme dread of being caught, and trusts far more to cunning than to courage. He lives, in fact, by concealment, is powerless in the light of day, and when once outwitted, is undone. In those early days of which I have spoken, Mr. Wyatt, a magistrate of Lambeth, when asked if he had anything to suggest for the benefit of his district, said he would employ gaslights at the openings of the different courts and alleys, the known resorts of thieves in the streets, and which lights, of a different form from the ordinary lamp, would warn passengers to look about them. 'I consider gas,' said Mr. Wyatt, 'without presuming to play upon the word, essential to an enlightened police.' Mr. Lee, the High Constable of Westminster, also told us that the widening of the pavements had done more than anything to prevent pocket-picking.

"In like manner the invention of modern times, the Tandem Tricycle, could be pressed into the service of an enlightened police. The lamps could either be used to conceal the armed officers in their approach, or to throw light into dark courts, alleys, or lanes. Near a house threatened with burglars one can imagine no surer method of protection. The deterrent effect would be invincible.

"On occasions, as on the outburst of serious fires or of calamities, by telegraphing or telephoning to the police stations, more rapid concentrations of available force may be effected than is practicable with the single mounted police force, if the tricycle were brought into use for this purpose.

"Tricycles may be used with great economy for the collection and movement of volunteer forces, ordinarily, to the practice grounds, and for their return home from thence.

"Cycling has been pronounced to be an eminently sanitary exercise, as good at least as pony-riding. It would admit of much use for curative service, for the relief of the police from the diseases to which they are liable from long exposure to the lethal influences of the ill-conditioned urban districts,—a relief which may be given by changes of service and the tricycle patrolling of well-conditioned suburban or rural districts on the prescription of the health-officer.

"It is nine years ago since the idea of using the tricycle by the police was proposed by me, and I expected that by this time some practical application of it would have come into force. I am glad to say that the Chief Constable of Coventry has introduced the tricycle there, and finds it highly successful.

"He makes to me the following report :—

"'The Chief Constable of Coventry, Mr. John Norris, has much pleasure in stating that a tricycle ("Salvo") has been in use by the members of this force for the last six years, and he can endorse all that is said by Colonel Cobbe, one of the Inspectors of Constabulary, and even say more in its favour.'

"Extract from the Colonel's official report to the Home Office: 'Lately the Watch Committee have provided a tricycle, at a cost of eighteen guineas, for the use of the force. It is represented that it has been in constant use, and has been found most useful, easily ridden, and comparatively noiseless; the night inspector is able to visit all parts of the city in his supervision, very frequently and with ease ; it is considered a good substitute for a horse and cart where this conveyance is not provided, and is used for the purpose of officers serving summonses and making inquiries within a short radius of the city.'

" Mr. Norris adds further that the use of the tricycle in his district is in course of extension.

" The sanitary benefits that cyclists, as it appears to me, may achieve, would also accrue by their agitating, with the concurrence of the police, for the amendment of all our roads,—civic, suburban, and provincial,—so as to bring roads everywhere into the same uniform condition of solidity for saving of friction and consequent loss of power.

" The cycling fraternity, containing as it does so many thousand observers, must, I should assume, by this time have obtained a very accurate knowledge of the state of all the roads in the kingdom, and if the police could be made to adopt cycling as a part of their efficiency and equipment, the reconstruction of the roads, so as to bring them all into unity, would be found to be a national necessity that could not be set aside, because the reformation would be to the saving of traffic and locomotion of every kind.

" I was told by the great inventor of the modern tricycle, Starley, that he could produce a vehicle on which, on a level asphalte road, one man could move four men and two men eight. My own plan of such a road would be the provision of a wheel track of the hardest asphalte on the main road and the hardest concrete on the bye-roads. Three miles of the hardest asphalte wheel tracks could be laid at the cost of one mile of iron tramway, and with as good results in the saving of force ; and, in the end, the construction would lead to a great saving in the rates. In my own parish I found that the plan would save forty pounds a mile on our eight miles of road, whilst it would also save a third of the force now lost in propulsion of cycling machines and all other classes of wheel conveyances. At the same time there would be great saving from dust, which is as injurious to the lungs as to the clothes of those who meet it.

" I throw out these hints to show that cyclists have before them a larger economical and sanitary reform than has yet been thought of, in regard to roads, by political parties, and which has been ignored shamefully by vestry and local authorities

" The only objection that I can see to the use of the tricycle by the police force is the expense. But again I urge that expense for intelligent service is always the best economy in the long run. My friend, the late Field Marshal Sir John Burgoyne, was wont to say that the sappers and miners, as an intelligent force, were, notwithstanding their double pay, a cheap force when all the results obtained from them were considered. Before a select Committee of the House of Commons it was proved in detail in regard to the Essex Constabulary that, omitting the towns which diminished the economy, the total expense of all was within the expenses of the unpaid parish constabulary. The like conclusions were established in respect to the Hampshire Constabulary ; and I believe on testimony, in spite of the increased pay of men and officers, the police are, all results considered, as cheap a force as any in the public service.

" In conclusion I would point out, as another illustration of the value of the tricycle for police purposes, a rule I insisted upon so far back as the year 1829 —namely, that in order effectually to diminish the chances of success which so often form the motive to depredation, it is requisite that all practicable measures to insure detection should be taken upon

' each ' of the individual acts, from the aggregate of which those chances are made up.

" The speedy publication of any act of delinquency, by exciting general alarm, creates general vigilance, and thus increases to the depredator the danger and difficulty of all future depredations. By a speedy and complete collection and publication of information concerning all sorts of delinquency committed, more would be done in reducing crime, and at a cheaper rate, than by any possible increase of the existing establishments. For by this means the public at large will be converted into a police; and each individual member, by being put upon his guard, would perform unconsciously a great portion of the duties of a police officer."

FINIS.

Printed by Hazell, Watson, & Viney, Ld., London and Aylesbury.

Catalogue of Books

PUBLISHED BY

MESSRS. LONGMANS, GREEN, & CO.

39 PATERNOSTER ROW, LONDON, E.C.

Abbey.—*The English Church and its Bishops*, 1700-1800. By Charles J. Abbey, Rector of Checkendon. 2 vols. 8vo. 24*s.*

Abbey and Overton.—*The English Church in the Eighteenth Century.* By Charles J. Abbey, Rector of Checkendon, and John H. Overton, Rector of Epworth and Canon of Lincoln. Crown 8vo. 7*s.* 6*d.*

Abbott.—*The Elements of Logic.* By T. K. Abbott, B.D. 12mo. 3*s.*

Acton. — *Modern Cookery for Private Families.* By Eliza Acton. With 150 Woodcuts. Fcp. 8vo. 4*s.* 6*d.*

Æschylus. — *The Eumenides of Æschylus:* a Critical Edition, with Metrical English Translation. By John F. Davies, M.A. Professor of Latin in the Queen's College, Galway. 8vo. 7*s.*

A. K. H. B.—*The Essays and Contributions of A. K. H. B.*—Uniform Cabinet Editions in crown 8vo.

Autumn Holidays of a Country Parson, 3*s.* 6*d.*
Changed Aspects of Unchanged Truths, 3*s.* 6*d.*
Commonplace Philosopher, 3*s.* 6*d.*
Counsel and Comfort from a City Pulpit, 3*s.* 6*d.*
Critical Essays of a Country Parson, 3*s.* 6*d.*
Graver Thoughts of a Country Parson. Three Series, 3*s.* 6*d.* each.
Landscapes, Churches, and Moralities, 3*s.* 6*d.*
Leisure Hours in Town, 3*s.* 6*d.*
Lessons of Middle Age, 3*s.* 6*d.*
Our Little Life. Two Series, 3*s.* 6*d.* each.
Our Homely Comedy and Tragedy, 3*s.* 6*d.*
Present Day Thoughts, 3*s.* 6*d.*
Recreations of a Country Parson. Three Series, 3*s.* 6*d.* each.
Seaside Musings, 3*s.* 6*d.*
Sunday Afternoons in the Parish Church of a Scottish University City, 3*s.* 6*d.*

Allen.—*Flowers and their Pedigrees.* By Grant Allen. With 50 Illustrations engraved on Wood. Crown 8vo. 5*s.*

Amos.—*Works by Sheldon Amos.*

A Primer of the English Constitution and Government. Crown 8vo. 6*s.*

A Systematic View of the Science of Jurisprudence. 8vo. 18*s.*

Anstey.—*The Black Poodle,* and other Stories. By F. Anstey, Author of 'Vice Versâ.' With Frontispiece by G. Du Maurier and Initial Letters by the Author. Crown 8vo. 6*s.*

Aristophanes. — *The Acharnians of Aristophanes.* Translated into English Verse by Robert Yelverton Tyrrell, M.A. Crown 8vo. 2*s.* 6*d.*

Aristotle.—*The Works of.*

The Politics, G. Bekker's Greek Text of Books I. III. IV. (VII.) with an English Translation by W. E. Bolland, M.A. ; and short Introductory Essays by A. Lang, M.A. Crown 8vo. 7*s.* 6*d.*

The Politics; Introductory Essays. By Andrew Lang. (From Bolland and Lang's 'Politics.') Crown 8vo. 2*s.* 6*d.*

The Ethics; Greek Text, illustrated with Essays and Notes. By Sir Alexander Grant, Bart. M.A. LL.D. 2 vols. 8vo. 32*s.*

The Nicomachean Ethics, Newly Translated into English. By Robert Williams, Barrister-at-Law. Crown 8vo. 7*s.* 6*d.*

Armstrong.—*Works by George Francis Armstrong, M.A.*

Poems : Lyrical and Dramatic. Fcp. 8vo. 6s.

King Saul. (The Tragedy of Israel, Part I.) Fcp. 8vo. 5s.

King David. (The Tragedy of Israel, Part II.) Fcp. 8vo. 6s.

King Solomon. (The Tragedy of Israel, Part III.) Fcp. 8vo. 6s.

Ugone : A Tragedy. Fcp. 8vo. 6s.

A Garland from Greece ; Poems. Fcp. 8vo. 9s.

Stories of Wicklow ; Poems. Fcp. 8vo. 9s.

The Life and Letters of Edmund J. Armstrong. Fcp. 8vo. 7s. 6d.

Armstrong.—*Works by Edmund J. Armstrong.*

Poetical Works. Fcp. 8vo. 5s.

Essays and Sketches. Fcp. 8vo. 5s.

Arnold. — *Works by Thomas Arnold, D.D. Late Head-master of Rugby School.*

Introductory Lectures on Modern History, delivered in 1841 and 1842. 8vo. 7s. 6d.

Sermons Preached mostly in the Chapel of Rugby School. 6 vols. crown 8vo. 30s. or separately, 5s. each.

Miscellaneous Works. 8vo. 7s. 6d.

Arnold.—*A Manual of English Literature,* Historical and Critical. By Thomas Arnold, M.A. Crown 8vo. 7s. 6d.

Arnott.—*The Elements of Physics or Natural Philosophy.* By Neil Arnott, M.D. Edited by A. Bain, LL.D. and A. S. Taylor, M.D. F.R.S. Woodcuts. Crown 8vo. 12s. 6d.

Ashby. — *Notes on Physiology for the Use of Students Preparing for Examination.* With 120 Woodcuts. By Henry Ashby, M.D. Lond. Fcp. 8vo. 5s.

Atelier (Thé) du Lys; or, an Art Student in the Reign of Terror. By the Author of ' Mademoiselle Mori.' Crown 8vo. 2s. 6d.

Bacon.—*The Works and Life of.*

Complete Works. Edited by R. L. Ellis, M.A. J. Spedding, M.A. and D. D. Heath. 7 vols. 8vo. £3. 13s. 6d.

Letters and Life, including all his Occasional Works. Edited by J. Spedding. 7 vols. 8vo. £4. 4s.

The Essays ; with Annotations. By Richard Whately, D.D., 8vo. 10s. 6d.

The Essays ; with Introduction, Notes, and Index. By E. A. Abbott, D.D. 2 vols. fcp. 8vo. price 6s. Text and Index only, without Introduction and Notes, in 1 vol. fcp. 8vo. 2s. 6d.

The BADMINTON LIBRARY,

edited by the Duke of Beaufort, K.G. assisted by Alfred E. T. Watson.

Hunting. By the Duke of Beaufort, K.G. and Mowbray Morris. With Contributions by the Earl of Suffolk and Berkshire, Rev. E. W. L. Davies, Digby Collins, and Alfred E. T. Watson. With Coloured Frontispiece and 53 Illustrations by J. Sturgess, J. Charlton, and Agnes M. Biddulph. Crown 8vo. 10s. 6d.

Fishing. By H. Cholmondeley-Pennell. With Contributions by the Marquis of Exeter, Henry R. Francis, M.A., Major John P. Traherne, and G. Christopher Davies.

Vol. I. Salmon, Trout, and Grayling. With 150 Illustrations. Cr. 8vo. 10s. 6d.
Vol. II. Pike and other Coarse Fish. With 58 Illustrations. Cr. 8vo. 10s. 6d.

Racing and Steeplechasing. By the Earl of Suffolk, W. G. Craven, The Hon. F. Lawley, A. Coventry, and A. E. T. Watson. With Coloured Frontispiece and 56 Illustrations by J. Sturgess. Cr. 8vo. 10s. 6d.

Shooting. By Lord Walsingham and Sir Ralph Payne - Gallwey, with Contributions by Lord Lovat, Lord Charles Lennox Kerr, The Hon. G. Lascelles, and Archibald Stuart Wortley. With 21 full-page Illustrations and 149 Woodcuts in the text by A. J. Stuart-Wortley, Harper Pennington, C. Whymper, J. G. Millais, G. E. Lodge, and J. H. Oswald-Brown.

Vol. I. Field and Covert. Cr. 8vo. 10s. 6d.
Vol. II. Moor and Marsh. Cr. 8vo. 10s. 6d.

Cycling. By Viscount Bury, K.C.M.G. and G. Lacy Hillier. With a Contribution by Joseph Pennell. With numerous Illustrations by Viscount Bury and Joseph Pennell. Crown 8vo. 10s. 6d.

₊ Other volumes in preparation.

Bagehot.—*WORKS BY WALTER BAGEHOT, M.A.*

BIOGRAPHICAL STUDIES. 8vo. 12s.

ECONOMIC STUDIES. 8vo. 10s. 6d.

LITERARY STUDIES. 2 vols. 8vo. Portrait. 28s.

THE POSTULATES OF ENGLISH POLITICAL ECONOMY. Crown 8vo. 2s. 6d.

Bagwell. — *IRELAND UNDER THE TUDORS,* with a Succinct Account of the Earlier History. By RICHARD BAGWELL, M.A. Vols. I. and II. From the first invasion of the Northmen to the year 1578. 2 vols. 8vo. 32s.

Bain. — *WORKS BY ALEXANDER BAIN, LL.D.*

MENTAL AND MORAL SCIENCE; a Compendium of Psychology and Ethics. Crown 8vo. 10s. 6d.

THE SENSES AND THE INTELLECT. 8vo. 15s.

THE EMOTIONS AND THE WILL. 8vo. 15s.

PRACTICAL ESSAYS. Cr. 8vo. 4s. 6d.

LOGIC, DEDUCTIVE AND INDUCTIVE. PART I. *Deduction,* 4s. PART II. *Induction,* 6s. 6d.

JAMES MILL; a Biography. Cr. 8vo. 5s.

JOHN STUART MILL; a Criticism, with Personal Recollections. Crown 8vo. 2s. 6d.

Baker.—*WORKS BY SIR SAMUEL W. BAKER, M.A.*

EIGHT YEARS IN CEYLON. Crown 8vo. Woodcuts. 5s.

THE RIFLE AND THE HOUND IN CEYLON. Crown 8vo. Woodcuts. 5s.

Ball.—*THE REFORMED CHURCH OF IRELAND* (1537-1886). By the Right Hon. J. T. BALL, LL.D. D.C.L. 8vo. 7s. 6d.

Barrett.—*ENGLISH GLEES AND PART-SONGS.* An Inquiry into their Historical Development. By WILLIAM ALEXANDER BARRETT, Mus. Bac. Oxon., Vicar-Choral St. Paul's Cathedral. Crown 8vo. 7s. 6d.

Beaconsfield.—*WORKS BY THE EARL OF BEACONSFIELD, K.G.*

NOVELS AND TALES. The Hughenden Edition. With 2 Portraits and 11 Vignettes. 11 vols. Crown 8vo. 42s.

Endymion.
Lothair.	Henrietta Temple.
Coningsby.	Contarini Fleming, &c.
Sybil.	Alroy, Ixion, &c.
Tancred.	The Young Duke, &c.
Venetia.	Vivian Grey.

Beaconsfield.—*WORKS BY THE EARL OF BEACONSFIELD, K.G.*—continued.

NOVELS AND TALES. Cheap Edition, complete in 11 vols. Crown 8vo. 1s. each, boards; 1s. 6d. each, cloth.

SELECTED SPEECHES. With Introduction and Notes, by T. E. KEBBEL, M.A. 2 vols. 8vo. Portrait, 32s.

THE WIT AND WISDOM OF THE EARL OF BEACONSFIELD. Crown 8vo. 1s. boards, 1s. 6d. cloth.

Becker.—*WORKS BY PROFESSOR BECKER, translated from the German by the Rev. F. METCALF.*

GALLUS; or, Roman Scenes in the Time of Augustus. Post 8vo. 7s. 6d.

CHARICLES; or, Illustrations of the Private Life of the Ancient Greeks. Post 8vo. 7s. 6d.

Boultbee.—*WORKS BY THE REV. T. P. BOULTBEE, LL.D.*

A COMMENTARY ON THE 39 ARTICLES of the Church of England. Crown 8vo. 6s.

A HISTORY OF THE CHURCH OF ENGLAND; Pre-Reformation Period. 8vo. 15s.

Bourne. — *WORKS BY JOHN BOURNE, C.E.*

A TREATISE ON THE STEAM ENGINE, in its application to Mines, Mills, Steam Navigation, Railways, and Agriculture. With 37 Plates and 546 Woodcuts. 4to. 42s.

CATECHISM OF THE STEAM ENGINE in its various Applications in the Arts, to which is now added a chapter on Air and Gas Engines, and another devoted to Useful Rules, Tables, and Memoranda. Illustrated by 212 Woodcuts. Crown 8vo. 7s. 6d.

HANDBOOK OF THE STEAM ENGINE; a Key to the Author's Catechism of the Steam Engine. With 67 Woodcuts. Fcp. 8vo. 9s.

RECENT IMPROVEMENTS IN THE STEAM ENGINE. With 124 Woodcuts. Fcp. 8vo. 6s.

EXAMPLES OF STEAM AND GAS ENGINES, with 54 Plates and 356 Woodcuts. 4to. 70s.

Bowen. — *HARROW SONGS AND OTHER VERSES.* By EDWARD E. BOWEN, Assistant-Master at Harrow. Fcp. 8vo. 2*s*. 6*d*.; or printed on hand-made paper, 5*s*.

Brabazon.—*SOCIAL ARROWS.* By Lord BRABAZON. Crown 8vo. 5*s*.
₊ This book is a reprint of Articles on Open Spaces—Associations for the Benefit of Young Men and Women—Over Population—The Overworked Shop Assistant —Social Wants of London, &c.

Brabourne.—*FRIENDS AND FOES FROM FAIRYLAND.* By the Right Hon. LORD BRABOURNE. With 20 Illustrations by Linley Sambourne. Crown 8vo. 6*s*.

Brassey. — *WORKS BY LADY BRASSEY.*

A VOYAGE IN THE 'SUNBEAM,' OUR HOME ON THE OCEAN FOR ELEVEN MONTHS.
Library Edition. With 8 Maps and Charts, and 118 Illustrations, 8vo. 21*s*.
Cabinet Edition. With Map and 66 Illustrations, crown 8vo. 7*s*. 6*d*.
School Edition. With 37 Illustrations, fcp. 2*s*. cloth, or 3*s*. white parchment with gilt edges.
Popular Edition. With 60 Illustrations, 4to. 6*d*. sewed, 1*s*. cloth.

SUNSHINE AND STORM IN THE EAST.
Library Edition. With 2 Maps and 114 Illustrations, 8vo. 21*s*.
Cabinet Edition. With 2 Maps and 114 Illustrations, crown 8vo. 7*s*. 6*d*.
Popular Edition. With 103 Illustrations, 4to. 6*d*. sewed, 1*s*. cloth.

IN THE TRADES, THE TROPICS, AND THE 'ROARING FORTIES.'
Library Edition. With 8 Maps and Charts and 292 Illustrations, 8vo. 21*s*.
Cabinet Edition. With Map and 220 Illustrations, crown 8vo. 7*s*. 6*d*.
Popular Edition. With 183 Illustrations, 4to. 6*d*. sewed, 1*s*. cloth.

THREE VOYAGES IN THE 'SUNBEAM.'
Popular Edition. With 346 Illustrations, 4to. 2*s*. 6*d*.

Browne.—*AN EXPOSITION OF THE 39 ARTICLES,* Historical and Doctrinal. By E. H. BROWNE, D.D., Bishop of Winchester. 8vo. 16*s*.

Buckle.—*WORKS BY HENRY THOMAS BUCKLE.*
HISTORY OF CIVILISATION IN ENGLAND AND FRANCE, SPAIN AND SCOTLAND. 3 vols. crown 8vo. 24*s*.
MISCELLANEOUS AND POSTHUMOUS WORKS. A New and Abridged Edition. Edited by GRANT ALLEN. 2 vols. crown 8vo. 21*s*.

Buckton.—*WORKS BY MRS. C. M. BUCKTON.*
FOOD AND HOME COOKERY. With 11 Woodcuts. Crown 8vo. 2*s*. 6*d*.
HEALTH IN THE HOUSE. With 41 Woodcuts and Diagrams. Crown 8vo. 2*s*.
OUR DWELLINGS. With 39 Illustrations. Crown 8vo. 3*s*. 6*d*.

Bull.—*WORKS BY THOMAS BULL, M.D.*
HINTS TO MOTHERS ON THE MANAGEMENT OF THEIR HEALTH during the Period of Pregnancy and in the Lying-in Room. Fcp. 8vo. 1*s*. 6*d*.
THE MATERNAL MANAGEMENT OF CHILDREN IN HEALTH AND DISEASE. Fcp. 8vo. 1*s*. 6*d*.

Bullinger.—*A CRITICAL LEXICON AND CONCORDANCE TO THE ENGLISH AND GREEK NEW TESTAMENT.* Together with an Index of Greek Words and several Appendices. By the Rev. E. W. BULLINGER, D.D. Royal 8vo. 15*s*.

Burnside and Panton.—*THE THEORY OF EQUATIONS.* With an Introduction to the Theory of Binary Algebraic Forms. By WILLIAM SNOW BURNSIDE, M.A. and ARTHUR WILLIAM PANTON, M.A. 8vo. 12*s*. 6*d*.

Burrows.—*THE FAMILY OF BROCAS OF BEAUREPAIRE AND ROCHE COURT,* Hereditary Masters of the Royal Buck-hounds. With some account of the English Rule in Aquitaine. By MONTAGU BURROWS, M.A. F.S.A. With 26 Illustrations of Monuments, Brasses, Seals, &c. Royal 8vo. 42*s*.

Cabinet Lawyer, The; a Popular Digest of the Laws of England, Civil, Criminal, and Constitutional. Fcp. 8vo. 9*s*.

Caddy. — *THROUGH THE FIELDS WITH LINNÆUS.*—By Mrs. CADDY. With Frontispiece and Vignette to each volume. 2 vols. crown 8vo. 16*s*.

Carlyle. — *THOMAS AND JANE WELSH CARLYLE.*
THOMAS CARLYLE, a History of the first Forty Years of his Life, 1795–1835 By J. A. FROUDE, M.A. With 2 Portraits and 4 Illustrations, 2 vols. 8vo. 32*s*.
THOMAS CARLYLE, a History of his Life in London : from 1834 to his death in 1881. By J. A. FROUDE, M.A. 2 vols. 8vo. 32*s*.
LETTERS AND MEMORIALS OF JANE WELSH CARLYLE. Prepared for publication by THOMAS CARLYLE, and edited by J. A. FROUDE, M.A. 3 vols. 8vo. 36*s*.

Cates. — A DICTIONARY OF GENERAL BIOGRAPHY. Fourth Edition, with Supplement brought down to the end of 1884. By W. L. R. CATES. 8vo. 28s. cloth ; 35s. half-bound russia.

Cicero.—THE CORRESPONDENCE OF CICERO: a revised Text, with Notes and Prolegomena. By ROBERT V. TYRRELL, M.A. Fellow of Trinity College, Dublin. Vols. I. and II. 12s. each.

Clerk.—THE GAS ENGINE. By DUGALD CLERK. With 101 Illustrations and Diagrams. Crown 8vo. 7s. 6d.

Coats.—A MANUAL OF PATHOLOGY. By JOSEPH COATS, M.D. Pathologist to the Western Infirmary and the Sick Children's Hospital, Glasgow. With 339 Illustrations engraved on Wood. 8vo. 31s. 6d.

Colenso.—THE PENTATEUCH AND BOOK OF JOSHUA CRITICALLY EXAMINED. By J. W. COLENSO, D.D. late Bishop of Natal. Crown 8vo. 6s.

Comyn.—ATHERSTONE PRIORY: a Tale. By L. N. COMYN. Crown 8vo. 2s. 6d.

Conder. — A HANDBOOK TO THE BIBLE, or Guide to the Study of the Holy Scriptures derived from Ancient Monuments and Modern Exploration. By F. R. CONDER, and Lieut. C. R. CONDER, R.E. Post 8vo. 7s. 6d.

Conington. — WORKS BY JOHN CONINGTON, M.A.

THE ÆNEID OF VIRGIL. Translated into English Verse. Crown 8vo. 9s.

THE POEMS OF VIRGIL. Translated into English Prose. Crown 8vo. 9s.

Conybeare & Howson. — THE LIFE AND EPISTLES OF ST. PAUL. By the Rev. W. J. CONYBEARE, M.A. and the Very Rev. J. S. HOWSON, D.D.

Library Edition, with Maps, Plates, and Woodcuts. 2 vols. square crown 8vo. 21s.

Student's Edition, revised and condensed, with 46 Illustrations and Maps. 1 vol. crown 8vo. 7s. 6d.

Cooke. — TABLETS OF ANATOMY. By THOMAS COOKE, F.R.C.S. Eng. B.A. B.Sc. M.D. Paris. Fourth Edition, being a selection of the Tablets believed to be most useful to Students generally. Post 4to. 7s. 6d.

Cox. — THE FIRST CENTURY OF CHRISTIANITY. By HOMERSHAM COX, M.A. 8vo. 12s.

Cox.—A GENERAL HISTORY OF GREECE: from the Earliest Period to the Death of Alexander the Great; with a Sketch of the History to the Present Time. By the Rev. Sir G. W. COX, Bart., M.A. With 11 Maps and Plans. Crown 8vo. 7s. 6d.

⁎ For other Works, see 'Epochs of History,' p. 24.

Creighton. — HISTORY OF THE PAPACY DURING THE REFORMATION. By the Rev. M. CREIGHTON, M.A. 8vo. Vols. I. and II. 1378-1464, 32s. ; Vols. III. and IV. 1464-1518, 24s.

Crookes. — SELECT METHODS IN CHEMICAL ANALYSIS (chiefly Inorganic). By WILLIAM CROOKES, F.R.S. V.P.C.S With 37 Illustrations. 8vo. 24s.

Crump.—A SHORT ENQUIRY INTO THE FORMATION OF POLITICAL OPINION, from the Reign of the Great Families to the Advent of Democracy. By ARTHUR CRUMP. 8vo. 7s. 6d.

Culley.—HANDBOOK OF PRACTICAL TELEGRAPHY. By R. S. CULLEY, M. Inst. C.E. Plates and Woodcuts. 8vo. 16s.

Dante.—THE DIVINE COMEDY OF DANTE ALIGHIERI. Translated verse for verse from the Original into Terza Rima. By JAMES INNES MINCHIN. Crown 8vo. 15s.

Davidson.—AN INTRODUCTION TO THE STUDY OF THE NEW TESTAMENT. Critical, Exegetical, and Theological. By the Rev. S. DAVIDSON, D.D. LL.D. Revised Edition. 2 vols. 8vo. 30s.

Davidson.—WORKS BY WILLIAM L. DAVIDSON, M.A.

THE LOGIC OF DEFINITION EXPLAINED AND APPLIED. Crown 8vo. 6s.

LEADING AND IMPORTANT ENGLISH WORDS EXPLAINED AND EXEMPLIFIED. Fcp. 8vo. 3s. 6d.

Dead Shot, The, OR *SPORTSMAN'S COMPLETE GUIDE;* a Treatise on the Use of the Gun, with Lessons in the Art of Shooting Game of all kinds, and Wild-Fowl, also Pigeon-Shooting, and Dog-Breaking. By MARKSMAN. With 13 Illustrations. Crown 8vo. 10s. 6d.

Decaisne & Le Maout. — *A GENERAL SYSTEM OF BOTANY.* Translated from the French of E. LE MAOUT, M.D., and J. DECAISNE, by Mrs. HOOKER; with Additions by Sir J. D. HOOKER, C.B. F.R.S. Imp. 8vo. with 5,500 Woodcuts, 31s. 6d.

De Salis. — *SAVOURIES À LA MODE.* By Mrs. DE SALIS. Fcp. 8vo. 1s. boards.

De Tocqueville. — *DEMOCRACY IN AMERICA.* By ALEXIS DE TOCQUEVILLE. Translated by HENRY REEVE, C.B. 2 vols. crown 8vo. 16s.

Dickinson. — *ON RENAL AND URINARY AFFECTIONS.* By W. HOWSHIP DICKINSON, M.D. Cantab. F.R.C.P. &c. With 12 Plates and 122 Woodcuts. 3 vols. 8vo. £3. 4s. 6d.

Dixon. — *RURAL BIRD LIFE;* Essays on Ornithology, with Instructions for Preserving Objects relating to that Science. By CHARLES DIXON. With 45 Woodcuts. Crown 8vo. 5s.

Dowell. — *A HISTORY OF TAXATION AND TAXES IN ENGLAND, FROM THE EARLIEST TIMES TO THE PRESENT DAY.* By STEPHEN DOWELL, Assistant Solicitor of Inland Revenue. 4 vols. 8vo. 48s.

Doyle. — *THE OFFICIAL BARONAGE OF ENGLAND.* By JAMES E. DOYLE. Showing the Succession, Dignities, and Offices of every Peer from 1066 to 1885. Vols. I. to III. With 1,600 Portraits, Shields of Arms, Autographs, &c. 3 vols. 4to. £5. 5s.

Doyle. — *REMINISCENCES AND OPINIONS,* 1813-1885. By Sir FRANCIS HASTINGS DOYLE. 8vo. 16s.

Doyle. — *WORKS BY J. A. DOYLE,* Fellow of All Souls College, Oxford.

THE ENGLISH IN AMERICA: VIRGINIA, MARYLAND, AND THE CAROLINAS. 8vo. 18s.

THE ENGLISH IN AMERICA: THE PURITAN COLONIES. 2 vols. 8vo. 36s.

Dublin University Press Series (The): a Series of Works, chiefly Educational, undertaken by the Provost and Senior Fellows of Trinity College, Dublin :

Abbott's (T. K.) Codex Rescriptus Dublinensis of St. Matthew. 4to. 21s.

———— Evangeliorum Versio Antehieronymiana ex Codice Usseriano (Dublinensi). 2 vols. crown 8vo. 21s.

Burnside (W. S.) and Panton's (A. W.) Theory of Equations. 8vo. 12s. 6d.

Casey's (John) Sequel to Euclid's Elements. Crown 8vo. 3s. 6d.

———— Analytical Geometry of the Conic Sections. Crown 8vo. 7s. 6d.

Davies's (J. F.) Eumenides of Æschylus. With Metrical English Translation. 8vo. 7s.

Dublin Translations into Greek and Latin Verse. Edited by R. Y. Tyrrell. 8vo. 12s. 6d.

Graves's (R. P.) Life of Sir William Hamilton. (3 vols.) Vols. I. and II. 8vo. each 15s.

Griffin (R. W.) on Parabola, Ellipse, and Hyperbola, treated Geometrically. Crown 8vo. 6s.

Haughton's (Dr. S.) Lectures on Physical Geography. 8vo. 15s.

Hobart's (W. K.) Medical Language of St. Luke. 8vo. 16s.

Leslie's (T. E. Cliffe) Essays in Political and Moral Philosophy. 8vo. 10s. 6d.

Macalister's (A.) Zoology and Morphology of Vertebrata. 8vo. 10s. 6d.

MacCullagh's (James) Mathematical and other Tracts. 8vo. 15s.

Maguire's (T.) Parmenides of Plato, Greek Text with English Introduction, Analysis, and Notes. 8vo. 7s. 6d.

Monck's (W. H. S.) Introduction to Logic. Crown 8vo. 5s.

Purser's (J. M.) Manual of Histology. Fcp. 8vo. 5s.

Roberts's (R. A.) Examples in the Analytic Geometry of Plane Curves. Fcp. 8vo. 5s.

Southey's (R.) Correspondence with Caroline Bowles. Edited by E. Dowden. 8vo. 14s.

Thornhill's (W. J.) The Æneid of Virgil, freely translated into English Blank Verse. Crown 8vo. 7s. 6d.

Tyrrell's (R. Y.) Cicero's Correspondence. Vols. I. and II. 8vo. each 12s.

———— The Acharnians of Aristophanes, translated into English Verse. Crown 8vo. 2s. 6d.

Webb's (T. E.) Goethe's Faust, Translation and Notes. 8vo. 12s. 6d.

———— The Veil of Isis : a Series of Essays on Idealism. 8vo. 10s. 6d.

Wilkins's (G.) The Growth of the Homeric Poems. 8vo. 6s.

Dunster.—*HOW TO MAKE THE LAND PAY;* or, Profitable Industries connected with the Land. By H. P. DUNSTER, M.A. Crown 8vo. 5s.

Eastlake.—*HINTS ON HOUSEHOLD TASTE IN FURNITURE, UPHOLSTERY,* &c. By C. L. EASTLAKE, F.R.I.B.A. With 100 Illustrations. 8vo. 14s.

Edersheim.—*WORKS BY THE REV. ALFRED EDERSHEIM, D.D.*

THE LIFE AND TIMES OF JESUS THE MESSIAH. 2 vols. 8vo. 24s.

PROPHECY AND HISTORY IN RELATION TO THE MESSIAH: the Warburton Lectures, delivered at Lincoln's Inn Chapel, 1880-1884. 8vo. 12s.

Ellicott. — *WORKS BY C. J. ELLICOTT, D.D.* Bishop of Gloucester and Bristol.

A CRITICAL AND GRAMMATICAL COMMENTARY ON ST. PAUL'S EPISTLES. 8vo. Galatians, 8s. 6d. Ephesians, 8s. 6d. Pastoral Epistles, 10s. 6d. Philippians, Colossians, and Philemon, 10s. 6d. Thessalonians, 7s. 6d.

HISTORICAL LECTURES ON THE LIFE OF OUR LORD JESUS CHRIST. 8vo. 12s.

English Worthies. Edited by ANDREW LANG, M.A. Fcp. 8vo. 2s. 6d. each.

DARWIN. By GRANT ALLEN.

MARLBOROUGH. By G. SAINTSBURY.

SHAFTESBURY (The First Earl). By H. D. TRAILL.

ADMIRAL BLAKE. By DAVID HANNAY.

RALEIGH. By EDMUND GOSSE.

STEELE. By AUSTIN DOBSON.

BEN JONSON. By J. A. SYMONDS.

CANNING. By FRANK H. HILL.

*** Other Volumes are in preparation.

Epochs of Ancient History. 10 vols. fcp. 8vo. 2s. 6d. each. *See* p. 24.

Epochs of Modern History. 18 vols. fcp. 8vo. 2s. 6d. each. *See* p. 24.

Epochs of Church History. Fcp. 8vo. 2s. 6d. each. *See* p. 24.

Erichsen.—*WORKS BY JOHN ERIC ERICHSEN, F.R.S.*

THE SCIENCE AND ART OF SURGERY: Being a Treatise on Surgical Injuries, Diseases, and Operations. With 984 Illustrations. 2 vols. 8vo. 42s.

ON CONCUSSION OF THE SPINE, NERVOUS SHOCKS, and other Obscure Injuries of the Nervous System. Cr. 8vo. 10s. 6d.

Evans.—*THE BRONZE IMPLEMENTS, ARMS, AND ORNAMENTS OF GREAT BRITAIN AND IRELAND.* By JOHN EVANS, D.C.L. 540 Illustrations. 8vo. 25s.

Ewald. — *WORKS BY PROFESSOR HEINRICH EWALD,* of Göttingen.

THE ANTIQUITIES OF ISRAEL. Translated from the German by H. S. SOLLY, M.A. 8vo. 12s. 6d.

THE HISTORY OF ISRAEL. Translated from the German. 8 vols. 8vo. Vols. I. and II. 24s. Vols. III. and IV. 21s. Vol. V. 18s. Vol. VI. 8vo. 16s. Vol. VII. 8vo. 21s. Vol. VIII. with Index to the Complete Work. 8vo. 18s.

Fairbairn.—*WORKS BY SIR W. FAIRBAIRN, BART., C.E.*

A TREATISE ON MILLS AND MILLWORK, with 18 Plates and 333 Woodcuts. 1 vol. 8vo. 25s.

USEFUL INFORMATION FOR ENGINEERS. With many Plates and Woodcuts. 3 vols. crown 8vo. 31s. 6d.

Farrar. — *LANGUAGE AND LANGUAGES.* A Revised Edition of *Chapters on Language and Families of Speech.* By F. W. FARRAR, D.D. Crown 8vo. 6s.

Fitzwygram. — *HORSES AND STABLES.* By Major-General Sir F. FITZWYGRAM, Bart. With 19 pages of Illustrations. 8vo. 5s.

Fox.—*THE EARLY HISTORY OF CHARLES JAMES FOX.* By the Right Hon. Sir G. O. TREVELYAN, Bart. Library Edition, 8vo. 18s. Cabinet Edition, cr. 8vo. 6s.

Francis.—*A BOOK ON ANGLING;* or, Treatise on the Art of Fishing in every branch; including full Illustrated Lists of Salmon Flies. By FRANCIS FRANCIS. Post 8vo. Portrait and Plates, 15s.

Freeman.—*THE HISTORICAL GEOGRAPHY OF EUROPE.* By E. A. FREEMAN, D.C.L. With 65 Maps. 2 vols. 8vo. 31s. 6d.

Froude.—*WORKS BY JAMES A. FROUDE, M.A.*

THE HISTORY OF ENGLAND, from the Fall of Wolsey to the Defeat of the Spanish Armada. Cabinet Edition, 12 vols. cr. 8vo. £3. 12s. Popular Edition, 12 vols. cr. 8vo. £2. 2s.

SHORT STUDIES ON GREAT SUBJECTS. 4 vols. crown 8vo. 24s.

[*Continued on next page.*

Froude.—*WORKS BY JAMES A. FROUDE, M.A.*—continued.

CÆSAR: a Sketch. Crown 8vo. 6s.

THE ENGLISH IN IRELAND IN THE EIGHTEENTH CENTURY. 3 vols. crown 8vo. 18s.

OCEANA; OR, ENGLAND AND HER COLONIES. With 9 Illustrations. Crown 8vo. 2s. boards, 2s. 6d. cloth.

THOMAS CARLYLE, a History of the first Forty Years of his Life, 1795 to 1835. 2 vols. 8vo. 32s.

THOMAS CARLYLE, a History of His Life in London from 1834 to his death in 1881. With Portrait engraved on steel. 2 vols. 8vo. 32s.

Ganot.— *WORKS BY PROFESSOR GANOT.* Translated by E. ATKINSON, Ph.D. F.C.S.

ELEMENTARY TREATISE ON PHYSICS, for the use of Colleges and Schools. With 5 Coloured Plates and 923 Woodcuts. Large crown 8vo. 15s.

NATURAL PHILOSOPHY FOR GENERAL READERS AND YOUNG PERSONS. With 2 Plates and 471 Woodcuts. Crown 8vo. 7s. 6d.

Gardiner.— *WORKS BY SAMUEL RAWSON GARDINER, LL.D.*

HISTORY OF ENGLAND, from the Accession of James I. to the Outbreak of the Civil War, 1603-1642. Cabinet Edition, thoroughly revised. 10 vols. crown 8vo. price 6s. each.

A HISTORY OF THE GREAT CIVIL WAR, 1642-1649. (3 vols.) Vol. I. 1642-1644. With 24 Maps. 8vo. 21s.

OUTLINE OF ENGLISH HISTORY, B.C. 55-A.D. 1880. With 96 Woodcuts, fcp. 8vo. 2s. 6d.

*** For other Works, *see* 'Epochs of Modern History,' p. 24.

Garrod. — *WORKS BY ALFRED BARING GARROD, M.D. F.R.S.*

A TREATISE ON GOUT AND RHEUMATIC GOUT (RHEUMATOID ARTHRITIS). With 6 Plates, comprising 21 Figures (14 Coloured), and 27 Illustrations engraved on Wood. 8vo. 21s.

THE ESSENTIALS OF MATERIA MEDICA AND THERAPEUTICS. New Edition, revised and adapted to the New Edition of the British Pharmacopœia, by NESTOR TIRARD, M.D. Crown 8vo. 12s. 6d.

Goethe.—*FAUST.* Translated by T. E. WEBB, LL.D. 8vo. 12s. 6d.

FAUST. A New Translation, chiefly in Blank Verse; with Introduction and Notes. By JAMES ADEY BIRDS, B.A. F.G.S. Crown 8vo. 12s. 6d.

FAUST. The German Text, with an English Introduction and Notes for Students. By ALBERT M. SELSS, M.A. Ph.D. Crown 8vo. 5s.

Goodeve.—*WORKS BY T. M. GOODEVE, M.A.*

PRINCIPLES OF MECHANICS. With 253 Woodcuts. Crown 8vo. 6s.

THE ELEMENTS OF MECHANISM. With 342 Woodcuts. Crown 8vo. 6s.

A MANUAL OF MECHANICS: an Elementary Text-Book for Students of Applied Mechanics. With 138 Illustrations and Diagrams, and 141 Examples. Fcp. 8vo. 2s. 6d.

Grant.—*THE ETHICS OF ARISTOTLE.* The Greek Text illustrated by Essays and Notes. By Sir ALEXANDER GRANT, Bart. LL.D. D.C.L. &c. 2 vols. 8vo. 32s.

Gray. — *ANATOMY, DESCRIPTIVE AND SURGICAL.* By HENRY GRAY, F.R.S. late Lecturer on Anatomy at St. George's Hospital. With 569 Woodcut Illustrations, a large number of which are coloured. Re-edited by T. PICKERING PICK, Surgeon to St. George's Hospital. Royal 8vo. 36s.

Green.—*THE WORKS OF THOMAS HILL GREEN*, late Fellow of Balliol College, and Whyte's Professor of Moral Philosophy in the University of Oxford. Edited by R. L. NETTLESHIP, Fellow of Balliol College, Oxford (3 vols.) Vols I. and II.—Philosophical Works. 8vo. 16s. each.

Greville.—*WORKS BY C. C. F. GREVILLE.*

A JOURNAL OF THE REIGN OF QUEEN VICTORIA, from 1837 to 1852. 3 vols. 8vo. 36s.

A JOURNAL OF THE REIGN OF QUEEN VICTORIA, from 1852 to 1860. 2 vols. 8vo. 24s.

Grove. — *THE CORRELATION OF PHYSICAL FORCES.* By the Hon. Sir W. R. GROVE, F.R.S. &c. 8vo. 15s.

Gwilt.—*AN ENCYCLOPÆDIA OF ARCHITECTURE.* By JOSEPH GWILT, F.S.A. Illustrated with more than 1,100 Engravings on Wood. Revised, with Alterations and Considerable Additions, by WYATT PAPWORTH. 8vo. 52s. 6d.

Haggard.—*SHE: A HISTORY OF ADVENTURE.* By H. RIDER HAGGARD. Crown 8vo. 6s.

Halliwell-Phillipps.—*OUTLINES OF THE LIFE OF SHAKESPEARE.* By J. O. HALLIWELL-PHILLIPPS, F.R.S. 2 vols. Royal 8vo. 10s. 6d.

Hamilton.—*LIFE OF SIR WILLIAM R. HAMILTON*, Kt. LL.D. D.C.L. M.R.I.A. &c. Including Selections from his Poems, Correspondence, and Miscellaneous Writings. By the Rev. R. P. GRAVES, M.A. (3 vols.) Vols. I. and II. 8vo. 15s. each.

Harte.—*WORKS BY BRET HARTE.* *IN THE CARQUINEZ WOODS.* Fcp. 8vo. 2s. boards; 2s. 6d. cloth. *ON THE FRONTIER.* Three Stories. 16mo. 1s. *BY SHORE AND SEDGE.* Three Stories. 16mo. 1s.

Hartwig.—*WORKS BY DR. G. HARTWIG.* *THE SEA AND ITS LIVING WONDERS.* With 12 Plates and 303 Woodcuts. 8vo. 10s. 6d. *THE TROPICAL WORLD.* With 8 Plates, and 172 Woodcuts. 8vo. 10s. 6d. *THE POLAR WORLD;* a Description of Man and Nature in the Arctic and Antarctic Regions of the Globe. With 3 Maps, 8 Plates, and 85 Woodcuts. 8vo. 10s. 6d. *THE ARCTIC REGIONS* (extracted from the 'Polar World'). 4to. 6d. sewed. *THE SUBTERRANEAN WORLD.* With 3 Maps and 80 Woodcuts. 8vo. 10s. 6d. *THE AERIAL WORLD;* a Popular Account of the Phenomena and Life of the Atmosphere. With Map, 8 Plates, and 60 Woodcuts. 8vo. 10s. 6d.

Hassall.—*THE INHALATION TREATMENT OF DISEASES OF THE ORGANS OF RESPIRATION,* including Consumption. By ARTHUR HILL HASSALL, M.D. With 19 Illustrations of Apparatus. Cr. 8vo. 12s. 6d.

Haughton.—*SIX LECTURES ON PHYSICAL GEOGRAPHY,* delivered in 1876, with some Additions. By the Rev. SAMUEL HAUGHTON, F.R.S. M.D. D.C.L. With 23 Diagrams. 8vo. 15s.

Havelock.—*MEMOIRS OF SIR HENRY HAVELOCK, K.C.B.* By JOHN CLARK MARSHMAN. Crown 8vo. 3s. 6d.

Hearn.—*THE GOVERNMENT OF ENGLAND;* its Structure and its Development. By WILLIAM EDWARD HEARN, Q.C. 8vo. 16s.

Helmholtz.—*WORKS BY PROFESSOR HELMHOLTZ.* *ON THE SENSATIONS OF TONE AS A PHYSIOLOGICAL BASIS FOR THE THEORY OF MUSIC.* Translated by A. J. ELLIS, F.R.S. Royal 8vo. 28s. *POPULAR LECTURES ON SCIENTIFIC SUBJECTS.* Translated and edited by EDMUND ATKINSON, Ph.D. F.C.S. With a Preface by Professor TYNDALL, F.R.S. and 68 Woodcuts. 2 vols. Crown 8vo. 15s. or separately, 7s. 6d. each.

Herschel.—*OUTLINES OF ASTRONOMY.* By Sir J. F. W. HERSCHEL, Bart. M.A. With Plates and Diagrams. Square crown 8vo. 12s.

Hester's Venture: a Novel. By the Author of 'The Atelier du Lys.' Crown 8vo. 6s.

Hewitt. — *THE DIAGNOSIS AND TREATMENT OF DISEASES OF WOMEN, INCLUDING THE DIAGNOSIS OF PREGNANCY.* By GRAILY HEWITT, M.D. New Edition, in great part re-written and much enlarged, with 211 Engravings on Wood, of which 79 are new in this Edition. 8vo. 24s.

Historic Towns. Edited by E. A. FREEMAN, D.C.L. and Rev. WILLIAM HUNT, M.A. With Maps and Plans. Crown 8vo. 3s. 6d. each. *LONDON.* By W. E. LOFTIE. *EXETER.* By E. A. FREEMAN. *BRISTOL.* By Rev. W. HUNT. [*Nearly ready.*] *** Other Volumes in preparation.

Hobart.—*SKETCHES FROM MY LIFE.* By Admiral HOBART PASHA. With Portrait. Crown 8vo. 7s. 6d.

Hobart.—*THE MEDICAL LANGUAGE OF ST. LUKE:* a Proof from Internal Evidence that St. Luke's Gospel and the Acts were written by the same person, and that the writer was a Medical Man. By the Rev. W. K. HOBART, LL.D. 8vo. 16s.

Holmes.—*A SYSTEM OF SURGERY,* Theoretical and Practical, in Treatises by various Authors. Edited by TIMOTHY HOLMES, M.A. and J. W. HULKE, F.R.S. 3 vols. royal 8vo. £4. 4s.

Homer.—*THE ILIAD OF HOMER,* Homometrically translated by C. B. CAYLEY. 8vo. 12s. 6d. *THE ILIAD OF HOMER.* The Greek Text, with a Verse Translation, by W. C. GREEN, M.A. Vol. I. Books I.–XII. Crown 8vo. 6s.

A 3

Hopkins.—*CHRIST THE CONSOLER;* a Book of Comfort for the Sick. By ELLICE HOPKINS. Fcp. 8vo. 2s. 6d.

Howitt.—*VISITS TO REMARKABLE PLACES,* Old Halls, Battle-Fields, Scenes illustrative of Striking Passages in English History and Poetry. By WILLIAM HOWITT. With 80 Illustrations engraved on Wood. Crown 8vo. 7s. 6d.

Howley. — *THE OLD MORALITY, TRACED HISTORICALLY AND APPLIED PRACTICALLY.* By EDWARD HOWLEY, Barrister-at-Law. With Frontispiece, Raffaelle's School at Athens. Crown 8vo. 3s.

Hudson & Gosse.—*THE ROTIFERA OR 'WHEEL-ANIMALCULES.'* By C. T. HUDSON, LL.D. and P. H. GOSSE, F.R.S. With 30 Coloured Plates. In 6 Parts. 4to. 10s. 6d. each. Complete in 2 vols. 4to. £3. 10s.

Hullah.—*WORKS BY JOHN HULLAH, LL.D.*

COURSE OF LECTURES ON THE HISTORY OF MODERN MUSIC. 8vo. 8s. 6d.

COURSE OF LECTURES ON THE TRANSITION PERIOD OF MUSICAL HISTORY. 8vo. 10s. 6d.

Hume.—*THE PHILOSOPHICAL WORKS OF DAVID HUME.* Edited by T. H. GREEN, M.A. and the Rev. T. H. GROSE, M.A. 4 vols. 8vo. 56s. Or separately, Essays, 2 vols. 28s. Treatise of Human Nature. 2 vols. 28s.

In the Olden Time: a Tale of the Peasant War in Germany. By the Author of ' Mademoiselle Mori.' Crown 8vo. 2s. 6d.

Ingelow.—*WORKS BY JEAN INGELOW.*

POETICAL WORKS. Vols. 1 and 2. Fcp. 8vo. 12s. Vol. 3. Fcp. 8vo. 5s.

LYRICAL AND OTHER POEMS, Selected from the Writings of JEAN INGELOW. Fcp. 8vo. 2s. 6d. cloth plain; 3s. cloth gilt.

THE HIGH TIDE ON THE COAST OF LINCOLNSHIRE. With 40 Illustrations, drawn and engraved under the supervision of GEORGE T. ANDREW. Royal 8vo. 10s. 6d. cloth extra, gilt edges.

Jackson.—*AID TO ENGINEERING SOLUTION.* By LOWIS D'A. JACKSON, C.E. With 111 Diagrams and 5 Woodcut Illustrations. 8vo. 21s.

Jameson.—*WORKS BY MRS. JAMESON.*

LEGENDS OF THE SAINTS AND MARTYRS. With 19 Etchings and 187 Woodcuts. 2 vols. 31s. 6d.

LEGENDS OF THE MADONNA, the Virgin Mary as represented in Sacred and Legendary Art. With 27 Etchings and 165 Woodcuts. 1 vol. 21s.

LEGENDS OF THE MONASTIC ORDERS. With 11 Etchings and 88 Woodcuts. vol. 21s.

HISTORY OF THE SAVIOUR, His Types and Precursors. Completed by Lady EASTLAKE. With 13 Etchings and 281 Woodcuts. 2 vols. 42s.

Jeans.—*WORKS BY J. S. JEANS.*

ENGLAND'S SUPREMACY: its Sources, Economics, and Dangers. 8vo. 8s. 6d.

RAILWAY PROBLEMS: An Inquiry into the Economic Conditions of Railway Working in Different Countries. 8vo. 12s. 6d.

Johnson.—*THE PATENTEE'S MANUAL;* a Treatise on the Law and Practice of Letters Patent, for the use of Patentees and Inventors. By J. JOHNSON and J. H. JOHNSON. 8vo. 10s. 6d.

Johnston.—*A GENERAL DICTIONARY OF GEOGRAPHY,* Descriptive, Physical, Statistical, and Historical; a complete Gazetteer of the World. By KEITH JOHNSTON. Medium 8vo. 42s.

Jones. — *THE HEALTH OF THE SENSES: SIGHT, HEARING, VOICE, SMELL AND TASTE, SKIN;* with Hints on Health, Diet, Education, Health Resorts of Europe, &c. By H. MACNAUGHTON JONES, M.D. Crown 8vo. 3s. 6d.

Jordan. — *WORKS BY WILLIAM LEIGHTON JORDAN, F.R.G.S.*

THE OCEAN: a Treatise on Ocean Currents and Tides and their Causes. 8vo. 21s.

THE NEW PRINCIPLES OF NATURAL PHILOSOPHY: a Defence and Extension of the Principles established by the Author's treatise on Ocean Currents. With 13 plates. 8vo. 21s.

THE WINDS: an Essay in Illustration of the New Principles of Natural Philosophy. Crown 8vo. 2s.

THE STANDARD OF VALUE. Crown 8vo. 5s.

Jukes.—*WORKS BY ANDREW JUKES.*

THE NEW MAN AND THE ETERNAL LIFE. Crown 8vo. 6s.

THE TYPES OF GENESIS. Crown 8vo. 7s. 6d.

THE SECOND DEATH AND THE RE-STITUTION OF ALL THINGS. Crown 8vo. 3s. 6d.

THE MYSTERY OF THE KINGDOM. Crown 8vo. 2s. 6d.

Justinian.—*THE INSTITUTES OF JUSTINIAN;* Latin Text, chiefly that of Huschke, with English Introduction, Translation, Notes, and Summary. By THOMAS C. SANDARS, M.A. 8vo. 18s.

Kalisch.—*WORKS BY M. M. KALISCH, M.A.*

BIBLE STUDIES. Part I. The Prophecies of Balaam. 8vo. 10s. 6d. Part II. The Book of Jonah. 8vo. 10s. 6d.

COMMENTARY ON THE OLD TESTAMENT; with a New Translation. Vol. I. Genesis, 8vo. 18s. or adapted for the General Reader, 12s. Vol. II. Exodus, 15s. or adapted for the General Reader, 12s. Vol. III. Leviticus, Part I. 15s. or adapted for the General Reader, 8s. Vol. IV. Leviticus, Part II. 15s. or adapted for the General Reader, 8s.

HEBREW GRAMMAR. With Exercises. Part I. 8vo. 12s. 6d. Key, 5s. Part II. 12s. 6d.

Kant.—*WORKS BY EMMANUEL KANT.*

CRITIQUE OF PRACTICAL REASON. Translated by Thomas Kingsmill Abbott, B.D. 8vo. 12s. 6d.

INTRODUCTION TO LOGIC, AND HIS ESSAY ON THE MISTAKEN SUBTILTY OF THE FOUR FIGURES. Translated by Thomas Kingsmill Abbott, B.D. With a few Notes by S. T. Coleridge. 8vo. 6s.

Killick.—*HANDBOOK TO MILL'S SYSTEM OF LOGIC.* By the Rev. A. H. KILLICK, M.A. Crown 8vo. 3s. 6d.

Kolbe.—*A SHORT TEXT-BOOK OF INORGANIC CHEMISTRY.* By Dr. HERMANN KOLBE. Translated from the German by T. S. HUMPIDGE, Ph.D. With a Coloured Table of Spectra and 66 Illustrations. Crown 8vo. 7s. 6d.

Lang.—*WORKS BY ANDREW LANG.*

LETTERS TO DEAD AUTHORS. Fcp 8vo. 6s. 6d.

BOOKS AND BOOKMEN. With 2 Coloured Plates and 17 Illustrations. Cr. 8vo. 6s. 6d. or printed on hand-made paper, 10s. 6d.

CUSTOM AND MYTH; Studies of Early Usage and Belief. With 15 Illustrations. Crown 8vo. 7s. 6d.

THE PRINCESS NOBODY: a Tale of Fairyland. After the Drawings by Richard Doyle, printed in colours by Edmund Evans. Post 4to. 5s. boards.

Latham.—*HANDBOOK OF THE ENGLISH LANGUAGE.* By ROBERT G. LATHAM, M.A. M.D. Crown 8vo. 6s.

Lecky.—*WORKS BY W. E. H. LECKY.*

HISTORY OF ENGLAND IN THE EIGHTEENTH CENTURY. 8vo. Vols. I.–IV. 1700–1784, £3. 12s.

THE HISTORY OF EUROPEAN MORALS FROM AUGUSTUS TO CHARLEMAGNE. 2 vols. crown 8vo. 16s.

HISTORY OF THE RISE AND INFLUENCE OF THE SPIRIT OF RATIONALISM IN EUROPE. 2 vols. crown 8vo. 16s.

Lenormant.—*THE BOOK OF GENESIS.* A New Translation from the Hebrew. By FRANÇOIS LENORMANT. Translated from the French by the Author of 'Mankind; their Origin and Destiny.' 8vo. 10s. 6d.

Lewes.—*THE HISTORY OF PHILOSOPHY,* from Thales to Comte. By GEORGE HENRY LEWES. 2 vols. 8vo. 32s.

Liddell & Scott.—*A GREEK-ENGLISH LEXICON.* Compiled by HENRY GEORGE LIDDELL, D.D. Dean of Christ Church; and ROBERT SCOTT, D.D. Dean of Rochester. 4to. 36s.

Liveing.—*WORKS BY ROBERT LIVEING, M.A. and M.D. Cantab.*

HANDBOOK ON DISEASES OF THE SKIN. With especial reference to Diagnosis and Treatment. Fcp. 8vo. 5s.

NOTES ON THE TREATMENT OF SKIN DISEASES. 18mo. 3s.

Lloyd.—*A Treatise on Magnet-ism*, General and Terrestrial. By H. Lloyd, D.D. D.C.L. 8vo. 10s. 6d.

Lloyd.—*The Science of Agricul-ture.* By F. J. Lloyd. 8vo. 12s.

Longman.—*History of the Life and Times of Edward III.* By William Longman, F.S.A. With 9 Maps, 8 Plates, and 16 Woodcuts. 2 vols. 8vo. 28s.

Longman.—*Works by Frederick W. Longman, Balliol College, Oxon.*

Chess Openings. Fcp. 8vo. 2s. 6d.

Frederick the Great and the Seven Years' War. With 2 Coloured Maps. 8vo. 2s. 6d.

A New Pocket Dictionary of the German and English Lan-guages. Square 18mo. 2s. 6d.

Longman's Magazine. Published Monthly. Price Sixpence. Vols. 1-8, 8vo. price 5s. each.

Longmore.—*Gunshot Injuries*; Their History, Characteristic Features, Complications, and General Treatment. By Surgeon-General Sir T. Longmore, C.B., F.R.C.S. With 58 Illustrations. 8vo. 31s. 6d.

Loudon.—*Works by J. C. Loudon, F.L.S.*

Encyclopædia of Gardening; the Theory and Practice of Horticulture, Floriculture, Arboriculture, and Land-scape Gardening. With 1,000 Woodcuts. 8vo. 21s.

Encyclopædia of Agriculture; the Laying-out, Improvement, and Management of Landed Property; the Cultivation and Economy of the Produc-tions of Agriculture. With 1,100 Wood-cuts. 8vo. 21s.

Encyclopædia of Plants; the Specific Character, Description, Culture, History, &c. of all Plants found in Great Britain. With 12,000 Woodcuts. 8vo. 42s.

Lubbock.—*The Origin of Civili-zation and the Primitive Condition of Man.* By Sir J. Lubbock, Bart. M.P. F.R.S. With Illustrations. 8vo. 18s.

Lyra Germanica; Hymns Trans-lated from the German by Miss C. Winkworth. Fcp. 8vo. 5s.

Macalister.— *An Introduction to the Systematic Zoology and Morphology of Vertebrate Ani-mals.* By A. Macalister, M.D. With 28 Diagrams. 8vo. 10s. 6d.

Macaulay.—*Works and Life of Lord Macaulay.*

History of England from the Accession of James the Second:
Student's Edition, 2 vols. crown 8vo. 12s.
People's Edition, 4 vols. crown 8vo. 16s.
Cabinet Edition, 8 vols. post 8vo. 48s.
Library Edition, 5 vols. 8vo. £4.

Critical and Historical Essays, with Lays of Ancient Rome, in 1 volume :
Authorised Edition, crown 8vo. 2s. 6d. or 3s. 6d. gilt edges.
Popular Edition, crown 8vo. 2s. 6d.

Critical and Historical Essays:
Student's Edition, 1 vol. crown 8vo. 6s.
People's Edition, 2 vols. crown 8vo. 8s.
Cabinet Edition, 4 vols. post 8vo. 24s.
Library Edition, 3 vols. 8vo. 36s.

Essays which may be had separ-ately price 6d. each sewed, 1s. each cloth :
Addison and Walpole.
Frederick the Great.
Croker's Boswell's Johnson.
Hallam's Constitutional History.
Warren Hastings. (3d. sewed, 6d. cloth.)
The Earl of Chatham (Two Essays).
Ranke and Gladstone.
Milton and Machiavelli.
Lord Bacon.
Lord Clive.
Lord Byron, and The Comic Dramatists of the Restoration.

The Essay on Warren Hastings annotated by S. Hales, 1s. 6d.
The Essay on Lord Clive annotated by H. Courthope-Bowen, M.A. 2s. 6d.

Speeches:
People's Edition, crown 8vo. 3s. 6d.
[Continued on next page.

Macaulay—*WORKS AND LIFE OF LORD MACAULAY*—*continued.*

MISCELLANEOUS WRITINGS :

Library Edition, 2 vols. 8vo. 21*s.*
People's Edition, 1 vol. crown 8vo. 4*s.* 6*d.*

LAYS OF ANCIENT ROME, &c.

Illustrated by G. Scharf, fcp. 4to. 10*s.* 6*d.*
——————————— Popular Edition, fcp. 4to. 6*d.* sewed, 1*s.* cloth.
Illustrated by J. R. Weguelin, crown 8vo. 3*s.* 6*d.* cloth extra, gilt edges.
Cabinet Edition, post 8vo. 3*s.* 6*d.*
Annotated Edition, fcp. 8vo. 1*s.* sewed, 1*s.* 6*d.* cloth, or 2*s.* 6*d.* cloth extra, gilt edges.

SELECTIONS FROM THE WRITINGS OF LORD MACAULAY. Edited, with Occasional Notes, by the Right Hon. Sir G. O. TREVELYAN, Bart. Crown 8vo. 6*s.*

MISCELLANEOUS WRITINGS AND SPEECHES:

Student's Edition, in ONE VOLUME, crown 8vo. 6*s.*
Cabinet Edition, including Indian Penal Code, Lays of Ancient Rome, and Miscellaneous Poems, 4 vols. post 8vo. 24*s.*

THE COMPLETE WORKS OF LORD MACAULAY. Edited by his Sister, Lady TREVELYAN.

Library Edition, with Portrait, 8 vols. demy 8vo. £5. 5*s.*
Cabinet Edition, 16 vols. post 8vo. £4. 16*s.*

THE LIFE AND LETTERS OF LORD MACAULAY. By the Right Hon. Sir G. O. TREVELYAN, Bart.

Popular Edition, 1 vol. crown 8vo. 6*s.*
Cabinet Edition, 2 vols. post 8vo. 12*s.*
Library Edition, 2 vols. 8vo. 36*s.*

Macdonald.—*WORKS BY GEORGE MACDONALD, LL.D.*

UNSPOKEN SERMONS. First Series. Crown 8vo. 3*s.* 6*d.*

UNSPOKEN SERMONS. Second Series. Crown 8vo. 3*s.* 6*d.*

THE MIRACLES OF OUR LORD. Crown 8vo. 3*s.* 6*d.*

A BOOK OF STRIFE, IN THE FORM OF THE DIARY OF AN OLD SOUL: Poems. 12mo. 6*s.*

Macfarren. — *LECTURES ON HARMONY,* delivered at the Royal Institution. By Sir G. A. MACFARREN. 8vo. 12*s.*

Macleod.—*WORKS BY HENRY D. MACLEOD, M.A.*

PRINCIPLES OF ECONOMICAL PHILOSOPHY. In 2 vols. Vol. I. 8vo. 15*s.* Vol. II. PART 1. 12*s.*

THE ELEMENTS OF ECONOMICS. In 2 vols. Vol. I. crown 8vo. 7*s.* 6*d.* Vol. II. PART 1, crown 8vo. 7*s.* 6*d.*

THE ELEMENTS OF BANKING. Crown 8vo. 5*s.*

THE THEORY AND PRACTICE OF BANKING. Vol. I. 8vo. 12*s.* Vol. II. 14*s.*

ELEMENTS OF POLITICAL ECONOMY. 8vo. 16*s.*

McCulloch. — *THE DICTIONARY OF COMMERCE AND COMMERCIAL NAVIGATION* of the late J. R. McCULLOCH, of H.M. Stationery Office. Latest Edition, containing the most recent Statistical Information by A. J. WILSON. 1 vol. medium 8vo. with 11 Maps and 30 Charts, price 63*s.* cloth, or 70*s.* strongly half-bound in russia.

Mademoiselle Mori : a Tale of Modern Rome. By the Author of 'The Atelier du Lys.' Crown 8vo. 2*s.* 6*d.*

Mahaffy.—*A HISTORY OF CLASSICAL GREEK LITERATURE.* By the Rev. J. P. MAHAFFY, M.A. Crown 8vo. Vol. I. Poets, 7*s.* 6*d.* Vol. II. Prose Writers, 7*s.* 6*d.*

Malmesbury. — *MEMOIRS OF AN EX-MINISTER:* an Autobiography. By the Earl of MALMESBURY, G.C.B. Crown 8vo. 7*s.* 6*d.*

Manning.—*THE TEMPORAL MISSION OF THE HOLY GHOST ;* or, Reason and Revelation. By H. E. MANNING, D.D. Cardinal-Archbishop. Crown 8vo. 8*s.* 6*d.*

Martineau—*WORKS BY JAMES MARTINEAU, D.D.*

HOURS OF THOUGHT ON SACRED THINGS. Two Volumes of Sermons. 2 vols. crown 8vo. 7*s.* 6*d.* each.

ENDEAVOURS AFTER THE CHRISTIAN LIFE. Discourses. Crown 8vo. 7*s.* 6*d.*

Maunder's Treasuries.

BIOGRAPHICAL TREASURY. Reconstructed, revised, and brought down to the year 1882, by W. L. R. CATES. Fcp. 8vo. 6s.

TREASURY OF NATURAL HISTORY; or, Popular Dictionary of Zoology. Fcp. 8vo. with 900 Woodcuts, 6s.

TREASURY OF GEOGRAPHY, Physical, Historical, Descriptive, and Political. With 7 Maps and 16 Plates. Fcp. 8vo. 6s.

HISTORICAL TREASURY: Outlines of Universal History, Separate Histories of all Nations. Revised by the Rev. Sir G. W. Cox, Bart. M.A. Fcp. 8vo. 6s.

TREASURY OF KNOWLEDGE AND LIBRARY OF REFERENCE. Comprising an English Dictionary and Grammar, Universal Gazetteer, Classical Dictionary, Chronology, Law Dictionary, &c. Fcp. 8vo. 6s.

SCIENTIFIC AND LITERARY TREASURY: a Popular Encyclopædia of Science, Literature, and Art. Fcp. 8vo. 6s.

THE TREASURY OF BIBLE KNOWLEDGE; being a Dictionary of the Books, Persons, Places, Events, and other matters of which mention is made in Holy Scripture. By the Rev. J. AYRE, M.A. With 5 Maps, 15 Plates, and 300 Woodcuts. Fcp. 8vo. 6s.

THE TREASURY OF BOTANY, or Popular Dictionary of the Vegetable Kingdom. Edited by J. LINDLEY, F.R.S. and T. MOORE, F.L.S. With 274 Woodcuts and 20 Steel Plates. Two Parts, fcp. 8vo. 12s.

Maxwell.—*DON JOHN OF AUSTRIA;* or, Passages from the History of the Sixteenth Century, 1547–1578. By the late Sir WILLIAM STIRLING MAXWELL, Bart. K.T. With numerous Illustrations engraved on Wood. Library Edition. 2 vols. royal 8vo. 42s.

May.—*WORKS BY THE RIGHT HON. SIR THOMAS ERSKINE MAY, K.C.B.*

THE CONSTITUTIONAL HISTORY OF ENGLAND SINCE THE ACCESSION OF GEORGE III. 1760–1870. 3 vols. crown 8vo. 18s.

DEMOCRACY IN EUROPE; a History. 2 vols. 8vo. 32s.

Melville.—*NOVELS BY G. J. WHYTE MELVILLE.* 1s. each, boards; 1s. 6d. each, cloth.

The Gladiators.	Holmby House.
The Interpreter.	Kate Coventry.
Good for Nothing.	Digby Grand.
The Queen's Maries.	General Bounce.

Mendelssohn.—*THE LETTERS OF FELIX MENDELSSOHN.* Translated by Lady WALLACE. 2 vols. crown 8vo. 10s.

Merivale.—*WORKS BY THE VERY REV. CHARLES MERIVALE, D.D. Dean of Ely.*

HISTORY OF THE ROMANS UNDER THE EMPIRE. 8 vols. post 8vo. 48s.

THE FALL OF THE ROMAN REPUBLIC: a Short History of the Last Century of the Commonwealth. 12mo. 7s. 6d.

GENERAL HISTORY OF ROME FROM B.C. 753 TO A.D. 476. Crown 8vo. 7s. 6d.

THE ROMAN TRIUMVIRATES. With Maps. Fcp. 8vo. 2s. 6d.

Miles. — *WORKS BY WILLIAM MILES.*

THE HORSE'S FOOT, AND HOW TO KEEP IT SOUND. Imp. 8vo. 12s. 6d.

STABLES AND STABLE FITTINGS. Imp. 8vo. with 13 Plates, 15s.

REMARKS ON HORSES' TEETH, addressed to Purchasers. Post 8vo. 1s. 6d.

PLAIN TREATISE ON HORSE-SHOEING. Post 8vo. Woodcuts, 2s. 6d.

Mill.—*ANALYSIS OF THE PHENOMENA OF THE HUMAN MIND.* By JAMES MILL. With Notes, Illustrative and Critical. 2 vols. 8vo. 28s.

Mill.—WORKS BY JOHN STUART MILL.

PRINCIPLES OF POLITICAL ECONOMY.
Library Edition, 2 vols. 8vo. 30s.
People's Edition, 1 vol. crown 8vo. 5s.

A SYSTEM OF LOGIC, Ratiocinative and Inductive. Crown 8vo. 5s.

ON LIBERTY. Crown 8vo. 1s. 4d.

ON REPRESENTATIVE GOVERNMENT. Crown 8vo. 2s.

AUTOBIOGRAPHY. 8vo. 7s. 6d.

UTILITARIANISM. 8vo. 5s.

THE SUBJECTION OF WOMEN. Crown 8vo. 6s.

EXAMINATION OF SIR WILLIAM HAMILTON'S PHILOSOPHY. 8vo. 16s.

NATURE, THE UTILITY OF RELIGION, AND THEISM. Three Essays. 8vo. 5s.

Miller.— WORKS BY W. ALLEN MILLER, M.D. LL.D.

THE ELEMENTS OF CHEMISTRY, Theoretical and Practical. Re-edited, with Additions, by H. MACLEOD, F.C.S. 3 vols. 8vo.

Part I. CHEMICAL PHYSICS, 16s.
Part II. INORGANIC CHEMISTY, 24s.
Part III. ORGANIC CHEMISTRY, 31s. 6d.

AN INTRODUCTION TO THE STUDY OF INORGANIC CHEMISTRY. With 71 Woodcuts. Fcp. 8vo. 3s. 6d.

Mitchell.—A MANUAL OF PRACTICAL ASSAYING. By JOHN MITCHELL, F.C.S. Revised, with the Recent Discoveries incorporated. By W. CROOKES, F.R.S. 8vo. Woodcuts, 31s. 6d.

Monsell.—WORKS BY THE REV. J. S. B. MONSELL, LL.D.

SPIRITUAL SONGS FOR THE SUNDAYS AND HOLYDAYS THROUGHOUT THE YEAR. Fcp. 8vo. 5s. 18mo. 2s.

THE BEATITUDES. Eight Sermons. Crown 8vo. 3s. 6d.

HIS PRESENCE NOT HIS MEMORY. Verses. 16mo. 1s.

Mulhall.—HISTORY OF PRICES SINCE THE YEAR 1850. By MICHAEL G. MULHALL. Crown 8vo. 6s.

Müller. — WORKS BY F. MAX MÜLLER, M.A.

BIOGRAPHICAL ESSAYS. Crown 8vo. 7s. 6d.

SELECTED ESSAYS ON LANGUAGE, MYTHOLOGY AND RELIGION. 2 vols. crown 8vo. 16s.

LECTURES ON THE SCIENCE OF LANGUAGE. 2 vols. crown 8vo. 16s.

INDIA, WHAT CAN IT TEACH US? A Course of Lectures delivered before the University of Cambridge. 8vo. 12s. 6d.

HIBBERT LECTURES ON THE ORIGIN AND GROWTH OF RELIGION, as illustrated by the Religions of India. Crown 8vo. 7s. 6d.

INTRODUCTION TO THE SCIENCE OF RELIGION: Four Lectures delivered at the Royal Institution. Crown 8vo. 7s. 6d.

A SANSKRIT GRAMMAR FOR BEGINNERS, in Devanagari and Roman Letters throughout. Royal 8vo. 7s. 6d.

A SANSKRIT GRAMMAR FOR BEGINNERS. New and Abridged Edition, accented and transliterated throughout, with a chapter on Syntax and an Appendix on Classical Metres. By A. A. MACDONELL, M.A. Ph.D. Crown 8vo. 6s.

Murchison.—WORKS BY CHARLES MURCHISON, M.D. LL.D. &c.

A TREATISE ON THE CONTINUED FEVERS OF GREAT BRITAIN. Revised by W. CAYLEY, M.D. Physician to the Middlesex Hospital. 8vo. with numerous Illustrations, 25s.

CLINICAL LECTURES ON DISEASES OF THE LIVER, JAUNDICE, AND ABDOMINAL DROPSY. Revised by T. LAUDER BRUNTON, M.D. and Sir JOSEPH FAYRER, M.D. 8vo. with 43 Illustrations, 24s.

Nelson.—*LETTERS AND DESPATCHES OF HORATIO, VISCOUNT NELSON.* Selected and arranged by JOHN KNOX LAUGHTON, M.A. 8vo. 16*s.*

Nesbit.—*LAYS AND LEGENDS.* By E. NESBIT. Crown 8vo. 5*s.*

Nevile.—*WORKS BY GEORGE NE-VILE, M.A.*

HORSES AND RIDING. With 31 Illustrations. Crown 8vo. 6*s.*

FARMS AND FARMING. With 13 Illustrations. Crown 8vo. 6*s.*

New Testament (The) of our Lord and Saviour Jesus Christ. Illustrated with Engravings on Wood after Paintings by the Early Masters. 4to. 21*s.* cloth extra.

Newman.—*WORKS BY CARDINAL NEWMAN.*

APOLOGIA PRO VITA SUA. Crown 8vo. 6*s.*

THE IDEA OF A UNIVERSITY DEFINED AND ILLUSTRATED. Crown 8vo. 7*s.*

HISTORICAL SKETCHES. 3 vols. crown 8vo. 6*s.* each.

DISCUSSIONS AND ARGUMENTS ON VARIOUS SUBJECTS. Crown 8vo. 6*s.*

AN ESSAY ON THE DEVELOPMENT OF CHRISTIAN DOCTRINE. Crown 8vo. 6*s.*

CERTAIN DIFFICULTIES FELT BY ANGLICANS IN CATHOLIC TEACHING CONSIDERED. Vol. I, crown 8vo. 7*s.* 6*d.*; Vol. 2, crown 8vo. 5*s.* 6*d.*

THE VIA MEDIA OF THE ANGLICAN CHURCH, ILLUSTRATED IN LECTURES &c. 2 vols. crown 8vo. 6*s.* each.

ESSAYS, CRITICAL AND HISTORICAL. 2 vols. crown 8vo. 12*s.*

ESSAYS ON BIBLICAL AND ON ECCLE-SIASTICAL MIRACLES. Crown 8vo. 6*s.*

AN ESSAY IN AID OF A GRAMMAR OF ASSENT. 7*s.* 6*d.*

Noble.—*HOURS WITH A THREE-INCH TELESCOPE.* By Captain W. NOBLE, F.R.A.S. &c. With a Map of the Moon. Crown 8vo. 4*s.* 6*d.*

Northcott.—*LATHES AND TURN-ING,* Simple, Mechanical, and Ornamental. By W. H. NORTHCOTT. With 338 Illustrations. 8vo. 18*s.*

O'Hagan.—*SELECTED SPEECHES AND ARGUMENTS OF THE RIGHT HON. THOMAS BARON O'HAGAN.* Edited by GEORGE TEELING. 8vo. 16*s.*

Oliphant.—*NOVELS BY MRS. OLI-PHANT.*

MADAM. Crown 8vo. 3*s.* 6*d.*

IN TRUST.—Crown 8vo. 2*s.* boards ; 2*s.* 6*d.* cloth.

Outlines of Jewish History.—From B.C. 586 to C.E. 1885. By the Author of 'About the Jews since Bible Times.' Revised by M. Friedländer, Ph.D. With 3 Maps. Crown 8vo. 3*s.* 6*d.*

Overton.—*LIFE IN THE ENGLISH CHURCH* (1660–1714). By J. H. OVER-TON, M.A. Rector of Epworth. 8vo. 14*s.*

Owen. — *THE COMPARATIVE ANA-TOMY AND PHYSIOLOGY OF THE VERTEBRATE ANIMALS.* By Sir RICHARD OWEN, K.C.B. &c. With 1,472 Woodcuts. 3 vols. 8vo. £3. 13*s.* 6*d.*

Paget. — *WORKS BY SIR JAMES PAGET, BART. F.R.S. D.C.L. &c.*

CLINICAL LECTURES AND ESSAYS. Edited by F. HOWARD MARSH, Assistant-Surgeon to St. Bartholomew's Hospital. 8vo. 15*s.*

LECTURES ON SURGICAL PATHO-LOGY. Re-edited by the AUTHOR and W. TURNER, M.B. 8vo. with 131 Woodcuts, 21*s.*

Pasteur.—*LOUIS PASTEUR,* his Life and Labours. By his SON-IN-LAW. Translated from the French by Lady CLAUD HAMILTON. Crown 8vo. 7*s.* 6*d.*

Payen.—*INDUSTRIAL CHEMISTRY;* a Manual for Manufacturers and for Colleges or Technical Schools ; a Translation of PAYEN's 'Précis de Chimie Indus-trielle.' Edited by B. H. PAUL. With 698 Woodcuts. Medium 8vo. 42*s.*

Payn.—*NOVELS BY JAMES PAYN.*

THE LUCK OF THE DARRELLS: Crown 8vo. 3*s.* 6*d.*

THICKER THAN WATER. Crown 8vo. 2*s.* boards ; 2*s.* 6*d.* cloth.

Pears.—*THE FALL OF CONSTANTI-NOPLE:* being the Story of the Fourth Crusade. By EDWIN PEARS, LL.B. Barrister-at-Law, late President of the European Bar at Constantinople, and Knight of the Greek Order of the Saviour. 8vo. 16*s.*

Pease.—*THE CLEVELAND HOUNDS AS A TRENCHER-FED PACK.* By A. E. PEASE. With Map of the Cleveland Hunt and Facsimiles of the original Rules of the Roxby and Cleveland Hunt (1817) &c. Royal 8vo. 18s.

Perring.—*HARD KNOTS IN SHAKES-PEARE.* By Sir PHILIP PERRING, Bart. 8vo. 7s. 6d.

Piesse.—*THE ART OF PERFUMERY,* and the Methods of Obtaining the Odours of Plants; with Instructions for the Manufacture of Perfumes, &c. By G. W. S. PIESSE, Ph.D. F.C.S. With 96 Woodcuts, square crown 8vo. 21s.

Pole.—*THE THEORY OF THE MODERN SCIENTIFIC GAME OF WHIST.* By W. POLE, F.R.S. Fcp. 8vo. 2s. 6d.

Proctor.—*WORKS BY R. A. PROCTOR.*

THE SUN; Ruler, Light, Fire, and Life of the Planetary System. With Plates and Woodcuts. Crown 8vo. 14s.

THE ORBS AROUND US; a Series of Essays on the Moon and Planets, Meteors and Comets. With Chart and Diagrams, crown 8vo. 5s.

OTHER WORLDS THAN OURS; The Plurality of Worlds Studied under the Light of Recent Scientific Researches. With 14 Illustrations, crown 8vo. 5s.

THE MOON; her Motions, Aspects, Scenery, and Physical Condition. With Plates, Charts, Woodcuts, and Lunar Photographs, crown 8vo. 6s.

UNIVERSE OF STARS; Presenting Researches into and New Views respecting the Constitution of the Heavens. With 22 Charts and 22 Diagrams, 8vo. 10s. 6d.

LARGER STAR ATLAS for the Library, in 12 Circular Maps, with Introduction and 2 Index Pages. Folio, 15s. or Maps only, 12s. 6d.

NEW STAR ATLAS for the Library, the School, and the Observatory, in 12 Circular Maps (with 2 Index Plates). Crown 8vo. 5s.

LIGHT SCIENCE FOR LEISURE HOURS; Familiar Essays on Scientific Subjects, Natural Phenomena, &c. 3 vols. crown 8vo. 5s. each.

CHANCE AND LUCK; a Series of Reprinted Articles. Crown 8vo. 5s.

STUDIES OF VENUS-TRANSITS; an Investigation of the Circumstances of the Transits of Venus in 1874 and 1882. With 7 Diagrams and 10 Plates. 8vo. 5s.

The 'KNOWLEDGE' LIBRARY. Edited by RICHARD A. PROCTOR.

CHANCE AND LUCK. By R. A. PROCTOR. Crown 8vo. 5s.

HOW TO PLAY WHIST: WITH THE LAWS AND ETIQUETTE OF WHIST. By R. A. PROCTOR. Crown 8vo. 5s.

HOME WHIST: an Easy Guide to Correct Play. By R. A. PROCTOR. 16mo. 1s.

THE POETRY OF ASTRONOMY. A Series of Familiar Essays. By R. A. PROCTOR. Crown 8vo. 6s.

NATURE STUDIES. By GRANT ALLEN, A. WILSON, T. FOSTER, E. CLODD, and R. A. PROCTOR. Crown 8vo. 6s.

LEISURE READINGS. By E. CLODD, A. WILSON, T. FOSTER, A. C. RUNYARD, and R. A. PROCTOR. Crown 8vo. 6s.

THE STARS IN THEIR SEASONS. An Easy Guide to a Knowledge of the Star Groups, in 12 Large Maps. By R. A. PROCTOR. Imperial 8vo. 5s.

STAR PRIMER. Showing the Starry Sky Week by Week, in 24 Hourly Maps. By R. A. PROCTOR. Crown 4to. 2s. 6d.

THE SEASONS PICTURED IN 48 SUN-VIEWS OF THE EARTH, and 24 Zodiacal Maps, &c. By R. A. PROCTOR. Demy 4to. 5s.

STRENGTH AND HAPPINESS. By R. A. PROCTOR. Crown 8vo. 6s.

ROUGH WAYS MADE SMOOTH. Familiar Essays on Scientific Subjects. By R. A. PROCTOR. Crown 8vo. 6s.

OUR PLACE AMONG INFINITIES. A Series of Essays contrasting our Little Abode in Space and Time with the Infinities Around us. By R. A. PROCTOR. Crown 8vo. 5s.

THE EXPANSE OF HEAVEN. Essays on the Wonders of the Firmament. By R. A. PROCTOR. Crown 8vo. 5s.

PLEASANT WAYS IN SCIENCE. By R. A. PROCTOR. Crown 8vo. 6s.

MYTHS AND MARVELS OF ASTRONOMY. By R. A. PROCTOR. Cr. 8vo. 6s.

Pryce.—*THE ANCIENT BRITISH CHURCH:* an Historical Essay. By JOHN PRYCE, M.A. Canon of Bangor. Crown 8vo. 6s.

Quain's Elements of Anatomy. The Ninth Edition. Re-edited by ALLEN THOMSON, M.D. LL.D. F.R.S.S. L. & E. EDWARD ALBERT SCHÄFER, F.R.S. and GEORGE DANCER THANE. With upwards of 1,000 Illustrations engraved on Wood, of which many are Coloured. 2 vols. 8vo. 18s. each.

Quain.—*A DICTIONARY OF MEDICINE.* By Various Writers. Edited by R. QUAIN, M.D. F.R.S. &c. With 138 Woodcuts. Medium 8vo. 31s. 6d. cloth, or 40s. half-russia; to be had also in 2 vols. 34s. cloth.

Reader.—*WORKS BY EMILY E. READER.*

THE GHOST OF BRANKINSHAW and other Tales. With 9 Full-page Illustrations. Fcp. 8vo. 2s. 6d. cloth extra, gilt edges.

VOICES FROM FLOWER-LAND, in Original Couplets. A Birthday-Book and Language of Flowers. 16mo. 2s. 6d. limp cloth; 3s. 6d. roan, gilt edges, or in vegetable vellum, gilt top.

FAIRY PRINCE FOLLOW-MY-LEAD; or, the *MAGIC BRACELET.* Illustrated by WM. READER. Cr. 8vo. 5s. gilt edges; or 6s. vegetable vellum, gilt edges.

Reeve. — *COOKERY AND HOUSEKEEPING.* By Mrs. HENRY REEVE. With 8 Coloured Plates and 37 Woodcuts. Crown 8vo. 7s. 6d.

Rich.—*A DICTIONARY OF ROMAN AND GREEK ANTIQUITIES.* With 2,000 Woodcuts. By A. RICH, B.A. Cr. 8vo. 7s. 6d.

Rivers. — *WORKS BY THOMAS RIVERS.*

THE ORCHARD-HOUSE. With 25 Woodcuts. Crown 8vo. 5s.

THE MINIATURE FRUIT GARDEN; or, the Culture of Pyramidal and Bush Fruit Trees, with Instructions for Root Pruning. With 32 Illustrations. Fcp. 8vo. 4s.

Robinson. — *THE NEW ARCADIA,* and other Poems. By A. MARY F. ROBINSON. Crown 8vo. 6s.

Roget.—*THESAURUS OF ENGLISH WORDS AND PHRASES,* Classified and Arranged so as to facilitate the Expression of Ideas and assist in Literary Composition. By PETER M. ROGET. Recomposed throughout, enlarged and improved, partly from the Author's Notes, and with a full Index by the Author's Son, JOHN LEWIS ROGET. Crown 8vo. 10s. 6d.

Ronalds. — *THE FLY-FISHER'S ENTOMOLOGY.* By ALFRED RONALDS. With 20 Coloured Plates. 8vo. 14s.

Schäfer. — *THE ESSENTIALS OF HISTOLOGY, DESCRIPTIVE AND PRACTICAL.* For the use of Students. By E. A. SCHÄFER, F.R.S. With 281 Illustrations. 8vo. 6s. or Interleaved with Drawing Paper, 8s. 6d.

Schellen. — *SPECTRUM ANALYSIS IN ITS APPLICATION TO TERRESTRIAL SUBSTANCES,* and the Physical Constitution of the Heavenly Bodies. By Dr. H. SCHELLEN. Translated by JANE and CAROLINE LASSELL. Edited by Capt. W. DE W. ABNEY. With 14 Plates (including Angström's and Cornu's Maps) and 291 Woodcuts. 8vo. 31s. 6d.

Seebohm.—*WORKS BY FREDERIC SEEBOHM.*

THE OXFORD REFORMERS—JOHN COLET, ERASMUS, AND THOMAS MORE; a History of their Fellow-Work. 8vo. 14s.

THE ENGLISH VILLAGE COMMUNITY Examined in its Relations to the Manorial and Tribal Systems, &c. 13 Maps and Plates. 8vo. 16s.

THE ERA OF THE PROTESTANT REVOLUTION. With Map. Fcp. 8vo. 2s. 6d.

Sennett. — *THE MARINE STEAM ENGINE;* a Treatise for the use of Engineering Students and Officers of the Royal Navy. By RICHARD SENNETT, Chief Engineer, Royal Navy. With 244 Illustrations. 8vo. 21s.

Sewell. — *STORIES AND TALES.* By ELIZABETH M. SEWELL. Crown 8vo. 1s. each, boards; 1s. 6d. each, cloth plain; 2s. 6d. each, cloth extra, gilt edges:—

Amy Herbert.	Margaret Percival.
The Earl's Daughter.	Laneton Parsonage.
The Experience of Life.	Ursula.
A Glimpse of the World.	Gertrude.
Cleve Hall.	Ivors.
Katharine Ashton.	

Shakespeare. — *BOWDLER'S FAMILY SHAKESPEARE.* Genuine Edition, in 1 vol. medium 8vo. large type, with 36 Woodcuts, 14s. or in 6 vols. fcp. 8vo. 21s.

OUTLINES OF THE LIFE OF SHAKESPEARE. By J. O. HALLIWELL-PHILLIPPS, F.R.S. 2 vols. Royal 8vo. 10s. 6d.

Short.—*SKETCH OF THE HISTORY OF THE CHURCH OF ENGLAND TO THE REVOLUTION OF* 1688. By T. V. SHORT, D.D. Crown 8vo. 7s. 6d.

Smith, H. F.—*THE HANDBOOK FOR MIDWIVES.* By HENRY FLY SMITH, M.B. Oxon. M.R.C.S. late Assistant-Surgeon at the Hospital for Sick Women, Soho Square. With 41 Woodcuts. Crown 8vo. 5s.

Smith, R. A.—*AIR AND RAIN;* the Beginnings of a Chemical Climatology. By R. A. SMITH, F.R.S. 8vo. 24s.

Smith, R. Bosworth. — *CARTHAGE AND THE CARTHAGINIANS.* By R. BOSWORTH SMITH, M.A. Maps, Plans, &c. Crown 8vo. 10s. 6d.

Smith, Rev. Sydney.—*THE WIT AND WISDOM OF THE REV. SYDNEY SMITH.* Crown 8vo. 1s. boards; 1s. 6d. cloth.

Smith, T.—*A MANUAL OF OPERATIVE SURGERY ON THE DEAD BODY.* By THOMAS SMITH, Surgeon to St. Bartholomew's Hospital. A New Edition, re-edited by W. J. WALSHAM. With 46 Illustrations. 8vo. 12s.

Southey.—*THE POETICAL WORKS OF ROBERT SOUTHEY,* with the Author's last Corrections and Additions. Medium 8vo. with Portrait, 14s.

Stanley. — *A FAMILIAR HISTORY OF BIRDS.* By E. STANLEY, D.D. Revised and enlarged, with 160 Woodcuts. Crown 8vo. 6s.

Steel.—*A TREATISE ON THE DISEASES OF THE OX;* being a Manual of Bovine Pathology specially adapted for the use of Veterinary Practitioners and Students. By J. H. STEEL, M.R.C.V.S. F.Z.S. With 2 Plates and 116 Woodcuts. 8vo. 15s.

Stephen. — *ESSAYS IN ECCLESIASTICAL BIOGRAPHY.* By the Right Hon. Sir J. STEPHEN, LL.D. Crown 8vo. 7s. 6d.

Stevenson.—*WORKS BY ROBERT LOUIS STEVENSON.*

A CHILD'S GARDEN OF VERSES. Small fcp. 8vo. 5s.

THE DYNAMITER. Fcp. 8vo. 1s. swd. 1s. 6d. cloth.

STRANGE CASE OF DR. JEKYLL AND MR. HYDE. Fcp. 8vo. 1s. sewed; 1s. 6d. cloth.

'Stonehenge.' — *THE DOG IN HEALTH AND DISEASE.* By 'STONEHENGE.' With 78 Wood Engravings. Square crown 8vo. 7s. 6d.

THE GREYHOUND. By 'STONEHENGE.' With 25 Portraits of Greyhounds, &c. Square crown 8vo. 15s.

Stoney. — *THE THEORY OF THE STRESSES ON GIRDERS AND SIMILAR STRUCTURES.* With Practical Observations on the Strength and other Properties of Materials. By BINDON B. STONEY, LL.D. F.R.S. M.I.C.E. With 5 Plates, and 143 Illustrations in the Text. Royal 8vo. 36s.

Sully.—*WORKS BY JAMES SULLY.*

OUTLINES OF PSYCHOLOGY, with Special Reference to the Theory of Education. 8vo. 12s. 6d.

THE TEACHER'S HANDBOOK OF PSYCHOLOGY, on the Basis of 'Outlines of Psychology.' Crown 8vo. 6s. 6d.

Supernatural Religion ; an Inquiry into the Reality of Divine Revelation. Complete Edition, thoroughly revised. 3 vols. 8vo. 36s.

Swinburne. — *PICTURE LOGIC;* an Attempt to Popularise the Science of Reasoning. By A. J. SWINBURNE, B.A. Post 8vo. 5s.

Swinton. — *THE PRINCIPLES AND PRACTICE OF ELECTRIC LIGHTING.* By ALAN A. CAMPBELL SWINTON. With 54 Illustrations engraved on Wood. Crown 8vo. 5s.

Taylor. — *STUDENT'S MANUAL OF THE HISTORY OF INDIA,* from the Earliest Period to the Present Time. By Colonel MEADOWS TAYLOR, C.S.I. Crown 8vo. 7s. 6d.

Text-Books of Science: a Series of Elementary Works on Science, adapted for the use of Students in Public and Science Schools. Fcp. 8vo. fully illustrated with Woodcuts. *See* p. 23.

Thomson's Conspectus.—Adapted to the British Pharmacopœia of 1885. Edited by NESTOR TIRARD, M.D. Lond. F.R.C.P. New Edition, with an Appendix containing notices of some of the more important non-official medicines and preparations. 18mo. 6*s.*

Thomson.—*AN OUTLINE OF THE NECESSARY LAWS OF THOUGHT;* a Treatise on Pure and Applied Logic. By W. THOMSON, D.D. Archbishop of York. Crown 8vo. 6*s.*

Three in Norway. By Two of THEM. With a Map and 59 Illustrations on Wood from Sketches by the Authors. Crown 8vo. 6*s.*

Trevelyan.—*WORKS BY THE RIGHT HON. SIR G. O. TREVELYAN, BART.*

THE LIFE AND LETTERS OF LORD MACAULAY.

    LIBRARY EDITION, 2 vols. 8vo. 36*s.*

    CABINET EDITION, 2 vols. crown 8vo. 12*s.*

    POPULAR EDITION, 1 vol. crown 8vo. 6*s.*

THE EARLY HISTORY OF CHARLES JAMES FOX. Library Edition, 8vo. 18*s.* Cabinet Edition, crown 8vo. 6*s.*

Trollope.—*NOVELS BY ANTHONY TROLLOPE.* Fcp. 8vo. 1*s.* each, boards; 1*s.* 6*d.* cloth.

    The Warden.
    Barchester Towers.

Twiss.—*WORKS BY SIR TRAVERS TWISS.*

THE RIGHTS AND DUTIES OF NATIONS, considered as Independent Communities in Time of War. 8vo. 21*s.*

THE RIGHTS AND DUTIES OF NATIONS IN TIME OF PEACE. 8vo. 15*s.*

Tyndall.—*WORKS BY JOHN TYNDALL, F.R.S. &c.*

FRAGMENTS OF SCIENCE. 2 vols. crown 8vo. 16*s.*

HEAT A MODE OF MOTION. Crown 8vo. 7*s.* 6*d.*

SOUND. With 204 Woodcuts. Crown 8vo. 10*s.* 6*d.*

ESSAYS ON THE FLOATING-MATTER OF THE AIR in relation to Putrefaction and Infection. With 24 Woodcuts. Crown 8vo. 7*s.* 6*d.*

LECTURES ON LIGHT, delivered in America in 1872 and 1873. With 57 Diagrams. Crown 8vo. 5*s.*

LESSONS IN ELECTRICITY AT THE ROYAL INSTITUTION, 1875-76. With 58 Woodcuts. Crown 8vo. 2*s.* 6*d.*

NOTES OF A COURSE OF SEVEN LECTURES ON ELECTRICAL PHENOMENA AND THEORIES, delivered at the Royal Institution. Crown 8vo. 1*s.* sewed, 1*s.* 6*d.* cloth.

NOTES OF A COURSE OF NINE LECTURES ON LIGHT, delivered at the Royal Institution. Crown 8vo. 1*s.* sewed, 1*s.* 6*d.* cloth.

FARADAY AS A DISCOVERER. Fcp. 8vo. 3*s.* 6*d.*

Ure.—*A DICTIONARY OF ARTS, MANUFACTURES, AND MINES.* By Dr. URE. Seventh Edition, re-written and enlarged by R. HUNT, F.R.S. With 2,064 Woodcuts. 4 vols. medium 8vo. £7. 7*s.*

Verney.—*CHESS ECCENTRICITIES.* Including Four-handed Chess, Chess for Three, Six, or Eight Players, Round Chess for Two, Three, or Four Players, and several different ways of Playing Chess for Two Players. By Major GEORGE HOPE VERNEY. Crown 8vo. 10*s.* 6*d.*

Ville.—*ON ARTIFICIAL MANURES,* their Chemical Selection and Scientific Application to Agriculture. By GEORGES VILLE. Translated and edited by W. CROOKES, F.R.S. With 31 Plates. 8vo. 21*s.*

Virgil.—*PUBLI VERGILI MARONIS BUCOLICA, GEORGICA, ÆNEIS;* the Works of VIRGIL, Latin Text, with English Commentary and Index. By B. H. KENNEDY, D.D. Crown 8vo. 10s. 6d.

THE ÆNEID OF VIRGIL. Translated into English Verse. By J. CONINGTON, M.A. Crown 8vo. 9s.

THE ÆNEID OF VIRGIL FREELY TRANSLATED INTO ENGLISH BLANK VERSE. By WILLIAM J. THORNHILL, B.A. Crown 8vo. 7s. 6d.

THE POEMS OF VIRGIL. Translated into English Prose. By JOHN CONINGTON, M.A. Crown 8vo. 9s.

Walker. — *THE CORRECT CARD;* or, How to Play at Whist; a Whist Catechism. By Major A. CAMPBELL-WALKER, F.R.G.S. Fcp. 8vo. 2s. 6d.

Walpole.—*HISTORY OF ENGLAND FROM THE CONCLUSION OF THE GREAT WAR IN 1815.* By SPENCER WALPOLE. 5 vols. 8vo. Vols. I. and II. 1815–1832, 36s.; Vol. III. 1832–1841, 18s.; Vols. IV. and V. 1841–1858, 36s.

Watts.—*A DICTIONARY OF CHEMISTRY AND THE ALLIED BRANCHES OF OTHER SCIENCES.* Edited by HENRY WATTS, F.R.S. 9 vols. medium 8vo. £15. 2s. 6d.

Webb.—*CELESTIAL OBJECTS FOR COMMON TELESCOPES.* By the Rev. T. W. WEBB. Map, Plate, Woodcuts. Crown 8vo. 9s.

Webb. — *THE VEIL OF ISIS:* a Series of Essays on Idealism. By THOMAS W. WEBB, LL.D. 8vo. 10s. 6d.

Wellington.—*LIFE OF THE DUKE OF WELLINGTON.* By the Rev. G. R. GLEIG, M.A. Crown 8vo. Portrait, 6s.

West.—*WORKS BY CHARLES WEST, M.D. &c.* Founder of, and formerly Physician to, the Hospital for Sick Children.

LECTURES ON THE DISEASES OF INFANCY AND CHILDHOOD. 8vo. 18s.

THE MOTHER'S MANUAL OF CHILDREN'S DISEASES. Crown 8vo. 2s. 6d.

Whately. — *ENGLISH SYNONYMS.* By E. JANE WHATELY. Edited by her Father, R. WHATELY, D.D. Fcp. 8vo. 3s.

Whately.—*WORKS BY R. WHATELY, D.D.*

ELEMENTS OF LOGIC. Crown 8vo. 4s. 6d.

ELEMENTS OF RHETORIC. Crown 8vo. 4s. 6d.

LESSONS ON REASONING. Fcp. 8vo. 1s. 6d.

BACON'S ESSAYS, with Annotations. 8vo. 10s. 6d.

White and Riddle.—*A LATIN-ENGLISH DICTIONARY.* By J. T. WHITE, D.D. Oxon. and J. J. E. RIDDLE, M.A. Oxon. Founded on the larger Dictionary of Freund. Royal 8vo. 21s.

White.—*A CONCISE LATIN-ENGLISH DICTIONARY,* for the Use of Advanced Scholars and University Students By the Rev. J. T. WHITE, D.D. Royal 8vo. 12s.

Wilcocks.—*THE SEA FISHERMAN.* Comprising the Chief Methods of Hook and Line Fishing in the British and other Seas, and Remarks on Nets, Boats, and Boating. By J. C. WILCOCKS. Profusely Illustrated. Crown 8vo. 6s.

Wilkins. — *THE GROWTH OF THE HOMERIC POEMS:* a Discussion of their Origin and Authorship. By GEORGE WILKINS, M.A. late Scholar, Trinity College, Dublin. 8vo. 6s.

Wilkinson.—*THE FRIENDLY SOCIETY MOVEMENT:* Its Origin, Rise, and Growth; its Social, Moral, and Educational Influences.—*THE AFFILIATED ORDERS.* —By the Rev. JOHN FROME WILKINSON, M.A. Crown 8vo. 2s. 6d.

Williams. — *MANUAL OF TELEGRAPHY.* By W. WILLIAMS, Superintendent of Indian Government Telegraphs. Illustrated by 93 Wood Engravings. 8vo. 10s. 6d.

Willich. — *POPULAR TABLES* for giving Information for ascertaining the value of Lifehold, Leasehold, and Church Property, the Public Funds, &c. By CHARLES M. WILLICH. Edited by H. BENCE JONES. Crown 8vo. 10s. 6d.

Wilson.—*A MANUAL OF HEALTH-SCIENCE.* Adapted for Use in Schools and Colleges, and suited to the Requirements of Students preparing for the Examinations in Hygiene of the Science and Art Department, &c. By ANDREW WILSON, F.R.S.E. F.L.S. &c. With 74 Illustrations. Crown 8vo. 6d.

Witt.—*WORKS BY PROF. WITT.* Translated from the German by FRANCES YOUNGHUSBAND.

THE TROYAN WAR. With a Preface by the Rev. W. G. RUTHERFORD, M.A. Head-Master of Westminster School. Crown 8vo. 2s.

MYTHS OF HELLAS; or, Greek Tales. Crown 8vo. 3s. 6d.

THE WANDERINGS OF ULYSSES. Crown 8vo. 3s. 6d.

Wood.—*WORKS BY REV. J. G. WOOD.*

HOMES WITHOUT HANDS; a Description of the Habitations of Animals, classed according to the Principle of Construction. With 140 Illustrations. 8vo. 10s. 6d.

INSECTS AT HOME; a Popular Account of British Insects, their Structure, Habits, and Transformations. With 700 Illustrations. 8vo. 10s. 6d.

INSECTS ABROAD; a Popular Account of Foreign Insects, their Structure, Habits, and Transformations. With 600 Illustrations. 8vo. 10s. 6d.

BIBLE ANIMALS; a Description of every Living Creature mentioned in the Scriptures. With 112 Illustrations. 8vo. 10s. 6d.

STRANGE DWELLINGS; a Description of the Habitations of Animals, abridged from 'Homes without Hands.' With 60 Illustrations. Crown 8vo. 5s. Popular Edition, 4to. 6d.

HORSE AND MAN: their Mutual Dependence and Duties. With 49 Illustrations. 8vo. 14s.

ILLUSTRATED STABLE MAXIMS. To be hung in Stables for the use of Grooms, Stablemen, and others who are in charge of Horses. On Sheet, 4s.

OUT OF DOORS; a Selection of Original Articles on Practical Natural History. With 11 Illustrations. Crown 8vo. 5s.

COMMON BRITISH INSECTS: BEETLES, MOTHS, AND BUTTERFLIES. With 130 Illustrations. Crown 8vo. 3s. 6d.

PETLAND REVISITED. With 33 Illustrations. Crown 8vo. 7s. 6d.

Wood-Martin. — *THE LAKE DWELLINGS OF IRELAND:* or Ancient Lacustrine Habitations of Erin, commonly called Crannogs. By W. G. WOOD-MARTIN, M.R.I.A. Lieut.-Colonel 8th Brigade North Irish Division, R.A. With 50 Plates. Royal 8vo. 25s.

Wylie. — *HISTORY OF ENGLAND UNDER HENRY THE FOURTH.* By JAMES HAMILTON WYLIE, M.A. one of Her Majesty's Inspectors of Schools. (2 vols.) Vol. I, crown 8vo. 10s. 6d.

Wylie. — *LABOUR, LEISURE, AND LUXURY;* a Contribution to Present Practical Political Economy. By ALEXANDER WYLIE, of Glasgow. Crown 8vo. 6s.

Youatt. — *WORKS BY WILLIAM YOUATT.*

THE HORSE. Revised and enlarged by W. WATSON, M.R.C.V.S. 8vo. Woodcuts, 7s. 6d.

THE DOG. Revised and enlarged. 8vo. Woodcuts. 6s.

Younghusband.—*THE STORY OF OUR LORD TOLD IN SIMPLE LANGUAGE FOR CHILDREN.* By FRANCES YOUNGHUSBAND. With numerous Illustrations from 'Longmans' Illustrated New Testament.' Crown 8vo. 2s. 6d. cloth plain, 3s. 6d. cloth extra, gilt edges.

Zeller. — *WORKS BY DR. E. ZELLER.*

HISTORY OF ECLECTICISM IN GREEK PHILOSOPHY. Translated by SARAH F. ALLEYNE. Crown 8vo. 10s. 6d.

THE STOICS, EPICUREANS, AND SCEPTICS. Translated by the Rev. O. J. REICHEL, M.A. Crown 8vo. 15s.

SOCRATES AND THE SOCRATIC SCHOOLS. Translated by the Rev. O. J. REICHEL, M.A. Crown 8vo. 10s. 6d.

PLATO AND THE OLDER ACADEMY. Translated by SARAH F. ALLEYNE and ALFRED GOODWIN, B.A. Crown 8vo. 18s.

THE PRE-SOCRATIC SCHOOLS; a History of Greek Philosophy from the Earliest Period to the time of Socrates. Translated by SARAH F. ALLEYNE. 2 vols. crown 8vo. 30s.

OUTLINES OF THE HISTORY OF GREEK PHILOSOPHY. Translated by SARAH F. ALLEYNE and EVELYN ABBOTT. Crown 8vo. 10s. 6d.

TEXT-BOOKS OF SCIENCE.

PHOTOGRAPHY. By Captain W. DE WIVE-LESLIE ABNEY, F.R.S. late Instructor in Chemistry and Photography at the School of Military Engineering, Chatham. With 105 Woodcuts. 3s.6d.

ON THE STRENGTH OF MATERIALS AND Structures: the Strength of Materials as depending on their quality and as ascertained by Testing Apparatus; the Strength of Structures, as depending on their form and arrangement, and on the materials of which they are composed. By Sir J. ANDERSON, C.E. 3s. 6d.

INTRODUCTION TO THE STUDY OF ORGANIC Chemistry; the Chemistry of Carbon and its Compounds. By HENRY E. ARMSTRONG, Ph.D. F.C.S. With 8 Woodcuts. 3s. 6d.

ELEMENTS OF ASTRONOMY. By Sir R. S. BALL, LL.D. F.R.S. Andrews Professor of Astronomy in the Univ. of Dublin, Royal Astronomer of Ireland. With 136 Figures and Diagrams. 6s.

RAILWAY APPLIANCES. A Description of Details of Railway Construction subsequent to the completion of Earthworks and Masonry, including a short Notice of Railway Rolling Stock. By J. W. BARRY. With 207 Woodcuts. 3s. 6d.

SYSTEMATIC MINERALOGY. By HILARY BAUERMAN, F.G.S. Associate of the Royal School of Mines. With 373 Diagrams. 6s.

DESCRIPTIVE MINERALOGY. By the same Author. With 236 Woodcuts and Diagrams. 6s.

METALS, THEIR PROPERTIES AND TREAT-ment. By C. L. BLOXAM and A. K. HUNTINGTON, Professors in King's College, London. With 130 Wood Engravings. 5s.

PRACTICAL PHYSICS. By R. T. GLAZE-BROOK, M.A. F.R.S. and W. N. SHAW, M.A. With 62 Woodcuts. 6s.

PHYSICAL OPTICS. By R. T. GLAZEBROOK, M.A. F.R.S. Fellow and Lecturer of Trin. Coll. Demonstrator of Physics at the Cavendish Laboratory, Cambridge. With 183 Woodcuts of Apparatus, &c. 6s.

THE ART OF ELECTRO-METALLURGY, including all known Processes of Electro-Deposition. By G. GORE, LL.D. F.R.S. With 56 Woodcuts. 6s

ALGEBRA AND TRIGONOMETRY. By the Rev. WILLIAM NATHANIEL GRIFFIN, B.D. 3s. 6d.

NOTES ON THE ELEMENTS OF ALGEBRA and Trigonometry. With Solutions of the more difficult Questions. By the Rev. W. N. GRIFFIN, B.D. 3s. 6d.

THE STEAM ENGINE. By GEORGE C. V. HOLMES, Whitworth Scholar; Secretary of the Institution of Naval Architects. Fully Illustrated. 6s.

ELECTRICITY AND MAGNETISM. By FLEEM-ING JENKIN, F.R.SS. L. & E. late Professor of Engineering in the University of Edinburgh. 3s. 6d.

THEORY OF HEAT. By J. CLERK MAXWELL, M.A. LL.D. Edin. F.R.SS. L. & E. With 41 Woodcuts. 3s. 6d.

TECHNICAL ARITHMETIC AND MENSURA-tion. By CHARLES W. MERRIFIELD, F.R.S. 3s. 6d.

KEY TO MERRIFIELD'S TEXT-BOOK OF Technical Arithmetic and Mensuration. By the Rev. JOHN HUNTER, M.A. formerly Vice-Principal of the National Society's Training College, Battersea. 3s. 6d.

INTRODUCTION TO THE STUDY OF INOR-ganic Chemistry. By WILLIAM ALLEN MILLER M.D. LL.D. F.R.S. With 71 Woodcuts. 3s. 6d.

TELEGRAPHY. By W. H. PREECE, C.E. and J. SIVEWRIGHT, M.A. With 160 Woodcuts. 5s.

THE STUDY OF ROCKS, an Elementary Text-Book of Petrology. By FRANK RUTLEY, F.G.S. of Her Majesty's Geological Survey. With 6 Plates and 88 Woodcuts. 4s. 6d.

WORKSHOP APPLIANCES, including Descriptions of some of the Gauging and Measuring Instruments—Hand Cutting Tools, Lathes, Drilling, Planing, and other Machine Tools used by Engineers. By C. P. B. SHELLEY, M.I.C.E. With 291 Woodcuts. 4s. 6d.

STRUCTURAL AND PHYSIOLOGICAL BOTANY. By Dr. OTTO WILHELM THOMÉ, Professor of Botany, School of Science and Art, Cologne. Translated by A. W. BENNETT, M.A. B.Sc. F.L.S. With 600 Woodcuts. 6s.

QUANTITATIVE CHEMICAL ANALYSIS. By T. E. THORPE, F.R.S.E. Ph.D. Professor of Chemistry in the Andersonian University, Glasgow. With 88 Woodcuts. 4s. 6d.

MANUAL OF QUALITATIVE ANALYSIS AND Laboratory Practice. By T. E. THORPE, Ph.D. F.R.S.E. Professor of Chemistry in the Andersonian University, Glasgow; and M. M. PATTISON MUIR. 3s. 6d.

INTRODUCTION TO THE STUDY OF CHEM-ical Philosophy; the Principles of Theoretical and Systematical Chemistry. By WILLIAM A. TILDEN, B.Sc. London, F.C.S. With 5 Woodcuts. 3s. 6d. With Answers to Problems, 4s. 6d.

ELEMENTS OF MACHINE DESIGN; an Introduction to the Principles which determine the Arrangement and Proportion of the Parts of Machines, and a Collection of Rules for Machine Designs. By W. CAWTHORNE UNWIN, B.Sc. Assoc. Inst. C.E. With 325 Woodcuts. 6s.

PLANE AND SOLID GEOMETRY. By the Rev. H. W. WATSON, formerly Fellow of Trinity College, Cambridge. 3s. 6d.

EPOCHS OF HISTORY.

EPOCHS OF ANCIENT HISTORY.

Edited by the Rev. Sir G. W. Cox, Bart. M.A. and by C. SANKEY, M.A. 10 Volumes, fcp. 8vo. with numerous Maps, Plans, and Tables, price 2s. 6d. each volume.

THE GRACCHI, MARIUS, AND SULLA. By A. H. BEESLY, M.A.

THE EARLY ROMAN EMPIRE. From the Assassination of Julius Cæsar to the Assassination of Domitian. By the Rev. W. WOLFE CAPES, M.A.

THE ROMAN EMPIRE OF THE SECOND CENtury, or the Age of the Antonines. By the Rev. W. WOLFE CAPES, M.A.

THE ATHENIAN EMPIRE. From the Flight of Xerxes to the Fall of Athens. By the Rev. Sir G. W. Cox, Bart. M.A.

THE GREEKS AND THE PERSIANS. By the Rev. Sir G. W. Cox, Bart. M.A.

THE RISE OF THE MACEDONIAN EMPIRE. By ARTHUR M. CURTEIS, M.A.

ROME TO ITS CAPTURE BY THE GAULS. By WILHELM IHNE.

THE ROMAN TRIUMVIRATES. By the Very Rev. CHARLES MERIVALE, D.D.

THE SPARTAN AND THEBAN SUPREMACIES. By CHARLES SANKEY, M.A.

ROME AND CARTHAGE, THE PUNIC WARS. By R. BOSWORTH SMITH, M.A.

EPOCHS OF MODERN HISTORY.

Edited by C. COLBECK, M.A. 18 vols. fcp. 8vo. with Maps, price 2s. 6d. each volume.

THE NORMANS IN EUROPE. By Rev. A. H. JOHNSON, M.A.

THE CRUSADES. By the Rev. Sir G. W. Cox, Bart. M.A.

THE BEGINNING OF THE MIDDLE AGES. By R. W. CHURCH, D.D. Dean of St. Paul's.

THE EARLY PLANTAGENETS. By W. STUBBS, D.D. Bishop of Chester.

EDWARD THE THIRD. By the Rev. W. WARBURTON, M.A.

THE HOUSES OF LANCASTER AND YORK. By JAMES GAIRDNER.

THE EARLY TUDORS. By the Rev. C. E. MOBERLY, M.A.

THE ERA OF THE PROTESTANT REVOLUtion. By F. SEEBOHM.

THE FIRST TWO STUARTS AND THE PURItan Revolution, 1603-1660. By SAMUEL RAWSON GARDINER.

THE AGE OF ELIZABETH. By the Rev. M. CREIGHTON, M.A. LL.D.

THE FALL OF THE STUARTS; AND WESTERN Europe from 1678 to 1697. By the Rev. EDWARD HALE, M.A.

THE AGE OF ANNE. By E. E. MORRIS, M.A.

THE THIRTY YEARS' WAR, 1618-1648. By SAMUEL RAWSON GARDINER.

THE EARLY HANOVERIANS. By E. E. MORRIS, M.A.

FREDERICK THE GREAT AND THE SEVEN Years' War. By F. W. LONGMAN.

THE WAR OF AMERICAN INDEPENDENCE, 1775-1783. By J. M. LUDLOW.

THE FRENCH REVOLUTION, 1789-1795. By Mrs. S. R. GARDINER.

THE EPOCH OF REFORM, 1830-1850. By JUSTIN M'CARTHY, M.P.

EPOCHS OF ENGLISH HISTORY.

Edited by the Rev. MANDELL CREIGHTON, M.A.

EARLY ENGLAND TO THE NORMAN CONquest. By F. YORK POWELL, M.A. 1s.

ENGLAND A CONTINENTAL POWER, 1066-1216. By Mrs. MANDELL CREIGHTON. 9d.

RISE OF THE PEOPLE AND THE GROWTH OF Parliament, 1215-1485. By JAMES ROWLEY, M.A. 9d.

TUDORS AND THE REFORMATION, 1485-1603. By the Rev. MANDELL CREIGHTON. 9d.

STRUGGLE AGAINST ABSOLUTE MONARCHY, 1603-1688. By Mrs. S. R. GARDINER. 9d.

SETTLEMENT OF THE CONSTITUTION, from 1689 to 1784. By JAMES ROWLEY, M.A. 9d.

ENGLAND DURING THE AMERICAN AND European Wars, from 1765 to 1820. By the Rev. O. W. TANCOCK, M.A. 9d.

MODERN ENGLAND FROM 1820 TO 1874. By OSCAR BROWNING, M.A. 9d.

₀ Complete in One Volume, with 27 Tables and Pedigrees, and 23 Maps. Price 5s.

THE SHILLING HISTORY OF ENGLAND; being an Introductory Volume to the Series of 'Epochs of English History.' By the Rev. MANDELL CREIGHTON, M.A. Fcp. 8vo. 1s.

EPOCHS OF CHURCH HISTORY.

Edited by the Rev. MANDELL CREIGHTON, M.A. Fcp. 8vo. price 2s. 6d. each volume.

THE ENGLISH CHURCH IN OTHER LANDS; or, the Spiritual Expansion of England. By Rev. W. H. TUCKER, M.A.

THE HISTORY OF THE REFORMATION IN England. By GEORGE G. PERRY, M.A.

THE EVANGELICAL REVIVAL IN THE Eighteenth Century. By the Rev. JOHN HENRY OVERTON, M.A.

THE HISTORY OF THE UNIVERSITY OF Oxford. By the Hon. G. C. BRODRICK, D.C.L.

₀ Other Volumes in preparation.

Spottiswoode & Co. Printers, New-street Square, London.

CPSIA information can be obtained
at www.ICGtesting.com
Printed in the USA
BVHW041953250819
556750BV00005B/18/P

9 781358 370649